D1218067

Chicago Public Library

REFERENCE

Form 178 rev. 11-00

Data Mining:
A Heuristic Approach

Hussein A. Abbass
Ruhul A. Sarker
Charles S. Newton

University of New South Wales, Australia

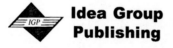 **Idea Group
Publishing**

 **Information Science
Publishing**

Hershey • London • Melbourne • Singapore • Beijing

Acquisitions Editor:	Mehdi Khosrowpour
Managing Editor:	Jan Travers
Development Editor:	Michele Rossi
Copy Editor:	Maria Boyer
Typesetter:	Tamara Gillis
Cover Design:	Debra Andree
Printed at:	Integrated Book Technology

Published in the United States of America by
    Idea Group Publishing
    1331 E. Chocolate Avenue
    Hershey PA 17033-1117
    Tel: 717-533-8845
    Fax: 717-533-8661
    E-mail: cust@idea-group.com
    Web site: http://www.idea-group.com

and in the United Kingdom by
    Idea Group Publishing
    3 Henrietta Street
    Covent Garden
    London WC2E 8LU
    Tel: 44 20 7240 0856
    Fax: 44 20 7379 3313
    Web site: http://www.eurospan.co.uk

Library of Congress Cataloging-in-Publication Data

Data mining : a heuristic approach / [edited by] Hussein Aly Abbass, Ruhul Amin Sarker, Charles S. Newton.
    p. cm.
  Includes index.
  ISBN 1-930708-25-4
  1. Data mining. 2. Database searching. 3. Heuristic programming. I. Abbass, Hussein.
II. Sarker, Ruhul. III. Newton, Charles, 1942-

QA76.9.D343 D36 2001
006.31--dc21   2001039775

British Cataloguing in Publication Data
A Cataloguing in Publication record for this book is available from the British Library.

NEW from Idea Group Publishing

- **Data Mining: A Heuristic Approach**
  Hussein Aly Abbass, Ruhul Amin Sarker and Charles S. Newton/ 1-930708-25-4
- **Managing Information Technology in Small Business: Challenges and Solutions**
  Stephen Burgess/ 1-930708-35-1
- **Managing Web Usage in the Workplace: A Social, Ethical and Legal Perspective**
  Murugan Anandarajan and Claire A. Simmers/ 1-930708-18-1
- **Challenges of Information Technology Education in the 21st Century**
  Eli Cohen/ 1-930708-34-3
- **Social Responsibility in the Information Age: Issues and Controversies**
  Gurpreet Dhillon/ 1-930708-11-4
- **Database Integrity: Challenges and Solutions**
  Jorge H. Doorn and Laura Rivero/ 1-930708-38-6
- **Managing Virtual Web Organizations in the 21st Century: Issues and Challenges**
  Ulrich Franke/ 1-930708-24-6
- **Managing Business with Electronic Commerce: Issues and Trends**
  Aryya Gangopadhyay/ 1-930708-12-2
- **Electronic Government: Design, Applications and Management**
  Åke Grönlund/ 1-930708-19-X
- **Knowledge Media in Health Care: Opportunities and Challenges**
  Rolf Grutter/ 1-930708-13-0
- **Internet Management Issues: A Global Perspective**
  John D. Haynes/ 1-930708-21-1
- **Enterprise Resource Planning: Global Opportunities and Challenges**
  Liaquat Hossain, Jon David Patrick and M. A. Rashid/ 1-930708-36-X
- **The Design and Management of Effective Distance Learning Programs**
  Richard Discenza, Caroline Howard, and Karen Schenk/ 1-930708-20-3
- **Multirate Systems: Design and Applications**
  Gordana Jovanovic-Dolecek/ 1-930708-30-0
- **Managing IT/Community Partnerships in the 21st Century**
  Jonathan Lazar/ 1-930708-33-5
- **Multimedia Networking: Technology, Management and Applications**
  Syed Mahbubur Rahman/ 1-930708-14-9
- **Cases on Worldwide E-Commerce: Theory in Action**
  Mahesh Raisinghani/ 1-930708-27-0
- **Designing Instruction for Technology-Enhanced Learning**
  Patricia L. Rogers/ 1-930708-28-9
- **Heuristic and Optimization for Knowledge Discovery**
  Ruhul Amin Sarker, Hussein Aly Abbass and Charles Newton/ 1-930708-26-2
- **Distributed Multimedia Databases: Techniques and Applications**
  Timothy K. Shih/ 1-930708-29-7
- **Neural Networks in Business: Techniques and Applications**
  Kate Smith and Jatinder Gupta/ 1-930708-31-9
- **Information Technology and Collective Obligations: Topics and Debate**
  Robert Skovira/ 1-930708-37-8
- **Managing the Human Side of Information Technology: Challenges and Solutions**
  Edward Szewczak and Coral Snodgrass/ 1-930708-32-7
- **Cases on Global IT Applications and Management: Successes and Pitfalls**
  Felix B. Tan/ 1-930708-16-5
- **Enterprise Networking: Multilayer Switching and Applications**
  Vasilis Theoharakis and Dimitrios Serpanos/ 1-930708-17-3
- **Measuring the Value of Information Technology**
  Han T. M. van der Zee/ 1-930708-08-4
- **Business to Business Electronic Commerce: Challenges and Solutions**
  Merrill Warkentin/ 1-930708-09-2

Excellent additions to your library!

**Receive the Idea Group Publishing catalog with descriptions of these books by
calling, toll free 1/800-345-4332
or visit the IGP Online Bookstore at: http://www.idea-group.com!**

Data Mining: A Heuristic Approach

Table of Contents

Preface

The last decade has witnessed a revolution in interdisciplinary research where the boundaries of different areas have overlapped or even disappeared. New fields of research emerge each day where two or more fields have integrated to form a new identity. Examples of these emerging areas include bioinformatics (synthesizing biology with computer and information systems), data mining (combining statistics, optimization, machine learning, artificial intelligence, and databases), and modern heuristics (integrating ideas from tens of fields such as biology, forest, immunology, statistical mechanics, and physics to inspire search techniques). These integrations have proved useful in substantiating problem-solving approaches with reliable and robust techniques to handle the increasing demand from practitioners to solve real-life problems. With the revolution in genetics, databases, automation, and robotics, problems are no longer those that can be solved analytically in a feasible time. Complexity arises because of new discoveries about the genome, path planning, changing environments, chaotic systems, and many others, and has contributed to the increased demand to find search techniques that are capable of getting a good enough solution in a reasonable time. This has directed research into heuristics.

During the same period of time, databases have grown exponentially in large stores and companies. In the old days, system analysts faced many difficulties in finding enough data to feed into their models. The picture has changed and now the reverse picture is a daily problem–how to understand the large amount of data we have accumulated over the years. Simultaneously, investors have realized that data is a hidden treasure in their companies. With data, one can analyze the behavior of competitors, understand the system better, and diagnose the faults in strategies and systems. Research into statistics, machine learning, and data analysis has been resurrected. Unfortunately, with the amount of data and the complexity of the underlying models, traditional approaches in statistics, machine learning, and traditional data analysis fail to cope with this level of complexity. The need therefore arises for better approaches that are able to handle complex models in a reasonable amount of time. These approaches have been named data mining (sometimes data farming) to distinguish them from traditional statistics, machine learning, and other data analysis techniques. In addition, decision makers were not interested in techniques that rely too much on the underlying assumptions in statistical models. The challenge is to not have any assumptions about the model and try to come up with something new, something that is not obvious or predictable (at least from the decision makers' point of view). Some unobvious thing may have significant values to the decision maker. Identifying a hidden trend in the data or a buried fault in the system is by all accounts a treasure for the investor who knows that avoiding loss results in profit and that knowledge in a complex market is a key criterion for success and continuity. Notwithstanding, models that are free from assumptions–or at least have minimum assumptions–are expensive to use. The dramatic search space cannot be navigated using traditional search techniques. This has highlighted a natural demand for the use of heuristic search methods in data mining.

This book is a repository of research papers describing the applications of modern heuristics to data mining. This is a unique–and as far as we know, the first–book that provides up-to-date research in coupling these two topics of modern heuristics and data mining. Although it is by all means an incomplete coverage, it does provide some leading research in this area.

This book contains open-solicited and invited chapters written by leading researchers in the field. All chapters were peer reviewed by at least two recognized researchers in the field in addition to one of the editors. Contributors come from almost all the continents and therefore, the book presents a global approach to the discipline. The book contains 13 chapters divided into five parts as follows:

- Part 1: General Heuristics
- Part 2: Evolutionary Algorithms
- Part 3: Genetic Programming
- Part 4: Ant Colony Optimization and Immune Systems
- Part 5: Parallel Data Mining

Part 1 gives an introduction to modern heuristics as presented in the first chapter. The chapter serves as a textbook-like introduction for readers without a background in heuristics or those who would like to refresh their knowledge.

Chapter 2 is an excellent example of the use of hill climbing for clustering. In this chapter, Vladimir Estivill-Castro and Michael E. Houle from the University of Newcastle and the University of Sydney, respectively, provide a methodical overview of clustering and hill climbing methods to clustering. They detail the use of proximity information to assess the scalability and robustness of clustering.

Part 2 covers the well-known evolutionary algorithms. After almost three decades of continuous research in this area, the vast amount of papers in the literature is beyond a single survey paper. However, in Chapter 3, Erick Cantú-Paz and Chandrika Kamath from Lawrence Livermore National Laboratory, USA, provide a brave and very successful attempt to survey the literature describing the use of evolutionary algorithms in data mining. With over 75 references, they scrutinize the data mining process and the role of evolutionary algorithms in each stage of the process.

In Chapter 4, Beatriz de la Iglesia and Victor J. Rayward-Smith, from the University of East Anglia, UK, provide a superb paper on the application of Simulated Annealing, Tabu Search, and Genetic Algorithms (GA) to nugget discovery or classification where an important class is under-represented in the database. They summarize in their chapter different measures of performance for the classification problem in general and compare their results against 12 classification algorithms.

Iñaki Inza, Pedro Larrañaga, and Basilio Sierra from the University of the Basque Country, Spain, follow, in Chapter 5, with an outstanding piece of work on feature subset selection using a different type of evolutionary algorithms, the Estimation of Distribution Algorithms (EDA). In EDA, a probability distribution of the best individuals in the population is maintained to sample the individuals in subsequent generations. Traditional crossover and mutation operators are replaced by the re-sampling process. They applied EDA to the Feature Subset Selection problem and showed that it significantly improves the prediction accuracy.

In Chapter 6, Jorge Muruzábal from the University of Rey Juan Carlos, Spain, presents the brilliant idea of evolving teams of local Bayesian learners. Bayes theorem was resurrected as a result of the revolution in computer science. Nevertheless, Bayesian approaches, such as

Bayesian Networks, require large amounts of computational effort, and the search algorithm can easily become stuck in a local minimum. Dr. Muruzábal combined the power of the Bayesian approach with the ability of Evolutionary Algorithms and Learning Classifier Systems for the classification process.

Neil Dunstan from the University of New England, and Michael de Raadt from the University of Southern Queensland, Australia, provide an interesting application of the use of evolutionary algorithms for the classification and detection of Unexploded Ordnance present on military sites in Chapter 7.

Part 3 covers the area of Genetic Programming (GP). GP is very similar to the traditional GA in its use of selection and recombination as the means of evolution. Different from GA, GP represents the solution as a tree, and therefore the crossover and mutation operators are adopted to handle tree structures. This part starts with Chapter 8 by Peter W.H. Smith from City University, UK, who provides an interesting introduction to the use of GP for data mining and the problems facing GP in this domain. Before discarding GP as a useful tool for data mining, A.P. Engelbrecht and L Schoeman from the University of Pretoria, South Africa along with Sonja Rouwhorst from the University of Vrije, The Netherlands, provide a building block approach to genetic programming for rule discovery in Chapter 9. They show that their proposed GP methodology is comparable to the famous C4.5 decision tree classifier–a famous decision tree classifier.

Part 4 covers the increasingly growing areas of Ant Colony Optimization and Immune Systems. Rafael S. Parpinelli and Heitor S. Lopes from Centro Federal de Educacao Tecnologica do Parana, and Alex A. Freitas from Pontificia Universidade Catolica do Parana, Brazil, present a pioneer attempt, in Chapter 10, to apply ant colony optimization to rule discovery. Their results are very promising and through an extremely interesting approach, they present their techniques.

Jon Timmis and Thomas Knight, from the University of Kent at Canterbury, UK, introduce Artificial Immune Systems (AIS) in Chapter 11. In a notable presentation, they present the AIS domain and how can it be used for data mining. Leandro Nunes de Castro and Fernando J. Von Zuben, from the State University of Campinas, Brazil, follow in Chapter 12 with the use of AIS for clustering. The chapter presents a remarkable metaphor for the use of AIS with an outstanding potential for the proposed algorithm.

In general, the data mining task is very expensive, whether we are using heuristics or any other technique. It was therefore impossible not to present this book without discussing parallel data mining. This is the task carried out by David Taniar from Monash University and J. Wenny Rahayu from La Trobe University, Australia, in Part 5, Chapter 13. They both have written a self-contained and detailed chapter in an exhilarating style, thereby bringing the book to a close.

It is hoped that this book will trigger great interest into data mining and heuristics, leading to many more articles and books!

Acknowledgments

We would like to express our gratitude to the contributors without whose submissions this book would not have been born. We owe a great deal to the reviewers who reviewed entire chapters and gave the authors and editors much needed guidance. Also, we would like to thank those dedicated reviewers, who did not contribute through authoring chapters to the current book or to our second book Heuristics and Optimization for Knowledge Discovery–Paul Darwen, Ross Hayward, and Joarder Kamruzzaman.

A further special note of thanks must go also to all the staff at Idea Group Publishing, whose contributions throughout the whole process from the conception of the idea to final publication have been invaluable. In closing, we wish to thank all the authors for their insights and excellent contributions to this book. In addition, this book would not have been possible without the ongoing professional support from Senior Editor Dr. Mehdi Khosrowpour, Managing Editor Ms. Jan Travers and Development Editor Ms. Michele Rossi at Idea Group Publishing. Finally, we want to thank our families for their love, support, and patience throughout this project.

Hussein A. Abbass, Ruhul Sarker, and Charles Newton
Editors (2001)

PART ONE:

GENERAL HEURISTICS

Chapter I

From Evolution to Immune to Swarm to ...? A Simple Introduction to Modern Heuristics

Hussein A. Abbass
University of New South Wales, Australia

The definition of heuristic search has evolved over the last two decades. With the continuous success of modern heuristics in solving many combinatorial problems, it is imperative to scrutinize the success of these methods applied to data mining. This book provides a repository for the applications of heuristics to data mining. In this chapter, however, we present a textbook-like simple introduction to heuristics. It is apparent that the limited space of this chapter will not be enough to elucidate each of the discussed techniques. Notwithstanding, our emphasis will be conceptual. We will familiarize the reader with the different heuristics effortlessly, together with a list of references that should allow the researcher to find his/her own way in this large area of research. The heuristics that will be covered in this chapter are simulated annealing (SA), tabu search (TS), genetic algorithms (GA), immune systems (IS), and ant colony optimization (ACO).

INTRODUCTION

Problem solving is the core of many disciplines. To solve a problem properly, we need first to represent it. *Problem representation* is a critical step in problem solving as it can help in finding good solutions quickly and it can make it almost impossible not to find a solution at all.

In practice, there are many different ways to represent a problem. For example, *operations research* (OR) is a field that represents a problem quantitatively. In *artificial intelligence* (AI), a problem is usually represented by a graph, whether this graph is a network, tree, or any other graph representation. In computer science and engineering, tools such as system charts are used to assist in the problem representation. In general, deciding on an appropriate representation of a problem influences the choice of the appropriate approach to solve it. Therefore, we need somehow to choose the problem solving approach before representing the problem. However, it is often difficult to decide on the problem solving approach before completing the representation. For example, we may choose to represent a problem using an optimization model, then we find out that this is not suitable because there are some qualitative aspects that also need to be captured in our representation.

Once a problem is represented, the need arises for a search algorithm to explore the different alternatives (solutions) to solve the problem and to choose one or more good possible solutions. If there are no means of evaluating the solutions' quality, we are usually just interested in finding any solution. If there is a criterion that we can use to differentiate between different solutions, we are usually interested in finding the best or optimal solution. Two types of optimality are generally distinguished: local and global. A local optimal solution is the best solution found within a region (*neighborhood*) of the search space, but not necessarily the best solution in the overall search space. A global optimal solution is the best solution in the overall search space.

To formally define these concepts, we need first to introduce one of the definitions of a neighborhood. A neighborhood $B_\delta(x)$ in the search space $\theta(X)$ defined on $X \subseteq R^n$ and centered on a solution x is defined by the Euclidean distance δ; that is $B_\delta(x) = \{x \in R^n \mid ||x - x|| < \delta, \delta > 0\}$. Now, we can define local and global optimality as follows:

Definition 1: Local optimality A solution $x \in \theta(X)$ is said to be a local minimum of the problem iff $\exists\ \delta > 0$ such that $f(x) \le f(x) \forall x \in (B_\delta(x) \cap \theta(X))$.

Definition 2: Global optimality A solution $x \in \theta(X)$ is said to be a global minimum of the problem iff $\exists\ \delta > 0$ such that $f(x) \le f(x) \forall x \in \theta(X)$.

Finding a global optimal solution in most real-life applications is difficult. The number of alternatives that exist in the search space is usually enormous and cannot be searched in a reasonable amount of time. However, we are usually interested in good enough solutions—or what we will call from now on, *satisfactory solutions*. To search for a local, global, or satisfactory solution, we need to use a search mechanism.

Search is an important field of research, not only because it serves all disciplines, but also because problems are getting larger and more complex; therefore, more efficient search techniques need to be developed every day. This is true whether a problem is solved quantitatively or qualitatively.

In the literature, there exist three types of search mechanisms (Turban, 1990), *analytical*, *blind*, and *heuristic* search techniques. These are discussed below.

- **Analytical Search:** An analytical search algorithm is guided using some mathematical function. In optimization, for example, some search algorithms are guided using the gradient, whereas others the Hessian. These types of algorithms guarantee to find the optimal solution if it exists. However, in most cases they only guarantee to find a local optimal solution and not the global one.
- **Blind Search:** Blind search—sometimes called unguided search - is usually categorized into two classes: complete and incomplete. A complete search technique simply enumerates the search space and exhaustively searches for the optimal solution. An incomplete search technique keeps generating a set of solutions until an optimal one is found. Incomplete search techniques do not guarantee to find the optimal solution since they are usually biased in the way they search the problem space.
- **Heuristic Search:** It is a guided search, widely used in practice, but does not guarantee to find the optimal solution. However, in most cases it works and produces high quality (satisfactory) solutions.

To be concise in our description, we need to distinguish between a general purpose search technique (such as all the techniques covered in this chapter), which can be applied to a wide range of problems, and a special purpose search technique which is domain specific (such as GSAT for the propositional satisfiability problem and back-propagation for training artificial neural networks) which will not be addressed in this chapter.

A general search algorithm has three main phases: initial start, a method for generating solutions, and a criterion to terminate the search. Logically, to search a space, we need to find a starting point. The choice of a starting point is very critical in most search algorithms as it usually biases the search towards some area of the search space. This is the first type of bias introduced into the search algorithm, and to overcome this bias, we usually need to run the algorithm many times with different starting points.

The second stage in a search algorithm is to define how a new solution can be generated, another type of bias. An algorithm, which is guided by the gradient, may become stuck in a saddle point. Finally, the choice of a stopping criterion depends on the problem on hand. If we have a large-scale problem, the decision maker may not be willing to wait for years to get a solution. In this case, we may end the search even before the algorithm stabilizes. From some researchers' points of view, this is unacceptable. However in practice, it is necessary.

An important issue that needs to be considered in the design of a search algorithm is whether it is population based or not. Most traditional OR and AI methods maintain a single solution at a time. Therefore, the algorithm starts with a solution and then moves from it to another. Some heuristic search methods, however, use a population(s) of solutions. In this case, we try to improve the population as a whole, rather than improving a single solution at a time. Other heuristics maintain a probability distribution of the population instead of storing a large number of individuals (solutions) in the memory.

Another issue when designing a search algorithm is the balance between intensification and exploration of the search. Early intensification of the search increases the probability that the algorithm will return a local optimal solution. Late intensification of the search may result in a waste of resources.

The last issue which should be considered in designing a search algorithm is the type of knowledge used by the algorithm and the type of search strategy. Positive knowledge means that the algorithm rewards good solutions and negative knowledge means that the algorithm penalizes bad solutions. By rewarding or penalizing some solutions in the search space, an algorithm generates some belief about the good or bad areas in the search. A positive search strategy biases the search towards a good area of the search space, and a negative search strategy avoids an already explored area to explore those areas in the search space that have not been previously covered. Keeping these issues of designing a search algorithm in mind, we can now introduce heuristic search.

The word *heuristic* originated from the Greek root $\varepsilon\upsilon\rho\iota\sigma\kappa\omega$, or to discover. In problem solving, a heuristic is a rule of thumb approach. In artificial intelligence, a heuristic is a procedure that may lack a proof. In optimization, a heuristic is an approach which may not be guaranteed to converge. In all previous fields, a heuristic is a type of search that may not be guaranteed to find a solution, but put simply "*it works*". About heuristics, Newell and Simon wrote (Simon 1960): "*We now have the elements of a theory of heuristic (as contrasted with algorithmic) problem solving; and we can use this theory both to understand human heuristic processes and to simulate such processes with digital computers.*"

The area of Heuristics has evolved rapidly over the last two decades. Researchers, who are used to working with conventional heuristic search techniques, are becoming interested in finding a new $A*$ algorithm for their problems. $A*$ is a search technique that is guided by the solution's cost estimate. For an algorithm to qualify to be $A*$, a proof is usually undertaken to show that this algorithm guarantees to find the minimum solution, if it exists. This is a very nice characteristic. However, it does not say anything regarding the efficiency and scalability of these algorithms with regard to large-scale problems.

Nowadays, heuristic search left the cage of conventional AI-type search and is now inspired by biology, statistical mechanics, neuroscience, and physics, to name but a few. We will see some of these heuristics in this chapter, but since the field is evolving rapidly, a single chapter can only provide a simple introduction to the topic. These new heuristic search techniques will be called modern heuristics, to distinguish them from the $A*$-type heuristics.

A core issue in many modern heuristics is the process for generating solutions from within the neighborhood. This process can be done in many different ways. We will propose one way in the next section. The remaining sections of this chapter will then present different modern heuristics.

GENERATION OF NEIGHBORHOOD SOLUTIONS

In our introduction, we defined the neighborhood of a solution x as all solutions within an Euclidean distance of at most δ from x. This might be suitable for continuous domains. However, for discrete domains, the Euclidean distance is not the best choice. One metric measure for discrete binary domains is the hamming distance, which is simply the number of corresponding bits with different values in the two solutions. Therefore, if we have a solution of length n, the number of solutions in the neighborhood (we will call it the *neighborhood size*) defined by a hamming distance of 1 is simply n. We will call the distance, δ, that defines a neighborhood, the *neighborhood length or radius*. Now, we can imagine the importance of the neighborhood length. If we assume a large-scale problem with a million binary variables, the smallest neighborhood length for this problem (a neighborhood length of 1) defines a *neighborhood size* of one million. This size will obviously influence the amount of time needed to search a neighborhood.

Let us now define a simple neighborhood function that we can use in the rest of this chapter. A solution x is generated in the neighborhood of another solution x by changing up to ζ variables of x, where ζ is the neighborhood length. The neighborhood length is measured in terms of the number of cells with different values in both solutions. Figure 1 presents an algorithm for generating solutions at random from the neighborhood of x.

Figure 1: Generation of neighborhood solutions

```
function neighborhood(x,ζ)
    x ← x
    i = 0
    while i < ζ
            k= random(0,1) x n
            x[k] = random(0,1)
            i = i + 1
    Loop
    return x
end function
```

Figure 2: Hill climbing algorithm

initialize the neighborhood length to ζ
initialize optimal solution $x_{opt} \in \theta(x)$ and its objective value $f_{opt} = f(x_{opt})$
    repeat
        $x \in neighbourhood(x_{opt}, \zeta), f = f(x)$
        if $f < f_{opt}$ **then** $x_{opt} = x, f_{opt} = f$
    until *loop condition is satisfied*
return $x_{opt \, and} f_{opt}$

HILL CLIMBING

Hill climbing is the greediest heuristic ever. The idea is simply not to accept a move unless it improves the best solution found so far. This represents a pure search intensification without any chance for search exploration; therefore the algorithm is more likely to return a local optimum and be very sensitive in relating to the starting point.

In Figure 2, the hill climbing algorithm is presented. The algorithm starts by initializing a solution at random. A loop is then constructed to generate a solution in the neighborhood of the current one. If the new solution is better than the current one, it is accepted; otherwise it is rejected and a new solution from the neighborhood is generated.

SIMULATED ANNEALING

In the process of physical annealing (Rodrigues and Anjo, 1993), a solid is heated until all particles randomly arrange themselves forming the liquid state. A slow cooling process is then used to crystallize the liquid. That is, the particles are free to move at high temperatures and then will gradually lose their mobility when the temperature decreases (Ansari and Hou, 1997). This process is described in the early work in statistical mechanics of Metropolis (Metropolis et al., 1953) and is well known as the Metropolis algorithm (Figure 3).

Figure 3: Metropolis algorithm.

define the transition of the substance from state i with energy $E(i)$ to state j with energy $E(j)$ to be $i \rightarrow j$
define T to be a temperature level
if $E(i) \le E(j)$ **then** accept $i \rightarrow j$
if $E(i) > E(j)$ **then** accept $i \rightarrow j$ with probability $\exp\left(\dfrac{E(i) - E(j)}{KT}\right)$
    where K is the Boltzmann constant

Kirkpatrick et al. (1998) defined an analogy between the Metropolis algorithm and the search for solutions in complex combinatorial optimization problems where they developed the idea of *simulated annealing* (SA). Simply speaking, SA is a stochastic computational technique that searches for global optimal solutions in optimization problems. In complex combinatorial optimization problems, it is usually easy to be trapped in a local optimum. The main goal here is to give the algorithm more time in the search space exploration by accepting moves, which may degrade the solution quality, with some probability depending on a parameter called the *"temperature."* When the temperature is high, the algorithm behaves like random search (*i.e.,* accepts all transitions whether they are good or not, to enable search exploration). A cooling mechanism is used to gradually reduce the temperature. The algorithm performs similar to a greedy hill-climbing algorithm when the temperature reaches zero (enabling search intensification). If this process is given sufficient time, there is a high probability that it will result in a global optimal solution (Ansari and Hou, 1997). The algorithm escapes a local optimal solution by moving with some probability to those solutions which degrade the current one and accordingly gives a high opportunity to explore more of the search space. The probability of accepting a bad solution, *p(T)*, follows a Boltzmann (also known as the Gibbs) distribution of:

$$\pi(T) = \exp\left(\frac{E(i) - E(j)}{KT} \right) \qquad (1)$$

where *E(i)* is the energy or objective value of the current solution, E(j) is the previous solution's energy, *T* is the temperature, and *K* is a Boltzmann constant. In actual implementation, *K* can be taken as a scaling factor to keep the temperature between 0 and 1, if it is desirable that the temperature falls within this interval. Unlike most heuristic search techniques, there is a proof for the convergence of SA (Ansari and Hou, 1997) assuming that the time , *L*, spent at each temperature level, *T*, is sufficient, usually when $T \to 0, L \to \infty$.

The Algorithm

There are two main approaches in SA: homogeneous and non-homogeneous (Vidal, 1993). In the former, the temperature is not updated after each step in the search space, although for the latter it is. It is found that in homogeneous SA, the transitions or generations of solutions for each temperature level represent a Markov chain of length equal to the number of transitions at that temperature level. The proof for the convergence of SA uses the homogenous version. The Markov chain length represents the time taken at each temperature level. The homogeneous algorithm is shown in Figure 4.

The homogeneous algorithm starts with three inputs from the user, the initial temperature *T*, the initial Markov chain length *L*, and the neighborhood length ζ. Then, it generates an initial solution, evaluates it, and stores it as the best solution found so far. After that, for each temperature level, a new solution is generated from

Figure 4: General homogeneous simulated annealing algorithm

initialize the temperature to T
initialize the chain length to L
initialize the neighborhood length to ζ
$x_0 \in \theta(x), f_0 = f(x_0)$
initialize optimal solution x_{opt} to be x_0 and its objective value $f_{opt} = f_0$
initialize current solution $\hat{x}$ to be x_0 and its objective value $\hat{f} = f_0$
repeat
    for $j = 0$ **to** L
        $i = i+1$
        $x_i \in neighbourhood(\hat{x}, \zeta), f_i = f(x_i)$
        $\Delta(f) = f_i - \hat{f}$
        if $f_i < f_{opt}$ **then** $x_{opt} = x_i,, f_{opt} = f_i$
        if $f_i < \hat{f}$ **then** $\hat{x} = x_i,, \hat{f} = f_i$ **else if** $\exp(-\Delta(f)/T) > random(0,1)$
        then $\hat{x} = x_i,, \hat{f} = f_i$
    next j
    update L and T
until loop condition is satisfied
return x_{opt} and f_{opt}

the current solution neighborhood function *neighbourhood*$(\hat{x}, \zeta)$, tested, and replaces the current optimal solution if it is better than it. The new solution is then tested against the previous solution—if it is better, the algorithm accepts it; otherwise it is accepted with a certain probability as specified in Equation 1. After completing each Markov chain of length L, the temperature and the Markov chain length are updated. The question now is: how to update the temperature T or the cooling schedule.

Cooling Schedule

In the beginning of the simulated annealing run, we need to find a reasonable value of T such that most transitions are accepted. This value can first be guessed. We then increase T with some factor until all transitions are accepted. Another way is to generate a set of random solutions and find the minimum temperature T that guarantees the acceptance of these solutions. Following the determination of the starting value of T, we need to define a cooling schedule for it. Two methods are usually used in the literature. The first is static, where we need to define a discount parameter. After the completion of each Markov chain, k, adjust T as follows (Vidal, 1993):

$$T_{k+1} = \alpha \times T_k, 0 < \alpha < 1 \tag{2}$$

The second is dynamic, where one of its versions was introduced by Huang, Romeo, and Sangiovanni-Vincetilli (1986). Here,

$$T_{K+1} = T_k e^{\left(-\frac{T_k \Delta(E)}{\sigma_{T_k}^2}\right)} \tag{3}$$

$$\Delta(E) = E_{T_k} - E_{T_{k-1}} \tag{4}$$

where is the variance of the accepted solutions at temperature level . When $\sigma_{T_k}^2$ is large—which will usually take place at the start of the search while the algorithm is behaving like a random search - the change in the temperature will be very small. When $\sigma_{T_k}^2$ is small—which will usually take place at the end of the search while intensification of the search is at its peak—the temperature will diminish to zero quickly.

TABU SEARCH

Glover (1989, 1990) introduced *tabu search* (TS) as a method for escaping local optima. The goal is to obtain a list of forbidden (tabu) solutions/directions in the neighborhood of a solution to avoid cycling between solutions while allowing a direction, which may degrade the solution although it may help in escaping from the local optimum. Similar to SA, we need to specify how to generate solutions in the current solution's neighborhood. Furthermore, the temperature parameter in SA is replaced with a list of forbidden solutions/directions updated after each step. When generating a solution in the neighborhood, this solution should not be in any of the directions listed in the tabu-list, although a direction in the tabu-list may be chosen with some probability if it results in a solution which is better than the current one. In essence, the tabu-list aims at constraining or limiting the search scope in the neighborhood while still having a chance to select one of these directions.

Figure 5: The tabu search algorithm

```
initialize the neighborhood length to ζ
initialize the memory, M, to empty
x₀ ∈ θ(x), f₀ = f(x₀)
x_opt = x₀, f_opt = f₀
x̄ = x₀, f̂ = f₀
i=1
repeat
    i = i + 1
    xᵢ ∈ neighborhood(x̄,ζ), fᵢ = f(xᵢ)
    if fᵢ < f_opt then x_opt = x,ᵢ, f_opt = fᵢ
    if fᵢ < f̂ then x̄ = x,ᵢ, f̂ = fᵢ else if x_k ∉ M then x̄ = x,ᵢ, f̂ = fᵢ
    update M with x_k
until loop condition is satisfied
return x_opt and f_opt
```

The Algorithm

The TS algorithm is presented in Figure 5. A new solution is generated within the current solution's neighborhood function $neighborhood(x,\zeta)$. If the new solution is better than the best solution found so far, it is accepted and saved as the best found. If the new solution is better than the current solution, it is accepted and saved as the current solution. If the new solution is not better than the current solution and it is not in a direction within the tabu list M, it is accepted as the current solution and the search continues from there. If the solution is tabu, the current solution remains unchanged and a new solution is generated. After accepting a solution, M is updated to forbid returning to this solution again.

The list M can be a list of the solutions visited in the last n iterations. However, this is a memory-consuming process and it is a limited type of memory. Another possibility is to define the neighborhood in terms of a set of moves. Therefore, instead of storing the solution, the reverse of the move, which produced this solution, is stored instead. Clearly, this approach prohibits, not only returning to where we came from, but also many other possible solutions. Notwithstanding, since the tabu list is a short-term memory list, at some point in the search, the reverse of the move will be eliminated from the tabu list, therefore, allowing to explore this part of the search space which was tabu.

A very important parameter here, in addition to the neighborhood length which is a critical parameter for many other heuristics such as SA, is the choice of the tabu-list size which is referred to in the literature as the *adaptive memory*. This is a problem-dependent parameter, since the choice of a large size would be inefficient in terms of memory capacity and the time required to scan the list. On the other hand, choosing the list size to be small would result in a cycling problem; that is, revisiting the same state again (Glover, 1989). In general, the tabu-list's size is a very critical issue for the following reasons:

1. The performance of tabu search is sensitive to the size of the tabu-list in many cases.
2. There is no general algorithm to determine the optimal tabu-list size apart from experimental results.
3. Choosing a large tabu-list is inefficient in terms of speed and memory.

GENETIC ALGORITHM

The previous heuristics move from a single solution to another single solution, one at a time. In this section, we introduce a different concept where we have a population of solutions and we would like to move from one population to another. Therefore, a group of solutions evolve towards the good area(s) in the search space.

In trying to understand evolutionary mechanisms, Holland (1998) devised a new search mechanism, which he called a genetic algorithm, based on Darwin's (1859) principle of natural selection. In its simple form, a genetic algorithm recursively applies the concepts of *selection*, *crossover*, and *mutation* to a randomly generated population of promising solutions with the best solution found being reported. In a comparison to analytical optimization techniques (Goldberg,1989), a number of strings are generated with each finite-length string representing a solution vector coded into some finite alphabet. Instead of using derivatives or similar information, as in analytical optimization techniques, the fitness of a solution is measured relative to all other solutions in the population, and natural operators, such as crossover and mutation, are used to generate new solutions from existing ones. Since GA is contingent upon coding the parameters, the choice of the right representation is a crucial issue (Goldberg, 1989). In its early stage, Holland (1998) coded the strings in GA using the binary set of alphabets {0,1}, that is the binary representation. He introduced the *Schema Theorem*, which provides a lower bound on the change in the sampling rate for a hyperplane (representing a group of adjacent solutions) from one generation to another. A schema is a subset of the solution space whose elements are identical in particular loci. It is a building block that samples one or more hyperplanes. Other representations use integer or real numbers. A generic GA algorithm is presented in Figure 6.

Reproduction strategies

A reproduction strategy is the process of building a population of individuals in a generation from a previous generation. There are a number of reproduction strategies presented in the literature, among them, *canonical*, *simple*, and *breedN*. Canonical GA (Whitley, 1994) is similar to Schwefel's (1981) evolutionary strategy where the offspring replace all the parents; that is, the crossover probability is 1. In simple GA (Goldberg, 1989), two individuals are selected and the crossover occurs with a certain probability. If the crossover takes place, the offspring are placed in the

Figure 6: A generic genetic algorithm

```
let G denote a generation, P a population of size M, and x^l the l^th
chromosome in P
initialize the initial population P_{G=0} = {x^1_{G=0}, ..., x^M_{G=0}}
evaluate every x^l ∈ P_{G=0}, l = 1, ..., M
k=1
while the stopping criteria is not satisfied do
     select P^\ (an intermediate population) from P_{G=k-1}
     P_{G=k} ← crossover elements in P^\
     mutate elements in P_{G=k}
     evaluate every x^l ∈ P_{G=0,} l = 1, ..., M
     k = k+1
end while
return the best encountered solution
```

new population; otherwise the parents are cloned. The *breeder genetic algorithm* (Mühlenbein and Schlierkamp-Voosen, 1993; Mühlenbein and Schlierkamp-Voosen 1994) or the breedN strategy is based on quantitative genetics. It assumes that there is an imaginary breeder who performs a selection of the best N strings in a population and breeds among them. Mühlenbein (1994) comments that if "GA is based on natural selection", then "breeder GA is based on artificial selection."

Another popular reproduction strategy, the *parallel genetic algorithm* (Mühlenbein et al. 1988; Mühlenbein 1991), employs parallelism. In parallel GA, a number of populations evolve in parallel but independently, and migration occurs among the populations intermittently. A combination of the breeder GA and parallel GA is known as the *distributed breeder genetic algorithm (*Mühlenbein and Schlierkamp-Voosen 1993). In a comparison between parallel GA and breeder GA, Mühlenbein (1993) states that "parallel GA models evolution which self-organizes" but "breeder GA models rational controlled evolution."

Selection

There are many alternatives for selection in GA. One method is based on the principle of "living for the fittest" or *fitness-proportionate selection* (Jong, 1975), where the objective functions' values for all the population's individuals are scaled and an individual is selected in proportion to its fitness. The fitness of an individual is the scaled objective value of that individual. The objective values can be scaled in differing ways, such as linear, sigma, and window scaling.

Another alternative is the *stochastic-Baker selection* (Goldberg, 1989), where the objective values of all the individuals in the population are divided by the average to calculate the fitness, and the individual is copied into the intermediate population a number of times equal to the integer part, if any, of the fitness value. The population is then sorted according to the fraction part of the fitness, and the intermediate population is completed using a fitness-proportionate selection.

Tournament selection is another famous strategy (Wetzel, 1983), where N chromosomes are chosen uniformly irrespective of their fitness, and the fittest of these is placed into the intermediate population. As this is usually expensive, a modified version called the *modified tournament selection* works by selecting an individual at random and up to N trials are made to pick a fitter one. The first fitter individual encountered is selected; otherwise, the first individual wins.

Crossover

Many crossover operators have been developed in the GA literature. Here, four crossover operators (one-point, two-point, uniform, and even-odd) are reported. To disentangle the explication, assume that we have two individuals that we would like to crossover, $x = (x_1, x_2, \ldots, x_n)$ and $y = (y_1, y_2, \ldots, y_n)$ to produce two children, *c1* and *c2*.

In *one-point crossover* (sometimes written 1-point) (Holland, 1998), a cut point, p_1, is generated at random in the range [1,n) and the corresponding parts to the right and left of the cut-point are swapped. Assuming that $\rho_1=2$, the two children are formulated as $c_1 = (x_1, x_2, y_3, \ldots, y_n)$ and $c_2 = (y_1, y_2, x_3, \ldots, x_n)$. In *two-point crossover* (sometimes written 2-points) (Holland 1998; Jong 1975), two cut points, $\rho_1 < \rho_2$, are generated at random in the range $[1,n)$ and the two middle parts in the two chromosomes are interchanged. Assuming that, the two children are formulated as $c_1 = (x_1, y_2, y_3, y_4, y_5, x_6, \ldots, x_n)$ and $c_2 = (y_1, x_2, x_3, x_4, x_5, y_6, \ldots, y_n)$. In *uniform crossover* (Ackley 1987), for each two corresponding genes in the parents' chromosomes, a coin is flipped to choose one of them (50-50 chance) to be placed in the same position as the child. In *even-odd crossover*, those genes in the even positions of the first chromosome and those in the odd positions of the second are placed in the first child and vice-versa for the second; that is, $c_1 = (y_1, x_2, y_3, \ldots, x_n)$ and $c_2 = (x_1, y_2, x_3, \ldots, y_n)$ assuming n is even.

Mutation

Mutation is a basic operator in GAs that introduces variation within the genetic materials, to maintain enough variations within the population, by changing the loci's value with a certain probability. If an allele is lost due to selection pressure, mutation increases the probability of retrieving this allele again.

IMMUNE SYSTEMS

In biological immune systems (Hajela and Yoo 1999), type-specific antibodies recognize and eliminate the antigens (*i.e.*, pathogens representing foreign cells and molecules). It has been estimated that the immune system is able to recognize at least 10^{16} antigens; an overwhelming recognition task given that the genome contains about 10^5 genes. For all possible antigens that are likely to be encountered, the immune system must use segments of genes to construct the necessary antibodies. For example, there are between 10^7 and 10^8 different antibodies in a typical mammal. In biological systems, this recognition problem translates into a complex geometry matching process. The antibody molecule region contains a specialized portion, the paratope, which is constructed from amino acids and is used for identifying other molecules. The amino acids determine the paratope as well as the antigen molecules' shapes that can be attached to the paratope. Therefore, the antibody can have a geometry that is specific to a particular antigen.

To recognize the antigen segment, a subset of the gene segments' library is synthesized to encode the genetic information of an antibody. The gene segments act cooperatively to partition the antigen recognition task. In immune, an individual's fitness is determined by its ability to recognize—through chemical binding and electrostatic charges—either a specific or a broader group of antigens.

The algorithm

There are different versions of the algorithms inspired by the immune system. This book contains two chapters about immune systems. In order to reduce the overlap between the chapters, we will restrict our introduction to a simple algorithm that hybridizes immune systems and genetic algorithms.

In 1998, an evolutionary approach was suggested by Dasgupta (1998) for use in the cooperative matching task of gene segments. The approach (Dasgupta, 1999) is based on genetic algorithms with a change in the mechanism for computing the fitness function. Therefore, in each GA generation, the top y% individuals in the population are chosen as antigens and compared against the population (antibodies) a number of times suggested to be twice the population size (Dasgupta, 1999). For each time, an antigen is selected at random from the set of antigens and compared to a population's subset. A similarity measure (assuming a binary representation, the measure is usually the hamming distance between the antigen and each individual in the selected subset) is calculated for all individuals in the selected subset. Then, the similarity value for the individual which has the highest similarity

Figure 7: The immune system algorithm

---

let G denote a generation and P a population

$$P_{G=0} = \left\{ x_{G=0}^{1}, \mathsf{K}, x_{G=0}^{M} \right\}$$

initialize the initial population of solutions

evaluate every $x^{l} \in P_{G=0}, l = 1, \mathsf{K}, M$
compare_with_antigen_and_update_fitness($P_{G=0}$)
k=1
while *the stopping criteria is not satisfied* **do**
    select P' (an intermediate population) from $P_{G=k-1}$
    mutate element in $P_{G=k}$
    evaluate every $x^{l} \in P_{G=k}$, *1, ..., M*
    compare _with_antigen_and_update_fitness ($P_{G=k}$)
    k=k+1
return $x = \arg \max l f(x^{l}), x^{l} \in P_{G=k}$, *the best encountered solution*

procedure *compare_with_antigen_and_update_fitness($P_{G=k}$)*
    antigen=top y% in ($P_{G=k}$)
    l=0
    while *l<2xM*
        antibodies $\subset P_{G=k}$
        randomly select $y \in antigen$
        find x where similarity(y, x) = $\arg \max_{\overline{x}} ximilarity(y, \overline{x}), \overline{x} \in antibodies$
        add similarity(y, x) to the fitness of $x \in P_{G=k}$
        l = l + 1
end procedure

to the antigen is added to its fitness value and the process continues. The algorithm is presented in Figure 7. Different immune concepts inspired other computational models. For further information, the reader may wish to refer to Dasgupta, 1999).

ANT COLONY OPTIMIZATION

Ant Colony Optimization (ACO) (Dorigo and Caro, 1999) is a branch of a newly developed form of artificial intelligence called *swarm intelligence*. Swarm intelligence is a field which studies "the emergent collective intelligence of groups of simple agents" (Bonabeau et al., 1999). In groups of insects which live in colonies, such as ants and bees, an individual can only do simple tasks on its own while the colony's cooperative work is the main reason determining the intelligent behavior it shows.

Real ants are blind. However, each ant, while it is walking, deposits a chemical substance on the ground called *pheromone* (Dorigo and Caro, 1999). Pheromone encourages the following ants to stay close to previous moves. The pheromone evaporates with time to allow search exploration. In a couple of experiments presented by Dorigo et al. (1996), the complex behavior of the ants' colony is illustrated. For example, a set of ants built a path to some food. An obstacle with two ends is then placed in their way where one end of the obstacle was more distant than the other. In the beginning, equal numbers of ants spread around the two ends of the obstacle. Since all ants have almost the same speed, the ants going around the nearer end of the obstacle return before the ants going around the farther end (differential path effect). With time, the amount of pheromone the ants deposit increases more rapidly on the shorter path and so more ants prefer this path. This positive effect is called *autocatalysis*. The difference between the two paths is called the *preferential path effect* and it is the cause of the pheromone between the two sides of the obstacle since the ants following the shorter path will make more visits to the source than those following the longer path. Because of pheromone evaporation, pheromone on the longer path vanishes with time.

The Algorithm

The *Ant System* (AS) (Dorigo et al., 1991) is the first algorithm based on the behavior of real ants for solving combinatorial optimization problems. The algorithm worked well on small problems but did not scale well for large-scale problems (Bonabeau et al., 1999). Many algorithms were developed to improve the performance of AS where two main changes were introduced. First, specialized local search techniques were added to improve the ants' performance. Second, allowing ants to deposit pheromone while they are building up the solution in addition to the normal rule of AS where an ant deposits pheromone after completing a solution. A generic updated version of the ACO algorithm presented in Dorigo, M. and G. Caro (1999) is presented in Figure 8. In Figure 9, a conceptual diagram of the ACO algorithm is presented.

In the figures, the pheromone table is initialized with equal pheromones. The pheromone table represents that amount of pheromone deposited by the ants between two different states (*i.e.*, nodes in the graph). Therefore, the table can be a square matrix with the dimension depending on the number of states (nodes) in the problem. While the termination condition is not satisfied, an ant is created and initialized with an initial state. The ant starts constructing a path from the initial state to its pre-defined goal state (generation of solutions, see Figure 9) using a probabilistic action choice rule based on the ant routing table. Depending on the pheromone update rule, the ant updates the ant routing table (reinforcement). This takes place either after each ant constructs a solution (*online update rule*) or after all ants have finished constructing their solutions (*delayed update rule*). In the following two sub-sections, different methods for constructing the ant routing table and pheromone update are given.

Figure 8: Generic ant colony optimization heuristic (Dorigo and Caro, 1999)

```
procedure ACO_heuristic()
    initialize pheromone_table
    while (termination_criterion_not_satisfied)
        foreach ant k do
            initialize _ant ();
            M ← update _ant _memory ();
            Ω ← a set of problem's constraints
            while (current _state ≠ target _state)
                A=read _local _ant – routing _table ();
                P=compute _transition _probabilit ies (A, M, Ω)
                next _state = apply _ant _decision _policy (P, Ω)
                move _to _next _state (next _state);
                if (online _step _by _step _pheronome _update)
                then
                    deposit _phermone _on _the _visited _arc ();
                    update _ant _routing _table ();
                    M ← update _int ernal _state ();
            if (online_delayed_pheromone_update)
            then foreach visited_arc do
                deposit _phermone _on _the _visited _arc ();
                update _ant _routing _table ();
            die();
            update_thepheromone_table();
    end procedure
```

Figure 9: The ant algorithm

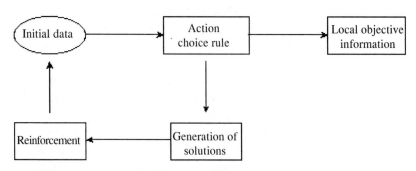

Ant Routing Table (Action Choice Rule)

The ant routing table is a normalization of the pheromone table where the ant builds up its route by a probabilistic rule based on the pheromone available at each possible step and its memory. There are a number of suggestions in the literature for the probabilistic decision (the element in row i column j in the matrix A (Figure 8) representing the probability that the ant will move from the current state i to the next potential state j). The first is the following rule:

$$\alpha_{ij} = \frac{\tau_{ij}(t)}{\sum_{l \in N_i} \tau_{il}(t)} \tag{5}$$

Here, the ant utilizes the pheromone information (τ_{ij} is the pheromone between the current state i and the next potential state j) only to decide on its next step (N_i is the set of possible transitions from state i). This rule does not require any parameter settings, however it is a biased exploratory strategy that can quickly lead to stagnation. Another rule suggested by Dorigo, Maniezzo and Colorni (1991) is:

$$\alpha_{ij} = \frac{[\tau_{ij}(t)]^{\alpha}[\eta_{ij}]^{\beta}}{\sum_{l \in N_i}[\tau_{ij}(t)]^{\alpha}[\eta_{ij}]^{\beta}} \tag{6}$$

where we need two parameters α and β. The heuristic value η_{ij} is used for the intensification of the search by means of a greedy behavior. For example, the heuristic value can be the immediate change in the objective resulting from increasing the value of a variable with 1 unit regardless of the effect of this increase on the overall solution. When $\beta=1$, $\alpha=0$ the algorithm behaves like a local search and when $\beta=0$, $\alpha=1$, stagnation may occur as previously mentioned. A balance is usually required between α (the pheromone information's weight) and β (the local search's weight). However, this rule is computationally expensive because of the exponents. As an attempt to overcome this, the following rule was suggested (Dorigo and Gambardella, 1997):

$$\alpha_{ij} = \frac{[\tau_{ij}(t)][\eta_{ij}]^{\beta}}{\sum_{l \in N_i}[\tau_{il}(t)][\eta_{il}]^{\beta}} \tag{7}$$

where only one parameter β is used.

Another alternative is to switch between any of the previous rules and the rule of choosing the transition with the maximum pheromone level, with some probability.

Pheromone update (reinforcement) rule

Each time a pheromone update is required, the ants use the following rule:

$$\tau_{ij}^{k}(t) \leftarrow (1-\rho)\tau_{ij}^{k}(t-1) + \Delta\tau_{ij}^{k}(t-1), \quad \forall i, j, k \tag{8}$$

where ρ is a discount factor for pheromone evaporation, ij represents a transition between state i and state j, and k is the number of ants. A number of suggestions were used in the literature for calculating the rate of pheromone's change $\Delta\tau_{ij}^{k}(t-1)$. For example, in MMAS-QAP system,

$$\Delta\tau_{ij}^{k}(t-1) = \begin{cases} 1/J^{best} & if\ ant\ k\ moves from\ state\ i\ to\ state\ j \\ 0 & otherwise \end{cases} \tag{9}$$

where J^{best} is the objective value of the best solution found by the colony. We may note here that when the objective value increases, the rate of pheromone change decreases, enabling the search's intensification. Another suggestion is to calculate $\Delta\tau_{ij}^{k}(t-1)$ (Bonabeau et al., 1999) as follows:

$$\Delta\tau_{ij}^{k}(t-1) = \begin{cases} \sum_{k \in K} C/J^{k} & if\ ant\ k\ moves\ from\ state\ i\ to\ state\ j \\ 0 & otherwise \end{cases} \tag{10}$$

where, K is the set of ants that visited transition ij, J^{k} is the objective value of the solution generated by ant k, C is a constant representing a lower bound on the solutions that will be generated by the algorithm.

To summarize, at the beginning of the algorithm, the pheromone matrix is initialized. In each step, the pheromone matrix is normalized to construct the ant routing table. The ants generate a set of solutions (one solution per ant) by moving from a state to another using the action choice rule. Each element in the pheromone matrix is then updated using the pheromone update step and the algorithm continues.

CONCLUSION

In this chapter, we have introduced a set of heuristic search techniques. Although our coverage was very sparse, it provides the reader with the basics of this research area and points to useful references concerning these heuristics. Notwithstanding, there are many general purpose heuristics that have not been covered in this chapter, such as evolutionary strategies, evolutionary programming, genetic programming, scatter search, and quantum computing to name but a few. Nevertheless, the heuristics covered in this chapter are the basic ones, and most of the others can be easily followed if the readers have comprehended the material briefly described in this chapter.

ACKNOWLEDGMENT

The author would like to thank the reviewers of this chapter and the other editors for their insightful comments. Also, we owe a great deal to E. Kozan, M. Towsey, and J. Diederich for their insights on an initial draft of this chapter.

REFERENCES

Ackley, D. (1987). *A connectionist machine for genetic hill climbing.* Kluwer Academic Publisher.

Ansari, N. and E. Hou (1997). *Computational intelligence for optimization.* Kluwer Academic Publisher.

Bonabeau, E., M. Dorigo, and G. Theraulaz (1999). *Swarm intelligence: from natural to artificial systems.* Oxford Press.

Darwin, C. (1859). *The origins of species by means of natural selection.* London, Penguin Classics.

Dasgupta, D. (1998). *Artificial immune systems and their applications.* Springer-Verlag.

Dasgupta, D. (1999). Information processing in immune system. In D. Corne, M. Dorigo, and F. Glover (Eds.), *New ideas in optimization,* pp. 161-166. McGraw-Hill.

Dorigo, M. and G. Caro (1999). *The ant colony optimization meta-heuristic.* In D. Corne, M. Dorigo, and F. Glover (Eds.), *New ideas in optimization,* pp. 11-32. McGraw-Hill.

Dorigo, M. and L. Gambardella (1997). *Ant colony system: a cooperative learning approach to the traveling salesman problem.* IEEE *Transactions on evolutionary computation* 1, 53-66.

Dorigo, M., V. Maniezzo, and A. Colorni (1991). *Positive feedback as a search strategy.* Technical Report 91-016, Deipartimento di Elettronica, politecnico do Milano, Italy.

Dorigo, M., V. Maniezzo, and A. Colorni (1996). *The ant system: optimization by a colony of cooperating agents. IEEE Transactions on Systems, Man, and Cybernetics* 26(1), 1-13.

Ferber, J. (1999). *Multi-agent systems: an introduction to distributed artificial intelligence.* Addison-Wesley.

Glover, F. (1989). Tabu search: Part 1. ORSA Journal on Computing 1(3), 190-206.

Glover, F. (1990). Tabu search: Part 2. ORSA Journal on Computing 2(1), 4-32.

Goldberg, D. (1989). *Genetic algorithms: in search, optimization and machine learning.* Addison Wesley.

Hajela, P. and J. Yoo (1999). *Immune network modeling in design optimization.* In D. Corne, M. Dorigo, and F. Glover (Eds.), *New ideas in optimization,* pp. 203-216. McGraw-Hill.

Holland, J. (1998). *Adaptation in natural and artificial systems.* MIT Press.

Jong, K. D. (1975). *An analysis of the behavior of a class of genetic adaptive systems.* PhD thesis, University of Michigan.

Kirkpatrick, S., D. Gelatt, and M. Vecchi (1983). *Optimization by simulated annealing.* Science 22, 671-680.

Laidlaw, H. and R. Page (1986). Mating Designs. In T. Rinderer (Ed.), *Bee Genetics and Breeding*, pp. 323-341. Academic Press, Inc.

Maniezzo, V. (1998). *Exact and approximate nondeterministic tree-search procedures for the quadratic assignment problem.* Technical Report CSR 98-1, Corso di Laurea in Scienze dell'Informazione, Universit di Bologna, Sede di Cesena, Italy.

Metropolis, N., A. Rosenbluth, M. Rosenbluth, A. Teller, and E. Teller (1953). Equations of state calculations by fast computing machines. *Chemical Physics* 21, 1087–1092.

Mühlenbein, H. (1991). Evolution in time and space: the parallel genetic algorithm. In G. Rawlins (Ed.), *Foundations of Genetic Algorithms,* pp. 316-337. San Mateo, CA: Morgan-Kaufman.

Mühlenbein, H., M. Gorges-Schleuter, and O. Krämer (1988). Evolutionary algorithms in combinatorial optimization. *Parallel Computing* 7, 65–88.

Mühlenbein, H. and D. Schlierkamp-Voosen (1993). Predictive models for the breeder genetic algorithms: continuous parameter optimization. *Evolutionary Computation* 1(1), 25–49.

Mühlenbein, H. and D. Schlierkamp-Voosen (1994). The science of breeding and its application to the breeder genetic algorithm bga. *Evolutionary Computation* 1 (4), 335–360.

Rodrigues, M. and A. Anjo (1993). On simulating thermodynamics. In R. Vidal (Ed.), *Applied Simulated annealing.* Springer-Verlag.

Ross, P. (1996). *Genetic algorithms and genetic programming: Lecturer Notes.* University of Edinburgh, Department of Artificial Intelligence.

Schwefel, H. (1981). *Numerical optimization of computer models.* Wiler, Chichester.

Simon, H. (1960). The new science of management decisions. Harper and Row, New York.

Storn, R. and K. Price (1995). *Differential evolution: a simple and efficient adaptive scheme for global optimization over continuous spaces.* Technical Report TR-95-012, International Computer Science Institute, Berkeley.

Turban, E. (1990). *Decision support and expert systems: management support systems.* Macmillan series in information systems.

Vidal, R. (1993). *Applied simulated annealing.* Springer-Verlag.

Wetzel, A. (1983). *Evaluation of the effectiveness of genetic algorithms in combinatorial optimization.* Technical report, University of Pittsburgh.

Whitley, D. (1994). A genetic algorithm tutorial. *Statistics and Computing* 4, 65–85.

Chapter II

Approximating Proximity for Fast and Robust Distance-Based Clustering

Vladimir Estivill-Castro, University of Newcastle, Australia
Michael E. Houle, University of Sydney, Australia

Distance-based clustering results in optimization problems that typically are NP-hard or NP-complete and for which only approximate solutions are obtained. For the large instances emerging in data mining applications, the search for high-quality approximate solutions in the presence of noise and outliers is even more challenging. We exhibit fast and robust clustering methods that rely on the careful collection of proximity information for use by hill-climbing search strategies. The proximity information gathered approximates the nearest neighbor information produced using traditional, exact, but expensive methods. The proximity information is then used to produce fast approximations of robust objective optimization functions, and/or rapid comparison of two feasible solutions. These methods have been successfully applied for spatial and categorical data to surpass well-established methods such as k-MEANS in terms of the trade-off between quality and complexity.

INTRODUCTION

A central problem in data mining is that of automatically summarizing vast amounts of information into simpler, fewer and more comprehensible categories. The most common and well-studied way in which this categorizing is done is by partitioning the data elements into groups called *clusters*, in such a way that members of the same cluster are as similar as possible, and points from different clusters are as dissimilar as possible. By examining the properties of elements from a common cluster, practitioners hope to discover rules and concepts that allow them to characterize and categorize the data.

The applications of clustering to knowledge discovery and data mining (KDDM) (Fayyad, Reina, & Bradley, 1998; Ng & Han, 1994; Wang, Yang, & Muntz, 1997) are recent developments in a history going back more than 30 years. In machine learning classical techniques for unsupervised learning are essentially those of clustering (Cheeseman et al, 1988; Fisher, 1987; Michalski & Stepp, 1983). In statistics, clustering arises in the analysis of mixture models, where the goal is to obtain statistical parameters of the individual populations (Titterington, Smith & Makov, 1985; Wallace & Freeman, 1987). Clustering methods appear in the literature of dimensionality reduction and vector quantization. Many textbooks have large sections devoted to clustering (Berry & Linoff, 1997; Berson & Smith, 1998; Cherkassky & Muller, 1998; Duda & Hart, 1973; Han & Kamber, 2000; Mitchell, 1997), and several are entirely devoted to the topic (Aldenderfer & Blashfield, 1984; Anderberg, 1973; Everitt, 1980; Jain & Dubes, 1998).

Although different contexts give rise to several clustering methods, there is a great deal of commonality among methods themselves. However, not all methods are appropriate for all contexts. Here, we will concentrate only on clustering methods that are suitable for the exploratory and early stages of a KDDM exercise. Such methods should be:

- *Generic*: Virtually every clustering method may be described as having two components: a search mechanism that generates candidate clusters, and an evaluation function that measures the quality of these candidates. In turn, an evaluation function may make use of a function that measures the similarity (or dissimilarity) between a pair of data points. Such methods can be considered generic if they can be applied in a variety of domains simply by substituting one measure of similarity for another.
- *Scalable*: In order to handle the huge data sets that arise in KDDM applications, clustering methods must be as efficient as possible in terms of their execution time and storage requirements. Given a data set consisting of n records on D attributes, the time and space complexity of any clustering method for the set should be sub-quadratic in n, and as low as possible in D (ideally linear). In particular, the number of evaluations of the similarity function must be kept as small as possible. Clustering methods proposed in other areas are completely unsuitable for data mining applications, due to their quadratic time complexities.
- *Incremental*: Even if the chosen clustering method is scalable, long execution times must be expected when the data sets are very large. For this reason, it is desirable to use methods that attempt to improve their solutions in an incremental fashion. Incremental methods allow the user to monitor their progress, and to terminate the execution early whenever a clustering of

sufficient quality is found, or when it is clear that no suitable clustering will be found.

- *Robust*: A clustering method must be robust with respect to noise and outliers. No method is immune to the effects of erroneous data, but it is a feature of good clustering methods that the presence of noise does not greatly affect the result.

Finding clustering methods that satisfy all of these desiderata remains one main challenge in data mining today. In particular, very few of the existing methods are scalable to large databases of records having many attributes, and those that are scalable are not robust. In this work, we will investigate the trade-offs between scalability and robustness for a family of hill-climbing search strategies known to be both generic and incremental. We shall propose clustering methods that seek to achieve both scalability and robustness by mimicking the behavior of existing robust methods to the greatest possible extent, while respecting a limit on the number of evaluations of similarity between data elements.

The functions that measure similarity between data points typically satisfy the conditions of a metric. For this reason, it is convenient to think of the evaluation of these functions in terms of nearest-neighbor calculations in an appropriate metric space. We will see how the problem of efficiently finding a robust clustering can essentially be reduced to that of efficiently gathering proximity information. We will propose new heuristics that gather approximate but useful nearest-neighbor information while still keeping to a budget on the number of distance calculations performed.

Although these heuristics are developed with data mining and interchange hill-climbers in mind, they are sufficiently general that they can be incorporated into other search strategies. Our nearest-neighbor heuristics will be illustrated in examples involving both spatial data and categorical data. We shall now briefly review some of the existing clustering methods and search strategies.

Overview of Clustering Methods

For exploratory data mining exercises, clustering methods typically fall into two main categories, agglomerative and partition-based.

Agglomerative clustering methods

Agglomerative clustering methods begin with each item in its own cluster, and then, in a bottom-up fashion, repeatedly merge the two closest groups to form a new cluster. To support this merge process, nearest-neighbor searches are conducted. Agglomerative clustering methods are often referred to as hierarchical methods for this reason.

A classical example of agglomerative clustering is the iterative determination of the closest pair of points belonging to different clusters, followed by the merging of their corresponding clusters. This process results in the minimum spanning tree (MST) structure. Computing an MST can be performed very quickly. However, because the decision to merge two clusters is based only on information provided by a single pair of points, the MST generally provides clusters of poor quality.

The first agglomerative algorithm to require sub-quadratic expected time, albeit in low-dimensional settings, is DBSCAN (Ester, Kriegel, Sander, & Xu, 1996). The algorithm is regulated by two parameters, which specify the density of the clusters to be retrieved. The algorithm achieves its claimed performance in an amortized sense, by placing the points in an R^*-tree, and using the tree to perform u-nearest-neighbor queries, u is typically 4. Additional effort is made in helping the users determine the density parameters, by presenting the user with a profile of the distances between data points and their 4-nearest neighbors. It is the responsibility of the user to find a valley in the distribution of these distances; the position of this valley determines the boundaries of the clusters. Overall, the method requires $Q(n \log n)$ time, given n data points of fixed dimension.

Another subfamily of clustering methods impose a grid structure on the data (Chiu, Wong & Cheung, 1991; Schikuta, 1996; Wang et al, 1997; Zhang, Ramakrishnan, & Livny, 1996). The idea is a natural one: grid boxes containing a large number of points would indicate good candidates for clusters. The difficulty is in determining an appropriate granularity. Maximum entropy discretization (Chiu et al., 1991) allows for the automatic determination of the grid granularity, but the size of the grid generally grows quadratically in the number of data points. Later, the BIRCH method saw the introduction of a hierarchical structure for the economical storage of grid information, called a Clustering Feature Tree (CF-Tree) (Zhang et al., 1996).

The recent STING method (Wang et al., 1997) combines aspects of these two approaches, again in low-dimensional spatial settings. STING constructs a hierarchical data structure whose root covers the region of analysis. The structure is a variant of a quadtree (Samet, 1989). However, in STING, all leaves are at equal depth in the structure, and represent areas of equal size in the data domain. The structure is built by finding information at the leaves and propagating it to the parents according to arithmetic formulae. STING's data structure is similar to that of a multidimensional database, and thus can be queried by OLAP users using an SQL-like language. When used for clustering, the query proceeds from the root down, using information about the distribution to eliminate branches from consideration. As only those leaves that are reached are relevant, the data points under these leaves can be agglomerated. It is claimed that once the search structure is in place, the time taken by STING to produce a clustering will be sub-linear. However, determining the depth of the structure is problematic.

STING is a statistical parametric method, and as such can only be used in limited applications. It assumes the data is a mixture model and works best with knowledge of the distributions involved. However, under these conditions, non-agglomerative methods such as EM (Dempster, Laird & Rubin, 1977), AutoClass (Cheeseman et al, 1988), MML (Wallace & Freeman, 1987) and Gibb's sampling are perhaps more effective.

For clustering two-dimensional points, $O(n \log n)$ time is possible (Krznaric & Levcopoulos, 1998), based on a data structure called a dendrogram or proximity tree, which can be regarded as capturing the history of a merge process based on nearest-neighbor information. Unfortunately, such hierarchical approaches had generally been disregarded for knowledge discovery in spatial databases, since it is often unclear how to use the proximity tree to obtain associations (Ester et al, 1996).

While variants emerge from the different ways in which the distance between items is extended to a distance between groups, the agglomerative approach as a whole has three fundamental drawbacks. First, agglomeration does not provide clusters naturally; some other criterion must be introduced in order to halt the merge process and to interpret the results. Second, for large data sets, the shapes of clusters formed via agglomeration may be very irregular, so much so that they defy any attempts to derive characterizations of their member data points. Third, and perhaps the most serious for data mining applications, hierarchical methods usually require quadratic time when applied in general dimensions. This is essentially because agglomerative algorithms must repeatedly extract the smallest distance from a dynamic set that originally has a quadratic number of values.

Partition-based clustering methods

The other main family of clustering methods searches for a partition of the data that best satisfies an evaluation function based on a given set of optimization criteria. Using the evaluation function as a guide, a search mechanism is used to generate good candidate clusters. The search mechanisms of most partition-based clustering methods are variants of a general strategy called hill-climbing. The essential differences among partition-based clustering methods lie in their choice of optimization criteria.

The optimization criteria of all partition-based methods make assumptions, either implicitly or explicitly, regarding the distribution of the data. Nevertheless, some methods are more generally applicable than others in the assumptions they make, and others may be guided by optimization criteria that allow for more efficient evaluation.

One particularly general optimization strategy is that of expectation maximization (EM) (Dempster et al., 1977), a form of inference with maximum likelihood. At each step, EM methods search for a representative point for each cluster in a candidate cluster. The distances from the representatives to the data elements in their clusters are used as estimates of the error in associating the data elements with this representative. In the next section, we shall focus on two variants of EM, the first being the well-known and widely used k-MEANS heuristic (MacQueen, 1967). This algorithm exhibits linear behavior and is simple to implement; however, it typically produces poor results, requiring complex procedures for initialization (Aldenderfer & Blashfield, 1984; Bradley, Fayyad, & Reina, 1998; Fayyad et al., 1998). The second variant is k-MEDOIDS, which produces clusters of much higher quality, but requires quadratic time.

Another partition-based clustering method makes more assumptions regarding the underlying distribution of the data. AutoClass (Cheeseman et al., 1998) partitions the data set into classes using a Bayesian statistical technique. It requires an explicit declaration of how members of a class should be distributed in order to form a probabilistic class model. AutoClass uses a variant of EM, and thus is a randomized hill-climber similar to k-MEANS, with additional techniques for escaping local maxima. It also has the capability of identifying some data points as noise.

Similarly, minimum message length (MML) methods (Wallace & Freeman, 1987) require the declaration of a model. The declaration allows an encoding of parameters of a statistical mixture model; the second part of the message is an encoding of the data given these statistical parameters. There is a trade-off between the complexity of the MML model and the quality of fit to the data. There are also difficult optimization problems that must be solved heuristically when encoding parameters in the fewest number of bits.

One of the advantages of partition-based clustering is that the optimization criteria lend themselves well to interpretation of the results. However, the family of partition-based clustering strategies includes members that require linear time as well as other members that require more than quadratic time. The main reason for this variation lies in the complexity of the optimization criteria. The more complex criteria tend to be more robust to noise and outliers, but also more expensive to compute. Simpler criteria, on the other hand, may have more local optima where the hill-climber can become trapped.

Nearest-neighbor searching

As we can see, many if not most clustering methods have at their core the computation of nearest neighbors with respect to some distance metric d. To conclude this section, we will formalize the notion of distance and nearest neighbors, and give a brief overview of existing methods for computing nearest neighbors.

Let us assume that we have been given a set $S=\{s_1,\dots,s_n\}$ of n objects to be clustered into k groups, drawn from some universal set of objects X. Let us also assume that we have been given a function $d:X{\times}X{\rightarrow}\Re$ for measuring the pairwise similarity between objects of X. If the objects of X are records having D attributes (numeric or otherwise), the time taken to compute d would be independent of n, but dependent on D. The function d is said to be a *metric* if it satisfies the following conditions:

1. *Non-negativity*: $x,y{\in}X$, $d(x,y)>0$ whenever $x{\neq}y$, and $d(x,y)=0$ whenever $x=y$.
2. *Symmetry*: $x,y{\in}X$, $d(x,y)=d(y,x)$.
3. *Triangular inequality*: $x,y,z{\in}X$, $d(x,z){\leq}d(x,y)+d(y,z)$.

Metrics are sometimes called distance functions or simply distances. Well-known metrics include the usual Euclidean distance and Manhattan distances in spatial settings (both special cases of the Lagrange metric), and the Hamming distance in categorical settings.

Formally, a nearest neighbor of $s{\in}S$ is an element $a{\in}S$ such that $d(s,a){\leq}d(s,b)$ for all $b{\in}X$, $a{\neq}b$. The notion can be extended to that of a *u*-nearest-neighbor set

$NN_u(s)=\{a_1,a_2,\ldots,a_u\}$, where $d(s,a_i)\leq d(s,b)$ for all $b\in S\backslash NN_u(s)$. Computation of nearest and u-nearest neighbors are well-studied problems, with applications in such areas as pattern recognition, content-based retrieval of text and images, and video compression, as well as data mining. In two-dimensional spatial settings, very efficient solutions based on the Delaunay triangulation (Aurenhammer, 1991) have been devised, typically requiring $O(\log n)$ time to process nearest-neighbor queries after $O(n \log n)$ preprocessing time. However, the size of Delaunay structures can be quadratic in dimensions higher than two.

For higher-dimensional vector spaces, again many structures have been proposed for nearest-neighbor and range queries, the most prominent ones being kd-trees (Bentley, 1975, 1979), quad-trees (Samet, 1989), R-trees (Guttmann, 1984), R^*-trees (Beckmann, Kriegel, Schneider & Seeger, 1990), and X-trees (Berchtold, Keim, & Kriegel, 1996). All use the coordinate information to partition the space into a hierarchy of regions. In processing a query, if there is any possibility of a solution element lying in a particular region, then that region must be searched. Consequently, the number of points accessed may greatly exceed the number of elements sought. This effect worsens as the number of dimensions increases, so much so that the methods become totally impractical for high-dimensional data mining applications. In their excellent survey on searching within metric spaces, Chávez, Navarro, Baeza-Yates and Marroquín (1999) introduce the notion of intrinsic dimension, which is the smallest number of dimensions in which the points may be embedded so as to preserve distances among them. They claim that none of these techniques can cope with intrinsic dimension more than 20.

Another drawback of these search structures is that the Lagrange similarity metrics they employ cannot take into account any correlation or 'cross-talk' among the attribute values. The M-tree search structure (Ciaccia, Patella & Zezula, 1997) addresses this by organizing the data strictly according to the values of the metric d. This generic structure is also designed to reduce the number of distance computations and page I/O operations, making it more scalable than structures that rely on coordinate information. However, the M-tree still suffers from the 'curse of dimensionality' that prevents all these methods from being effective for higher-dimensional data mining.

If one were to insist (as one should) on using only generic clustering methods that were both scalable and robust, a reasonable starting point would be to look at the optimization criteria of robust methods, and attempt to approximate the choices and behaviors of these methods while still respecting limits on the amount of computational resources used. This is the approach we take in the upcoming sections.

Optimization Criteria

Some of the most popular clustering strategies are based on optimization criteria whose origins can be traced back to induction principles from classical statistics. Such methods appeal to the user community because their goals and choices can be explained in light of these principles, because the methods are largely easy to implement and understand, and often because the optimization functions can be evaluated quickly. However, the optimization criteria generally have not been designed with robustness in mind, and typically sacrifice robustness for the sake of simplicity and efficiency. In this section, we will look at some optimization criteria derived from statistical induction principles, and show how the adoption of some of these criteria has led to problems with robustness.

We begin by examining a classical distance-based criterion for representative-based clustering. Assuming the data is a set of attribute-vectors $S=\{s_1,...,s_n\}$, the statistical theory of multivariate analysis of variance suggests the use of the *total scatter matrix T* (Duda & Hart, 1963) for evaluating homogeneity, based on the use of the mean as an estimator of location. Formally, the matrix is $T = \Sigma_{i=1...n} (s_i-\mu)(s_i-\mu)^T$, where μ is the total observed mean vector; that is, $\mu=\Sigma_{i=1...n} s_i/n$. Similarly, the scatter matrix T_{Cj} of a cluster C_j is simply $T_{Cj} =\Sigma_{s_i\in Cj} (s_i-\mu_j)(s_i-\mu_j)^T$, where μ_j is the observed mean vector of C_j.

Each cluster scatter matrix captures the variance – or dissimilarity – of the cluster with respect to its representative, the mean. One can thus use as a clustering goal the minimization of the sum of some function of the cluster scatter matrices, where the function attempts to capture the overall magnitude of the matrix elements. Although one is tempted to take into account all entries of the matrix, this would result in a quadratic number of computations, too high for data mining purposes. A traditional and less costly measure of the magnitude is the *trace*, which for a symmetric matrix is simply the sum of the elements along its diagonal. The sum of the traces of the cluster scatter matrices is exactly the least sum of squares loss function (known in the statistics literature as L_2 [Rousseeuw & Leroy, 1987]):

$$L_2(C) = \Sigma_{i=1...n} Euclid^2 (s_i, rep[s_i,C]) \qquad (1)$$

where $Euclid(x,y)=[(x-y)(x-y)^T]^{1/2}$ is the Euclidean metric $C=\{c_1,...,c_k\}$ is a set of *k centers*, or representative points of $\Re^D$; and $i=1,\&\...,n$, $rep[s_i,C]$ is the closest representative point in C to s_i. The optimization problem is then to minimize $L_2(C)$. Note that Equation (1) measures the quality of a set C of k cluster representatives, according to the partition into clusters defined by assigning each s_i to its $rep[s_i,C]$. The minimum value is achieved when the cluster representatives coincide with the cluster means.

It is interesting that seeking to minimize the variance within a cluster leads to the evaluation of Euclidean distances. While the proponents of robust statistics (Rousseeuw and Leroy,1987) attribute this to the relationship of the Euclidean distance to the standard normal distribution, others point to the fact that Equation (1) corresponds to minimizing the sum of the average squared Euclidean distance between cluster points and their representatives (Duda & Hart, 1973): that is, if $S_1,...,S_k$ denotes a partition of S, then the problem of minimizing Equation (1) is equivalent to

$$minimize \ L_2(S_1,...,S_k) = \Sigma_{j=1,...,k} 1// \|S_j\| \Sigma_{s_i\in Sj}\Sigma_{s_{i'}\in Sj} Euclid^2(s_i,s_{i'}). \qquad (2)$$

Note that this last criterion does not explicitly rely on the notion of a representative point. Thus, when the metric is the Euclidean distance, we find that minimizing the intra-cluster pairwise squared dissimilarity is equivalent to minimizing the expected squared dissimilarity between items and their cluster representative. This property seems to grant special status to the use of sums of squares of the Euclidean metric, and to heuristics such k-MEANS that are based upon them. This relationship does not hold for general metrics.

The literature has proposed many iterative heuristics for computing approximate solutions to Equation (1), and to Equation (2) (Anderberg, 1973; Duda & Hart, 1973; Hartigan, 1975; Späth, 1980). All can be considered variants of the k-MEANS heuristic (MacQueen, 1967), which is in turn a form of expectation maximization (EM) (Dempster et al., 1977). The generic maximization step in EM involves estimating the distance of each data point to a representative, and using this estimate to approximate the probability of being a member of that cluster. In each iteration of k-MEANS, this is done by:

1. Given a set C of k representatives, assigning each data point to its closest representative in C.
2. For each cluster S_j in the resulting partition, replacing its representative in C by the arithmetic mean of its elements, $\underline{s} = \Sigma_{s_i \in S_j}\ s_i / \|S_j\|$.

One point of concern is that the Euclidean metric is biased towards spherical clusters. Of more concern is that using the squares of Euclidean distances, rather than (say) the unsquared distances, renders the algorithms far more sensitive to noise and outliers, as their contribution to the sum is proportionally much higher. For exploratory data mining, it is more important that the clustering method be robust and generic, than for the cluster representatives to be generated by strict adherence to statistical principles. It stands to reason that effective clustering methods can be devised by reworking existing optimization criteria to be more generic and more robust. Still, it is not immediately clear that these methods can compete in computational efficiency with k-MEANS.

Problems and Solutions

We will investigate two optimization criteria related to Equations (1) and (2), one representative-based and the other non-representative-based. After formally defining the problems and their relationship with k-MEANS, we discuss heuristic solutions. Although the heuristics are inherently more generic and robust than k-MEANS, the straightforward use of hill-climbers leads to quadratic-time performance. We then show how scalability can be achieved with little loss of robustness by restricting the number of distance computations performed.

The first optimization criterion we will study follows the form of Equation (1), but with three important differences: (1) unsquared distance is used instead of squared distance; (2) metrics other than the Euclidean distance may be used; and (3) cluster representatives are restricted to be elements of the data set. This third condition ensures that each representative can be interpreted as a valid, 'typical' element of its cluster. It also allows the method to be applied to categorical data as well as spatial data. With this restriction on the representatives, the problem is no

longer one of continuous optimization (where solutions may not even be comput-
able (Estivill-Castro & Yang, 2000)), but rather one of discrete optimization. From
the perspective of spatial statistics, the formulation below is simply a replacement
of means by medians (a much more robust estimator of location), and the L_2 loss
function by the L_1 loss function (Rousseeuw & Leroy, 1987).

Definition 1 Let $S=\{s_1,s_2,\ldots,s_n\}\subseteq X$ be a set of n objects and let $d:X\times X\to\Re^{\geq 0}$ be a
metric on X. The L_1-problem is:

$$minimize\ L_1(C)\quad=\quad \Sigma_{i=1,\ldots,n}\ w_i\,d(s_i,rep[s_i,C]),\qquad(3)$$
$$=\quad \Sigma_{j=1,\ldots,n}\,\Sigma_{si\in Si}\,w_i\,d(s_i,c_j),$$

where $C=\{c_1,\ldots,c_k\}\subset S$ is a set of k *centers* in S, w_i is a weight for the relevance of
s_i, the point $rep[s_i,C]$ is the closest point in C to s_i, and S_j is the set of elements having
c_j as its closest representative; that is $S_j=\{s_i\in S\mid rep[s_i,C]=c_j\}$.

The problem was first introduced to the data mining literature by Ng and Han
(1994) as medoid clustering, although it was in fact already well known to
researchers in facility location as the *p*-median problem (Densham & Rushton,
1992; Rosing, ReVelle & Rosing-Voyelaar, 1979). It can also be viewed as a
generalization of other representative-based EM variants for the Euclidean and
other metrics. Examples include the Generalized Lloyd Algorithm (GLA)
[Cherkassky & Muller, 1998], fuzzy-*c*-clustering (Cherkassky & Muller, 1998;
Hall, Özyurt & Bezdek, 1999) and *k*-C-*L*$_1$-MEDIANS (Bradley, Mangasarian, &
Street, 1997; Estivill-Castro & Yang, 2000).

The second optimization criterion we will investigate attempts to minimize the
total pairwise dissimilarity within clusters in the same fashion as Equation (2), but
again with the metric values unsquared. This criterion has been studied by researchers since the 1960s, under such names as the *Grouping* (Vinod, 1969), the *Full-
Exchange* (Rosing & ReVelle, 1986) the *Interaction* (Murray and Estivill-Castro,
1998), and the *Total Within-Group Distance(TWGD)* (Rao, 1971). Here we will
refer to this criterion as TWGD, as this latter term seems to be the best description
of the measure.

Definition 2 Let $S=\{s_1,s_2,\ldots,s_n\}$ be a set of n objects and $d:X\times X\to\Re^{\geq 0}$ be a metric
(which is symmetric). The TWGD problem is:

$$minimize\ TWGD(P)\quad=\quad \Sigma_{m=1,\ldots,k}\,\Sigma_{i<j\wedge\ si,sj\in Sm}\,w_i w_j\,d(s_i,s_j),\qquad(4)$$

where $P=S_i|\ldots|S_k$ is a partition of S and w_i is a weight for the relevance of s_i, but
which may have other specific interpretations. Intuitively, this criterion not only
minimizes the dissimilarity between items in a group, but also uses all interactions
between items in a group to assess cohesiveness, (thus, uses all the available
information). Also, it implicitly maximizes the distance between groups (and
thereby minimizes coupling), since the terms $d(s_i, s_j)$ not included in the sum are
those for which the items belong to different groups. However, the TWGD problem
is NP-hard (Brucker, 1978; Krivánek, 1986). One interesting aspect of TWGD is
that, even in Euclidean space, the optimal solution can be a partition where the
convex hulls of the groups overlap. This is sometimes used to suggest the number
k of groups.

Hill-climbing strategies

Both the L_1-problem (Def. 1) and the TWGD problem (Def. 2) are NP-hard discrete optimization problems. The techniques to be described are widely applicable to other loss functions. Thus, we will refer to a generic loss function $L(P)$ based on a partition P of the data. Note that claims regarding $L(P)$ will apply to $L_1(C)$ and $TWGD(P)$.

The minimization of $L(P)$ is typically solved approximately using interchange heuristics based on a hill-climbing search strategy (Densham & Rushton, 1992; Horn, 1996; Murray & Church, 1996; Murray, 2000; Teitz & Bart, 1968). Hill-climbers search the space of all partitions $P=S_1|...|S_k$ of S by treating the space as if it were a graph. Every node of the graph can be thought to correspond to a unique partition of the data; an edge exists between two nodes if the corresponding two partitions differ slightly. Typically, the difference involves the interchange or promotion of one item. For L_1, two solutions (sets of k representatives) C and C' are adjacent if they differ in exactly one representative (that is, $||C \cap C'||=k-1$). For the TWGD problem, two nodes P and P' are adjacent if and only if their corresponding partitions coincide in all but one data point (clearly, the resulting graphs are connected).

Interchange heuristics start at a randomly chosen solution P^0, and explore by moving from the current solution to one of its neighbors. Letting P^t be the current solution at time step t, the heuristic examines a set $N(P^t)$ of solutions neighboring P^t, and considers the best alternative to P^t in this neighborhood: the node for which $L(P^{t+1})= \min_{P \in N(P_t)} L(P)$. Provided that the new node P^{t+1} is an improvement over the old (that is, if $L(P^{t+1})<L(P^t)$), P^{t+1} becomes the current node for time step $t+1$. Hill-climbers define the neighborhood set $N(P^t)$ in varying ways (Kaufman & Rousseeuw, 1990; Murray & Church, 1996; Ng & Han, 1994; Rolland, Schilling & Current, 1996). One general interchange heuristic, originally proposed for the L_1-problem by Teitz and Bart (1968), is a hill-climber that is regarded as the best known benchmark (Horn, 1996). It has been remarkably successful in finding local optima of high quality in applications to facility location problems (Murray & Church, 1996; Rolland, et al, 1996), and very accurate for the clustering of large sets of low-dimensional spatial data (Estivill-Castro & Murray, 1998), even in the presence of noise or outliers. We refer to this heuristic as TAB.

When searching for a profitable interchange, TAB considers the points in turn, according to a circular ordering $(s_1,s_2,...,s_n)$ of the data. Whenever the turn belonging to a point s_i comes up, it is used to determine a number of neighboring solutions. In the case of L_1, provided that s_i is not already a representative, the feasible solutions in $N(P^t)$ are constructed by swapping s_i with each of the k current representatives of C^T. For TWGD, the data point s_i is considered for changing its group. The most advantageous interchange P_j of these alternatives is determined, and if it is an improvement over P^t, then P_j becomes the new current solution P^{t+1}; otherwise, $P^{t+1}=P^t$. In either case, the turn then passes to the next point in the circular list, s_{i+1} (or s_1 if $i=n$). If a full cycle through the data set yields no improvement, a local optimum has been reached, and the search halts.

The TAB heuristic forbids the reconsideration of s_i for inclusion until all other data points have been considered as well. The heuristic can, therefore, be regarded as a local variant of *Tabu search* (Glover, 1986), whose design balances the need to explore possible interchanges against the 'greedy' desire to improve the solution as quickly as possible.

We now begin our discussion of the computational complexity of interchange heuristics. First, in the case of TWGD, we note that given a current partition P^t and one of its k--1 neighbors P_j, a naive approach would compute $TWGD(P_j)$ and $TWGD(P^t)$ explicitly in order to decide whether $TWGD(P_j)<TWGD(P^t)$. However, this would potentially require $\Theta(kn^2)$ time, simply because Equation (4) shows that each cluster involves the sum of distances between all pairs. A more efficient way is to compute the discrete gradient $\nabla(P^t,P_j)=TWGD(P^t) - TWGD(P_j)$ for $P_j \in N(P^t)$. since only s_i is changing its cluster membership. $TWGD(P^t)$ and $TWGD(P_j)$ differ only in $O(n)$ terms, and therefore only $O(n)$ evaluations of the distance metric are required to compute $\nabla(P^t,P_j)$. Therefore, the number of evaluations of the distance metric required to test all interchanges suggested by s_i is in $O(kn)$. This bound is easily seen to hold for L_1 as well. The generic TAB heuristic thus requires $\Omega(n^2)$ time per complete scan through the list. At least one complete scan is needed for the heuristic to terminate, although empirical evidence suggests that the total number of scans is constant.

Limiting the number of distance computations

We have just presented a generic local search heuristic for two versions of distance-based clustering. Although the methods are robust, they require quadratic time. By limiting the total number of distance evaluations, the time cost can be substantially reduced.

The first fundamental idea is to allow modifications to the objective functions that result in scalable new functions that still respect the optimization goals of the originals. As long as the approximation is sufficiently accurate for the operation of the hill-climber to be effective, the results will be satisfactory. To achieve this approximation, we note that the distance-based criteria attempt to evaluate the total weighted discrepancies in each cluster and then add them together. The L_1 objective function measures the discrepancy between cluster items and their representatives, whereas the *TWGD* function can be seen as an assessment of the expected variance within a cluster. For the purposes of the hill-climber, it is enough to assess these functions approximately.

The purpose of clustering is to identify subsets, each of whose records are highly similar to one another. Loss functions implicitly or explicitly assess whether near neighbors of points have been assigned to the same cluster: the more points grouped in the same cluster as its near neighbors, the better the clustering. However, the greatest individual contributions to that portion of the loss function $L(P)$ associated with a cluster S_j are made by outliers assigned to S_j, records which exhibit the least similarities to other records, and which often should not be considered to be part of any cluster.

To eliminate the inappropriate contributions of outliers towards the expected discrepancy within clusters, the strategy we adopt is to estimate the expected discrepancy among non-outlier points only. Instead of finding a clustering which best summarizes the entire set of points S, we propose that clusterings be found that best represent the sets of points *in their own vicinities*.

In order to be able to efficiently determine the set of those points in the vicinity of a given data item, we preprocess the full set of n records as follows:

1. For each $s_i \in S$, we find u records that rank highly among the nearest neighbors of s_i.

2. We construct a *proximity directed graph PD(S)* of regular out-degree u, with the $s_1, \ldots, s_n$ as nodes. Two records s_i and $s_{i'}$ in the proximity digraph are adjacent if $s_{i'}$ is one of the u records found to be close to s_i in the previous step. The adjacency representation of this regular graph has $O(un)$ size.

3. In order to avoid a potential bias from the use of local information, we also construct a *random influence graph RI(S)* of regular degree r having node set S. The r nodes adjacent to s_i in $RI(S)$ are chosen randomly from S.

During the hill-climbing process, whenever the hill-climber evaluates a candidate solution s_i, the computation of distances will ordinarily be restricted to those with the nodes in its adjacency lists in $PD(S)$ and $RI(S)$. However, since two data items may share neighbors $PD(S)$, the situation may arise where fewer than $uk+\rho k$ nearby records may be evaluated. In order for the hill-climber not to be attracted simply to sets with fewer neighbors in the proximity digraph, two strategies can be applied to pad the number of evaluations out to exactly $uk+\rho k$:

1. Fill the quota of $uk+\rho k$ items by randomly selecting from the remaining items.

2. Fill the quota from among the records of the proximity graph by repeatedly adding the largest distance contribution as many times as is necessary.

In our implementations, we have opted for the latter strategy to assure convergence. Unlike the former strategy, the latter is deterministic, and preserves the hill-climbing nature of TAB.

The time required by the hill-climber is typically much less than the time required to build the graphs $PD(S)$ and $RI(S)$ in high-dimensional settings, where the cost of distance computation dominates. The total number of distances needed would be at most $un++\rho n$, and if the graphs are pre-computed, no distance would be evaluated more than once. Nevertheless, it can be advantageous to generating the random influence graph during the hill-climbing process, as continual sampling can result in a clustering of better quality. However, care must be taken to control any oscillations that would prevent convergence. One way would be to gradually reduce the effect of $RI(S)$ by reducing the value of ρ in later iterations of the algorithm, in a manner similar to simulated annealing. In what follows, we assume that ρ is chosen to be commensurate with u.

We are now left with the problem of efficiently computing a list of near neighbors for each of the data elements. To complete the description of our approach, we will examine how this can be accomplished in three different contexts: two-dimensional spatial data, categorical data in low dimensions and generic data sets in higher dimensions.

Low-dimensional spatial data

In the two-dimensional spatial setting, we need only be concerned with the scalability of clustering methods with respect to n, the number of records. Still, care must be taken to avoid paying quadratic time in computing the approximate near-neighbor information required for the hill-climber methods we have just seen. For this exercise, we will consider only the L_1-problem.

Given a set of data points $S=\{s_1,\dots,s_n\}$ in the two-dimensional Euclidean space $\Re^2$, the Voronoi region of $s_i \in S$ is the locus of points of $\Re^2$ that have s_i as a nearest neighbor; that is $\{x \in \Re^2 \,|\, \forall.\ i' \neq i,\ d(x,s_i) \leq d(x,s_{i'})\}$. Taken together, the n Voronoi regions of S form the Voronoi diagram of S (also called the Dirichlet tessellation or the proximity map). The regions are (possibly unbounded) convex polygons, and their interiors are disjoint.

The Delaunay triangulation $D(S)$ of S is a planar embedding of a graph defined as follows: the nodes of $D(S)$ consist of the data points of S, and two nodes s_i and $s_{i'}$ are joined by an edge if the boundaries of the corresponding Voronoi regions share a line segment. Delaunay triangulations capture in a very compact form the proximity relationships among the points of S. They have many useful properties (Okabe, Boots, & Sugihara, 1992; O'Rourke, 1994), some of which are:

1. The 1-nearest neighbor digraph is a subgraph of the Delaunay triangulation.
2. The number of edges in $D(S)$ is at most $3n$-6.
3. The triangulation $D(S)$ can be robustly computed in $O(n \log n)$ time.
4. The minimum spanning tree is a subgraph of the Delaunay triangulation.

Under the Euclidean distance, the u nearest neighbors of a point s_i can be found via a search in $D(S)$ in $O(u \log u)$ expected time (Dickerson, Drysdale, & Sack, 1992). The algorithm is simple and practical. Place the Delaunay neighbors of $s_i \in S$ in a priority queue using Euclidean distances to s_i as key values. Repeatedly extract the item with smallest key and insert its yet-unexamined Delaunay neighbors into the priority queue. When u items have been extracted, then terminate; these are the u-nearest neighbors.

The construction of $PD(S)$ can be accomplished in sub-quadratic time. The total time required to generate u neighbors for each data point s_i is in $O(un \log u)$, and $\Theta(n \log n)$ time is required for computing a Delaunay triangulation. Choosing u to be in $\Theta(\log n \,/\, \log \log n)$ allows the proximity directed graph $PD(S)$ to be constructed in $O(n \log n)$ total time. Thereafter, each evaluation of $L(C)$ would take $\Theta(k \log n \,/\, \log \log n)$ time. The total time bound simplifies to $O(kn \log n)$ per complete scan of TAB, and since the number of complete scans is typically constant, the overall observed complexity is $O(kn \log n)$.

Of course, the user is free to choose larger or smaller values of u. The larger the value of u, the closer the performance becomes to that of the original TAB heuristic, and the more time is taken. Small choices of u result in very fast execution times, at the cost of a degradation in quality. In practice, the user could base the choice of u according to a time budget. Even when u is chosen to be very small, experimental evaluation of the implementation of this hill-climber variant shows that the method is much more robust to noise and outliers than k-MEANS, even if k-MEANS is given the advantage of an initial clustering based on the MST (Estivill-Castro & Houle, forthcoming).

Categorical data with Hamming distance

We next consider the situation for categorical data, where the dimension D of the set is relatively low. For this example, we will assume the use of the Hamming distance as the metric, defined as follows: $Hamming(\pmb{x},\pmb{y}) = \Sigma_{j=1,...,D} \chi(x_j,y_j)$, where $\chi(x_j,y_j)$ equals 1 if $x_j \neq y_j$, and equals 0 otherwise. The method we shall present scales well in terms of the number n of records, but less so with respect to D.

The proximity digraph $PD(S)$ will be built up in several stages, with the help of several auxiliary graphs. The first auxiliary graph we consider is the *nearest-neighbor* digraph, defined as follows: the arc $(s_i,s_{i'})$ is in the digraph if there exists no record s distinct from s_i and $s_{i'}$ such that $d(s_i,s)<d(s_i,s_{i'})$. For each item s_i of S, we include in $PD(S)$ at least one nearest-neighbor digraph arc from s_i.

The second auxiliary graph is the Δ-*graph*, where $1 \leq \Delta \leq m$ is a density parameter. For the Hamming distance in low dimensions (less than 20), we suggest that Δ be set to 2. The edge $(s_i,s_{i'})$ is in the Δ-graph if and only if the distance $d(s_i,s_{i'})$ is at most Δ. An edge $(s_i,s_{i'})$ of the Δ-graph will cause the insertion of $(s_i,s_{i'})$ and $(s_{i'}, s_i)$ into the proximity digraph, provided that the resulting out-degree of s_i and $s_{i'}$ does not exceed u.

Third, the digraph that results from the union of edges chosen from the nearest-neighbor digraph and the Δ-graph is extended by transitive closure, in such a way that each node has out-degree no more than u. Using breadth-first search initialized with s_i (for $i=1,...,n$), and stopping when u nodes have been found, requires $O(Du^2n)$ time overall. Note that we are using the fact that if s_a is the nearest neighbor of s_b, and s_b is the nearest neighbor of s_c, then s_c usually ranks highly among the u nearest neighbors of s_a. Intuitively speaking, the 'nearness' relationship tends to be transitive along short paths in the nearest-neighbor digraph.

As soon as we find u outgoing edges for each s_i, we have the desired edges for s_i in the proximity graph. Unfortunately, breadth-first search may find less than u outgoing edges for some s_i, if the graph is not strongly connected. This happens whenever a strongly connected component has less than u records (such connected components are in essence small isolated clusters). However, connected components of size less than u are identified as a byproduct of the search.

The situation may be remedied by joining the connected components into one, by adding carefully chosen edges to the graph. This can be done by computing a spanning tree and a representative node for each component, in total time in $O(Dun)$. As a representative node of a component, we may choose its (graph) 1-median, since the 1-median problem in a tree can be solved in linear time.

Once representatives of strongly connected components are selected, the process of adding arcs into the proximity graph is resumed by computing nearest neighbors among the representatives of components. Every nearest-neighbor edge generated, when added to the proximity graph, serves to merge two of the connected components. As the number of connected components after the merge is at most half the original number, repeating this process until all components are connected will take linear time in n. Once the graph is connected, resumption of the breadth-first transitive closure computation will complete the list of u out-going arcs for each record s_i.

We now describe how to find the nearest neighbor, and the list of neighbors at distance at most Δ, for each of the n data records. We insert all records in linked lists at the leaves of a digital tree (or trie) (Gonnet & Baeza-Yates, 1991), a variant of the well-known kd-tree search structure. The root of a standard tree discriminates according to the first attribute, and has a child for every possible categorical value of the attribute in the domain. Nodes at depth i discriminate by the values of the i-th attribute. The leaf nodes store a linked list of labels for data records arriving at that node. Although this trial can have a path of depth equal to the number of attributes — that is, D – in practice, the number of nodes of the trie is bounded by Dn. Moreover, a path from the root to a leaf may terminate before all attributes are tested if only one data record reaches that leaf.

The trie is constructed by incremental insertions, in $O(Dn)$ time. The records at distance Δ from a given record s_i are then found in time independent of n, by appending the lists at those leafs whose path from the root differs in at most Δ links to the path from the root to the leaf holding s_i (however, as this requires $O(\Delta^D)$ time, the choice of $\Delta \leq 2$ is strongly advised). Finding neighbors at distance at most Δ is repeated for each data record s_i whose nearest neighbor is again at distance no more than Δ, for a total time in $\cup(\Delta^{D+1}n)$.

Note that, because the digital tree has depth dependent only on D, a nearest neighbor for every node can be found in time proportional to D^2n. Thus, the total complexity of the preprocessing step that constructs the proximity graph is $O((D^\Delta+u^2)Dn)$ time. At first, it may seem that if D is not small, this preprocessing is costly. However, $O(Dn)$ time is also required by adaptations of k-MEANS to categorical data. Thus, the preprocessing step of our approach requires time of an order of magnitude comparable to that of k-MEANS, provided that u and Δ are chosen to be small.

Experimental evaluation of this implementation on categorical data again shows that the hill-climber exhibits more robustness to noise and outliers and is scalable in the number n of records (Estivill-Castro & Houle, 1999).

Generic data using random sampling

In the previous two examples, we showed how approximate near-neighbor information could be gathered in low-dimensional settings to support a robust clustering algorithm, while still scaling well in terms of n. For our third example, we will aim for a method that scales very well with respect to the dimension, but still achieves sub-quadratic time. The method makes no assumptions on the distance metric used; however, since the dimension is presumed to be relatively high, the number of distance calculations will dominate the time complexity. Accordingly, we will measure the complexity of the method in terms of the number of these distance calculations.

The method relies on a random sampling to reduce the number of distance computations. The idea is that if a sample R of sufficient size is chosen from the points of S, then most points of S would have a point of R among its near neighbors. Two data points s_i and $s_{i'}$ that are both close to the same element of R are more likely to be near neighbors of one another; conversely, two near neighbors are more likely to have a common point of R near to them. The sample points can serve the role of intermediaries, informing pairs of points of S that they lie close to one another.

In order to allow the user some control of the trade-offs between scalability and robustness, Algorithm NNSampler (stated below) allows two parameters: the size r of the sample, and the number m of sample points that can serve as intermediates for a given data point of S. The algorithm produces a proximity $PD(S)$ as defined earlier, with each adjacency list containing u elements. After stating the basic algorithm, we will discuss modifications that will further improve the performance of the method.

Algorithm NNSampler

1. Select a subset $R=\{y_1,\ldots,y_r\}$ uniformly at random from among all subsets of S of size r. This requires $O(r)$ time.
2. For each $s\in S$, find its m nearest elements in R. Let $C_i = \{y\in R \mid y$ is one of the m nearest elements of R to $s_i\}$.
3. For each $y_j\in R$, construct a list or 'bucket' B_j of the elements S for $y_j\in C_i$.
4. For each $s_i\in S$, compute the union U_i of the m buckets to which it belongs (that is $U_i=\acute{O}_{s_i\in B_j} B_j$).
5. For each $s_i\in S$, find the u closest points of U_i to s_i, and use them to form the adjacency list of s_i in $PD(S)$.

Note that the distance between any pair of data points need be computed no more than twice. Consequently, the total number of distance computations required by the basic method is in $O(rn+\Sigma_{i=1,\ldots,n} |U_i|)$. If the points of S are distributed evenly among the r buckets, the number of distance calculations simplifies to $O(rn++mn^2/ /r)$. This is minimized when r is chosen to be $(mn)^{1/2}$, yielding $O(n(mn)^{1/2})$ distance calculations.

However, in practice, some buckets could receive more elements than others; if any one bucket were to receive a linear number of elements, the number of distance computations would become quadratic. On the other hand, any bucket that receives a disproportionately large number of elements immediately indicates a cluster in the data, as it would have been chosen as one of the m near neighbors of many data points. If the user is unwilling or unable to declare the existence of a cluster based on this sample point, the overfull bucket can simply be discarded, and a new random point selected to replace it. By managing the process carefully, it is not hard to see that a replacement bucket can be generated using n distance computations.

Another complication that can arise in practice is when the U_i contains fewer than u points. In this case, it is a simple matter to expand the number of buckets contributing to U_i until it contains at least u points. If this is done carefully, no additional distance computations are required for this.

Algorithm NNSampler was implemented and tested on the Reuters data set, which has previously been used in the analysis of several data mining applications (Bradley & Fayyad, 1998; Fayyad 1998). The Reuters set consists of records of categorical data coded as integers, each record having 302 attributes. Two sets of runs were performed, one set with $n=1000$ records, and the other with $n=10,000$. The sample sizes were chosen to be roughly $n^{1/2}$: $r=32$ for the first set, and $r=100$ for the second. For each set, the number of near neighbors computed was $u=10$ and $u=20$.

To test the accuracy of the near-neighbor generation, the full set of distances was calculated, and the true u nearest neighbor lists were compared with the approximate lists. The accuracy of the approximate lists are shown in Table 1, along with the time needed to compute the lists, in CPU seconds (the confidence intervals shown are at 95%). In the case where $u=20$, the accuracy rate of the closest 10 elements on the approximate list are compared with the 10 elements on the exact list. The lower accuracy rate in the case of $n=10,000$ and $u=10$ is due to the high number of neighbors having identical distances—in cases of an overabundance of near neighbors with the same distance to a given data point, the selection of u near neighbors is performed arbitrarily.

Random partitioning for the TWGD-problem

We now illustrate a general non-representative randomized clustering strategy, based on a two-phase enhanced version of the interchange heuristic for the TWGD-problem. The strategy is divide-and-conquer: in the first phase, we partition the set of points randomly, and compute a clustering of each partition set. For the merge step, we perform an aggregation of the elements based on the clusters generated in the first phase. Before giving the details of the method, we require some terminology and notation.

The assignment of a data element to a cluster can be viewed as a labeling of that data element with the index associated with that cluster. Each modification per-

Table 1: Testing algorithm NNSampler versus brute force calculation

	Execution Time		Precision	
	$n=1000$	$n=10,000$	$n=1000$	$n=10,000$
Brute Force	38.5 s	3765.9 s	100%	100%
NNSampler ($u=10$)	12.6 s	360 ± 20 s	91%	$73 \pm 3\%$
NNSampler ($u=20$)	18.6 s	720 ± 35 s	98%	$90 \pm 4\%$

formed by an interchange heuristic would thus result in a re-labeling of one of the data elements. The cluster to which s_i belongs in P^t will be denoted by $C_t[s_i]$. Conversely, the elements of j-th cluster at time t will be denoted by $C_{t,j}$. We also evaluate s_i for its quality as a discrete representative of the j-th cluster in P^t, using the L_1 loss function: $L_1(s_i,t,j) = \Sigma_{si' \in Ct,j} w_{i'} d(s_i,s_{i'})$. In the preprocessing step of the first phase, data structures are constructed that maintain information about the partition in a feasible solution P^t, and the sum of distances of each point to items of a cluster. A linear array of indices is used to maintain $C_t[s_i]$, the assignment of data elements to clusters for the current solution P^t. A table $M[i,j]$ of k columns and n rows will be used to store the set of loss function values $L_1(s_i,t,j)$. Since the initialization L_{si} requires $O(n)$ distance calculations, initializing the entire table would require $\Theta(n^2)$ calculations, but only $O(kn)$ space.

The matrix M facilitates the implementation of the heuristics for the $TWGD(P)$-problem. That is, for the interchange at time t for item s_i, we find the index j_{min} that is the smallest value in the row for s_i in M; that is, $L_1(s_i,t,j_{min}) = \min_{j=1,...,k} L_1(s_i,t,j)$. This clearly can be done in $O(k)$ time. If $j_{min} = C_t[s_i]$, the point s_i does not change cluster membership, and $P^{t+1} = P^t$. However, if $j_{min} \neq C_t[s_i]$, we have found an improvement over the current partition P^t, with s_i assigned to cluster j_{min}. We let $j_{old} \leftarrow C_t[s_i]$ and $C_{t+1}[s_i] \leftarrow j_{min}$. We also update the information in the matrix M. For all $s_{i'}$, we update its column $M_{i',*}$ by setting

$M_{i'jold} \leftarrow M_{i'jold} - w_i d(s_i,s_{i'})$, $M_{i'jmin} \leftarrow M_{i'jmin} + w_i d(s_i,s_{i'})$. In either case, the total number of distance calculations in one interchange is in $O(n)$.

Clearly, the clustering computed is the same as for the standard TWGD interchange heuristic. This matrix-based variant (referred to as TWGD-median) is apparently more complex than the standard interchange heuristic. But TWGD-median will allow us to develop a faster approximation algorithm for the TWGD-problem. The algorithm starts by first randomly partitioning S into smaller $Y_1,...,Y_r$. This can be achieved by generating a permutation S' of S uniformly at random (in $O(n)$ time). We let $r \in \{1,...,n\}$ be an integer parameter and determine the random partition by dividing the sequence S' into r consecutive blocks $Y_1,...,Y_r$, each containing roughly n/r elements.

We will operate the interchange heuristic separately for each of the blocks Y_b, $b=1,...,r$. The result will be a collection of r clusters, each consisting of k clusters. In the second phase, this collection of clusters $C_1^b,...,C_k^b$ of the blocks Y_b, $b=1,...,r$, are used in turn to influence the construction of a clustering for the entire set S. The execution proceeds as if we were using the TWGD interchange on the whole set, except that the distance calculations to arbitrary points are replaced by calculations to their representative discrete medians, defined below.

The first step of the second phase is the extraction of the discrete median of each cluster C_j^b of each block ($j=1,...,k$ and $b=1,...,r$). Formally, the discrete median c_j^b is a point $s_i \in T_b \subseteq S$ belonging to cluster C_j^b such that $L_1(c_j^b,t,j) \leq L_1(s,t,j)$ for all data points s in C_j^b. Computing the discrete median can be done simply by finding the smallest value in the j-th column for matrix M_b of the block Y_b, and identifying the row where that occurs. Since c_j^b will be used to represent all points in C_j^b, we will assign to it the aggregation of weights in C_j^b; that is, $w(c_j^b) = \Sigma_{si' \in Cj}{}^b w_{i'}$.

Next, on the collection of rk discrete medians obtained, a TWGD-style k-clustering is performed. The k groups of medians indicate which block clusters C_j^b could be merged to produce the best clustering of S into k groups.

The aggregation interchange heuristic uses this information as follows. When a point s_i in group j is being assessed for migration to group j', we consider whether the contribution $\Sigma_{si \neq si' \wedge si' \in \text{cluster } j}\, w(s_i)\, w(s_{i'})\, d(s_i, s_{i'})$ is larger than $\Sigma_{si \neq si' \wedge si' \in \text{cluster } j'}\, w(s_i)$ $w(s_{i'})\, d(s_i, s_{i'})$. In the case that the former is larger than the latter, s_i is migrated from cluster j to group j'. This new gradient is one where the sum of all pairs of distances between points represented by s_i and points represented by $s_{i'}$ are approximated by the aggregated information from the matrices M_b.

Since the blocks have size $\Theta(n/r)$, the application of the aggregation version of TWGD-median to all blocks Y_b requires $O(rn^2/r^2) = O(n^2/r)$ distance computations. The aggregation version of the hill-climber integrating these results will work with rk items per data element, and thus will require $O(rkn)$ distance computations per complete scan through S. The overall number of distance computations is therefore in $O((rk++n/r)n)$. This is minimized when r is chosen to be $O((n/k)^{1/2})$, yielding $O(n^{3/2}k^{1/2})$ computations.

To illustrate the scalability of our methods, we implemented the three algorithms discussed here, namely the original interchange method for TWGD (which we will call TWGD-quadratic), then our enhanced version TWGD-median and finally, our final randomized approximation algorithm (which we will call TWGD-random). We used synthetic data, generated as a mixture of 10 probability distributions in 2D. We generated data sets of different sizes, from $n=4000$ data items to $n=1,000,000$. The results are displayed graphically in Figure 1. Data in Figure 1 is on a logarithmic scale. Algorithm TWGD-median is 4 to 5 times faster than TWGD-

Figure 1: Illustration of CPU-time requirements of TWGD-quadratic, TWGD-median and TWGD-random

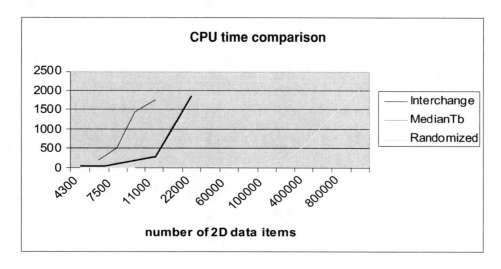

quadratic, and for n=5000 it requires only 48s, while TWGD-quadratic requires 207s. However, both have quadratic time complexity. Our divide-and-conquer TWGD-random is radically faster, being able to cluster 1,000,000 points in the same CPU time that TWGD-median takes for only slightly more than 20,000, and the original TWGD-quadratic takes for just over 11,000. Both TWGD-quadratic and TWGD-median exhibit quadratic time complexity. An example illustrating clustering of mixture models for 3D data appears in Estivill-Castro & Houle (2001).

CONCLUSION AND FUTURE TRENDS

In this work, we have put forward a case for approximation of objective criteria and of proximity information as keys to the development of generic, scalable and robust methods for clustering for data mining applications. In particular, randomized sampling and partition techniques seem to hold the greatest promise for pushing back the barrier of scalability for these important problems.

Although some of the solutions we have presented are specific to certain problem settings, others can be applied in a wide variety of settings, both inside and beyond the field of data mining clustering. The idea of using approximations to full proximity information is a very general one, and there is much potential for the application of these ideas in other settings. The underlying spirit of these solutions is the same: obtain the highest quality possible subject to a rigid observation of time constraints.

There are other settings in which approximation to the full proximity information has been used to good effect. In physics, researchers applied simulated annealing to predict the motion of particles in 2D and 3D used a hierarchical structure to aggregate distance computations (Carrier, Greengard & Rokhlin, 1988; Barnes & Hut, 1986), reducing the cost of an iteration of the simulation from $\Theta(n^2)$ to $O(n \log n)$. These structures have been taken up and extended to the area of graph drawing, where graphs are treated as linkages of stretchable springs between nodes with repulsive charges. Layouts of these graphs are generated by simulating the effect of forces along springs and between nodes, also using simulated annealing (Quigley & Eades, 2000). Similar structures have also been used in facility location (Belbin, 1987). Although scalability with respect to dimension is not an issue in these fields, the techniques presented here provide yet more opportunities for the development of fast and robust algorithms.

Our techniques contribute to the area of robust statistics. We showed (Estivill-Castro & Houle, 2000) that robust estimators of location could be computed in subquadratic time using random sampling and partitioning. Even though the statistic itself is a random variable, its robustness can be proved according to several standards.

Finally, there is great potential for our techniques to be hybridized with other search strategies, such as genetic algorithms (Estivill-Castro, 2000; Estivill-Castro & Torres-Velázquez, 1998; Estivill-Castro & Murray, 2000; and references) and simulated annealing [Murray & Church, 1996]. Genetic algorithms and simulated annealing have extended the power of local search hill-climbers due to their ability to escape from and improve over local optima, at the cost of an increase in the computation time. These areas can also benefit from a stricter management of the distance computations performed.

REFERENCES

Aldenderfer, M.S. and R.K. Blashfield (1973.) *Cluster Analysis*. Sage, Beverly Hills, 1984.

M.R. Anderberg. *Cluster Analysis with Applications*. Academic Press, NY.

Aurenhammer, F. (1991). Voronoi diagrams: A survey of a fundamental geometric data structure. *ACM Comput. Surv.*, 23(3):345-405.

Barnes, J. and P. Hut (1986). A hierarchical $O(n \log n)$ force-calculation algorithm. *Nature*, 324(4), 446-449.

Beckmann, N., H.-P. Kriegel, R. Schneider, and B. Seeger (1990). The R^*-tree: An efficient and robust access method for points and rectangles. In *Proc. ACM SIGMOD Conf. on Management of Data*, 322-331.

Belbin, L. (1987). The use of non-hierarchical allocation methods for clustering large sets of data. *The Australian Computer Journal*, 19(1), 32-41.

Bentley, J.L. (1975). A survey of techniques for fixed radius near neighbor searching. Report STAN-CS-78-513, Dept. Comput. Sci., Stanford Univ., Stanford, CA.

Bentley, J.L. (1979). Decomposable searching problems. *Information Processing Letters*, 8, 244-251.

Berchtold, S. D.A. Keim, and H.-P. Kriegel(1996).. The X-tree: An index structure for higher dimensional data. In *Proc. 22nd VLDB Conference*, 28-39.

Berry, M.J.A. and G. Linoff (1997). *Data Mining Techniques - for Marketing, Sales and Customer Support*. John Wiley & Sons, NY, USA.

Berson, A. and S.J. Smith (1998). *Data Warehousing, Data Mining, & OLAP*. Series on Data Warehousing and Data Management. McGraw-Hill, NY, USA.

Bradley, P.S. and U. Fayyad (1998). Refining the initial points in k-means clustering. In *Proc. of the 15th Int. Con.e on Machine Learning*, Morgan Kaufmann, 91-99.

Bradley, P.S., U. Fayyad, and C. Reina (1998). Scaling clustering algorithms to large databases. In R. Agrawal and P. Stolorz, eds., *Proc. of the 4th Int. Conference on Knowledge Discovery and Data Mining*, AAAI Press, 9-15.

Bradley, P.S., O.L. Mangasarian, and W.N. Street (1997). Clustering via concave minimization. *Advances in neural information processing systems*, 9:368.

Brucker, P. (1978). On the complexity of clustering problems. In R. Henn, B.H.B. Korte, and W.W. Oetti, eds., *Optimization and Operations Research: Proceedings of the workshop held at the University of Bonn*, Berlin. Springer Verlag Lecture Notes in Economics and Mathematical Systems.

Carrier, J., L. Greengard, and V. Rokhlin (1988). A fast adaptive multipode algorithm for particle simulation. *SIAM J. of Science and Statistical Computing*, 9:669-686.

Chávez, E., G. Navarro, R. Baeza-Yates, and J. Marroquín (1999). Searching in metric spaces. Report TR/DCC-99-3, Dept. of Comp. Science, U. of Chile, Santiago.

Cheeseman, P., M. Self, J. Kelly, W. Taylor, D. Freeman, and J. Stutz (1988). Bayesian classification. In *Proc. Seventh National Conference on Artificial Intelligence*, 607-611, Palo Alto, CA, AAAI, Morgan Kaufmann.

Cherkassky, V., and F. Muller (1998). *Learning from Data - Concept, Theory and Methods.* John Wiley & Sons, NY, USA.

Chiu, D.K.Y., A.K.C. Wong, and B. Cheung (1991). Information discovery through hierarchical maximum entropy discretization and synthesis. In G. Piatetsky-Shapiro and W.J. Frawley, eds., *Knowledge Discovery in Databases*, pages 125-140, Menlo Park, CA. AAAI, AAAI Press.

Ciaccia, P., M. Patella, and P. Zezula (1997). M-tree: an efficient access method for similarity search in metric spaces. In *Proc. 23rd VLDB Conference*, pages 426-435.

Dempster, A.P., N.M. Laird, and D.B. Rubin (1977). Maximum likelihood from incomplete data via the EM algorithm. *Journal of the Royal Statistical Society B*, 39:1-38.

Densham, P. and G. Rushton (1992). A more efficient heuristic for solving large p-median problems. *Papers in Regional Science*, 71:307-329.

Dickerson, M.T., R.L.S. Drysdale, and J.-R. Sack (1992). Simple algorithms for enumerating interpoint distances and finding k nearest neighbours. *International Journal of Computational Geometry & Applications*, 2(3):221-239, 1992.

Duda, R.O. and P.E. Hart (1973). *Pattern Classification and Scene Analysis.* John Wiley & Sons, NY, USA.

Ester, M., H.P. Kriegel, S. Sander, and X. Xu (1996). A density-based algorithm for discovering clusters in large spatial databases with noise. E. Simoudis, J. Han, and U. Fayyad, eds., *Proc. 2nd Int. Conf. Knowledge Discovery and Data Mining* 226-231, Menlo Park, CA, AAAI, AAAI Press.

Estivill-Castro, V. (2000). Hybrid genetic algorithms are better for spatial clustering. In R. Mizoguchi and J. Slaney, eds., *Proc. 6th Pacific Rim Int. Conf. on Artificial Intelligence,* 424-434, Melbourne, Australia,Springer-Verlag LNAI 1886.

Estivill-Castro, V. and M.E. Houle (forthcoming). Robust distance-based clustering with applications to spatial data mining. *Algorithmica.* In press - Special Issue on Algorithms for Geographic Information.

Estivill-Castro, V. and M.E. Houle (1999). Robust clustering of large data sets with categorical attributes. In J. Roddick, editor, *Database Systems - Australian Computer Science Communications*, 21(2), 165-176, Springer Verlag, Singapore.

Estivill-Castro, V. and M.E. Houle (2000). Fast randomized algorithms for robust estimation of location. In J. Roddick and K. Hornsby, eds., *Proc. Int. Workshop on Temporal, Spatial and Spatio-Temporal Data Mining, in conjunction with the 4th European Conf. on Principles and Practices of Knowledge Discovery and Databases*, 74-85, Lyon, France, 2000. Springer-Verlag LNAI 2007.

Estivill-Castro, V. and M.E. Houle (2001). Fast minimization of total within-group distance. M. Ng, ed., *Proc. Int. Workshop Spatio-Temporal Data Mining in conjunction with 5th Pacific-Asia Conf. Knowledge Discovery and Data Mining*, Hong Kong 2001.

Estivill-Castro, V. and A.T. Murray (1998). Discovering associations in spatial data - an efficient medoid based approach. In X. Wu, R. Kotagiri, and K.K. Korb, eds., *Proc. 2nd Pacific-Asia Conf. on Knowledge Discovery and Data Mining*, 110-121, Melbourne, Australia, Springer-Verlag LNAI 1394.

Estivill-Castro, V. and A.T. Murray (2000). Weighted facility location and clustering via hybrid optimization. In F. Naghdy, F. Kurfess, H. Ogata, E. Szczerbicki, and H. Bothe, eds., *Proc. Int. Conf. on Intelligent Systems and Applications* (*ISA-2000*), Paper 1514-079, Canada, 2000. ICSC, ICSC Academic Press. CD-ROM version.

Estivill-Castro, V. and R. Torres-Velázquez (1999). Hybrid genetic algorithm for solving the p-median problem. In A Yao, R.I. McKay, C.S. Newton, J.-H Kim, and T. Furuhashi, eds., *Proc. of Second Asia Pacific Conference On Simulated Evolution and Learning SEAL-98*, 18-25. Springer Verlag LNAI 1585.

Estivill-Castro, V. and J. Yang (2000).. A fast and robust general purpose clustering algorithm. R. Mizoguchi & J. Slaney, eds, *Proc. 6th Pacific Rim Int. Conf. Artificial Intelligence*, 208-218, Melbourne, Australia, 2000. Springer-Verlag LNAI 1886.

Everitt,B. (1980). *Cluster Analysis*. Halsted Press, New York, USA, 2nd. edition, 1980.

Fayyad, U., C. Reina, and P.S. Bradley (1998). Initialization of iterative refinement clustering algorithms. R. Agrawal and P. Stolorz, eds., *Proc. 4th Int. Conf. on Knowledge Discovery and Data Mining*, 194-198. AAAI Press.

Fisher, D.H.(1987). Knowledge acquisition via incremental conceptual clustering. *Machine Learning*, 2(2):139-172.

Glover, F. (1986). Future paths for integer programming and links to artificial intelligence. *Computers and Operations Research*, 5:533-549.

Gonnet, G.H. and R. Baeza-Yates (1991). *Handbook of Algorithms and Data Structures*, 2nd edition. Addison-Wesley Publishing Co., Don Mills, Ontario.

Guttmann, A. (1984). R-trees: a dynamic index structure for spatial searching. In *Proc. ACM SIGMOD International Conference on Management of Data*, pages 47-57, 1984.

Hall, I.B. (1999). L.O. Özyurt and J.C. Bezdek. Clustering with a genetically optimized approach. *IEEE Transactions on Evolutionary Computation*, 3(2):103-112, July 1999.

Han, J. and M. Kamber (2000). *Data Mining: Concepts and Techniques*. Morgan Kaufmann Publishers, San Mateo, CA.

Hartigan, J.A. (1975). *Clustering Algorithms*. Wiley, NY.

Horn, M. (1996). Analysis and computation schemes for p-median heuristics. *Environment and Planning A*, 28:1699-1708.

Jain, A.K. and R.C. Dubes (1998). *Algorithms for Clustering Data*. Prentice-Hall, Inc., Englewood Cliffs, NJ, Advanced Reference Series: Computer Science.

Kaufman, L. and P.J. Rousseuw (1990).. *Finding Groups in Data: An Introduction to Cluster Analysis*. John Wiley & Sons, NY, USA.

Krivánek, M. (1986). Hexagonal unit network — a tool for proving the NP-completeness results of geometric problems. *Information Processing Letters*, 22:37-41.

Krznaric, D. and C. Levcopoulos (1998). Fast algorithms for complete linkage clustering. *Discrete & Computational Geometry*, 19:131-145.

MacQueen, J.(1967). Some methods for classification and analysis of multivariate observations. L. Le Cam and J. Neyman, eds., *5th Berkley Symposium on Mathematical Statistics and Probability*, volume 1, 281-297.

Michalski, R.S. and R.E. Stepp (1983). Automated construction of classifications: clustering versus numerical taxonomy. *IEEE Tran. on Pattern Analysis and Machine Intelligence*, 5:683-690.

Mitchell, T.M. (1997). *Machine Learning*. McGraw-Hill, Boston, MA, 1997.

Murray, A.T. (2000). Spatial characteristics and comparisons of interaction and median clustering models. *Geographical Analysis*, 32(1):1-.

Murray, A.T. and R.L. Church (1996). Applying simulated annealing to location-planning models. *Journal of Heuristics*, 2:31-53, 1996.

Murra, A.T. and V. Estivill-Castro (1998). Cluster discovery techniques for exploratory spatial data analysis. *Int. J. of Geographic Information Systems*, 12(5):431-443.

Ng, R.T. and J. Han (1994). Efficient and effective clustering methods for spatial data mining. In J. Bocca, M. Jarke, and C. Zaniolo, eds., *Proc. 20th VLDB Conference*, 144-155, San Francisco, CA, Santiago, Chile, Morgan Kaufmann.

Okabe,A., B. Boots, and K. Sugihara (1992). *Spatial Tesselations - Concepts and applications of Voronoi diagrams*. John Wiley & Sons, NY, USA.

O'Rourke, J. (1994). *Computational Geometry in C*. Cambridge University Press, UK.

Quigley, A.J. and P. Eades (1984). FADE: Graph drawing, clustering and visual abstraction. In J. Marks, editor, *Proc. 8ht Int. Symposium on Graph Drawing*, Williamsburg Virginia, USA, 2000. Springer Verlag Lecture Notes in Computer Science.

Rao, M. (1971). Cluster analysis and mathematical programming. *Journal of the American Statistical Association*, 66:622-626.

Rolland, D., E. Schilling and J. Current (1996). An efficient Tabu search procedure for the *p*-median problem. *European Journal of Operations Research*, 96:329-342.

Rosing, K. and C. ReVelle (1986). Optimal clustering. *Environment and Planning A*, 18:1463-1476.

Rosing, K.E., C.S. ReVelle, and H. Rosing-Voyelaar (1979). The *p*-median and its linear programming relaxation: An approach to large problems. *Journal of the Operational Research Society*, 30:815-823.

Rousseeuw, P.J. and A.M. Leroy (1987). *Robust regression and outlier detection*. John Wiley & Sons, NY, USA.

Samet, H. (1989). *The Design and Analysis of Spatial Data Structures*. Addison-Wesley Publishing Co., Reading, MA.

Schikuta, E. (1996). Grid-clustering: an efficient hierarchical clustering method for very large data sets. In *Proc. 13th Int. Conf. on Pattern Recognition*, vol. 2, 101-105.

Späth, H. (1980). *Cluster Analysis Algorithms for data reduction and classification of objects*. Ellis Horwood Limited, Chinchester, UK.

Teitz, M.B. and P. Bart (1968). Heuristic methods for estimating the generalized vertex median of a weighted graph. *Operations Research*, 16, 955-961.

Titterington, D.M., A.F.M. Smith, and U.E. Makov (1985). *Statistical Analysis of Finite Mixture Distributions*. John Wiley & Sons, UK.

Vinod, H.(1969). Integer programming and the theory of grouping. *Journal of the American Statistical Association*, 64, 506-517.

Wallace, C.S. and P.R. Freeman (1987). Estimation and inference by compact coding. *Journal of the Royal Statistical Society, Series B*, 49(3), 240-265, 1987.

Wang, W., J. Yang, and R. Muntz (1997). STING: a statistical information grid approach to spatial data mining. In M. Jarke, editor, *Proc. 23rd VLDB Conference*, pages 186-195, Athens, Greece. VLDB, Morgan Kaufmann Publishers.

Zhang, T., R. Ramakrishnan, and M. Livny (1996). BIRCH: an efficient data clustering method for very large databases. *SIGMOD Record*, 25(2),103-114.

PART TWO:

EVOLUTIONARY ALGORITHMS

Chapter III

On the Use of Evolutionary Algorithms in Data Mining

Erick Cantú-Paz and Chandrika Kamath
Center for Applied Scientific Computing
Lawrence Livermore National Laboratory, USA

With computers becoming more pervasive, disks becoming cheaper, and sensors becoming ubiquitous, we are collecting data at an ever-increasing pace. However, it is far easier to collect the data than to extract useful information from it. Sophisticated techniques, such as those developed in the multi-disciplinary field of data mining, are increasingly being applied to the analysis of these datasets in commercial and scientific domains. As the problems become larger and more complex, researchers are turning to heuristic techniques to complement existing approaches. This survey chapter examines the role that evolutionary algorithms (EAs) can play in various stages of data mining. We consider data mining as the end-to-end process of finding patterns starting with raw data. The chapter focuses on the topics of feature extraction, feature selection, classification, and clustering, and surveys the state of the art in the application of evolutionary algorithms to these areas. We examine the use of evolutionary algorithms both in isolation and in combination with other algorithms including neural networks, and decision trees. The chapter concludes with a summary of open research problems and opportunities for the future.

INTRODUCTION

Data mining is increasingly being accepted as a viable means of analyzing massive data sets. With commercial and scientific datasets approaching the terabyte and even petabyte range, it is no longer possible to manually find useful information in this data. As the semi-automated techniques of data mining are applied in various domains, it is becoming clear that methods from statistics, artificial intelligence, optimization, etc., that comprise data mining, are no longer sufficient to address this problem of data overload. Often, the data is noisy and has a high level of uncertainty. It could also be dynamic, with the patterns in the data evolving in space and time. To address these aspects of data analysis, we need to incorporate heuristic techniques to complement the existing approaches.

In this chapter, we survey the role that one category of heuristic algorithms, namely, evolutionary algorithms (EAs), plays in the various steps of the data mining process. After a brief definition of both the data mining process and evolutionary algorithms, we focus on the many ways in which these algorithms are being used in data mining. This survey is by no means exhaustive. Rather, it is meant to illustrate the diverse ways in which the power of evolutionary algorithms can be used to improve the techniques being applied to the analysis of massive data sets. Following a survey of current work in the use of EAs for data mining tasks such as feature extraction, feature selection, classification, and clustering, we describe some challenges encountered in applying these techniques. We conclude with the exciting opportunities that await future researchers in the field.

AN OVERVIEW OF DATA MINING

Data mining is a process concerned with uncovering patterns, associations, anomalies and statistically significant structures in data (Fayyad et al., 1996). It typically refers to the case where the data is too large or too complex to allow either a manual analysis or analysis by means of simple queries. Data mining consists of two main steps, data pre-processing, during which relevant high-level features or attributes are extracted from the low level data, and pattern recognition, in which a pattern in the data is recognized using these features (see Figure 1). Pre-processing the data is often a time-consuming, yet critical, first step. To ensure the success of the data-mining process, it is important that the features extracted from the data are

Figure 1: Data mining—An iterative and interactive process

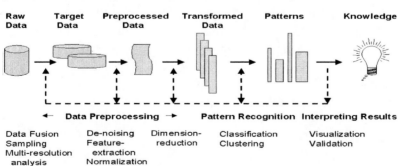

Figure 1: Data Mining - an iterative and interactive process

relevant to the problem and representative of the data.

Depending on the type of data being mined, the pre-processing step may consist of several sub-tasks. If the raw data is very large, we could use sampling and work with fewer instances, or use multi-resolution techniques and work with data at a coarser resolution. Next, noise in the data is removed to the extent possible, and relevant features are extracted. In some cases, where data from different sources or sensors are available, data fusion may be required to allow the miner to exploit all the data available for a problem. At the end of this first step, we have a feature vector for each data instance. Depending on the problem and the data, we may need to reduce the number of features using feature selection or dimension reduction techniques such as principal component analysis (PCA) (Jackson, 1991) or its non-linear versions. After this pre-processing, the data is ready for the detection of patterns through the use of algorithms such as classification, clustering, regression, etc. These patterns are then displayed to the user for validation. Data mining is an iterative and interactive process. The output of any step, or feedback from the domain experts, could result in an iterative refinement of any, or all, of the sub-tasks.

While there is some debate about the exact definition of data mining (Kamath 2001), most practitioners and proponents agree that data mining is a multi-disciplinary field, borrowing ideas from machine learning and artificial intelligence, statistics, high performance computing, signal and image processing, mathematical optimization, pattern recognition, etc. What is new is the confluence of the mature offshoots of these technologies at a time when we can exploit them for the analysis of massive data sets. As data mining has been applied to new problem domains, this technology mix has grown as well. For example, the growth of the Internet and the World Wide Web has resulted in tasks such as clustering text documents, multimedia searches, or mining a user's Web surfing patterns to predict what page they are likely to visit next or to target the advertising on a Web page. This has added natural language processing and privacy issues to the technological mix that comprises data mining.

Data mining techniques are being applied for the analysis of data in a variety of fields including remote sensing, bio-informatics, medical imaging, astronomy, Web mining, text mining, customer relationship management, and market-basket analysis. While much of the focus in the data mining process tends to be on pattern recognition algorithms, the data pre-processing steps are more influential in the success of the data mining endeavor (Langley and Simon, 1995; Burl et al., 1998). Unfortunately, the pre-processing steps often depend on the domain and problem. As a result, given the space limitations of this chapter, any discussion of the role of evolutionary algorithms in data pre-processing is likely to be limited in scope. Rather than ignore this important subject altogether, we will discuss aspects of this subject that are broadly applicable to several problem domains.

AN OVERVIEW OF EVOLUTIONARY ALGORITHMS

Evolutionary algorithms are randomized search procedures inspired by the mechanics of genetics and natural selection. EAs are often used as optimization algorithms, and this is the role that they play in most data mining applications. EAs work on a population of individuals that represent possible solutions to a problem in their chromosomes. Each individual can be as simple as a string of zeroes and ones, or as complex as a computer program. The initial population of individuals may be created entirely at random, or some knowledge about previously known solutions may be used to seed the population. The algorithm evaluates the individuals to determine how well they solve the problem at hand with an objective function, which is unique to each problem and must be supplied by the user. The individuals with better performance are selected to serve as parents of the next generation. Evolutionary algorithms create new individuals using simple randomized operators that are similar to sexual recombination and mutation in natural organisms. The new solutions are evaluated, and the cycle of selection and creation of new individuals is repeated until a satisfactory solution is found or a predetermined time limit has elapsed.

There are several major types of evolutionary algorithms: genetic algorithms (GAs), genetic programming (GP), evolution strategies (ES), and evolutionary programming (EP). All evolutionary algorithms share the same basic concepts, but differ in the way they encode the solutions and on the operators they use to create the next generation.

Evolutionary algorithms are controlled by several inputs, such as the size of the population, and the rates that control how often mutation and crossover are used. In general, there is no guarantee that the evolutionary algorithm will find the optimal solution to an arbitrary problem, but a careful manipulation of the inputs and choosing a representation that is adequate to the problem increase the chances of success.

There are many ways to encode a potential solution as a chromosome, and there are many variations of selection methods, crossover, and mutation operators. Some of these choices are better suited to a particular problem than others, and no single choice is the best for all problems. Traditionally, genetic algorithms use chromosomes composed of zeroes and ones, but other encodings may be more natural to the problem and may facilitate the search for good solutions. Genetic programming encodes solutions as computer programs. ES and EP use floating-point numbers, which may be more suitable for function optimization problems where the parameters to optimize are real numbers, but may be an awkward match to a problem of finding the shortest route between multiple cities.

The choice of encoding is related to the operators that are used to produce new solutions from the selected ones. The simplest operator is mutation, and it acts by randomly changing a short piece of the chromosome. For example, when applied to strings of binary digits, it randomly chooses a location in the chromosome of an individual and flips a bit from zero to one or vice-versa. ES and EP use more sophisticated mutation operators.

Taking a cue from nature, genetic algorithms do not use mutation very often. The primary mechanism in GAs to create new individuals is crossover. In its simplest form, crossover randomly chooses two individuals from the pool that were selected to be parents, and exchanges segments of their two chromosomes around a single randomly chosen point. The result is two new individuals, each with a segment of chromosome from each parent. Other variants of crossover exchange material around more than one point, and some researchers have experimented with recombining chromosomes from more than two parents. Some of the new solutions will be more fit than the parents, but others will be less fit. Evolutionary algorithms cannot avoid creating solutions that turn out to be unfit, but the selection process eliminates the bad solutions and keeps the best.

The selection of the parents can occur in many ways, but all selection methods have the same objective of preserving good individuals and discarding the less fit ones. Roughly, there are two kinds of selection: hard and soft. Soft selection methods assign to each individual a probability of survival based on their fitness, so that individuals with high fitness are more likely to be selected than individuals with low fitness. The soft selection methods then use the probabilities to select the parents. The hard methods do not involve any probabilities; they choose deterministically a fixed number of the best solutions available.

THE ROLE OF EVOLUTIONARY ALGORITHMS IN DATA MINING

After the brief overview of data mining and evolutionary algorithms, we next discuss the important role these algorithms can play in the various steps of data mining. In the following sections, we discuss how evolutionary algorithms can be used to improve the robustness and accuracy of the more traditional techniques used in feature extraction, feature selection, classification, and clustering.

In our survey, we view data mining as a multi-step process, focusing on the role that EAs can play in each step. However, we would be remiss if we did not include the work of those authors who blur the separation between the different steps and use EAs to perform data mining as a whole on the input data. For example, in an early paper, Tackett (1993) identifies targets in a cluttered image by combining simple features extracted from the segmented image through linear and non-linear operations. If the resulting single value at the root of the tree is greater than zero, the object is classified as a target. Stanhope and Daida (1998) use a similar approach in their work on target classification using Synthetic Aperture Radar (SAR) images. Sherrah, Bogner, and Bouzerdoum (1996) also use non-linear pre-processing functions to create new features from primitive features. In addition, they associate one of three simple classifiers with each individual. The objective function is to minimize the number of errors made by each individual (a parse tree + a classifier) on the training data, with smaller trees being favored as a tie-breaker. In the process, the classifier is selected automatically.

EVOLUTIONARY ALGORITHMS IN FEATURE EXTRACTION

The process of extracting features that are relevant to the problem being addressed in data mining is very problem- and data-dependent. In some types of data, the features are relatively easy to identify. For example, in text data, the features are the words in the text, and in market-basket analysis, the features are the items bought in a transaction. In each case, some processing of these raw features may be required. In text mining, words that do not represent the content of the text (e.g., articles) are removed and stemming of words performed so that similar words such as "computers" and "computing" are not considered as different (Frakes and Baeza-Yates, 1992). In market-basket analysis, we may need to convert the units so that all items bought by weight are measured in ounces.

While some types of data lend themselves easily to feature extraction, this task is more difficult in other cases. A typical example is image data, where feature extraction is far more challenging. In the past, image data was restricted to a few domains such as astronomy and remote sensing; however, it is now becoming more pervasive. With data mining being applied to domains such as medical imaging, multimedia on the Web, and video images, it is important that we have robust techniques to identify features representing an image. Since images tend to vary widely, even within a domain, the adaptive nature of evolutionary algorithms can be exploited very effectively to address this important and difficult problem of feature extraction in image data.

An image is a rectangular array of pixels, where each pixel has either a gray-scale value, or a real value representing some physical quantity. In image mining, the first task is to identify an object in the image, followed by extraction of features that represent the object. Object identification is often the more difficult of these two tasks, as it involves the conversion of the low-level representation (i.e., pixels) into a higher-level representation (i.e., objects). It is here that evolutionary algorithms can be used very efficiently and effectively. Two techniques that are traditionally used to identify an object in an image are *segmentation*, where the image is separated into several regions based on some desired criteria, and *edge detection*, where edges or contours in an image are identified (Weeks, 1996).

Several authors have exploited the use of evolutionary algorithms for image segmentation to deal with large and complex search spaces where limited information is available about the objective function. As Bhanu, Lee, and Ming (1995) point out, a key challenge in image segmentation is that most algorithms require the selection of several control parameters for optimal performance. This results in a high-dimensional search space, where the interactions between the parameters are complex and non-linear. Further, variations between images could cause the objective function representing the quality of segmentation to vary from one image to another. The problem is worsened by the fact that there is no single, universally accepted measure of the quality of the segmented image. To address these problems, Bhanu and Lee (1994) have explored the use of genetic algorithms to adaptively find the optimal set of control parameters for the Phoenix segmentation algorithm. The genetic algorithm selects an initial set of parameters based on the statistics of an image along with the conditions under which the image was obtained (time of day, cloud cover, etc.). The performance is evaluated using multiple measures of segmentation quality that include both global characteristics of the image and local features of the object. The system is adaptive as a global population of images, their associated characteristics, and the optimal control parameters. It is maintained and used to seed the population each time a new image is analyzed. This global population is also constantly updated with higher strength individuals. Using scene images, Bhanu, Lee, and Ming (1995) show that their approach provides high quality results in a minimal number of cycles.

Another approach to segmentation using genetic algorithms is the work done in three-dimensional medical imaging by Cagnoni, Dobrzeniecki, Poli, and Yanch (1997). They too observe that the extreme variability of the features in biological structures causes the solutions generated by general-purpose algorithms to be unacceptable. As a result, some degree of adaptivity is required when segmenting medical images. Their approach identifies the contours of an object by first identifying the edge points using a filter whose parameters are optimized by a GA. These edge points are then used to seed an interpolation process, where the interpolation parameters are also generated by a GA. The fitness function is proportional to the degree of similarity between the contours generated by the GA and the contours identified in manually generated training examples. These filter and interpolation parameters are obtained for each new class of problems. Results on three-dimensional MRI images show that the GA-based techniques are insensitive to significant changes in shape across a sequence of images as well as the inter- and intra-slice variability in the contours, thus illustrating the power of these techniques.

The task of edge detection can also benefit from the use of evolutionary algorithms. Most edge detectors use simple first- and second-order derivatives to identify an edge. However, these operators are sensitive to noise and are not very general. In addition, they identify a pixel as an edge pixel based on the response of the edge detector at that pixel, ignoring the edge structure around the pixel. To overcome this disadvantage, several authors, including Tan, Gelfand, and Delp (1989) and Bhandarkar, Zhang, and Potter (1994) have proposed an approach based on cost minimization, where the cost takes into account issues such as local edge structure, continuity of the edge, and fragmentation. This lends itself very naturally to the use of genetic algorithms for minimizing the cost. Bhandarkar et al. (1994) first define edge pixels as those that satisfy certain constraints, and then define the corresponding cost functions based on the local edge structure. Since the data is an image, the most natural representation of a chromosome is a two dimensional sequence of zeroes and ones, where an edge pixel is a one, and a non-edge pixel is a zero. The crossover operator is defined in two dimensions, with two-dimensional sub-images swapped between individuals. Their results show that both simulated annealing and an integrated GA (which includes elitism, intelligent mutation, etc.) are better at detecting edges than a local search or a simple GA for both noisy and noise-free images.

This idea of using evolutionary algorithms to find an optimal set of parameters has also been used for image registration, where points in one image are mapped to corresponding points in another image of the same scene taken under different conditions. For example, Mandava, Fitzpatrick, and Pickens (1989) use GAs to find the parameters of a non-linear transformation that warps the four corners of one sub-image and maps them to another sub-image. To reduce the time, the quality of the transformation is evaluated using only a select sample of pixels in the sub-image.

In addition to genetic algorithms, several authors have used genetic programming to address image-processing problems. In particular, GP is often used for constructing image-processing operators for specific tasks. The idea is to start with a set of basic primitive functions such as a median filter applied to an image or the square of an image, and use GP to create a new operation. The fitness of the parse tree is usually evaluated by comparison with training examples, where the task to be achieved has been performed manually. Ebner and Zell (1999) describe how this approach can be used to measure optical flow, which requires the establishment of corresponding points between one image and the next. Brumby et al. (1999) use a similar approach for finding open water, such as rivers and lakes, amidst vegetation in remote sensing images. Their approach implements several checks to reduce unnecessary computation, and also gives credit for finding the anti-feature, that is, everything but the open water. Poli (1996) illustrates how GP can be used to find effective filters for medical images. He considers several ways of specifying the fitness function to account for the fact that any algorithm that uses filters for tasks such as image segmentation will give rise to false positives and false negatives. Depending on the application, the fitness function could assign weights to each, thus emphasizing appropriately the costs associated with either the false positives or the false negatives.

EVOLUTIONARY ALGORITHMS IN FEATURE SELECTION

Once the relevant features representing the data items have been extracted, it is often helpful to reduce this set of features. There are several reasons for this. In many situations, it is not possible to know a priori which features extracted from the data will be relevant to the problem at hand. Including features that are irrelevant not only increases the time complexity of many algorithms, but also increases the time needed to extract the features. Further, as the number of examples needed for learning a concept is proportional to the dimension of the feature space, fewer training examples will be required if the number of features is reduced. In addition, some features may have costs or risks associated with them, and these should be weighted accordingly during the process of data mining. This leads to the problem of feature subset selection which is the task of identifying and selecting a useful subset of features to be used to represent patterns from a larger set of often mutually redundant, possibly irrelevant, features with different associated measurement costs and risks (Yang and Honavar, 1997). Note that we use the term feature to indicate the attributes that represent an object or a data instance—these may be obtained directly from the original data, or derived by processing the original data.

The simplest way to remove irrelevant features is to apply domain knowledge. For example, if we are interested in clustering text documents, it is obvious that articles, such as "a," "an" and "the" are irrelevant variables (Frakes and Baeza-Yates, 1992). However, this approach is feasible only when a domain scientist can easily identify irrelevant attributes, which is rarely the case. More complex techniques such as principal component analysis can also be used to obtain linear combinations of attributes by projecting them along the directions of the greatest variance. We next discuss the ways in which evolutionary algorithms can be used to address the problem of feature selection.

The evolutionary approach most often used for feature selection is to combine the selection with the learning algorithm, in what is referred to as the wrapper approach. In this approach, the fitness of the feature subsets obtained during the evolutionary computation is evaluated using the learning algorithm itself. While this is more computationally intensive than selecting the features independent of the learning algorithm, it preserves any inductive and representational biases of the learning algorithm. Early work by Siedlecki and Sklansky (1989) with genetic algorithms identified an individual in the population as a series of zeros and ones, where a one indicated that a feature was included in the classification, and a zero indicated that it was not. The k-nearest-neighbor algorithm was chosen to evaluate how good each individual was based on its classification accuracy and the number of the features (i.e., ones) used. Others have applied the same basic binary encoding to select features in classification problems using neural networks (Brill, Brown and Martin, 1990; Brotherton and Simpson, 1995)

Punch et al. (1993) extended the simple binary feature selection idea by representing an individual by a series of weights between zero and ten, thus weighting some features as more important than others. They found that their extension appeared to work better than the zero/one approach of Siedlecki and Sklansky (1989) on noisy real-world datasets. Vafaie and DeJong (1998) also investigated a similar approach to feature selection using decision trees for classification. However, in their work, instead of just weighting each feature, they allowed the combination of existing features to form new features through simple operations such as add, subtract, multiply, and divide. This adaptive feature-space transformation led to a significant reduction in the number of features and improved the classification accuracy. Other related work in this area is that of Yang and Honavar (1997) who used neural networks as the classifier and a simple zero/one strategy for weighting each feature.

A very different use of genetic algorithms in feature selection is in the generation of ensembles of classifiers. Recent work by several authors (see, for example, Dietterich, 2000) has shown that it is possible to improve classification accuracy by combining the prediction of multiple classifiers. These ensembles of classifiers differ in the ways in which the classifiers are generated and their results are combined. Early work of Ho (1998), which used a random selection of features to create an ensemble, was extended by Guerra-Salcedo and Whitley (1999). They replaced the random selection with a more intelligent approach using genetic algorithms, and showed empirically that their idea was more accurate.

EVOLUTIONARY ALGORITHMS IN CLASSIFICATION

In this section, we describe how evolutionary algorithms can be used in conjunction with classification algorithms such as rule-based systems, neural networks, and decision trees.

Rule-Based Systems

Representing concepts as sets of rules has long been popular in machine learning, because, among other properties, rules are easy to represent and humans can interpret them easily. In EAs there are two main ways to represent rule sets. In the "Michigan" approach (Holland, 1975; Booker, Goldberg and Holland 1989), each individual in the population represents one fixed-length rule, and the entire population represents the target concept. In contrast, in the "Pittsburgh" approach (Smith, 1980, 1983; DeJong, Spears and Gordon, 1993), each variable-sized individual represents an entire set of rules. The two representations have their merits and drawbacks and have been used successfully in classifier systems, which are rule-based systems that combine reinforcement learning and evolutionary algorithms.

The basic loop in a classifier system is that the system is presented with inputs from the environment, the inputs are transformed into messages that are added into a message list, and the strongest rules that match any message in the list are fired (possibly adding more messages to the list or acting on the environment). Rules are assigned a fitness value based on a reward returned by the environment. A genetic algorithm is used as the discovery component of the system, creating new rules based on the current best.

This is not the place to describe classic classifier systems or their relatives in detail. The interested reader should consult the book by Goldberg (1989) for a good introduction to classic CS, or the papers by Wilson (1995; 2000a) that describe some extensions. Wilson and Goldberg (1989) present an early critical review of classifier systems, and Wilson (2000b) presents a summary and outlook of research on XCS.

Classifier systems are commonly used as control systems in changing or uncertain environments, where there may not be sufficient or clear expert knowledge to produce a more conventional control (e.g., Goldberg, 1983). Closer to our interests in data mining, classifier systems have been used to learn Boolean functions (Wilson, 1995), which are of significance because they illustrate the ability of the system to learn complex non-linear concepts. Other applications include the classification of letters (Frey, 1991), and breast cancer diagnosis (Wilson, 2000a).

In classifier systems, the left side of rules is a conjunctive expression. This limits the descriptive power of the rules compared to, for example, first-order logic statements. First-order logic is important because it permits expression of relationships between entities in databases. As Augier et al. (1995) noted, most of the machine learning algorithms that use first-order logic discover new rules using deterministic or heuristic approaches that can get trapped in local optima. To address this problem one can try to use EAs. A critical problem is to represent the rules, so that the evolutionary operators can act on them effectively and produce rules that make sense. Giordana and Neri (1995) proposed to use a user-defined template to specify the predicates. The EA finds the specific values that will be used in the rules. Their scheme has the advantage that the EA does not require modifications, because chromosomes are of fixed length and all combinations form valid rules. They also proposed two specialized crossover operators that are designed to promote specialization and generalization.

Another advantage of Giordana and Neri's system is also one of its main disadvantages: the dependence on the user to supply a template for the rules. Although this permits the incorporation of domain knowledge into the algorithm, the user must have a rough idea of the desired result. Augier et al. (1995) proposed an algorithm that addresses this issue by manipulating both the predicates and their values. The algorithm begins with a single rule that matches a single example. Specialized evolutionary operators modify the rule and create offspring that are added to the population until a limit is reached. The best rule after the execution of the EA is selected to form part of the final rule set, and the examples covered by the rule are deleted from the training set. The algorithm is repeated until there are no examples left.

Evolutionary Algorithms and Neural Networks

Genetic algorithms and artificial neural networks (ANNs) have been used together in two major ways. First, EAs have been used to train or to aid in the training of ANNs. In particular, EAs have been used to search for the weights of the network, to search for appropriate learning parameters, or to reduce the size of the training set by selecting the most relevant features. The second major type of collaboration has been to use EAs to design the structure of the network. The structure largely determines the efficiency of the network and the problems that it can solve. It is well known that to solve non–linearly separable problems, the network must have at least one layer between the inputs and outputs; but determining the number and the size of the hidden layers is mostly a matter of trial and error. EAs have been used to search for these parameters, as well as for the pattern of connections and for developmental instructions for the network. The interested reader may consult the reviews by Branke (1995), Whitley (1995) or Yao (1999).

Training an ANN is an optimization task with the goal of finding a set of weights that minimizes some error measure. The search space has many dimensions and it is likely to contain multiple local optima. Some traditional network training algorithms, such as backpropagation, use some form of gradient search, and may get trapped in local optima. In contrast, EAs do not use any gradient information, and are likely to avoid getting trapped in a local optimum by sampling simultaneously multiple regions of the space.

A straightforward combination of evolutionary algorithms and neural networks is to use the EAs to search for weights that make the network perform as desired. In this approach, each individual in the EA is a vector with all the weights of the network. Assessing the fitness of each network involves measuring the accuracy of classification or regression on the training set, so for each fitness evaluation, the training set is passed through the network. This can be inefficient if the training set is large, but the fitness may be estimated using a sample of the training set. Although the fitness would change over different samples, EAs are known to search well using such noisy evaluations.

There are three main variants of the training method:

- Start from a random population and use the weights found by the EA in the network without any further refinement (Caudell and Dolan,1989; Montana and Davis, 1989; Whitley and Hanson, 1989). This method may be particularly useful when the activation function of the neurons is non-differentiable.

- Use backpropagation or other methods to refine the weights found by the EA (Kitano, 1990; Skinner and Broughton, 1995). The motivation for this approach is that EAs quickly identify promising regions of the search space, but they do not fine-tune parameters very fast. So, EAs are used to find a promising set of initial weights from which a gradient-based method can quickly reach an optimum. This involves additional passes through the training data (for each epoch of backpropagation, for example), extending the processing time per individual, but sometimes the overall training time can be reduced because fewer individuals may need to be processed.

- Use the EA to refine results found by an NN learning algorithm. Although EAs do not refine solutions very fast, there have been some attempts to seed the initial population of the EA with solutions found with backpropagation (Kadaba and Nygard, 1990).

These approaches suffer from several problems. First, the length of the individuals grows rapidly with the size of the network. Since adjacent layers in a network are usually fully connected, the total number of weights that need to be represented is $O(n^2)$ (where n is the number of neurons). Longer individuals usually require larger populations, which in turn result in higher computational costs. For small networks, EAs can be used to search for good weights efficiently, but this method may not scale up to larger networks.

Another drawback is the so-called permutations problem (Radcliffe, 1990). The problem is that if the order of the hidden nodes is permuted, the representation of the weights would be different, so functionally equivalent networks can be represented in various ways. Some orderings may not be very suitable for EAs that use recombination because it might disrupt some favorable combinations of weights. To ameliorate this problem, Thierens et al. (1991) suggest that incoming and outgoing weights of a hidden node should be encoded next to each other. Hancock (1992) has done some analysis that suggests that the permutation problem is not as hard as it is often presented. Later, Thierens (1995) presented an encoding that completely avoids the permutations problem.

There are two basic approaches to using EAs to design the topology of an ANN: use a direct encoding to specify each connection of the network or evolve an indirect specification of the connectivity. The resulting network may be trained with a traditional learning algorithm (e.g., backpropagation), or the EA may be used to search the configuration and the weights simultaneously.

The key idea behind direct encodings is that a neural network may be regarded as a directed graph where each node represents a neuron and each edge is a connection. A common method of representing directed graphs is with a binary connectivity matrix: the (i, j)-th element of the matrix is one if there is an edge between nodes i and j, and zero otherwise. The connectivity matrix can be represented in the EA simply by concatenating its rows or columns. Several researchers have used this approach successfully (e.g., Miller, Todd, and Hegde 1989; and Belew, McInerney, and Schraudolph, 1990). Using this method, Whitley, Starkweather, and Bogart (1990) showed that the EA could find topologies that learn faster than the typical fully connected feedforward network. The EA can be explicitly biased to favor smaller networks, which can be trained faster. However, since each connection is explicitly coded, the length of the individuals is $O(n^2)$, and the algorithm may not scale up to large problems.

Although direct encoding is straightforward to implement, it is not a good analogy of the way things work in nature. The genome of an animal does not specify every connection in its nervous system. Instead, the genome contains instructions that—in conjunction with environmental factors—determine the final structure of the network. Many interesting combinations of EAs with NNs imitate nature's indirect specification of nervous systems, and use a developmental approach to construct the networks.

A simple method to avoid specifying all the connections is to commit to a particular topology (feedforward, recurrent, etc.) and a particular learning algorithm, and then use the EA to set the parameters that complete the network specification. For example, with a fully connected feedforward topology, the EA may be used to search for the number of layers and the number of neurons per layer. Another example would be to code the parameters of a particular learning algorithm such as the momentum and learning rate for backpropagation (Belew, McInerney, and Schraudolph, 1990; Marshall and Harrison, 1991). By specifying only the parameters for a given topology, the coding is very compact and well suited for a evolutionary algorithm, but this method is constrained by the initial choice of topology and learning algorithm.

A more sophisticated approach to indirect representations is to use a grammar to encode rules that govern the development of a network. Kitano (1990) introduced the earliest grammar-based approach. He used a connectivity matrix to represent the network, but instead of coding the matrix directly in the chromosome, he used a graph rewriting grammar to generate the matrix. The chromosomes contain rules that rewrite scalar matrix elements into 2 x 2 matrices. To evaluate the fitness, the rules are decoded from the chromosomes, and the connectivity matrix is created applying all the rules that match non-terminal symbols. Then, the connectivity matrix is interpreted to build a network, which is trained by backpropagation, and the fitness is measured. Perhaps the major drawback in this approach is that the size of the network must be 2^i (where i is any non-negative integer that represents the number of rewriting steps), because after each rewriting step the size of the matrix doubles in each dimension.

Another example of a grammar-based developmental system is the work of Boers and Kuiper (1992). Each individual contains the rules for one Lindenmayer system (L-system), which are parallel string rewriting grammars (every applicable rule is used at each derivation step). L-systems have been used to model the development of living organisms. To evaluate the fitness, the system uses the rules of the L-system to generate a string that represents the structure of a neural network. Then, the network is trained using backpropagation and the fitness is determined by combining the accuracy of the classifications on separate training and testing sets.

Gruau (1992) invented a "cellular encoding" method to evolve the topology and the weights of the network simultaneously. His objective was to produce a coding for modular networks that would scale up to large and interesting problems naturally. Gruau (1994) proved that cellular encoding has many desirable properties for a neural network representation. For example, all possible networks are representable, and only valid networks result after applying the genetic operators. Each cell in the network has a copy of a grammar tree (a grammar encoded as a tree), a read head, and some internal registers. The development of the network starts with a single cell. The grammar tree contains instructions that make the cell divide, increment or decrement its bias or some weights, cut a connection, and stop reading the tree. At each step, every cell executes the instruction pointed to by its head, and the development finishes when all the cells reach stop instructions. Gruau solved large parity and symmetry problems, and his approach compares favorably to direct encoding (Gruau, Whitley and Pyeatt, 1996).

Nolfi, Elman, and Parisi (1994) developed another grammar-based encoding. Their objective was to simulate cell growth, migration and differentiation, three processes involved in the development of natural neural networks. Their networks may contain up to 16 types of cells, and for each type there is a rule that governs how the cell reproduces. The rules are encoded in the chromosome, and they specify the types of the daughter cells and their relative spatial locations. After a fixed number of divisions, the cells grow artificial axons to reach other cells. Cells live in a two-dimensional space that is partitioned into three regions. The developmental process begins with a cell placed near the center. The neurons that end up in the lower and upper regions serve as the inputs and outputs, respectively. The cells in the middle region function as hidden units.

The grammar-based methods share several properties. First, the developmental process begins with a single cell, just as in nature. Second, all the methods are very sensitive to changes in parts of the genome that govern early development (e.g., the initial cell's type or the first rule to be applied).

Decision Trees and Evolutionary Algorithms

Decision trees are a popular classification method because they are easy to build and experts can interpret them easily. The internal nodes represent tests on the features that describe the data, and the leaf nodes represent the class labels. A path from the root node to one of the leaves represents a conjunction of tests. Since genetic programming traditionally uses trees to represent solutions, it seems well suited for the task of finding decision trees. Koza (1992) offered an early example of this use of GP in classification, where the fitness of each decision tree is based on its accuracy on a training set. Nicolaev and Slavov (1997) extended the fitness measure to include terms related to the tree size, and determined that GP could find small trees that were comparable in accuracy to those found by C4.5 in several test cases. Folino, Spizzuti, and Spezzano (2000) demonstrate that a fine-grained GP system can find trees that are smaller and comparatively accurate to those found with C4.5 on several test problems. Their system was designed with the intention of implementing it on a parallel computer to shorten the computation time.

The trees considered above used tests on a single attribute of the data. These tests are equivalent to hyperplanes that are parallel to one of the axes in the attribute space, and therefore the resulting trees are called axis-parallel. Axis-parallel trees are easy to interpret, but may be complex and inaccurate if the data is partitioned best by hyperplanes that are not axis-parallel. Oblique decision trees use linear combinations of attributes in the tests in each of the internal nodes. Cantú-Paz and Kamath (2000) used evolution strategies and genetic algorithms to find the coefficients for the tests. They used the traditional top-down construction method, where the algorithm determines the test of each node, splits the data according to the test, and applies itself recursively to each of the resulting subsets. Cantú-Paz and Kamath compared their methods against axis-parallel and other oblique tree algorithms. They found that when the data was best split by oblique hyperplanes, the evolutionary methods were in general faster and more accurate than the existing oblique algorithms, but when the target concepts were well represented by axis-parallel hyperplanes, the existing methods were superior.

Other approaches to build oblique decision trees consider the entire tree at a time, just as Koza's original method. Bot and Langdon (2000) use traditional GP complemented with a multi-objective selection method that attempts to minimize the tree size and the classification errors simultaneously. When compared to other algorithms, the classification accuracy results were mixed, but GP was consistently slower.

Venturini et al. (1997) presented an interactive evolutionary algorithm that permits the user to evaluate combinations of the attributes that describe the data. The objective of the system is to find new variables that can describe the data concisely and that can be used in a traditional classification algorithm afterwards. Each individual in the algorithm uses two GP trees to represent new variables that are a transformation of the original attributes. The two new variables can be regarded as new axes on which the training set is projected and the result is displayed as a scatter plot. All the individuals are processed in this way and presented to the user who decides which projections show some interesting structures. The selected individuals undergo crossover and mutation, and the cycle is repeated. Venturini et al. (1997) present mixed results on several data sets from the UCI repository, but suggest several interesting extensions of their system, such as allowing the user to create rules directly by specifying thresholds on the screen.

EVOLUTIONARY ALGORITHMS IN CLUSTERING

We can distinguish two major methods to apply evolutionary algorithms to clustering problems. In the first method, each position in the chromosome represents an item in the training set. The task of the EA is to find the right cluster for each data item. If the number of clusters, k, is known a priori, each position in the chromosomes can take a value in [1,k]. This method is somewhat analogous to the direct encoding of neural nets. It is easy to implement, as there is no need for special evolutionary operators, but it suffers from a severe scalability problem: the length of the individuals is exactly the size of the training set, and for large problems this option may not be practical. Examples of this approach include the work by Murthy and Chowdhury (1996).

Park and Song (1998) created a variation of the direct representation. They recognized that the clustering problem could be cast as a graph-partitioning problem. The objective is to consider the items in the data set as nodes in a graph and the objective is to use a GA to find connected sub-graphs that represent clusters. Each data item has a corresponding position in the chromosomes, but the alleles are not the cluster labels, but the indices of other data items. So if position i contains the value j, there is a link in the graph between the nodes that represent items i and j. The values for each position are limited to the nearest neighbors of each data item, and the number of neighbors is an input parameter to the algorithm. Park and Song tested their algorithm on the problem of generating a thesaurus of word meanings and compared their results to other clustering algorithms. An advantage of their algorithm is that the number of clusters does not have to be specified in advance. The problem of scalability is still present as the individual's length is the size of the data set, and since this algorithm computes the nearest neighbors of all the data items, the algorithm may not be very efficient on data sets with many dimensions.

Another use of EAs in clustering is to identify the cluster centroids. Hall, Ozyurt and Bezdek (1999) described an evolutionary approach where the individuals represent the coordinates of the centers of the k desired clusters. They used a standard genetic algorithm, trying both floating point and binary representations, but did not observe a clear advantage to either approach. Their study considered both fuzzy and hard clustering, and their fitness functions included terms to penalize degenerate solutions (with fewer than k clusters). Hall et al. compared their algorithm to conventional clustering algorithms (FCM/HCM) and observed that their evolutionary approach usually found solutions as good as the other methods, and avoided degenerate solutions when the other methods did not. They experimented with adaptive methods to set the parameters of the algorithm and found the results encouraging. This is important because it facilitates the use of the evolutionary algorithm in practice. However, Hall et al. also reported that the execution time of the evolutionary method can take up to two orders of magnitude more than FCM/HCM. Despite the efficiency problem, Hall et al. noted that the evolutionary approach could be useful to evaluate other clustering fitness functions for which no optimization method has been devised. A similar approach is to use the EA to search for the optimal initial seed values for the cluster centroids and then run a clustering algorithm (Babu and Murty, 1993).

As in other problems, in clustering we can use domain knowledge in several ways to try to improve the performance of the algorithm. For example, we could design specialized evolutionary operators or we can hybridize the evolutionary algorithm with a conventional clustering algorithm. Fränti et al. (1997) tried both approaches. Their clustering algorithm represented the coordinates of the centroids. They used five different crossover methods (three of their own invention) and after crossover each new individual underwent two iterations of the k-means clustering algorithm. Later they extended the algorithm to include self-adaptation of parameters and automatic choice of operators (Kivijärvi, 2000). Fränti et al. (1997) observed that adding the k-means iterations was critical for obtaining good results, and although there can be a considerable increase of the computation time if many iterations are used, their experiments suggest that only a few iterations are needed. Along these lines, Krishna and Murty (1999) used a single k-means iteration. The hybridization raises the question of how to allocate the computing time: should we use many generations of the EA and a few iterations of the local methods, or run the EAs for a few generations and use the local methods to improve the solutions considerably?

As we saw in the neural networks section, another way to use domain knowledge in GAs is to initialize the population with good known solutions. One way to do this in clustering problems would be to use the output of independent runs of the k-means algorithm to create at least part of the initial population (Murthy and Chowdhury, 1996).

In principle, the centroid-based representation has the advantage that the individuals are shorter, because they only need to represent the coordinates of the k centroids. This means that the length of the individuals is proportional to the dimensionality of the problem and not to the size of the training set as in the partitioning-based encoding. In addition, using the GA to assign the right cluster labels to each data item allows more flexibility in the shape of the clusters. For example, nonadjacent regions of the data space can belong to the same cluster.

PERFORMANCE OF EVOLUTIONARY ALGORITHMS

Evolutionary algorithms are proving themselves in solving real problems in data mining, especially in cases where the data is noisy, or requires the solution of a multi-objective optimization problem. However, they are not without their drawbacks.

A key concern expressed by several authors is that evolutionary algorithms can be very time consuming. For example, Poli (1996) comments that the tremendous computational demands of fitness evaluations in the use of genetic programming for image processing has prevented researchers from doing an extensive study of the behavior of these algorithms in solving real problems. A similar sentiment is expressed by Ebner and Zell (1999) who observe that the evolution of an image processing operator typically takes several days to complete on a single PC, making it difficult to use their algorithm in an adaptive vision system that adapts to changing environmental conditions.

Several approaches have been proposed to address this need for enormous computational resources. For example, Mandava, Fitzpatrick, and Pickens (1989) and Poli (1996) suggest that, in image processing, instead of using all pixels in an image to evaluate the fitness of an operator, only a small sample of pixels could be used in order to reduce the time required. Other authors, such as Bhanu, Lee, and Ming (1995) keep a global population of fit individuals, which can be used to seed the genetic algorithm for each image. This not only makes the system adaptive, but also reduces the computation time. Bhandarkar, Zhang, and Potter (1994) propose exploiting the inherent parallelism in genetic algorithms to reduce the time for edge detection operators in image analysis.

Researchers using evolutionary algorithms for feature selection also echo this need for extensive computer resources. Since the approach requires the classification step to be performed for each fitness evaluation, it can be time consuming. A common solution in this case is the use of parallel processing (Punch et al., 1993).

Of course, sampling and parallel processing can also aid in classification and clustering problems. In addition, in previous sections we also hinted that using representations that are more appropriate for the problems at hand or designing custom operators could result in a more scalable algorithm. For example, directly encoding each weight in a neural network or each possible assignment of a data item to a cluster will not scale up to large and interesting problems.

RESOURCES FOR EVOLUTIONARY ALGORITHMS IN DATA MINING

With evolutionary algorithms rapidly gaining acceptance in data mining, there are a variety of resources that the interested researcher can refer to for the most recent advances in the field. There are several conferences held on the various topics covered in this chapter, including the EvoIASP conferences organized by the Working Group on Evolutionary Algorithms in Image Analysis and Signal Processing (2001), Knowledge Discovery and Data Mining (KDD), International Conference on Machine Learning (ICML), and the Genetic and Evolutionary Computation Conference (GECCO). The journals *Evolutionary Computation, Genetic Programming and Evolvable Machines, IEEE Transactions on Systems, Man, and Cybernetics*, and the *IEEE Transactions on Evolutionary Computation* are also excellent resources. There are several resources available on the Internet as well. A comprehensive bibliography on genetic algorithms by Alander (2000) includes their use in classifier systems, image processing, signal processing, neural networks, etc.

SUMMARY

In this survey chapter, we have shown that evolutionary algorithms can complement many existing data mining algorithms. They can extract and select features, train neural networks, find classification rules, and build decision trees. Evolutionary algorithms are particularly useful when the problems involve the optimization of functions that are not smooth and differentiable, or functions where the objective value changes over time, which can happen in data mining as more data becomes available or if sampling is used to reduce the computation time.

While evolutionary algorithms enable us to solve some difficult problems, they come at a price, namely a need for high computational resources. However, with processors becoming faster and the increasing acceptance of parallel systems, we hope that this problem will be minimized in the future.

ACKNOWLEDGMENTS

We would like to thank the anonymous reviewers and the editors for their constructive comments on an earlier draft of this chapter.

UCRL-JC-141872. This work was performed under the auspices of the U.S. Department of Energy by the University of California Lawrence Livermore National Laboratory under contract No. W-7405-Eng-48.

REFERENCES

Alander, J. (2000). *Indexed bibliography of genetic algorithms and artificial intelligence.* Technical Report No. 94-1-AI. University of Vaasa, Department of Information Technology and Production Economics. ftp://ftp.vaasa.fi/cs/report94-1/gaAIbib.ps.Z.

Augier, S., Venturini, G., Kodratoff, Y. (1995). Learning first order rules with a genetic algorithm. In *Proceedings of the First International Conference on Knowledge Discovery in Databases.* (pp. 21-26). Menlo Park, CA: AAAI Press.

Babu, G. P., & Murty, M. N. (1993). Clustering with evolution strategies. *Pattern Recognition,* 27 (2), 321-329.

Belew, R., McInerney, J., & Schraudolph, N. (1990). Evolving networks: Using the genetic algorithm with connectionist learning (Tech. Rep. No. CS90-174). San Diego: University of California, Computer Science and Engineering Department.

Bhandarkar, S., Zhang, Y., & Potter, W. (1994). An edge detection technique using genetic algorithm based optimization. *Pattern Recognition* 27, 1159-1180.

Bhanu, B. & Lee, S. (1994). *Genetic learning for adaptive image segmentation.* Boston, MA: Kluwer Academic Publishers.

Bhanu, B., Lee, S. & Ming, J. (1995). Adaptive image segmentation using a genetic algorithm. *IEEE Transactions on Systems, Man, and Cybernetics,* 25, 1543-1567.

Boers, J. W., & Kuiper, H. (1992). Biological metaphors and the design of modular artificial neural networks. Unpublished Master's Thesis, Leiden University, The Netherlands.

Booker, L. B., Goldberg, D. E., & Holland, J. H. (1989). Classifier systems and genetic algorithms. *Artificial Intelligence,* 40 (1/3), 235-282.

Bot, M.C.J. & Langdon, W.B. Application of genetic programming to induction of linear classification trees. In *European Conference on Genetic Programming,* (pp. 247-258). Berlin: Springer-Verlag.

Branke, J. (1995). Evolutionary algorithms for neural network design and training (Technical Report). Karlsruhe, Germany: Institute AIFB, University of Karlsruhe.

Brill, F.Z., Brown, D.E., & Martin, W.N. (1990) *Genetic algorithms for feature selection for counterpropagation networks.* (Tech. Rep. No. IPC-TR-90-004). Charlottesville, VA: University of Virginia, Institute of Parallel Computation.

Brotherton, T.W., & Simpson, P.K. (1995). Dynamic feature set training of neural nets for classification. In McDonnell, J.R., Reynolds, R.G., & Fogel, D.B. (Eds.). *Evolutionary Programming IV* (pp. 83-94). Cambridge, MA: MIT Press.

Brumby, S., Theiler, J., Perkins, S., Harvey, N., Szymanski, J., Bloch, J. and Mitchell, M., (1999). Investigation of image feature extraction by a genetic algorithm. Bellingham, WA: *Procedings of the International Society for Optical Engineering,* vol. 3812, 24-31

Burl, M., Asker, L., Smyth, P., Fayyad, U., Perona, P., Crumpler, L, & Aubele, J. (1998). Learning to recognize volcanoes on Venus. *Machine Learning,* 30, 165-195.

Cagnoni S., Dobrzeniecki, A., Poli, R., & Yanch, J. (1997). Segmentation of 3D medical images through genetically-optimized contour-tracking algorithms. Univ. of Birmingham School of Computer Science Tech. Report CSRP-97-28.

Cantú-Paz, E., & Kamath, C. (2000). Using evolutionary algorithms to induce oblique decision trees. In Whitley, D., Goldberg, D. E., Cantú-Paz, E., Spector, L., Parmee, L., & Beyer, H.-G. (Eds.), *Proceedings of the Genetic and Evolutionary Computation Conference 2000* (pp. 1053-1060). San Francisco, CA: Morgan Kaufmann Publishers.

Caudell, T. P., & Dolan, C. P. (1989). Parametric connectivity: Training of constrained networks using genetic algorithms. In Schaffer, J. D. (Ed.), *Proceedings of the Third International Conference on Genetic Algorithms* (pp. 370-374). San Mateo, CA: Morgan Kaufmann.

De Jong, K. A., Spears, W. M., & Gordon, D. F. (1993). Using genetic algorithms for concept learning. *Machine Learning*, 13, 161-188.

Dietterich, T., (2000). An experimental comparison of three methods for constructing ensembles of decision trees: bagging, boosting, and randomization. *Machine Learning*, 40 (2), 139-158.

Ebner, M. & Zell, A. (1999). Evolving a task specific image operator. In Poli, R. et al. (ed.), *Evolutionary Image Analysis, Signal Processing and Telecommunications*, First European Workshop (pp.74-89). Berlin: Springer-Verlag.

Fayyad, U., Piatetsky-Shapiro, G., Smyth, P. & Uthurusamy, R. (1996). *Advances in knowledge discovery and data mining*. Menlo Park, CA: AAAI Press/ The MIT Press.

Folino, G., Pizzuti, C. & Spezzano, G. (2000). Genetic programming and simulated annealing: A hybrid method to evolve decision trees. In Poli, R., Banzhaf, W., Langdon, W. B., Miller, J., Nordin, P., & Fogarty, T. C. (Eds.), *Genetic Programming: Third European Conference* (pp. 294-303). Berlin: Springer-Verlag.

Frakes, W.B. & Baeza-Yates, R. (1992). *Information Retrieval: Data Structures and Algorithms*. Englewood Cliffs, NJ: Prentice Hall.

Fränti, P., Kivijärvi, J., Kaukoranta, T., & Nevalainen, O. (1997). Genetic algorithms for large-scale clustering problems. *The Computer Journal*, 40 (9), 547-554.

Frey, P. W., & Slate, D. J. (1991). Letter recognition using Holland-style adaptive classifiers. *Machine Learning*, 6 , 161-182.

Giordana, A., & Neri, F. (1995). Search-intensive concept induction. *Evolutionary Computation*, 3 (4), 375-416.

Goldberg, D. E. (1983). Computer-aided gas pipeline operation using genetic algorithms and rule learning. *Dissertation Abstracts International*, 44 (10), 3174B. Doctoral dissertation, University of Michigan.

Goldberg, D. E. (1989). *Genetic algorithms in search, optimization, and machine learning*. Reading, MA: Addison-Wesley.

Gruau, F. (1992). Cellular encoding of genetic neural networks (Tech. Rep. No. 92-21). Lyon Cedex, France: Ecole Normale Superieure de Lyon.

Gruau, F. (1994). Neural network synthesis using cellular encoding and the genetic algorithm. Unpublished doctoral dissertation, L'Universite Claude Bernard-Lyon I.

Gruau, F., Whitley, D., & Pyeatt, L. (1996). A comparison between cellular encoding and direct encoding for genetic neural networks. *In Proceedings of the First Annual Conference on Genetic Programming* (pp. 81-89). Cambridge, MA: MIT Press.

Guerra-Salcedo, C. & Whitley, D. (1999). Genetic approach to feature selection for ensemble creation. *Proceedings of the Genetic and Evolutionary Computation Conference*, 236-243.

Hall, L., Ozyurt, B., & Bezdek, J. (1999). Clustering with a genetically optimized approach. *IEEE Transactions on Evolutionary Computation*, 3(2), 103-112.

Hancock, P. J. B. (1992). Recombination operators for the design of neural nets by genetic algorithm. In Männer, R., & Manderick, B. (Eds.), *Parallel Problem Solving from Nature, 2* (pp. 441-450). Amsterdam: Elsevier Science.

Ho, T. (1998). The random subspace method for constructing decision forests. *IEEE Transactions on Pattern Analysis and Machine Intelligence*, 20(8), 832-844.

Holland, J. H. (1975). *Adaptation in natural and artificial systems*. Ann Arbor, MI: University of Michigan Press.

Jackson, J. E. (1991). *A user's guide to principal components*. New York, NY: John Wiley & Sons.

Kadaba, N., & Nygard, K. E. (1990). Improving the performance of genetic algorithms in automated discovery of parameters. *Machine Learning: Proceedings of the Seventh International Conference*, 140-148.

Kamath, C. (2001). On mining scientific data sets. To appear in *Data Mining in Scientific and Engineering Applications*, Norwell, MA: Kluwer Academic Publishers.

Kitano, H. (1990). Designing neural networks using genetic algorithms with graph generation system. *Complex Systems*, 4 (4), 461-476.

Kivijärvi, J., Fränti, P., & Nevalainen, O. (2000). Efficient clustering with a self-adaptive genetic algorithm. In Whitley, D., Goldberg, D. E., Cantú-Paz, E., Spector, L., Parmee, L., & Beyer, H.-G. (Eds.), *Proceedings of the Genetic and Evolutionary Computation Conference 2000* (pp. 377). San Francisco, CA: Morgan Kaufmann Publishers.

Koza, J. R. (1992). *Genetic programming: on the programming of computers by means of natural selection*. Cambridge, MA: The MIT Press.

Krishna, K., & Murty, M. N. (1999). Genetic k-means algorithm. *IEEE Transactions on Systems, Man, and Cybernetics-Part B*, 29 (3), 433-439.

Langley, P. & Simon, H. A. (1995). Applications of machine learning and rule induction. *Communications of the ACM*, 38 (11), 55-64.

Mandava, V., Fitzpatrick, J. & Pickens, D. (1989). Adaptive search space scaling in digital image registration. *IEEE Transactions on Medical Imaging*, 8, 251-262.

Marshall, S.J., & Harrison, R.F. (1991) Optimization and training of feedforward neural networks by genetic algorithms. In *Proceedings of the Second International Conference on Artificial Neural Networks and Genetic Algorithms* (pp. 39-43). Berlin: Springer-Verlag.

Miller, G. F., Todd, P. M., & Hegde, S. U. (1989). Designing neural networks using genetic algorithms. In Schaffer, J. D. (Ed.), *Proceedings of the Third International Conference on Genetic Algorithms* (pp. 379-384). San Mateo, CA: Morgan Kaufmann.

Montana, D. J., & Davis, L. (1989). Training feedforward neural networks using genetic algorithms. In *Proceedings 11th International Joint Conference on Artificial Intelligence* (pp. 762—767). San Mateo, CA: Morgan Kaufmann.

Murthy, C. A., & Chowdhury, N. (1996). In search of optimal clusters using genetic algorithms. *Pattern Recognition Letters*, 17, 825-832.

Nikolaev, N. I., & Slavov, V. (1998). Inductive genetic programming with decision trees. *Intelligent Data Analysis*, 2 (1).

Nolfi, S., Elman, J. L., & Parisi, D. (1994). Learning and evolution in neural networks (Tech. Rep. No. 94-08). Rome, Italy: Institute of Psychology, National Research Council.

Park, Y., & Song, M. (1998). A genetic algorithm for clustering problems. In Koza, J. R., Banzhaf, W., Chellapilla, K., Deb, K., Dorigo, M., Fogel, D. B., Garzon, M. H., Goldberg, D. E., Iba, H., & Riolo, R. L. (Eds.). *Genetic Programming 98* (pp. 568-575). San Francisco: Morgan Kaufmann Publishers.

Poli, R., (1996). Genetic programming for feature detection and image segmentation. In Fogarty, T. (ed.), *Evolutionary Computing*, in Lecture Notes in Computer Science, number 1143, pp 110—125. Springer-Verlag.

Punch, W., Goodman, E., Pei, M., Lai, C., Hovland, P. & Enbody, R. (1993). Further research on feature selection and classification using genetic algorithms, In *Proceedings of the Fifth International Conference on Genetic Algorithms*, 557-564.

Radcliffe, N. J. (1990). Genetic neural networks on MIMD computers. Unpublished doctoral dissertation, University of Edinburgh, Scotland.

Sherrah, J., Bogner, R. & Bouzerdoum, B. (1996). Automatic selection of features for classification using genetic programming. In *Proceedings of the 1996 Australian New Zealand Conference on Intelligent Information Systems*, Adelaide, Australia, November 1996, 284 - 287.

Siedlecki, W. & Sklansky, J. (1989). A note on genetic algorithms for large-scale feature selection. *Pattern Recognition Letters* (10), pp 335-347.

Skinner, A., & Broughton, J.Q. (1995). Neural networks in computational material science: training algorithms. *Modeling and Simulation in Material Science and Engineering*, 3, 371-390.

Smith, S. F. (1980). A learning system based on genetic adaptive algorithms. *Dissertation Abstracts International,* 41 , 4582B. (University Microfilms No. 81-12638).

Smith, S. F. (1983). Flexible learning of problem solving heuristics through adaptive search. *In Proceedings of the 8th International Joint Conference on Artificial Intelligence* (pp. 422-425).

Stanhope, S. & Daida, J. (1998). Genetic programming for automatic target classification and recognition in synthetic aperture radar imagery. In *Evolutionary Programming VII: Proceedings of the Seventh Annual Conference on Evolutionary Programming*, V.W. Porto, N. Saravan, D. Waagen, and A.E. Eiben (Eds.). Berlin: Springer-Verlag, pp. 735-744.

Tackett, W. (1993). Genetic Programming for Feature Discovery and Image Discrimination, In *Proceedings of the Fifth International Conference on Genetic Algorithms*, Morgan Kaufmann Publishers, 303 – 309.

Tan, H., Gelfand, S. & Delp, E. (1989). A comparative cost function approach to edge detection. *IEEE Transactions on Sytems, Man, and Cybernetics* 19, 1337-1349.

Thierens, D., Suykens, J., Vanderwalle, J., & Moor, B.D. (1991). Genetic weight optimization of a feedforward neural network controller. In *Proceedings of the Second International Conference on Artificial Neural Networks and Genetic Algorithms* (pp. 658-663). Berlin: Springer-Verlag.

Thierens, D. (1995). Analysis and design of genetic algorithms. Unpublished doctoral dissertation. Leuven, Belgium: Katholieke Universiteit Leuven.

Vafaie, H. and DeJong, K. (1998). Feature space transformation using genetic algorithms. *IEEE Intelligent Systems and their Applications*, 13(2), 57-65.

Venturini, G., Slimane, M., Morin, F., & Asselin de Beauville, J.-P. (1997). On using interactive genetic algorithms for knowledge discovery in databases. In Bäck, T. (Ed.), *Proceedings of the Seventh International Conference on Genetic Algorithms* (pp. 696-703). San Francisco: Morgan Kaufmann.

Weeks, A. (1996). *Fundamentals of electronic image processing*. Bellingham, WA: The International Society for Optical Engineering Press.

Whitley, D. (1995). Genetic algorithms and neural networks. In Winter, G., Periaux, J., Galan, M., & Cuesta, P. (Eds.), *Genetic Algorithms in Engineering and Computer Science* (Chapter 11, pp. 203-221). Chichester: John Wiley and Sons.

Whitley, D., & Hanson, T. (1989). Optimizing neural networks using faster, more accurate genetic search. In Schaffer, J. D. (Ed.), *Proceedings of the Third International Conference on Genetic Algorithms* (pp. 391-397). San Mateo, CA: Morgan Kaufmann.

Whitley, D., Starkweather, T., & Bogart, C. (1990). Genetic algorithms and neural networks: Optimizing connections and connectivity. *Parallel Computing*, 14 , 347-361.

Wilson, S. W., & Goldberg, D. E. (1989). A critical review of classifier systems. In Schaffer, J. D. (Ed.), *Proceedings of the Third International Conference on Genetic Algorithms* (pp. 244-255). San Mateo, CA: Morgan Kaufmann.

Wilson, S. W. (1995). Classifier fitness based on accuracy. *Evolutionary Computation*, 3 (2), 149-175.

Wilson, S. W. (2000a). Mining oblique data with XCS. IlliGAL Technical Report No 2000028, University of Illinois at Urbana-Champaign.

Wilson, S. W. (2000b). State of XCS classifier system research. In Lanzi, P., Stolzmann, W., & Wilson, S. W. (Eds.), *Learning Classifier Systems: From Foundations to Applications*. Berlin: Springer-Verlag.

Yang, J. and Honavar, V. (1997). Feature subset selection using a genetic algorithm, *Proceedings of the Second Annual Conference on Genetic Programming*, pp 380-385.

Yao, X. (1999). Evolving artificial neural networks. *Proceedings of the IEEE*, 87 (9), 1423-1447.

Chapter IV

The Discovery of Interesting Nuggets Using Heuristic Techniques

Beatriz de la Iglesia
Victor J. Rayward-Smith
University of East Anglia, UK

Knowledge Discovery in Databases (KDD) is an iterative and interactive process involving many steps (Debuse, de la Iglesia, Howard & Rayward-Smith, 2000). Data mining (DM) is defined as one of the steps in the KDD process. According to Fayyad, Piatetsky-Shapiro, Smyth and Uthurusamy (1996), there are various data mining tasks including: classification, clustering, regression, summarisation, dependency modeling, and change and deviation detection. However, there is a very important data mining problem identified previously by Riddle, Segal and Etzioni (1994) and very relevant in the context of commercial databases, which is not properly addressed by any of those tasks: *nugget discovery*. This task has also been identified as *partial classification* (Ali, Manganaris & Srikant, 1997). Nugget discovery can be defined as the search for relatively rare, but potentially important, patterns or anomalies relating to some pre-determined class or classes. Patterns of this type are called *nuggets*.

This chapter will present and justify the use of heuristic algorithms, namely Genetic Algorithms (GAs), Simulated Annealing (SA) and Tabu Search (TS), on the data mining task of nugget discovery. First, the concept of nugget discovery will be introduced. Then the concept of the *interest* of a nugget will be discussed. The necessary properties of an interest measure for nugget discovery will be presented. This will include a partial ordering of nuggets based on those properties. Some of the existing measures for nugget discovery will be reviewed in light of the properties established, and it will be shown that they do not display the required properties. A suitable evaluation function for nugget discovery, the *fitness* measure, will then be discussed and justified according to the required properties.

A number of algorithms, including the heuristic algorithms, will be introduced briefly. Experiments using those algorithms on some of the UCI repository databases (Merz & Murphy, 1998) will be reported. Conclusions about the suitability of the different algorithms on datasets with different characteristics can be drawn from these experiments. The three heuristics–Genetic Algorithms, Simulated Annealing and Tabu Search–will also be compared in terms of their implementation, results and performance.

THE DATA MINING TASK OF NUGGET DISCOVERY

In any KDD project, one of the first decisions that has to be made is what is the primary task that the user wants to achieve. The "high level" primary tasks of the KDD process are defined in the literature (Fayyad, Piatetsky-Shapiro & Smyth, 1996) as *prediction* and *description*. Prediction involves using some variables or fields in the database to predict unknown or future values of other variables of interest. Description focuses on finding human-interpretable patterns describing the data. The main distinction between prediction and description is who interprets the discovered knowledge. In prediction the system interprets the knowledge, whereas in description, it is the analyst or the user that interprets it.

Once the high-level goal of the process is established, the particular data mining task to be undertaken has to be chosen. This is known as the "low-level" task. As mentioned in the previous section, the most commonly recognised tasks are: classification, clustering, regression, summarisation, dependency modeling, and change and deviation detection. We will focus on the task of classification.

The type of data used for classification contains a pre-defined class assignment for each case or record in the database. This type of data is often encountered in commercial databases. The high-level goal of the user, when analysing this type of data, is sometimes prediction. This is when the user wants to infer a model that will allow him/her to assign a class to new data. For a predictive goal, a complete classification (that is, a complete model that assigns a class to each case or record in the database) may be necessary and appropriate. This would definitely fall under the heading of a classification task. An example of a classification task may be to build a decision tree (Quinlan, 1986) to differentiate between those customers that represent a good credit risk and those that do not, based on a database of financial information. The database must contain some classification of customers into good and bad credit risks, based on their past performance.

When the high-level goal is descriptive, it is not always necessary to provide a complete classification. This may indeed be detrimental to obtaining interesting and understandable patterns. The objective in many cases is to identify relatively rare, but potentially important, patterns or anomalies relating to some class or classes. We will call this type of pattern a *nugget*, and hence we will call this task *nugget discovery*. For instance, in the previous example, the bank may be particularly interested in understanding what characterises the worst type of loan defaulters, and they may be a minority in the database. In that case, building a complete classifier could seriously obscure the nuggets that we are looking for.

Of course, a decision tree, for example, will contain nuggets but, as Quinlan (1987) explains, algorithms that produce such models often produce very large and complex knowledge structures that are suitable for the goal of prediction, but cannot be easily interpreted by humans. For any sizeable database, a complete classification that is accurate will contain many specific patterns that describe noise, or uninteresting cases. Work is required to extract nuggets that are truly interesting (according to some pre-defined measure) for a particular class. We will have to look through the tree to extract a few good branches representing the knowledge in which we are interested. Furthermore, complete classifications are often assessed in terms of the overall accuracy on classifying new instances (those reserved for testing the model), and the metrics used to build the model are often biased towards overall accuracy. But high accuracy of a complete classification model does not guarantee accuracy in classifying all of the classes. Hence a complete classification may not contain interesting nuggets for all classes, and complete classification algorithms may guide the search towards an overall good classification, and not towards interesting nuggets. Nugget discovery and complete classification are different tasks, with different goals.

It is worth noting here that there is another class of algorithms that may also be used to deliver nuggets: association rule algorithms (Agrawal, Imielinski & Swami, 1993; Agrawal Mannila, Srikant, Toivonen & Verkamo, 1996). They were developed for transaction data (also known as basket data). This type of data contains information on transactions, for example, showing items that have been purchased together. Association rule mining algorithms deliver a set of association rules, often containing all associations between items above certain support and confidence thresholds. The association rules are generally of the form "customers that purchase bread and butter also get milk, with 98 % confidence." This type of rule is not constrained to have a particular value as output, or indeed to refer to any particular attribute. Delivering all association rules in transactional data is a suitable approach, since transactional data tends to contain few associations. Classification datasets, however, tend to contain many associations, so delivering all association rules for a classification dataset results in output of overwhelming size. Also classification datasets often contain many numeric continuous attributes, and association rule induction algorithms are not designed to cope with this type of data. Therefore, although association rules can be used for classification (Bayardo, 1997; Liu, Hsu & Ma, 1998), and even for partial classification or nugget discovery (Ali et al., 1997), work is required to adapt the association algorithms to cope with classification data, and with the problem of partial classification or nugget discovery.

DEFINING A NUGGET

The type of nuggets that will be sought (Rayward-Smith, Debuse & de la Iglesia, 1995) are simple rules of the following format:

$$\alpha \Rightarrow \beta$$

where α, the precondition, or antecedent, of the rule represents a conjunction or disjunction of tests on the attributes or fields of the database, D, and β, the postcondition, or consequent, of the rule, represents the class assignment. In the case of conjunctive rules, the antecedent is a conjunction of the following form:

$$\alpha_1 \wedge \alpha_2 \wedge \ldots \wedge \alpha_m.$$

For a categorical attribute, a conjunct, α_i, is a test that can take the following forms:

- Simple value: $AT_j = v$, where AT_j represents the jth attribute, and $v \in Dom_{ATj}$, $1 \le j \le n$ (n is the number of attributes in the database). A record x meets this test if $x[AT_j] = v$.
- Subset of values: $AT_j \in \{v_1, \ldots, v_k\}$, where $\{v_1, \ldots, v_k\} \in Dom_{ATj}$, $1 \le j \le n$. A record x satisfy this test if $x[AT_j] \in \{v_1, \ldots, v_k\}$.
- Inequality test: $AT_j \ne v$, $1 \le j \le n$. A record x meets this test if $x[AT_j] \ne v$.

For a numeric attribute a conjunct, α_i, is a test that can take the following form:

- Simple value: $AT_j = v$, as for categorical attributes.

- Binary partition: $AT_j \le v$ or $AT_j \ge v$, $v \in Dom_{ATj}$ and $1 \le j \le n$. A record x meets these tests if $x[AT_j] \le v$ or $x[AT_j] \ge v$ respectively.

- Range of values: $v_1 \le AT_j \le v_2$ or $AT_j \in [v_1, v_2]$, $v_1, v_2 \in Dom_{ATj}$ and $1 \le j \le n$. A record x meets this test if $v_1 \le x[AT_j] \le v_2$.

A record, x, meets a conjunction of tests, $\alpha_1 \wedge \alpha_2 \wedge \ldots \wedge \alpha_m$, if x satisfies all the tests $\alpha_1\ \alpha_2, \ldots, \alpha_m$. In the case of disjunctive preconditions, x will have to satisfy some (at least one) tests.

The consequent of the rule is just the specification of the class that the rule is describing, chosen from a set of predefined classes. For the purpose of simplicity, we can assume that the problem to be solved is always a two-class problem. Any other problem with more than two classes can simply be transformed to the two-class problem by labelling as positive examples any records that belong to the class of interest and as negative examples all other records. If the class of interest changes, then the labelling is changed to reflect this. This simplification is perfectly valid in nugget discovery, since the search is directed to find a good description of a class, so as long as the target class is distinguishable from other classes, a description of

Figure 1: Venn diagram for simple rule

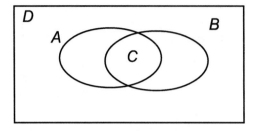

it can be found. Note that in nugget discovery, we are interested in describing the target class as accurately as possible, and so an accurate description of the negative examples, although interesting in some contexts, is not the required output.

For the simple rule described, we can define some simple measures based on the cardinalities of the different sets defined by the rule. Each conjunct defines a set of data points (or records) for which the test specified by the conjunct is true, and the intersection of all those sets, or the set of points for which all the conjuncts are true is the support of the rule in the database. This is represented in Figure 1. We will refer to this set as A, and to its cardinality by $|A| = a$. The set of data points for which the consequent of the rule is true, or, in other words, the set of data points that belong to the class specified by the rule, will be referred to as B, and $|B| = b$. Finally, the set of points for which both the antecedent and consequent of the rule are true will be called C, and $|C| = c$. In summary,

$$A = \{x \mid \alpha(x)\}, \quad B = \{x \mid \beta(x)\} \text{ and } C = \{x \mid \alpha(x) \wedge \beta(x)\}.$$

Note that $c \leq a$ and $c \leq b$, as $C \subseteq A$ and $C \subseteq B$. Also, $a \leq d$ and $b \leq d$, since $A, B \subseteq D$.

Properties of a Nugget

On the simple nuggets just introduced, we can define some important properties. The properties of a nugget can be expressed in terms of a, b, c and d. In fact, most of the interest measure that are described in the following section either use some of these properties on their own, or represent combinations of them. The fundamental properties of a nugget or rule, r, of the form $\alpha \Rightarrow \beta$ are:

Accuracy (Confidence): $Acc(r) = \dfrac{c}{a}$

This measure represents the proportion of records for which the prediction of the rule (or model in the case of a complete classification) is correct, and it is one of the most widely quoted measures of quality, particularly in the context of complete classification.

Applicability (Support): $App(r) = \dfrac{a}{d}$

This is the proportion of records of the whole database for which the rule applies. This measure is often quoted in conjunction with accuracy, to establish the quality of individual rules.

Coverage: $Cov(r) = \dfrac{c}{b}$

This measure is defined here as the proportion of the target class covered by the rule. When the target class represents a small proportion of the database, the coverage is more expressive than the applicability of a nugget because it gives a more accurate view of the worth of a nugget. In such case, high coverage of the class may be indicative of an interesting rule, which may still have very low applicability due to the size of the class under scrutiny.

Default Accuracy: $DefAcc(class) = \dfrac{b}{d}$

This measure represents the proportion of the database that belongs to the target class, or class of interest, and it is equivalent to the accuracy of the default rule for the given class (that is, the rule that has no pre-conditions and predicts the target class). The accuracy of the default rule gives a yardstick by which to measure other rules predicting the same class. We expect a nugget to be of interest for a given class if the accuracy is considerably higher than that of the default rule for that class. This leads to the next measure.

Loading: $Load(r) = \dfrac{Acc(r) - DefAcc(class)}{1 - DefAcc(class)}$

This measure is an alternative to the accuracy measure. It uses the default accuracy of the target class to "normalise" accuracy in terms of it. It is sometimes used as an alternative to accuracy because it can be more representative than a simple accuracy measure when the target class accounts for a small proportion of the database. For example, a rule that has low accuracy may be interesting if the loading is high.

In order to assess the quality of a nugget some of the above properties may be examined. Accuracy and coverage are commonly used in the literature. If the accuracy and coverage of a nugget are known, as the default accuracy of the class is also normally known, it is not difficult to calculate the applicability or loading of the same nugget. So once results are presented using one set of measures, it would be a matter of some simple calculations to present them in the alternative way. The presentation below therefore uses accuracy and coverage to order rules.

A PARTIAL ORDERING OF NUGGETS

The accuracy and coverage properties of a rule are very important. In fact, they are fundamental properties of a nugget, because they allow us to establish a *partial ordering*, $\leq_{ca}$, of rules. The partial ordering $\leq_{ca}$ can be defined as follows:

- Given rules r_1 and r_2, $r_1 <_{ca} r_2$ if and only if
$Cov\,(r_1) \leq Cov\,(r_2)$ and $Acc\,(r_1) < Acc(r_2)$, or
$Cov\,(r_1) < Cov\,(r_2)$ and $Acc\,(r_1) \leq Acc(r_2)$

- Also, $r_1 =_{ca} r_2$ if and only if
$Cov(r_1) = Cov(r_2)$ and $Acc(r_1) = Acc(r_2)$

The partial ordering $\leq_{ca}$, illustrated in Figure 2, was also proposed independently by Bayardo and Agrawal (1999). In this simple graph, the coverage of a rule is represented by the x-axis, and the accuracy is represented by the y-axis. Rules r_1 and r_2 have the same coverage with r_2 having higher accuracy. r_2 is the "preferred" rule, as it is higher in the partial ordering $\leq_{ca}$. Similarly, r_3 and r_4 have the same accuracy, but r_4 has higher coverage, so r_4 is higher in the partial ordering than r_3. r_5 has less accuracy and coverage than both r_2 and r_4, and hence r_5 is lower in the partial ordering than both r_2 and r_4. This ordering is called partial because it cannot order all rules. In fact, each rule defines a rectangular area as marked by the dotted line in Figure 2, and a rule can only be ordered with respect to another if it falls within the perimeter of the other rule's area. For example, rules r_2 and r_4 cannot be ordered with respect to one another using $\leq_{ca}$ as they belong to different accuracy/coverage areas. The simple ordering of rules established by $\leq_{ca}$ may appear to be obvious. It seems safe to assume that with equal accuracy a rule of more coverage represents a more interesting concept. Similarly, with equal coverage, a rule of higher accuracy is a more interesting concept. The partial ordering $\leq_{ca}$ is therefore important and must be enforced by any measure of interest that is used to guide the search for nuggets. Surprisingly, many of the measures of interest proposed in the literature do not support this partial ordering.

The partial ordering establishes that the more covering and the more accurate a rule is, the more interesting it is. However, there is often a trade-off in real-world datasets between accuracy and coverage. In commercial databases, a completely accurate description of a class can often not be found. The more general a pattern is (i.e., the higher the coverage), the lower the accuracy tends to be. Very specific patterns, capturing the behaviour of a few world entities, may achieve very high levels of accuracy. As the patterns become more general and capture the behaviour for a whole target class, we can expect the accuracy of those patterns to drop to reflect the levels of noise present in the real environment. Hence, when a completely

Figure 2: Partial rule ordering

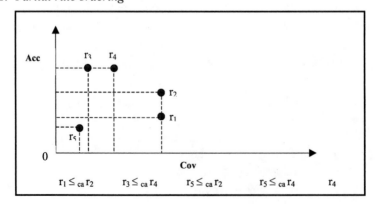

covering and accurate description for a class cannot be found, the interest measure needs to balance the trade-off between both properties. In other words, it needs to be able to select one of the defined areas or accuracy/coverage as the target for the discovery.

Interest measures should therefore contain some criteria for selecting one of the areas of accuracy/coverage as the more interesting area. Which then should be the criteria for selecting high accuracy areas or high coverage areas? The answer will vary from one application to another. For example, let us suppose that a medical database exists containing characteristics and history of patients with a particular disease. Let us also suppose that patients are divided into two classes: those that suffer the disease in its initial stages, and those that suffer it in an advanced stage. Let us assume that a drug is available, which may prevent the disease from spreading in the initial stages, but would have serious side effects for patients with the disease in an advanced stage. In this case, the description of the class "patient with disease in initial stage" to be used for the administration of the drug would have to be very accurate to be of use. In such a case, accuracy will be the most important property to be considered in an interest measure to guide the search for rules. If, however, the drug had no side effects for other patients, but was extremely effective at curing the disease if found in the initial stages, then it would be coverage of the class "patient with disease in initial stage" that should be the guiding force for nugget discovery.

A measure of interest for nugget discovery must therefore have two fundamental qualities:

- It must establish the $\leq_{ca}$ partial ordering between any two nuggets that can be compared or ordered under such ordering.

- It must also allow the search to be geared towards accurate rules or highly covering rules, depending on the preferences of the user or the application needs.

MEASURES OF INTEREST

The measure of interest commonly used in algorithms to guide the search for rules are presented next. They are presented in terms of a,b,c and d, and are given for the two-class problem. The algorithms in which they are applied will be mentioned in this section, but they will be introduced in the next section:

Accuracy (Confidence): Defined in the previous section, it often forms part of the rule extraction process in the form of a minimum accuracy constraint (Agrawal et al., 1996; Bayardo, Agrawal & Gunopulos, 1999), but sometimes it is used as the measure to be optimised (i.e., the measure of interest) (Fukuda, Morimoto, Morishita & Tokuyama, 1996; Rastogi & Shim, 1998). In terms of the algorithms presented later, Brute (Riddle et al., 1994) uses accuracy as a measure to rank rules (although Brute also provide other measures), 1R (Holte, 1993; Nevill-Manning, Holmes & Witten, 1995), T2 (Auer, Holte & Maass, 1995) and Rise

(Domingos, 1995, 1996) use it as a guiding criterion for the construction of a complete classification, and the Apriori algorithm (Agrawal et al., 1993, 1996) uses it in the form of a minimum accuracy constraint.

Laplace Accuracy: Laplace Accuracy (Clark & Boswell, 1991) is a variation of accuracy used by CN2 (Clark & Boswell, 1991;Clark & Niblett, 1989) and other rule induction algorithms. It is defined as

$$LapAcc(r) = \frac{c+1}{a+k}$$

where k is a number greater than 1, usually set to the number of classes in a classification problem.

Conviction: This is a measure of interest defined by Brin, Rastogi and Shim (1999). It can be expressed in terms of a,b,c and d as

$$Conv(r) = \frac{d-b}{d(1-Acc(r))} = \frac{a(d-b)}{d(a-c)}$$

Lift: This measure of interest is used by IBM Intelligent Miner (International Business Machines, 1997). It can be expressed as

$$Lift(r) = d\frac{Acc(r)}{b} = \frac{cd}{ab}$$

Piatetsky-Shapiro: This measure has the name of its proposer, and was introduced by Piatetsky-Shapiro (1991). The measure can be defined as

$$PS(r) = c - \frac{b}{d}a$$

J Measure: The J measure was proposed by Smyth and Goodman (1992) as a theoretic measure of the information content of a rule, and it is used by the GRI algorithm. It can be defined in terms of a,b,c and d as

$$J(r) = \frac{a}{d} \times \left(\frac{c}{a} \times \log\left(\frac{cd}{ab}\right) + \left(1-\frac{c}{a}\right) \times \log\left(\frac{d(a-c)}{a(d-b)}\right) \right)$$

Gini Index: This measure, along with the next two measures (χ^2 and entropy gain) are often used to indicate the extent to which a rule divides the data into segments whose target or class distribution is more skewed than that of the data as a whole. The Gini Index, used in the context of rule induction by Morimoto, Fukuda, Matsuzawa, Tokuyama and Yoda (1998), is also known as the *Mean Squared Error(MSE)*. For the two-class problem, the Gini Index can be expressed in terms of a,b,c and d as

$$Gini(r) = 1 - \left(\left(\frac{b}{d}\right)^2 + \left(\frac{d-b}{d}\right)^2 \right)$$

$$-\frac{a}{d} \times \left(1 - \left(\left(\frac{c}{a}\right)^2 + \left(\frac{a-c}{a}\right)^2 \right) \right)$$

$$-\frac{d-a}{d} \times \left(1 - \left(\left(\frac{b-c}{d-a}\right)^2 + \left(\frac{d-a-b+c}{d-a}\right)^2 \right) \right)$$

Entropy Gain: This measure, also known as Information Gain, behaves in an almost identical way to the Gini Index. It was the measure used initially by Quinlan (1993) in C4.5/C5. It is also used by the algorithms PART (Frank & Witten, 1998) and RIPPER (Cohen, 1995) in some of their rule building stages. The measure compares the mutual information gained by a rule, and for the two-class problem can be defined as

$$Ent(r) = -\left(\frac{b}{d} \times \log\left(\frac{b}{d} \right) + \frac{d-b}{d} \times \log\left(\frac{d-b}{d} \right) \right)$$

$$+ \frac{a}{d} \times \left(\frac{c}{a} \times \log\left(\frac{c}{a} \right) + \frac{a-c}{a} \times \log\left(\frac{a-c}{a} \right) \right)$$

$$+ \frac{d-a}{d} \times \left(\frac{b-c}{d-a} \times \log\left(\frac{b-c}{d-a} \right) + \frac{d-a-b+c}{d-a} \times \log\left(\frac{d-a-b+c}{d-a} \right) \right)$$

χ^2 *(chi-square)*: This measure is a statistical measure often used to determine if hypothesized results are verified by an experiment. It is used to rank rules in the algorithm KnowledgeSEEKER (Biggs, de Ville & Suen, 1991; de Ville, 1990) and is provided as one of the choices in Brute. The χ^2 test is again used to see whether the distribution of the classes for the records covered by a particular rule is significantly different to the overall distribution of classes in the database.

$$\chi^2(r) = \frac{d}{b} \times \left(c - a\frac{b}{d} \right)^2 + \frac{d}{d-b} \times \left((a-c) - a\frac{d-b}{d} \right)^2$$

$$+ \frac{d}{b(d-a)} \times \left((b-c) - (d-a)\frac{b}{d} \right)^2 + \frac{d}{(d-a)(d-b)} \left((d-a-b+c) - (d-a)\frac{d-b}{d} \right)^2$$

Of all the interest measures presented, only the Piatetsky-Shapiro measure establishes the $\leq_{ca}$ partial ordering under certain conditions. As this measure is closely related to the fitness measure presented later, the conditions under which the partial ordering is established for the PS measure will be discussed later. Proof of why the other measures do not establish the partial ordering is given by de la Iglesia (2001). None of the measures presented have any parameters or other means to allow the search to be directed towards more accurate or more general rules.

THE FITNESS MEASURE

The measure of interest proposed by Rayward-Smith et al. (1995), the fitness measure, is an individual quantity which displays the two important aspects of pattern quality: it establishes $\leq_{ca}$ partial ordering under certain conditions, and it also allows the search to be directed towards accuracy or generality for rules that cannot be compared under the $\leq_{ca}$ partial ordering. This measure is used as the basis for the implementation of some heuristic-based algorithms for solving the nugget discovery problem.

The simple measure that will be used to define the fitness of a rule is

$$f(r) = \lambda c - a,$$

where λ is a positive real number.

The fitness measure has a local maximum when $c = a$, and a global maximum when $c = a = b$.

Note that an equivalent measure, the gain measure was proposed by Fukuda et al. (1996), after the proposal of our measure. The gain measure is defined as

$$Gain(r) = c - \theta a,$$

where the parameter θ performs an equivalent function to the λ parameter. The gain measure is also identical to the Piatetsky-Shapiro measure for a fixed value of θ,

$$\theta = \frac{b}{d}.$$

Therefore, the following discussion regarding the fitness measure can equally be applied to the gain and to the Piatetsky-Shapiro measure by interpreting,

$$\lambda = \frac{d}{b}.$$

The parameter λ establishes an *accuracy threshold* above which the fitness measure orders rules correctly with respect to the $\leq_{ca}$ partial ordering. The accuracy threshold is defined by $1/\lambda$, and is represented in Figure 3.

The accuracy threshold is established by the following theorem:

Theorem 1: *For a given $\lambda > 1$, and for two rules* r_1 *and* r_2,

A1: *if $Acc(r_1) > \frac{1}{\lambda}$ and $Acc(r_2) > \frac{1}{\lambda}$ then*

$$r_1 <_{ca} r_2 \Rightarrow f(r_1) < f(r_2), \text{ and}$$
$$r_1 =_{ca} r_2 \Rightarrow f(r_1) = f(r_2);$$

A2: *if $Acc(r_1) = \frac{1}{\lambda}$ then $f(r_1) = 0$;*

A3: *if $Acc(r_1) > \frac{1}{\lambda}$ and $Acc(r_2) \leq \frac{1}{\lambda}$ then $f(r_1) > f(r_2)$.*

The proof of this theorem can be found in de la Iglesia (2001). A good approach to rule induction using the fitness measure is to start with a high threshold value, established by a λ value close to 1, in order to find very accurate rules. As all rules above the threshold accuracy are ordered correctly according to the $\leq_{ca}$ partial ordering, we should be able to find a rule of high accuracy and coverage, if one exists. If rules of positive fitness are not found, or if the rules found are too specific, then the threshold can be lowered by raising the value of λ, and the search restarted.

Figure 3: Accuracy Threshold

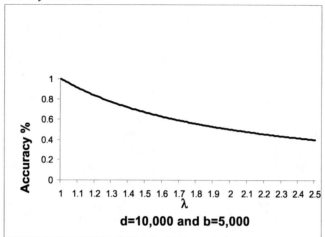

d=10,000 and b=5,000

We will then be searching a different accuracy/coverage area.

Hence, apart from the threshold established, the λ parameter has another effect on accuracy/generality of rules. For low values of the parameter λ, accuracy will have a greater weight on the fitness value, whereas for high values of λ, coverage will have a greater weight. In other words, at low λ values, rules with high accuracy, even if they have low coverage, may appear to be fitter over rules of low accuracy and higher coverage. As the lambda parameter is increased in value this effect is reversed. For example, for a database of $d = 10,000$ and $b = 5,000$:

r_1 has $c_1 = 200,$ $a_1 = 200,$ $Acc(r_1){=}1,$ $Cov(r_1) = 0.04,$
r_2 has $c_2 = 1000,$ $a_2 = 1085,$ $Acc(r_2){=}0.92$ $Cov(r_2) = 0.2.$

We find that at $\lambda = 1.1$, $f(r_1) = 20$ and $f(r_2) = 15$, hence r_1 is preferred. At $\lambda = 1.5$, $f(r_1) = 100$ and $f(r_2) = 415$, hence r_2 is preferred.

The λ parameter allows the analyst to focus the search on general but possibly less accurate patterns, or on more accurate but possibly more specific patterns. Therefore, the fitness measure establishes the $\leq_{ca}$ partial ordering, and also can encourage the production of patterns that are of high coverage or of high accuracy, depending on the application needs.

HEURISTIC TECHNIQUES TO SOLVE THE NUGGET DISCOVERY PROBLEM

Three modern heuristic techniques were adapted for the solution of the nugget discovery problem: Genetic Algorithms (GAs), Simulated Annealing (SA) and Tabu Search (TS).

The Genetic Algorithm for data mining was developed using a GA toolkit developed at the University of East Anglia. GAmeter (Smith & Mann, 1994) is an easy-to-use environment for the development of optimisation problems using GAs.

The GAmeter toolkit consists of an intuitive interface including binary, integer and floating point representations, various selection and replacement mechanisms, different cross-over and mutation operators and other features. The main code in GAmeter is implemented in the C programming language.

The simulated annealing toolkit, SAmson, developed in conjunction with GAmeter and described by Mann (1996), was used as the platform for the implementation of data mining using SA. SAmson shares most of the features of GAmeter, but uses a simulated annealing algorithm with its corresponding parameters to perform optimisation, instead of the genetic algorithm.

The TAbasco toolkit, implementing a very simple and naive Tabu Search strategy, was modified to perform the data mining tasks of nugget discovery. The only tabu search features implemented in the toolkit at the time of the research were simple recency and frequency memory structures and aspiration criteria. Hence this can only be considered as a very initial attempt at using TS for the problem of nugget discovery. A more sophisticated implementation is necessary in the future to establish the worth of TS for this problem, and some additional work in this area, soon to receive publication, is taking place within our group.

Solution Representation

One of the most important decisions for the implementation of heuristic algorithms is how to represent a solution. In this case, the solution to be represented is a conjunctive rule or nugget. The three heuristics presented all share the same solution representation: a nugget is represented by a binary string.

The first part of the string is used to represent the numeric fields or attributes. Each numeric attribute is represented by a set of gray-coded lower and upper limits, where each limit is allocated a user-defined number of bits, n ($n=10$ is the default). There is a scaling procedure that transforms any number in the range of possible values using n bits $[0,2^{n-1}]$ to a number in the range of values that the attribute can take. The procedure works as follows. When the data is loaded the maximum value, max_i, and minimum value, min_i, for each attribute i is stored. A weight for each attribute is then calculated as

$$w_i = \frac{max_i - min_i}{2^n - 1}$$

When the string representing a nugget is decoded, the upper and lower limit values for each attribute are calculated by

$$limit_i = (ss * w_i) + min_i,$$

where ss represents the decimal value of an n bit gray coded substring extracted from the binary string, which corresponds to one of the limits.

The second part of the string represents categorical attributes, with each attribute having v number of bits, where v is the number of distinct values (usually very small in number) or the number of labels that the categorical attribute can take. If a bit assigned to a categorical attribute is set to 0 in the bit string representation, then the corresponding label is included as an inequality in one of the conjuncts. For example, if the bit for the value "blue" of an attribute "colour" is set to 0, then one of the conjuncts would be "Colour ≠ blue".

When a bit string is decoded as a nugget it will acquire the following format:

IF $(l_1 \leq AT_1 \leq u_1)$ AND $(l_2 \leq AT_2 \leq u_2)$ AND...AND $(l_i \leq AT_i \leq u_i)$ AND $AT_p \neq label_a$ AND $AT_r \neq label_b$ THEN Class$_j$

where l_1, the lower limit for attribute 1, is given by the first n bits of the binary string, u_1, the upper limit, is given by the following n bits, etc. We have assumed for simplicity that the first i attributes are numeric, with the categorical attributes following. If a lower limit or any attribute i is set to its lowest possible value for the attribute, min_i, or the upper limit is set to its highest possible value, max_i, then there is no need to include that limit in the decoded nugget. If both limits are excluded in that way, then the attribute is obviously also excluded. Equally, if a categorical attribute has a value of 1 for all the bits allocated to its labels, then there is no need to include the attribute. Note that with this representation some solutions may translate to the empty rule, i.e., the rule that contains no records. This could happen, for example, if all the categorical labels are set to 0. Solutions of this kind were penalised with a very low fitness, to overcome the problem.

Other Details of the Nugget Discovery Implementation

Aside of the representation issues, the heuristic toolkits used (GAmeter, SAmson and TAbasco) handled the optimisation according to the chosen paradigm. The only implementation details left to be covered were the loading of a solution, the initialisation, the evaluation and the saving procedure.

The details of the loading and saving operations will not be discussed here, as they are reasonably trivial. The initialisation was achieved, after some experimentation, by use of the default rule. The default rule is the rule in which all limits are maximally spaced and all labels are included. In the case of SA and TS, the initial solution was set to the default rule, whereas in the case of the GAs all solutions were initialised to the default rule. This worked surprisingly better, more so for the GAs, than initialising some or all rules at random.

To evaluate a solution, the bit string is decoded, and the data is scanned through. For each record the values of the fields are compared against the nuggets, and the class is also compared. The counts of c and a are updated accordingly. Once all the data has been examined $f(r) = \lambda c - a$ is calculated. It is also possible, especially in the early stages, to approximate this by sampling.

Parameters

For each heuristic algorithm, extensive experimentation was conducted to find an adequate set of parameters. (The details of the experiments are given by de la Iglesia, 2001). The three algorithms were found fairly robust to parameter experimentation on the problem of nugget discovery tested, hence a set of parameters was chosen to run each algorithm in future exercises. Here is a summary of the parameters chosen for each algorithm:

For the GAs
− A pool of 10 solutions (an increase to 500 was an option for more accurate runs).
− A roulette selection mechanism with replacement. The number of solutions that are selected to create new solutions is a random number between a minimum and maximum value established by the user (note that min. must be at least two and max. can be at most equal to the population size).
− Offspring are merged into the population using the "best fit" method, which sequentially replaces the worst solution in the population with the best of the offspring until there is no child better than the next candidate for replacement.
− Consecutive pairs of parents are selected for one-point crossover with 60% probability (and so consequently replication at 40%). If an odd number of parents is chosen and crossover is applied to the last parent from the mating pool, it is mated with a solution in the mating pool chosen at random.
− Mutation rate 1%.
− The stopping condition was 500 generations without improvement.

For the SA
− A neighbourhood of a solution was generated by selecting a bit at random and inverting it.
− Initial temperature of 10, selected as an acceptable value after experimentation with different initial temperatures.
− Cooling schedule Lundy and Mees (1986), with a Beta value of 0.9 and 20 proposed moves spent at each temperature step.
− Non-monotonicity was introduced within the cooling schedule by means of a threshold parameter. This works by returning the temperature to half its value at the point of the last temperature rise when the threshold percentage of this value is reached. The temperature value at the point of the last temperature rise is considered to be the initial temperature if no rises have yet been performed. For example, if an initial temperature of 100 is used together with a threshold value of 10, the temperature will be raised to 50 (100 ÷2) once it reaches 10 (10% of 100). The temperature will next be raised to 25 (50 ÷2) when it falls to 5 (10% of 50) and so on.
− All experiments were halted once the temperature had fallen to 0.01.

For the TS
− A neighbourhood operator: flip one bit.
− Recency memory (implemented by recording whole solutions) with a tabu tenure of 10.
− Frequency memory (implemented by keeping a count of how many times each single bit of the solution representation had been changed) with a threshold of 20.

- A subset of 20 neighbours generated.
- Stopping after 250 iterations without change in the best solution value.

OTHER ALGORITHMS FOR NUGGET DISCOVERY

In the following section we will present the results of applying the heuristic algorithms for nugget discovery to some problems. Other algorithms available for classification or for nugget discovery were applied to the same problems so that the suitability of different approaches to the task of nugget discovery could be assessed. The algorithms tested ranged from complete classification algorithms, to nugget discovery algorithms and association rule algorithms. A description of each algorithm is not possible here due to space constraints, hence the reader is referred to appropriate papers. For each algorithm, extensive parameter experimentation was carried out and a set of good parameters was chosen, but again this is not reported here; see de la Iglesia (2001) for details.

The classification algorithms chosen were:

- *C5/C4.5*: This is the most prominent decision tree induction algorithm, which also contains functionality to extract a non-mutually exclusive set of rules (Quinlan, 1986, 1993). Each rule is a nugget of the form described previously. For categorical attributes the type of tests contained in the nuggets formed by the C5 algorithm are either a single value or a subset of values. For numeric attributes, the tests contained are binary partitions.

- *CN2*: This is a rule induction algorithm for complete classification described by Clark and Boswell (1991) and Clark and Niblett (1989). If an unordered rule set is extracted, each of the rules is a nugget that can be assessed on its own. For categorical attributes, it uses single-value tests only, whereas for numerical attributes it uses tests containing a range of values.

- *Brute*: This is a nugget discovery algorithm (Riddle et al., 1994) which performs an exhaustive depth-bounded search for conjunctive rules, guided by a chosen interest measure (the choices include Laplace accuracy, χ^2, and a weighted average of accuracy and coverage). The nuggets extracted use binary partitions for numeric attributes and either single value, subset of values or inequality tests for categorical attributes.

- *RIPPER*: Repeated Incremental Pruning to Produce Error Reduction (Cohen, 1995) is another rule induction algorithm that produces a complete classification. The rules that form part of the classification are conjunctive nuggets. The nuggets obtained have binary partitions for numeric attributes and either single value or inequality tests for categorical attributes.

- *KnowledgeSEEKER*: The commercial package KnowledgeSEEKER (Biggs et al., 1991; de Ville, 1994) is another tree induction algorithm which is based on the statistical approach to tree induction. Each branch (or even partial branch up to any node) of the tree can be considered as a nugget. For categorical attributes, the nuggets can contain single value or subsets of values, whereas for numerical attributes it uses tests containing a range of values.

- *1R*: This is a rule induction algorithm that produces rules which base the classification of examples upon a single attribute. The algorithm (Holte, 1993; Nevill-Manning et al., 1995) assumes categorical attributes, but can handle numeric attributes as they are discretised as a preprocessing operation. The interpretation of the classification produced by 1R as a set of nuggets can be done in various ways. If the attribute chosen for the classification is categorical, then each value of the attribute can be interpreted as a conjunctive test, or a subset of values can be considered together. In the experiment that follows all possibilities of individual tests or subsets of tests were considered as nuggets for the attribute chosen in each case. For a numerical attribute, each interval produced by the discretisation can be considered individually, or various intervals can be considered together as a disjunction. In the experiments that follow, both individual ranges and disjunction of ranges were evaluated.

- *T2*: This is a tree induction algorithm which produces a decision tree containing at most two levels (Auer et al., 1995). In the first level the tree contains a test on a single attribute, with numeric attributes using a binary partition and discrete attributes using a simple value. If there is a second level, a test on a numeric attribute will test on range of values instead of a binary partition. Each branch or partial branch of a T2 tree can be interpreted as a nugget.

- *PART*: This algorithm (Frank & Witten, 1998) generates rule sets and combines concepts of C4.5 and RIPPER. Each rule of the rule set can be considered as a nugget, but they need to be re-evaluated individually as they form part of an ordered rule set. PART uses simple value tests for categorical attributes, and binary partitions for numerical attributes.

- *RISE*: This algorithm (Domingos, 1995, 1996) combines rule induction with Instance Based Learning (IBL). Since IBL explicitly memorises some or all of the examples and attempts to find the most similar cases to the target one, the resulting classifier is made up of some abstractions formed by the rule induction part of the algorithm and some individual examples. It is only worth considering the abstractions as nuggets, and this is what was done in the following experiments. The abstractions are rules using range of values for tests on numeric attributes and simple value tests for categorical attributes.

  Also, the following association rule algorithms were chosen:

- *GRI*: Generalised Rule Induction (Mallen & Bramer, 1995) is described as an association rule algorithm, although it could also be considered as a partial classification algorithm. It builds a table of the best N association rules, as ranked by the J measure, where N is a parameter set by the user. In GRI the output attribute can be chosen, and each rule produced can be used as a nugget describing that output. They contain binary partitions for numeric attributes and tests on a simple value for categorical attributes.

– *Apriori*: The Apriori algorithm (Agrawal et al., 1993, 1996) is the most prominent association rule algorithm. Pre-discretisation of numeric attributes is necessary, since the algorithm can only handle categorical attributes. A simple equal width discretisation scheme was used for this. The output of this algorithm is not constraint to rules for a particular attribute, hence only the nuggets relating to the class under scrutiny need to be analysed for the task of nugget discovery. The Apriori rules contain simple value tests for categorical attributes.

EXPERIMENTS

The heuristic algorithms, as well as the 11 algorithms mentioned above, were applied to the problem of nugget discovery using four different databases extracted from the UCI repository of databases (Merz & Murphy, 1998). The databases chosen are briefly summarised in Table 1.

Full details of all the experiments carried out, and more details on each database, are presented in de la Iglesia (2001). Here only a summary of the findings is presented.

For the first three databases, patterns were sought for all the classes. For the last database, patterns were sought only for two of the classes, the majority class with 48.8% representative examples and the minority class with 0.5% representative examples. For the Adult database, records with missing values were removed, and for the mushroom database one of the attributes, which contains a high percentage of missing values, was also removed as a pre-processing step. The other datasets contained no missing values. Also, for the Apriori algorithm, numeric attributes were discretised using a simple equal-width bin scheme. In the case of the Forest Cover Type database, a balanced version of the data was produced for the extraction of nuggets for the minority class. This balanced version contained a reduced dataset, with records belonging to classes other than the minority class removed at random, until the minority class represented a higher percentage of the data (over 30%). Algorithms were tried on both the balanced and the complete data set, and the best

Table 1: Databases from the UCI repository chosen for nugget discovery

Name	Records	Attrib.	Classes	Numeric Attributes	Categorical Attributes
Adult	45,222	14	2	6	8
Mushroom	8,124	21	2	0	21
Contraception	1,473	9	3	2	7
Forest Cover Type	581,012	54	7	10	14

nuggets obtained by either were selected for comparison. The balanced version of the data was included because techniques such as C5 are known to give best results if balanced databases are used (de la Iglesia, Debuse and Rayward-Smith, 1996). The heuristics did not use the balanced dataset to induce the rules of best quality.

The databases used posed different challenges for the algorithms: the Adult database can be considered large and has some strong patterns; the Mushroom database has very obvious and strong patterns; the Contraception database has very weak patterns in particular for some classes; the Forest Cover database is large and contains a very good example of a minority or exceptional class. The databases chosen have a mixture of categorical and numeric attributes.

For each database, the data was partitioned into a train/test partition. Then the algorithms were applied using a set of parameters chosen previously as a result of parameter experimentation. For the algorithms that produce a complete classification, or a set of nuggets or rules, each rule was transformed into a fitness measure using a range of λ values. The λ values used were chosen to represent decreasing accuracy thresholds, and varied from dataset to dataset. At most six different λ values were experimented with for each dataset. Experimentation to find the right λ value for a particular problem is reasonably straightforward, and it involves starting with a high accuracy threshold (close to 100%) and decreasing it at approximately equal steps until the accuracy threshold is equal to the default accuracy for the class being targeted. The process of λ experimentation can be automated.

From the set of rules, or individual rules obtained by each algorithm, the one with the highest fitness measure for each λ value was chosen for comparison to the rules produced by other algorithms. For illustrative purposes, one set of result tables is reproduced in Table 2. In this table, N/R means that no rule was obtained. For each algorithm, the fitness, accuracy and coverage of the best (highest fitness) nugget produced are recorded in the table. The figures in brackets represent the accuracy and coverage obtained by testing the nugget on the test partition. The highest fitness results obtained, corresponding in this case to the heuristics, are highlighted in bold.

Similar tables are presented in de la Iglesia (2001) for each class examined in each database. All results cannot be reproduced here due to space constraints. As a summary, this is how algorithms performed on the different problems:

– *Adult database:* For this dataset, the heuristic techniques, C5, GRI and Brute produced fit nuggets for both classes consistently at different levels of accuracy and generality. The algorithms 1R and KnowledgeSEEKER produced good results in some cases, but not as consistently. The other algorithms produced results of lower fitness in most cases. The nuggets obtained by the best algorithms were simple rules that represented good descriptions of the classes, with high accuracy and coverage. The measures of accuracy and coverage of the same rules when applied to the test datasets showed that the patterns were not overfitting the training data, as the properties of the nuggets remained stable

Table 2: Results of nugget discovery for class '<=50K' in Adult dataset

Method	λ Acc T	1.1 91	1.2 83	1.3 77	1.4 71
CN2	Fitness Acc Cov	455.6 95.2(95.3) 40.9(40.9)	1381.2 95.2(95.3) 40.9(40.9)	2306.8 95.2(95.3) 40.9(40.9)	2232.4 95.2(95.3) 40.9(40.9)
RIPPER	Fitness Acc Cov	455.6 95.2(95.3) 40.9(40.9)	1381.2 95.2(95.3) 40.9(40.9)	2306.8 95.2(95.3) 40.9(40.9)	3322.6 93(92.5) 45.2(44.1)
BRUTE	Fitness Acc Cov	785.2 95.5(95.7) 65.2(65.5)	2262.4 95.5(95.7) 65.2(65.5)	3739.6 95.5(95.7) 65.2(65.5)	5216.8 95.5(95.7) 65.2(65.5)
C5	Fitness Acc Cov	798.7 95.5(95.7) 66.1(66.3)	2296.4 95.5(95.7) 66.1(66.3)	3794.1 95.5(95.7) 66.1(66.3)	5291.8 95.5(95.7) 66.1(66.3)
KS	Fitness Acc Cov	873.4 97.3(97.6) 53.3(53)	2132 94.8(95) 64.9(65)	3603 94.8(95) 64.9(65)	5074 94.8(95) 64.9(65)
T2	Fitness Acc Cov	57.5 96(96.1) 4.3(4.7)	268.6 85.7(85.8) 36.2(36.4)	1088.4 85.7(85.8) 36.2(36.4)	1908.2 85.7(85.8) 36.2(36.4)
1R	Fitness Acc Cov	28.6 100(100) 1.3(1.1)	57.2 100(100) 1.3(1.1)	866.9 79.3(79.5) 99.8(99.8)	3128.2 79.3(79.5) 99.8(99.8)
PART	Fitness Acc Cov	476.7 99.7(99.5) 21.7(21.2)	991.8 99.2(99.2) 22.8(22.8)	1508.2 99.2(99.2) 22.8(22.8)	2024.6 99.2(99.2) 22.8(22.8)
RISE	Fitness Acc Cov	163.9 99.8(99.4) 7.4(6.8)	330.8 99.8(99.4) 7.4(6.8)	497.7 99.8(99.4) 7.4(6.8)	664.6 99.8(99.4) 7.4(6.8)
GRI	Fitness Acc Cov	586.3 96.5(96.6) 40.3(40.3)	1499.6 96.5(96.6) 40.3(40.3)	2412.9 96.5(96.6) 40.3(40.3)	3326.2 96.5(96.6) 40.3(40.3)
Apriori	Fitness Acc Cov	N/R	N/R	N/R	N/R
GA	Fitness Acc Cov	954.1 97.7(97.7) 55.4(55.2)	2328.6 96.3(96.7) 63.5(63.3)	3793.2 95.6(95.8) 66(66.2)	5293.6 95.7(95.9) 65.8(65.9)
SA	Fitness Acc Cov	**954.7** 97.7(97.7) 55.4(55.2)	**2329.8** 96.3(96.7) 63.5(63.3)	**3803.2** 95.6(95.8) 66(66.2)	**5294.8** 95.7(95.9) 65.8(65.9)
TA	Fitness Acc Cov	930.1 97.7(97.9) 53.7(53.4)	**2329.8** 96.3(96.6) 63.6(63.4)	**3803.2** 95.7(95.9) 65.8(65.9)	**5294.8** 95.6(95.8) 66.1(66.3)

on new data.

- *Mushroom database:* This database contains very strong rules (nearly 100 % accurate and 100% covering rules).The heuristics–Brute, C5, KnowledgeSEEKER, and 1R–perform well for both classes, finding the strong rules present. Again, the rules found do not show signs of overfitting. RIPPER performs well for one class, but worse for the other. The other algorithms find rules of worse quality (in most cases rules that are very accurate but of considerably lower coverage) for both classes.

- *Contraception database*: This database does not contain strong patterns, especially for two of the classes. In particular, those classes do not seem to contain accurate rules of wide coverage, and the accurate rules found show signs of overfitting. The heuristics find good rules at different levels of accuracy/ coverage, for the more obvious class, and good rules of wide coverage for the other two classes, but not good accurate rules for those classes. C5 did not find very good rules, except for the class with the more obvious patterns. CN2 found some accurate rules, but did not find very general rules for any of the classes. BRUTE produced some reasonably good accurate rules, in particular for the class with the more obvious patterns, but they did show some signs of overfitting. The other algorithms only did well on some isolated cases.

- *Forest Cover Type database*: Some algorithms could not work with the size of this file so two random samples containing 10% and 5% of the data respectively were used subsequently as alternatives when an algorithm failed to run on the bigger file. In those cases, the rest of the data was used as a test set. For the majority class, the heuristics gave best performance, with C5, Brute and 1R performing well in some cases. The other algorithms presented poor performance for most cases. For the minority class, which presented a real challenge for the algorithms, the heuristic obtained the best rules for all except the highest level of accuracy sought. C5, found a good accurate rule for this class, and performed generally well. RIPPER and CN2 found good accurate rules but the wide coverage rules found by those algorithms were of worse quality. Brute, KnowledgeSEEKER and 1R performed well for the wide covering rules. The rest of the algorithms performed poorly in general.

The results obtained show that the heuristic techniques produce good nuggets for most problems and most λ values in terms of their fitness. This is perhaps not surprising, as they are designed to optimise the fitness measure. Other good performers are C5, Brute and KnowledgeSEEKER. Those algorithms extract rules of high coverage and accuracy and, in general, do not overfit the training data. However with the other algorithms, a way of selecting some interesting nuggets from the set of nuggets obtained is necessary. We have used the fitness measure to rank the rules, and we have selected in each case the fittest rule. But how good is the fitness measure as an assessment of the interest of a rule? The patterns obtained confirm that a higher fitness measure implies a higher ranking in the partial ordering for rules that can be ranked by the same partial ordering. This is definitely desirable. It can also be seen that the λ parameter allows for the variation of the search criteria between accurate and more general patterns. This also seems a good property, as it delivers patterns that go from the accurate or very accurate to the very general, for all databases and classes. Hence ranking patterns according to the fitness measure seems to deliver interesting patterns, and using the heuristic as a means of finding those patterns tends to deliver the fittest patterns.

We have previously said that the heuristic algorithms produce good nuggets for most classes and most λ values, generally outperforming other algorithms. In comparing the three heuristic, it is difficult to judge which is the best technique: SA, GA or TS. They all seem to perform well and mostly produce similarly good results so they would all be a good choice for nugget discovery. TS seems to offer a very robust performance, with the best results for many of the experiments. This is very encouraging considering that the implementation of TS used is quite naive and does not include many of the advanced Tabu Search features that can improve on the search process. A full implementation of TS, including for example aspiration criteria and good intensification and diversification techniques, may be the next step forward, given these results.

In terms of execution time, the three heuristic algorithms performed similarly for most of the experiments undertaken. All three algorithms were run with execution time limits given by similar conditions such as a fixed number of generations without change for the GA, or a fixed number of proposed moves without change for the TA/SA algorithms. Statistics for when the best solution was reached were kept and compared, finding similar performance for all three heuristics. Execution times are difficult to compare, given that experiments were conducted on different machines, and in competition with other machine users which produced variations in performance, but in general the time to run a single TA, SA or GA experiment was comparable to the time taken to produce, for example, a C5 set of rules. C5 offered one of the best performances when compared with the other algorithms (CN2, Brute, T2, etc.), hence the heuristics were competitive with all other algorithms in terms of execution times.

CONCLUSIONS

In this chapter, we have established nugget discovery as a data mining task in its own right. We have shown that it needs to be guided by a good measure of interest for nugget discovery. We have looked at the properties of a nugget that should be incorporated into a measure of interest. We have presented a partial ordering of rules that should be enforced by measures of interest for nugget discovery. We have then looked at the measures of interest that have traditionally been used by classification (complete or partial) algorithms. We have established that many do not uphold the partial ordering and hence they are not suitable for ordering and selecting nuggets. The fitness measure, a measure which establishes the partial ordering and allows for the variation of the search criteria towards more accurate or more general rules, has been established.

The heuristic algorithms for nugget discovery have been reviewed. Other algorithms, which can also be used for this task, were briefly introduced. They use the different measures of interest reviewed to produce complete or partial classifications.

Using four databases from the UCI repository, nugget discovery has been performed using all the algorithms presented. In each case, the fitness measure has been used to choose the most interesting nuggets from the set of rules produced by the algorithms. The examination of the nuggets obtained has established that algorithms such as C5, Brute and KnowledgeSEEKER are capable of obtaining good nuggets using their own guiding criteria for the search, and the fitness measure to choose the most interesting nugget from the set obtained. The heuristics have produced the best overall results, and since it is the delivery of interesting nuggets which is the guiding search criteria, they are the best choice for this task.

Tabu Search has shown great potential, and more sophisticated implementations of Tabu Search for data mining must be the focus of future research. Some further work, in particular using the Simulated Annealing algorithm, is also being implemented in the commercial data mining toolkit Datalamp (Howard, 1999) (*http://www.datalamp.com*). Adaptation of the techniques to databases with many missing values is also an area of research for the future. Algorithms that search for all conjunctive rules that are best according to some criteria of accuracy and applicability (Bayardo & Agrawal, 1999) have been proposed for categorical data. This is a promising area of research, which would also provide a good benchmark to analyse the performance of the heuristic algorithms, so some of the research efforts in our group have been directed to an all-rules search algorithm.

REFERENCES

Agrawal, R., Imielinski, T., and Swami, A. (1993). Database mining: A performance perspective. *IEEE Transactions on Knowledge and Data Engineering,* 5(6), 914-925.

Agrawal, R., Mannila, H., Srikant, R., Toivonen, H., and Verkamo, I. (1996). Fast discovery of association rules. In Fayyad et al., 307-328.

Ali, K. Manganaris, S. and Srikant, R. (1997). *Partial classification using association rules.* In Heckerman, Mannila, Pregibon and Uthurusamy, 115-118.

Auer, P., Holte, R., and Maass, W. (1995). *Theory and application of agnostic PAC-learning with small decision trees.* In Prieditis and Russell, 21-29.

Bayardo R. J. (1997). *Brute force mining of high-confidence classification rules.* In Heckerman et al., 123-126.

Bayardo, R. J. and Agrawal, R. (1999). *Mining the most interesting rules.* In Chaudhuri and Madigan, 145-154.

Bayardo, R. J., Agrawal, R., and Gunopulos, D. (1999). Constraint-based rule mining in large, dense datasets. In *Proc. of the 15th Int. Conf. On Data Engineering,* 188-197.

Biggs, D., de Ville, B., and Suen, E. (1991). A method of choosing multiway partitions for classification and decision trees. *Journal of Applied Statistics,* 18(1), 49-62.

Brin, S., Rastogi, R., and K. Shim. (1999). *Mining optimized gain rules for numeric attributes.* In Chaudhuri and Madigan, 135-144.

Clark, P. C. and Boswell, R. (1991). Rule induction with CN2: Some recent improvements. In Y. Kodratoff (Ed.), *Machine Learning – Proc. of the Fifth European Conf.* Berlin: Springer-Verlag, 151-163.

Clark, P. C. and Niblett, T. N. (1989). The CN2 induction algorithm. *Machine Learning,* 3(4), 261-283.

Chaudhuri, S. and Madigan, D., (Ed.).(1999). *Proceeding of the 5th ACM SIGKDD Int. Conf. On Knowledge Discovery and Data Mining.* New York: ACM.

Cohen, W. W. (1995). *Fast effective rule induction.* In Prieditis and Russell, 115-123.

de la Iglesia, B. (2001). *The development and application of heuristic techniques for the data mining task of nugget discovery.* PhD Thesis, University of East Anglia.

de la Iglesia, B., Debuse, J. C. W. and Rayward-Smith V. J. (1996). Discovering knowledge in commercial databases using modern heuristic techniques. In E. Simoudis, J. W. Han, and U. M. Fayyad (Ed.). *Proceeding of the Second Int. Conf. on Knowledge Discovery and Data Mining.* AAAI Press, 44-49.

de Ville, B. (1990). Applying statistical knowledge to database analysis and knowledge base construction. In *Proc. Of the 6th IEEE Conf. On Artificial Intelligence Applications.* Washington: IEEE Computer Society, 30-36.

Debuse, J. C. W., de la Iglesia, B., Howard, C. M., and Rayward-Smith, V.J. (2000). Building the KDD Roadmap: A Methodology for Knowledge Discovery. In R. Roy (Ed.). *Industrial Knowledge Management,* London: Springer-Verlag, 170-196.

Domingos, P. (1995). Rule induction and instance-based learning: A unified approach. In *Proc. Of the 14th Int. Joint Conf. on Artificial Intelligence.*

Domingos, P. (1996). From instances to rules: A comparison of biases. In *Proc. Of the 3rd Int. Workshop on Multistrategy Learning,* 147-54.

Fayyad, U. M., Piatetsky-Shapiro, G., and Smyth, P. (1996). *From Data Mining to Knowledge Discovery: An overview.* In Fayyad et al., 1-34.

Fayyad, U. M., Piatetsky-Shapiro, G., Smyth, P. and Uthurusamy, R., (Ed.) (1996). *Advances in Knowledge Discovery and Data Mining.* California: AAAI Press/ MIT Press.

Frank, E. and Witten, I. H. (1998). Generating accurate rule sets without global optimization. In *Proc. Of the Int. Conf. on Machine Learning.* Morgan Kaufmann, 144-151.

Fukuda, T. Morimoto, Y., Morishita, S. and Tokuyama, T. (1996). Data mining using two-dimensional optimized association rules: schemes, algorithms and visualisation. In *Proc. Of the ACM SIGMOD Conference on Management of Data,* 3-26.

Heckerman, D., Mannila, H., Pregibon, D. and Uthurusamy, R. (Eds) (1997). *Proceedings of the Third Int. Conf. on Knowledge Discovery and Data Mining.* California: AAAI Press.

Holte, R. C. (1993). Very simple classification rules perform well on most commonly used datasets. *Machine Learning,* 11(1), 63-91).

Howard, C. M. (1999). *DMEngine Class Reference.* SYS Technical Report SYS-C99-03, University of East Anglia.

International Business Machines. (1997). *IBM Intelligent Miner.* User's Guide, Version 1, Release 1.

Liu, B., Hsu, W. and Ma, Y. (1998). Integrating classification and association rule mining. In Agrawal, R. and Stolorz, P. (Ed.). *Proceedings of the Fourth Int. Conf. On Knowledge Discovery and Data Mining.* California: AAAI Press, 80-86.

Lundy, M. and Mees, A. (1986). Convergence of an annealing algorithm. *Mathematical Programming,* 34, 111-124.

Mallen, J. and Bramer, M. (1995). *Cupid – Utilising Domain Knowledge in Knowledge*

Discovery. In Expert Systems XI.

Mann, J. W. (1996). *X-SAmson v1.5 developers manual.* School of Information Systems Technical Report, University of East Anglia, UK.

Merz, C. J. and Murphy, P. M. (1998). *UCI repository of machine learning databases.* University of California, Irvine, Dept. of Information and Computer Sciences. *http// www.ics.uci.edu/~mlearn/MLRepository.html.*

Morimoto, Y., Fukuda, T., Matsuzawa, H., Tokuyama, T. and Yoda, K. (1998). Algorithms for mining association rules for binary segmentations of huge categorical databases. In *Proc. Of the 24ᵗʰ Very Large Data Bases conference,* 380-391.

Nevill-Manning, C., Holmes, G., and Witten, I. H. (1995) The development of Holte's 1R classifier. In *Proc. Artificial Neural Networks and Expert Systems,* Dunedin, NZ 239-242.

Piatetsky-Shapiro, G. (1991) Discovery, Analysis, and Presentation of Strong Rules. In *Knowledge Discovery in Databases,* (Chapter 13). California: AAAI/MIT Press.

Prieditis, A. and Russell, S. (Ed.) *Proc. Of the 12ᵗʰ International Conf. On Machine Learning.* Tahoe City, CA: Morgan Kaufmann Publishers, Inc.

Quinlan, J. R. (1986). Induction of decision trees. *Machine learning,* 1(1), 81-106. Reprinted in J. W. Shavlik and T. G. Dietterich (Ed.), *Readings in Machine Learning.* San Mateo, CA: Morgan Kaufmann, (1991). Reprinted in B. G. Buchanan, and D. Wilkins (Ed.), *Readings in Knowledge Acquisition and Learning.* San Mateo, CA: Morgan Kaufmann (1992).

Quinlan, J. R. (1987). Simplifying decision trees. *International Journal of Man-Machine Studies,* 27, 221-234.

Quinlan, J. R. (1993). *C4.5: Programs for Machine Learning.* San Mateo, CA: Morgan Kaufmann.

Rastogi, R. and Shim, K. (1998). Mining optimised association rules with categorical and numeric attributes. In *Proc. Of the 14ᵗʰ Int. Conf. On Data Engineering,* 503-512.

Rayward-Smith, V., Debuse, J. , and de la Iglesia, B. (1995). Using a Genetic Algorithm to data mine in the financial services sector. In Macintosh, A. and Cooper, C. (Ed). *Applications and innovations in Expert Systems III.* SGES Publications, 237-252.

Riddle, P., Segal, R., and Etzioni, O. (1994). Representation design and brute-force induction in a Boeing manufacturing domain. *Applied Artificial Intelligence,* 8, 125-147.

Smith, G. D. and Mann, J. W. (1994). Gameter: A genetic algorithm in X. In *Proceedings of the 5ᵗʰ Annual EXUG Conference.*

Smyth, P. and Goodman, R. M. (1992). An information theoretic approach to rule induction from databases. *IEEE Transactions on Knowledge and Data Engineering,* 4, 301-316.

Chapter V

Estimation of Distribution Algorithms for Feature Subset Selection in Large Dimensionality Domains

Iñaki Inza, Pedro Larrañaga and Basilio Sierra
University of the Basque Country, Spain

Feature Subset Selection (FSS) is a well-known task of Machine Learning, Data Mining, Pattern Recognition or Text Learning paradigms. Genetic Algorithms (GAs) are possibly the most commonly used algorithms for Feature Subset Selection tasks. Although the FSS literature contains many papers, few of them tackle the task of FSS in domains with more than 50 features. In this chapter we present a novel search heuristic paradigm, called Estimation of Distribution Algorithms (EDAs), as an alternative to GAs, to perform a population-based and randomized search in datasets of a large dimensionality. The EDA paradigm avoids the use of genetic crossover and mutation operators to evolve the populations. In absence of these operators, the evolution is guaranteed by the factorization of the probability distribution of the best solutions found in a generation of the search and the subsequent simulation of this distribution to obtain a new pool of solutions. In this chapter we present four different probabilistic models to perform this factorization. In a comparison with two types of GAs in natural and artificial datasets of a large dimensionality, EDA-based approaches obtain encouraging results with regard to accuracy, and a fewer number of evaluations were needed than used in genetic approaches.

ESTIMATION OF DISTRIBUTION ALGORITHMS FOR FEATURE SUBSET SELECTION IN LARGE DIMENSIONALITY DOMAINS

The basic problem of Supervised Classification in Data Mining is concerned with the induction of a model that classifies a given object into one of several known classes. In order to induce the classification model, each object is described by a pattern of 'd' features: $X_1, X_2, ..., X_d$. With advanced computer technologies, big data archives are usually formed and many features are used to describe the objects. Here, Data Mining and Machine Learning communities usually formulate the following question: *Are all of these 'd' descriptive features useful when learning the classification model?* On trying to respond to this question, we come up with the Feature Subset Selection (FSS) approach, which can be formulated as follows: given a set of candidate features, select the best subset in a classification task.

The dimensionality reduction made by an FSS process can provide several advantages for a classification system applied to a specific task:

- a reduction in the cost of data acquisition;
- an improvement of the final classification model's comprehensibility;
- a faster induction of the final classification model; and
- an improvement in classification accuracy.

The attainment of higher classification accuracies, coupled with a notable dimensionality reduction, is the common objective of Machine Learning and Data Mining processes.

It has long been proved that the classification accuracy of supervised classifiers is not monotonic with respect to the addition of features (Kohavi & John, 1997). Irrelevant or redundant features, depending on the specific characteristics of the supervised classifier, may degrade the predictive accuracy of the classification model.

FSS can be viewed as a search problem, with each state in the search space specifying a subset of the possible features of the task. Exhaustive evaluation of possible feature subsets is usually infeasible in practice because of the large amount of computational effort required. Due to its randomized, evolutionary and population-based nature, Genetic Algorithms (GAs) have been the most commonly used search engine in the FSS process (Kudo & Sklansky, 2000; Siedelecky & Sklansky, 1988; Vafaie & De Jong, 1993). Most of the theory of GAs deals with the so-called Building Blocks (BBs) (Goldberg, 1989): simply said, BBs are partial solutions of a problem, formed by groups of related variables. GAs reproduce BBs by an implicit manipulation of a large number of them through the mechanisms of selection and recombination. A crucial factor of the GA success resides in the proper growth and mixing of the optimal BBs of the problem. Problem-independent recombination operators often break these BBs and do not mix them efficiently; thus, this could delay the discovery of the global optima or produce a convergence to a local optima.

Linkage learning (LL) (Harik, Lobo & Goldberg, 1997) is the identification of the BBs to be conserved under recombination. Recently, various approaches to solve the LL problem have been proposed (Pelikan & Müehlenbein, 1999). Several proposed methods are based on the manipulation of the representation of solutions during the optimization to make the interacting components of partial solutions less likely to be broken. For this purpose, various reordering and mapping operators are used. One of these approaches is the well-known Messy Genetic Algorithm (MGA) (Goldberg, 1989).

Instead of extending the GA, in latter years, a new approach has strongly emerged under the EDA (Estimation of Distribution Algorithm) (Müehlenbein & Paab, 1996) to tackle the LL problem. The EDA approach explicitly learns the probabilistic structure of the problem and uses this information to ensure a proper mixing and growth of BBs that do not disrupt them. The further exploration of the search space is guided, instead of crossover and mutation operators as in GAs, by the probabilistic modeling of promising solutions.

Although the FSS literature contains many papers, few of them tackle the selection of features in domains of a large dimensionality (more than 50 features) (Aha & Bankert, 1994; Kudo & Sklansky, 2000; Mladenic, 1998). EDA-inspired techniques have shown good behavior with respect to sequential and genetic approaches in datasets of a smaller dimensionality (Inza, Larrañaga & Sierra, 2001). The use of sequential FSS techniques is not advised in large dimensionality datasets because of their exhaustive search of a specific part of the solution space, leaving the remaining large parts of the solution space unexplored (Kudo & Sklansky, 2000). Due to their randomized nature, population-based search algorithms allow a search with a larger degree of diversity, being the advised algorithms to solve large dimensionality FSS tasks (Kudo & Sklansky, 2000; Vafaie & De Jong, 1993). In this chapter, as an alternative to GAs (the most popular population-based paradigm (Goldberg, 1989)) we propose the use of four new EDA-inspired techniques to solve the FSS task in datasets of a large dimensionality: FSS-PBIL, FSS-BSC, FSS-MIMIC and FSS-TREE.

The chapter is organized as follows. The next section introduces the FSS problem and its basic components. We then introduce the EDA paradigm and the PBIL, BSC, MIMIC and TREE probabilistic models. That is followed by the details of the application of these probabilistic models to solve the FSS problem. The next section shows a comparison of these EDA approaches with respect to GAs in a set of real and artificial large dimensionality datasets. We finish the chapter with a brief set of conclusions and a description of possible avenues of future research in the field.

FEATURE SUBSET SELECTION TASK: A SEARCH PROBLEM

Our work is associated with Machine Learning and Data Mining, but FSS literature includes numerous works from other fields such as Pattern Recognition (Jain & Chandrasekaran, 1982; Kittler, 1978), Statistics (Miller, 1990; Narendra & Fukunaga, 1997) and Text-Learning (Mladenic, 1998; Yang & Pedersen, 1997). Thus, different research communities have exchanged and shared ideas on dealing with the FSS problem. A good review of FSS methods can be found in Liu and Motoda (1998).

The objective of FSS in a Machine Learning or a Data Mining framework (Aha & Bankert, 1994) is to *reduce the number of features used to characterize a dataset so as to improve a learning algorithm's performance on a given task*. Our objective will be the maximization of classification accuracy in a specific task for a specific learning algorithm; as a side effect, we will have a reduction in the number of features needed to induce the final classification model. The feature selection task can be viewed as a search problem, with each state in the search space identifying a subset of possible features. A partial ordering on this space, with each child having exactly one more feature than its parents, can be created.

The structure of FSS's search space suggests that any feature selection method must decide on four basic issues that determine the nature of the search process (Blum & Langley, 1997): a starting point in the search space, an organization of the search, an evaluation strategy for the feature subsets and a criterion for halting the search.

1. **The starting point in the space**. This determines the direction of the search. One might start with no features at all and successively add them, or one might start with all the features and successively remove them. One might also select an initial state somewhere in the middle of the search space.

2. **The organization of the search**. This determines the strategy for the search. Roughly speaking, search strategies can be *complete* or *heuristic*. The basis of the *complete* search is the systematic examination of every possible feature subset. Three classic complete search implementations are depth-first, breadth-first, and branch and bound search (Narendra & Fukunaga, 1977). On the other hand, among *heuristic* algorithms, there are *deterministic heuristic* algorithms and *non-deterministic heuristic* ones. Classic *deterministic heuristic* FSS algorithms are sequential forward selection and sequential backward elimination (Kittler, 1978), floating selection methods (Pudil, Novovicova & Kittler, 1994) and best-first search methods (Kohavi & John, 1997). They are deterministic in the sense that their runs always obtain the same solution. *Non-deterministic heuristic* search is used to escape from local optima. Randomness is used for this purpose and this implies that one should not expect the same solution from different runs. Two classic implementations of non-deterministic search engines are the frequently applied Genetic Algorithms

(Siedelecky & Sklansky, 1988) and Simulated Annealing (Doak, 1992).

3. **Evaluation strategy for feature subsets**. The evaluation function identifies promising areas of the search space by calculating the goodness of each proposed feature subset. The objective of the FSS algorithm is to maximize this function. The search algorithm uses the value returned by the evaluation function to guide the search. Some evaluation functions carry out this objective by looking only at the intrinsic characteristics of the data and measuring the power of a feature subset to discriminate between the classes of the problem: these evaluation functions are grouped under the title of *filter* strategies. These evaluation functions are usually monotonic and increase with the addition of features that can later damage the predictive accuracy of the final classifier. However, when the goal of FSS is maximization of classifier accuracy, the features selected should depend not only on the features and the target concept to be learned, but also on the special characteristics of the supervised classifier (Kohavi & John, 1997). The *wrapper* concept was proposed for this: it implies that the FSS algorithm conducts the search for a good subset by using the classifier itself as a part of the evaluation function, i.e., the same classifier that will be used to induce the final classification model. Once the classification algorithm is fixed, the idea is to train it with the feature subset found by the search algorithm, estimating the predictive accuracy on the training set and using that accuracy as the value of the evaluation function for that feature subset. In this way, any representational biases of the classifier used to construct the final classification model are included in the FSS process. The role of the supervised classification algorithm is the principal difference between the filter and wrapper approaches.

4. **Criterion for halting the search**. An intuitive criterion for stopping the search is the improvement of the evaluation function value of alternative subsets. Another classic criterion is to fix a limit on the number of possible solutions to be visited during the search.

THE EDA PARADIGM

Many combinatorial optimization algorithms have no mechanism for capturing the relationships among the variables of the problem. The related literature has many papers proposing different heuristics in order to implicitly capture these relationships. GAs implicitly capture these relationships by concentrating samples on combinations of high-performance members of the current population through the use of the crossover operator. Crossover combines the information contained within pairs of selected 'parent' solutions by placing random subsets of each parent's bits into their respective positions in a new 'child' solution. In GAs no explicit information is kept about which groups of variables jointly contribute to the quality of candidate solutions. The crossover operation is randomized and could disrupt many of these relationships among the variables; therefore, most of the crossover operations yield unproductive results and the discovery of the global optima could be delayed.

On the other hand, GAs are also criticized in the literature for three aspects (Larrañaga, Etxeberria, Lozano & Peña, 2000):

- the large number of parameters and their associated preferred optimal selection or tuning process (Grefenstette, 1986);
- the extremely difficult prediction of the movements of the populations in the search space; and
- their incapacity to solve the well-known deceptive problems (Goldberg, 1989).

Linkage Learning (LL) is the identification of groups of variables (or Building Blocks, BBs) that are related. Instead of extending the GA, the idea of the explicit discovery of these relationships during the optimization process itself has emerged from the roots of the GA community. One way to discover these relationships is to estimate the joint distribution of promising solutions and to use this estimate in order to generate new individuals. A general scheme of the algorithms based on this principle is called the Estimation of Distribution Algorithm (EDA) (Müehlenbein & Paab, 1996). In EDA there are no crossover nor mutation operators, and the new population of individuals (solutions) is sampled from a probability distribution which is estimated from the selected individuals. This is the basic scheme of the EDA paradigm:

1. $D_o \leftarrow$ Generate N individuals (the initial population) randomly
2. Repeat for $l = 1,2,...$ until a stop criterion is met:
   2.1 $DS_{l-1} \leftarrow$ Select $S \leq N$ individuals from D_{l-1} according to a selection method
   2.2 $p_l (\mathbf{x}) = p(\mathbf{x} \mid DS_{l-1}) \leftarrow$ Estimate the joint probability distribution of selected individuals
   2.3. $D_l \leftarrow$ Sample N individuals (the new population) from $p_l (\mathbf{x})$

However, estimating the distribution is a critical task in EDA. The simplest way to estimate the distribution of good solutions assumes the independence between the features of the problem. New candidate solutions are sampled by only regarding the proportions of the values of the variables independently to the remaining ones. Population Based Incremental Learning (PBIL) (Baluja, 1994), Compact Genetic Algorithm (cGA) (Harik, Lobo & Goldberg, 1997), Univariate Marginal Distribution Algorithm (UMDA) (Müehlenbein, 1997) and Bit-Based Simulated Crossover (BSC) (Syswerda, 1993) are four algorithms of this type. In our work we use the PBIL and BSC algorithms.

In PBIL, the probability distribution to sample each variable of an individual of the new population is learned in the following way:

$$p_l (x_i) = (1-\alpha) \cdot p_{l-1}(x_i \mid D_{l-1}) + \alpha \cdot p_{l-1}(x_i \mid DS_{l-1})$$

- x_i is the i-th value of the variable X_i;
- $p_{l-1}(x_i \mid D_{l-1})$ and $p_{l-1}(x_i \mid DS_{l-1})$ are the probability distributions of the variable

i in the old population and among selected individuals, respectively; and
- α is a user parameter which we fix it to 0.5.

For each possible value of every variable, BSC assigns a probability proportional to the evaluation function of those individuals that in the generation take the previous value:

$$p_l(x_i) = e(I_i) / e(I)$$

- $e(I_i)$ is the sum of the evaluation function values of the individuals with value x_i in the variable X_i; and
- $e(I)$ is the sum of the evaluation function values of all individuals.

The estimation of the joint probability distribution can also be done in a fast way without assuming the hypothesis of independence between the variables of the problem (which in some problems, is far away from the reality), and only taking into account dependencies between pairs of variables and discarding dependencies between groups of more variables.

Efforts covering pairwise interactions among the features of the problem have generated algorithms such as: MIMIC which uses simple chain distributions (De Bonet, Isbell & Viola, 1997), Baluja and Davies (1997) use the so-called dependency trees and the Bivariate Marginal Distribution Algorithm (BMDA) was created by Pelikan and Müehlenbein (1999). The method proposed by Baluja and Davies (1997) was inspired by the work of Chow and Liu (1968). In this chapter, we call TREE the dependency tree algorithm presented in the work of Chow and Liu (1968) . In our work we use the MIMIC and TREE algorithms.

In MIMIC, the joint probability distribution is factorized by a chain structure. Given a permutation of the numbers between 1 and d, $\Pi = i1 , i2 ,..., id$, MIMIC searches for the best permutation between the d variables in order to find the chain distribution which is closest with respect to the Kullback-Leibler distance to the set of selected individuals:

$$p_l(\mathbf{x}) = p(X_{i1} | X_{i2}) . p(X_{i2} | X_{i3}) ... p(X_{id-1} | X_{id}) . p(X_{id})$$

The TREE algorithm induces the optimal dependency tree structure in the sense that among all possible trees, its probabilistic structure maximizes the likelihood of selected individuals when they are drawn from any unknown distribution. See Figure 1 for a graphical representation of MIMIC and TREE models.

Figure 1: Graphical representation of MIMIC and TREE probabilistic models

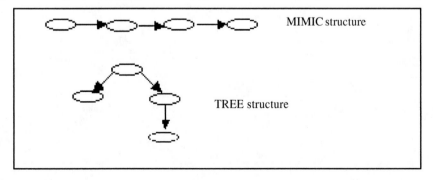

Several approaches covering higher order interactions include the use of Bayesian networks to factorize the joint probability distribution of selected individuals. In this way, the EBNA (Etxeberria & Larrañaga, 1999) and BOA (Pelikan, Goldberg & Cantú-Paz, 1999) are two algorithms of this type. The FDA (Müehlenbein & Mahning, 1999) multivariate algorithm uses a previously fixed factorization of the joint probability distribution. Harik (1999) presents an algorithm (Extend compact Genetic Algorithm, EcGA), whose basic idea consists of factorizing the joint probability distribution in a product of marginal distributions of variable size; these marginal distributions of variable size are related to the variables that are contained in the same group and to the probability distributions associated with them. For a more complete review of the different EDA approaches, see the work of Larrañaga, Etxeberria, Lozano, Sierra, Inza and Peña (1999).

FSS BY EDAS IN LARGE-SCALE DOMAINS: THE BASIC COMPONENTS

Many of the works related in the previous section notify of a faster discovery of the global optimum by EDA algorithms than GAs for certain combinatorial optimization problems. Harik (1999) and Pelikan and Müehlenbein (1999) show several intuitive and well-known problems where the GAs, when the crossover operator is applied, frequently disrupt optimum relationships (or Building Blocks) among features. In this way, these optimum relationships that appear in the parent solutions will disappear in the children solutions and the discovery of the global optimum will be delayed. Thus, these authors note that EDA approaches are able to

Figure 2: Application of the EDA paradigm to solve the FSS task

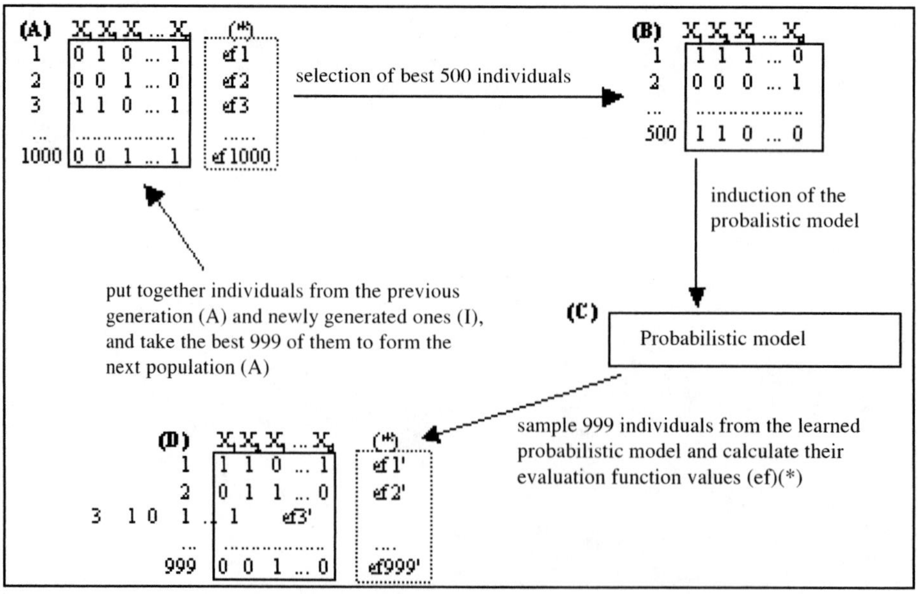

first discover and then maintain these relationships during the entire optimization process, producing a faster discovery of the global optimum than GAs.

In order to avoid the evaluation of larger amounts of possible solutions (and its associated CPU time), a fast discovery of high fitness areas in the search space is desired in the FSS problem. Bearing this purpose in mind, we use an EDA-inspired approach for FSS. We propose the use of the PBIL, BSC, MIMIC and TREE models to represent the probability distribution of the set of candidate solutions for the FSS problem, resulting in the FSS-PBIL, FSS-BSC, FSS-MIMIC and FSS-TREE algorithms. Although Bayesian networks are an attractive paradigm, the large dimensionality of the employed datasets discourages its use: a large number of individuals is needed to induce a reliable Bayesian network in domains of large dimensionality (Friedman & Yakhini, 1996). In this way, we prefer the use of simpler probabilistic models that avoid an increase in the number of individuals of the population such as PBIL, BSC, MIMIC and TREE.

In this way, we propose the use of these four EDA-inspired algorithms to tackle the FSS task. Using an intuitive notation to represent each individual (there are n bits in each possible solution, each bit indicating whether a feature is present (1) or absent (0)), we can see in Figure 2 an overview of the application of the EDA approach in the FSS problem: FSS-PBIL, FSS-BSC, FSS-MIMIC and FSS-TREE use this scheme and they only differ in the specific probabilistic model which factorizes the probability distribution of the best solutions in each generation of the search.

A population size of $1,000$ individuals is considered. Range-based selection is proposed, i.e., selecting the best 500 individuals of the population to induce the probabilistic model. Probabilistic Logic Sampling (PLS) (Henrion, 1988) is used to sample new individuals from the induced probabilistic model.

The way in which the new population is created must be pointed out. In the given procedure, all individuals from the previous population are discarded and the new population is composed of all newly created individuals (or 'offspring'). This has the problem of losing the best individuals that have been previously generated, therefore, the following minor change has been made: instead of discarding all the individuals, we maintain the best individual of the previous generation and create 999 new individuals.

An elitist approach is used to form iterative populations. Instead of directly discarding all the individuals from the previous generation by replacing them with 999 newly generated ones, all the individuals from the previous generation and the new ones are put together and the best 999 taken among them. These best 999 individuals form the new population together with the best individual of the previous generation. In this way, the population converges faster to the best individuals found; although this implies a risk of losing diversity within the population, when a wrapper evaluation approach is employed, a more relaxed approach for the selection of individuals could require prohibitive computation times.

Characteristics of the Evaluation Function

A wrapper approach is used here to calculate the evaluation function value of each proposed individual or feature subset. The value of the evaluation function of a feature subset found by the search technique, once the supervised classifier is fixed, is given by an accuracy estimation on training data. The accuracy estimation, seen as a random variable, has an intrinsic uncertainty. A 10-fold cross-validation multiple run, combined with a heuristic proposed by Kohavi and John (1997), is used to control the intrinsic uncertainty of the evaluation function. The heuristic works as follows:

• if the standard deviation of the accuracy estimate is above *1%*, another 10-fold cross-validation is executed; and

• this is repeated until the standard deviation drops below *1%*, up to a maximum of five times.

In this way, small datasets will be cross-validated many times, but larger ones may only be once. Although the search algorithm is independent of the specific supervised classifier used within its wrapper approach, in our set of experiments we will use the well-known Naive-Bayes (NB) (Cestnik, 1990) supervised classifier. This is a simple and fast classifier which uses Bayes rule to predict the class for each test instance, assuming that features are independent of each other given the class. Due to its simplicity and fast induction, it is commonly used on Data Mining tasks of high dimensionality (Kohavi & John, 1997; Mladenic, 1998). The probability of discrete features is estimated from data using maximum likelihood estimation and applying the Laplace correction. A normal distribution is assumed to estimate the class conditional probabilities for continuous attributes. Unknown values in the test instance are skipped. Despite its simplicity and its independence assumption among variables, the literature shows that the NB classifier gives remarkably high accuracy in many domains (Langley & Sage, 1994), and especially in medical ones. Despite its good scaling with irrelevant features, NB can improve its accuracy level by discarding correlated or redundant features. Because of its independence assumption of features to predict the class, NB is degraded by correlated features which violate this independence assumption. Thus, FSS can also play a 'normalization' role that discards these groups of correlated features, and ideally selects just one of them in the final model.

The Relevance of the Stopping Criteria

To stop the search algorithm, we have adopted an intuitive stopping criteria which takes the number of instances in the training set into account. In this way, we try to avoid the 'overfitting' problem (Jain & Zongker, 1997):

• for datasets with more than *2,000* instances, the search is stopped when in a sampled new generation no feature subset appears with an evaluation function value improving the best subset found in the previous generation. Thus, the best subset of the search, found in the previous generation, is returned as the search's solution; and

- for smaller datasets the search is stopped when in a sampled new generation no feature subset appears with an evaluation function value improving, at least with a p-value smaller than *0.1* (using a 10-fold cross-validated paired *t* test between the folds of both estimations, taking only the first run into account when 10-fold cross-validation is repeated multiple times), the value of the evaluation function of the best feature subset of the previous generation. Thus, the best subset of the previous generation is returned as the search's solution.

For larger datasets the 'overfitting' phenomenom has less impact and we hypothesize that an improvement in the accuracy estimation over the training set will be coupled with an improvement in generalization accuracy on unseen instances. On the contrary, for smaller datasets, in order to avoid the 'overfitting' risk, continuation of the search is only allowed when a significant improvement in the accuracy estimation of the best individuals of consecutive generations appears. We hypothesize that when this significant improvement appears, the 'overfitting' risk decays and there is a basis for further generalization accuracy improvement over unseen instances.

The work of Ng (1997) can be consulted to understand the essence of this stopping criterion. The author demonstrates that when cross-validation is used to select from a large pool of different classification models in a noisy task with too small a training set, it may not be advisable to pick the model with minimum cross-validation error, and a model with higher cross-validation error could have better generalization power over novel test instances.

Another concept to consider in this stopping criterion is the wrapper nature of the proposed evaluation function. The evaluation function value of each visited solution (the accuracy estimation of the NB classifier on the training set by 10-fold cross-validation multiple runs, using only the features proposed by the solution) needs several seconds to be calculated. As the creation of a new generation of individuals implies the evaluation of *1,000* new individuals, we only allow the search to continue when it demonstrates that it is able to escape from the local optima, discovering new 'best' solutions in each generation. When the wrapper approach is used, the CPU time must also be controlled: we hypothesize that when the search is allowed to continue by our stopping criterion, the CPU times to evaluate a new generation of solutions are justified. For a larger study about this stopping criterion, the work of Inza, Larrañaga, Etxeberria and Sierra (2000) can be consulted.

EMPIRICAL COMPARISON

In a first step we test the power of FSS-PBIL, FSS-BSC, FSS-MIMIC and FSS-TREE in six real and large-dimensionality datasets. Table 1 reflects the principal characteristics of the datasets. All except *Cloud* dataset (Aha & Bankert, 1994) can

Table 1: Details of experimental domains

Domain	Number of instances	Number of features
Audiology	226	69
Arrhythmia	452	279
Cloud	1,834	204
DNA	3,186	180
Internet advertisement	3,279	1,558
Spambase	4,601	57

be download from the *UCI Repository* (Murphy, 1995).

The power of four EDA algorithms is compared with two GAs:

* a GA with one-point crossover (FSS-GA-o);
* a GA with uniform crossover (FSS-GA-u).

Although the optimal selection of parameters is still an open problem on GAs (Grefenstette, 1986), for both GAs, guided by the recommendations of Bäck (1996), the probability of crossover is set to *1.0* and the mutation probability to *1/ (total_number_of_features)* (these values are so common in the literature). Fitness-proportionate selection is used to select individuals for crossover. In order to avoid any bias in the comparison, the remaining GA parameters are the same as EDA's: the exposed evaluation and stopping criteria, the population size is set to 1,000 and the new population is formed by the best members from both the old population and offspring.

Due to the non-deterministic nature of EDAs and GAs, five replications of twofold cross-validation (*5x2cv*) are applied to assess the predictive generalization accuracy of the compared FSS algorithms. In each replication, the available data are randomly partitioned into two equally sized sets S_1 and S_2. The FSS algorithm is trained on each set and tested on the other set. In this way, the reported accuracies are the mean of 10 accuracies. We extend the comparison by running the Naive-Bayes classifier without feature selection. Tables 2 and 3 show the accuracy results

Table 2: Accuracy percentages (and their standard deviation) of the Naive-Bayes (NB) classifier without feature selection and using FSS-GA-o and FSS-GA-u; the last row shows the average accuracy percentages for all six domains

Domain	without FSS	FSS-GA-o	FSS-GA-u
Audiology	52.39 ± 5.56 =	68.29 ± 2.98	68.44 ± 4.46
Arrhythmia	39.91 ± 8.50 =	63.23 ± 3.95	64.73 ± 3.52
Cloud	68.18 ± 2.09 =	74.49 ± 1.93	75.17 ± 1.22
DNA	93.93 ± 0.67	94.00 ± 0.75	95.01 ± 0.56
Internet adv.	95.23 ± 0.40 S	96.10 ± 0.12	96.38 ± 0.47
Spambase	81.71 ± 0.92 =	88.92 ± 1.45	88.77 ± 1.28
Average	71.88	80.83	81.41

Table 3: Accuracy percentages of the Naive-Bayes (NB) classifier using FSS-PBIL, FSS-BSC, FSS-MIMIC and FSS-TREE; the last row shows the average accuracy percentages for all six domains

Domain	FSS-PBIL	FSS-BSC	FSS-MIMIC	FSS-TREE
Audiology	70.22 ± 2.78	68.29 ± 3.18	68.88 ± 3.93	70.09 ± 4.12
Arrhythmia	64.62 ± 2.70	65.01 ± 2.22	64.33 ± 1.82	64.51 ± 2.59
Cloud	75.18 ± 1.30	76.24 ± 1.25	76.31 ± 0.95	75.84 ± 0.98
DNA	94.86 ± 0.64	95.40 ± 0.40	95.53 ± 0.29	95.40 ± 0.28
Internet adv.	96.49 ± 0.21	96.37 ± 0.41	96.46 ± 0.46	96.69 ± 0.63
Spambase	88.63 ± 1.36	89.52 ± 1.38	89.80 ± 0.79	89.60 ± 0.93
Average	81.66	81.80	81.88	82.02

Table 4: Cardinalities of finally selected feature subsets for the Naive-Bayes (NB) classifier without feature selection and using FSS-GA-o and FSS-GA-u; it must be taken into account that when no FSS is applied to NB, it uses all the features

Domain	without FSS	FSS-GA-o	FSS-GA-u
Audiology	69	14.00 ± 3.68	15.33 ± 3.50
Arrhythmia	279	15.40 ± 3.02	18.30 ± 4.71
Cloud	204	26.40 ± 4.45	27.60 ± 3.86
DNA	180	59.00 ± 8.35	55.80 ± 6.46
Internet adv.	1,558	113.10 ± 7.52	108.00 ± 5.35
Spambase	57	29.20 ± 3.88	29.00 ± 4.24

Table 5: Cardinalities of finally selected features subsets for the Naive-Bayes (NB) classifier using FSS-PBIL, FSS-BSC, FSS-MIMIC and FSS-TREE

Domain	FSS-PBIL	FSS-BSC	FSS-MIMIC	FSS-TREE
Audiology	10.66 ± 2.50	14.33 ± 4.67	13.33 ± 3.14	12.50 ± 2.34
Arrhythmia	13.60 ± 1.95	13.40 ± 2.36	17.60 ± 2.83	20.50 ± 6.13
Cloud	26.40 ± 3.47	30.00 ± 3.59	29.50 ± 4.83	30.60 ± 4.08
DNA	56.90 ± 5.83	56.90 ± 5.89	57.40 ± 7.04	59.40 ± 5.10
Internet adv.	114.30 ± 5.65	120.25 ± 18.00	122.25 ± 8.88	125.00 ± 17.60
Spambase	28.80 ± 3.82	29.10 ± 3.78	29.10 ± 3.41	30.50 ± 3.40

on the datasets and the corresponding standard deviation.

A deeper analysis of the accuracy results is carried out by means of statistical tests. The 5x2cv F test (Alpaydin, 1999) is performed to determine the significance degree of obtained accuracy differences among different approaches. In each dataset of Tables 2 and 3, the symbol '†' denotes a statistically significant difference to the algorithm with the best estimated accuracy at the $\alpha = 0.05$ confidence level; '*', significance at the $\alpha = 0.1$ confidence level. The meaning of these symbols is the same in all the tables of this chapter. Tables 4 and 5 show the average (and its standard deviation) number of features selected by each approach. Experiments are executed on an SGI-Origin 200 computer using the Naive-Bayes algorithm's implementation of the *MLC++* (Kohavi, Sommerfield & Dougherty, 1997) software.

With the use of FSS approaches, statistically significant accuracy improvements and notable dimensionality reductions are achieved relative to the no-FSS approach in all except the *DNA* dataset. All six FSS algorithms obtain similar accuracy results and dimensionality reductions in all the domains. Although five FSS approaches obtain similar accuracy results in all the datasets, we note significant differences in the number of generations needed to arrive at these similar accuracy levels. Table 6 shows which generation FSS algorithms halt in, using the explained stopping criteria.

Table 6 shows two notably different kinds of behavior. For each domain in Table 6, statistically significant differences relative to the algorithm which needs the lowest number of generations are noted. The results show that FSS-BSC, FSS-MIMIC and FSS-TREE arrive faster to similar fitness areas than FSS-PBIL and both of the GA approaches in all the domains. The capture of the underlying structure of the problem and the discovery and maintenance of feature relationships during the optimization process seems to be essential: as FSS-MIMIC and FSS-TREE are able to cover interactions of order-two among the features of the task, this could be the reason for their good behavior. Note the good behavior of FSS-BSC, a probabilistic algorithm which does not cover interactions among domain features: the explanation of these FSS-BSC results could be its direct use of the accuracy percentages to estimate the univariate probabilities, probabilities which are simulated to generate the new solutions of each EDA-generation. On the other hand, the behavior of FSS-PBIL, the other order-one probabilistic algorithm, is similar to that of the GA approaches. We suspect that the explanation of this result is the absence of a tuning process to select a value for the α parameter: previous studies indicate that a good selection of the PBIL α parameter is a critical task (González, Lozano & Larrañaga, 1999).

Because of the large dimensionality of the datasets, when the wrapper approach is employed to estimate the goodness of a feature subset, faster discovery of similar fitness solutions becomes a critical task. Despite the faster nature of the NB

Table 6: Mean stop-generation for FSS algorithms; the standard deviation of the mean is also reported; the initial generation is considered to be the zero generation

Domain	FSS-GA-o	FSS-GA-u	FSS-PBIL	FSS-BSC	FSS-MIMIC	FSS-TREE
Audiology	5.80 ± 0.42 =	4.60 ± 0.96 S	5.20 ± 1.03 S	2.50 ± 0.70	2.80 ± 0.78	2.80 ± 0.78
Arrhythmia	8.70 ± 0.48 =	8.80 ± 0.42 =	8.30 ± 0.48 S	7.10 ± 0.73	7.00 ± 0.66	7.20 ± 0.78
Cloud	10.50 ± 0.52 S	10.60 ± 1.07 S	10.40 ± 0.84	8.40 ± 0.51	8.40 ± 0.69	8.30 ± 0.82
DNA	12.80 ± 0.91 =	11.80 ± 0.42 =	11.30 ± 0.48 =	8.70 ± 0.82	8.10 ± 0.73	8.40 ± 0.69
Internet adv.	4.70 ± 1.41	5.00 ± 1.41	5.00 ± 0.66	4.40 ± 1.26	4.30 ± 0.67	4.00 ±1.63
Spambase	4.80 ± 1.03	5.20 ± 0.63	5.50 ± 1.17	4.20 ± 0.91	3.70 ± 0.82	4.20 ± 1.22

classifier, a large amount of CPU time is saved by avoiding the simulation of several generations of solutions. In order to understand the advantages of the EDA approach relative to the GA approach, CPU times for the induction of the probabilistic models must be studied: the EDA approach has the added overhead of the calculation of probabilistic models in each EDA-generation. Table 7 shows, for each domain, the average CPU times to induce the associated probabilistic model in each generation. The last column also shows the average CPU times needed to estimate the predictive accuracy of a single feature subset by the NB classifier: note that the times in the last column are not comparable with the previous columns, but they help to understand the magnitude of the CPU time savings when fewer generations are needed to achieve similar accuracy results.

As CPU times for the induction of probabilistic models are insignificant in all domains except *Internet advertisements*, the CPU time savings relative to GA approaches shown in Table 6 are maintained. In the case of the *Internet advertisements* domain, as order-two probabilistic approaches (MIMIC and TREE) need a large amount of CPU time in each generation, the advantage of using them (in CPU time savings) relative to GA approaches is considerably reduced. It must be noted that GA CPU times for recombination operations in each generation are nearly zero.

Experiments in Artificial Domains

In order to enrich the comparison among GA and EDA approaches, we have designed three artificial datasets of *2,000* instances each, where the feature subset which induces each domain is known; *Red60of1* and *Red30of3* have *100* and *Red30of2 80* continuous features in the range *(3,6)*. The target concept in all three domains is to determine whether an instance is nearer (using Euclidean distance) to *(0,0,...,0)* or *(9,9,...,9)*. At first, all *21* features participate in the distance calculation. As NB's predictive power is heavily damaged by redundant features, groups of repeated features are generated in the following way:

- no interactions appear among the features of the *Red60of1* domain. While *60* features induce the class of the domain, the remaining *40* features are

Table 7: Average CPU times (in seconds) for the induction of different probabilistic models (standard deviations are nearly zero) in each generation of the EDA search; the last column shows the average CPU time to estimate the predictive accuracy of a feature subset by the NB classifier

Domain	PBIL	BSC	MIMIC	TREE	Naive-Bayes
Audiology	1.2	1.3	1.8	2.2	1.0
Arrhythmia	4.0	4.2	12.2	25.3	2.6
Cloud	2.3	2.4	6.5	14.6	7.2
DNA	1.8	2.0	4.8	10.9	5.3
Internet adv.	101.1	106.4	808.5	1,945.6	9.8
Spambase	0.8	0.9	1.2	1.8	8.2

irrelevant;

- There are *30* groups of *two* repeated features each in the *Red30of2* domain while the remaining *20* features are not repeated. The class of the domain is induced by these *20* individual features and one feature from each of the *30* groups;
- There are *30* groups of *three* repeated features each in the *Red30of3* domain while the *10* individual features are not repeated. The class of the domain is induced by these single *10* features and one feature from each of the *30* groups.

While the degree of the relations among the features of *Red60of1* is well suited to be covered by probabilistic algorithms of order-one, approaches of order-two are needed for *Red30of2* and approaches of order three (i.e., Bayesian networks) for *Red30of3*; conditional probabilities for a variable given the value of another variable and also for a variable given values of a set of other variables should be considered in *Red30of3*.

Table 8 shows the generation where GA and EDA approaches discover a feature subset that equalizes or surpasses the estimated accuracy level of the feature subset which induces the domain. For each domain, statistically significant differences relative to the algorithm which needs the lowest number of generations are also shown in Table 8.

In *Red60of1*, a domain with no interactions among the variables of the problem, the good behavior of GA approaches relative to EDA order-two approaches must be noted. We think that the absence of a tuning process (González et al., 1999) to fix the *a* parameter of PBIL is critical to understanding its bad behavior in this domain. However, with the appearance of interacting features in the tasks *Red30of2* and *Red30of3*, the performance of order-two probabilistic approaches (MIMIC and TREE) is significantly better than the remaining algorithms; this superiority of EDA order-two approaches relative to GAs and order-one approaches in domains with interacting features is also noted in the literature (De Bonet et al., 1997; Pelikan & Müehlenbein, 1999). In this way, we hypothesize that in natural domains, the superior behavior of order-two probabilistic approaches relative to order-one approaches and GAs is due to the existence of interacting features in these tasks.

Table 8's results are achieved when the interacting variables of the same group are mapped together in the individual's representation. While GA-u and the EDA

Table 8: Number of generations needed on average (and their standard deviation) by FSS-GA-o, FSS-GA-u, FSS-PBIL, FSS-BSC, FSS-MIMIC and FSS-TREE to discover a feature subset that equalizes or surpasses the estimated accuracy level of the feature subset which induces the domain; the initial generation is considered to be the zero generation

Domain	FSS-GA-o	FSS-GA-u	FSS-PBIL	FSS-BSC	FSS-MIMIC	FSS-TREE
Red60of1	6.70 ± 0.48 =	4.10 ± 0.31	12.80 ± 0.91 =	7.60 ± 0.51 =	8.60 ± 0.51 =	8.00 ± 0.47 =
Red30of2	22.40 ± 4.22 =	73.50 ± 5.73 =	66.30 ± 7.52 =	36.40 ± 3.13 =	15.10 ± 2.33	10.90 ± 1.52
Red30of3	21.00 ± 2.26 =	119.00 ± 5.27 =	113.80 ± 8.76 =	89.50 ± 17.6 =	18.90 ± 2.13	16.30 ± 1.33

approach are not influenced by the positions of features in the individual's representation, GA-o noticeably suffers when interacting features are not coded together. When we perform the same set of experiments but randomly separating the interacting features in the individual's representation, FSS-GA-o needs the following number of generations to discover a feature subset which equalizes or surpasses the estimated accuracy level of the feature subset that induces the domain:

- 46.70 ± 6.53 in *Red30of2*;
- 48.00 ± 5.88 in *Red30of3*.

The results show a large increment in the number of generations needed by FSS-GA-o. This phenomenon is noted in the GA literature by many authors (Harik & Goldberg, 1996; Thierens & Goldberg, 1993), where a close encoding of related variables aids GA with one-point crossover to not disrupt these relationships during the recombination process. As the *Red60of1* domain has no interactions among the features of the task, it is not included in this comparison.

CONCLUSIONS AND FUTURE WORK

As an alternative to GAs, the application of the EDA paradigm to solve the well- known FSS problem on datasets of a large dimensionality has been studied. As the application of Bayesian networks is discarded in this kind of large dimensionality tasks, four simple probabilistic models (PBIL, BSC, MIMIC and TREE) have been used within the EDA paradigm to factorize the probability distribution of best individuals of the population of possible solutions. MIMIC and TREE are able to cover interactions between pairs of variables and PBIL and BSC assume the independence among the variables of the problem. We note that using three of these four probabilistic models (BSC, MIMIC and TREE), GA approaches need more generations than the EDA approach to discover similar fitness solutions. We show this behavior on a set of natural and artificial datasets where these three EDA approaches carry out a faster discovery than the other approaches of the feature relationships and the underlying structure of the problem. In this way, when the wrapper approach is used, this fast discovery of high fitness solutions is highly desirable to save CPU time. However, because of the high CPU times needed for the induction of order-two algorithms in the *Internet advertisements* domain, the CPU time savings produced by this reduction in the number of solutions relative to GA approaches is noticeably reduced.

As future work, we envision the use of other probabilistic models with large dimensionality datasets, models which assume small order dependencies among the variables of the domain. Another interesting possibility is the use of parallel algorithms to induce Bayesian networks in these kinds of tasks (Xiang & Chu, 1999). When dimensionalities are higher than *1,000* variables, research is also needed on the reduction of CPU times associated with the use of probabilistic order-two approaches.

Biological Data Mining is an interesting application area of FSS techniques

(Ben-Dor, Bruhn, Friedman, Nachman, Schummer, Yakhini, 2000). Ever since efficient and relatively cheap methods have been developed for the acquisition of biological data, data sequences of high dimensionality have been obtained. Thus, the application of an FSS procedure is an essential task.

REFERENCES

Aha, D.W., & Bankert, R.L. (1994). Feature selection for case-based classification of cloud types: An empirical comparison. In *Proceedings of the AAAI'94 Workshop on Case-Based Reasoning* (pp. 106-112).

Alpaydin, E. (1999). Combined 5x2cv *F* test for comparing supervised classification learning algorithms. *Neural Computation, 11,* 1885-1982.

Bäck, T. (1996). *Evolutionary Algorithms in Theory and Practice.* Oxford University Press.

Baluja, S. (1994). *Population-based incremental learning: A method for integrating genetic search based function optimization and competitive learning.* Pittsburgh, PA: Technical Report CMU-CS-94-163, Carnegie Mellon University.

Baluja, S., & Davies, S. (1997). Using optimal dependency-trees for combinatorial optimization: Learning the structure of the search space. In *Proceedings of the Fourteenth International Conference on Machine Learning,* 30-38.

Ben-Dor, A., Bruhn, L., Friedman, N., Nachman, I., Schummer, M., & Yakhini, Z. (2000). Tissue Classification with Gene Expression Profiles. *Journal of Computational Biology.*

Blum, A.L., & Langley, P. (1997). Selection of relevant features and examples in machine learning. *Artificial Intelligence, 97,* 245-271.

Cestnik, B. (1990). Estimating Probabilities: A crucial task in Machine Learning. In *Proceedings of the European Conference on Artificial Intelligence,* 147-149.

Chow, C., & Liu, C. (1968). Approximating discrete probability distributions with dependence trees. *IEEE Transactions on Information Theory, 14,* 462-467.

De Bonet, J.S., Isbell, C.L., & Viola, P. (1997). MIMIC: Finding optima by estimating probability densities. In *Advances in Neural Information Processing Systems,* Vol. 9. Cambridge, MA: MIT Press.

Doak, J. (1992). *An evaluation of feature selection methods and their application to computer security.* Davis, CA: Technical Report CSE-92-18, University of California at Davis.

Etxeberria, R., & Larrañaga, P. (1999). Global Optimization with Bayesian networks. In *Proceedings of the Second Symposium on Artificial Intelligence,* 332-339.

Friedman, N., & Yakhini, Z. (1996). On the Sample Complexity of Learning Bayesian Networks. In *Proceedings of the Twelveth Conference on Uncertainty in Artificial Intelligence,* 274-282.

Goldberg, D.E. (1989). *Genetic algorithms in search, optimization, and machine learning.* Reading, MA: Addison-Wesley.

González, C., Lozano, J.A., & Larrañaga, P. (1999). *The convergence behavior of PBIL algorithm: a preliminary approach.* Donostia - San Sebastián, Spain: Technical Report EHU-KZAA-IK-3/99, University of the Basque Country.

Harik, G. (1999). *Linkage Learning via Probabilistic Modelling in the ECGA.* Urbana-Champaign, ILL: IlliGAL Report 99010, University of Illinois at Urbana-Champaign, Illinois Genetic Algorithms Laboratory.

Harik, G.R., Lobo, F.G., & Goldberg, D.E. (1997). *The compact genetic algorithm*. Urbana-Champaign, ILL: IlliGAL Report 97006, University of Illinois at Urbana-Champaign, Illinois Genetic Algorithms Laboratory.

Henrion, M. (1988). Propagating uncertainty in Bayesian networks by probabilistic logic sampling. In *Uncertainty in Artificial Intelligence*, Vol. 2 (pp. 149-163). Amsterdam, The Netherlands: Elsevier Science Publishers, B.V.

Inza, I., Larrañaga, P., Etxeberria, R., & Sierra, B. (2000). Feature Subset Selection by Bayesian network based optimization. *Artificial Intelligence, 123 (1-2)*, 157-184.

Inza, I., Larrañaga, P., & Sierra, B. (2001). Feature Subset Selection by Bayesian networks: A comparison with genetic and sequential algorithms. I*nternational Journal of Approximate Reasoning*, 27(2), 143-164.

Jain, A.K., & Chandrasekaran, R. (1982). Dimensionality and sample size considerations in pattern recognition practice. In Krishnaiah, P.R. & Kanal, L.N. (Eds.), *Handbook of Statistics*, Vol. 2 (pp.835-855). Amsterdam, The Netherlands: North-Holland.

Jain, A., & Zongker, D. (1997). Feature Selection: Evaluation, Application, and Small Sample Performance. *IEEE Transactions on Pattern Analysis and Machine Intelligence, 19(2)*, 153-158.

Kittler, J. (1978). Feature Set Search Algorithms. In Chen, C.H. (Ed.), Pattern Recognition and Signal Processing (pp. 41-60). Alphen aan den Rijn, The Netherlands: Sithoff and Noordhoff.

Kohavi, R,. & John, G. (1997). Wrappers for feature subset selection. *Artificial Intelligence, 97(1-2)*, 273-324.

Kohavi, R., Sommerfield, D., & Dougherty, J. (1997). Data mining using MLC++, a Machine Learning Library in C++. *International Journal of Artificial Intelligence Tools, 6*, 537-566.

Kudo, M., & Sklansky, J. (2000). Comparison of algorithms that select features for pattern classifiers. *Pattern Recognition, 33*, 25-41.

Langley, P., & Sage, S. (1994). Induction of selective Bayesian classifiers. In *Proceedings of the Tenth Conference on Uncertainty in Artificial Intelligence*, 399-406.

Larrañaga, P., Etxeberria, R., Lozano, J.A., Sierra, B., Inza, I. &, Peña, J.M. (1999). A review of the cooperation between evolutionary computation and probabilistic graphical models. In *Proceedings of the Second Symposium on Artificial Intelligence*, 314-324.

Larrañaga, P., Etxeberria, R., Lozano, J.A., & Peña, J.M. (2000). Combinatorial Optimization by Learning and Simulation of Bayesian Networks. In *Proceedings of the Conference in Uncertainty in Artificial Intelligence*, 343-352.

Liu, H., & Motoda, H. (1998). *Feature Selection for Knowledge Discovery and Data Mining*. Norwell, MA: Kluwer Academic Publishers.

Miller, A.J. (1998). *Subset Selection in Regression*. Washington, DC: Chapman and Hall.

Mladenic, D. (1998). Feature subset selection in text-learning. In *Proceedings of the Tenth European Conference on Machine Learning*, 95-100.

Müehlenbein, H. (1996). The equation for response to selection and its use for prediction. *Evolutionary Computation, 5 (3)*, 303-346.

Müehlenbein, H., & Mahning, T. (1999). FDA: A scalable evolutionary algorithm of distributions. Binary parameters. *Evolutionary Computation, 7 (4)*, 353-376.

Müehlenbein, H., & Paab, G. (1996). From recombination of genes to the estimation of distributions. Binary parameters. In Lecture Notes in Computer Science 1411: Parallel Problem Solving from Nature - PPSN IV, 178-187.

Murphy, P. (1995). *UCI Repository of machine learning databases*. Irvine, CA: University of California, Department of Information and Computer Science.

Narendra, P., & Fukunaga, K. (1977). A branch and bound algorithm for feature subset selection. *IEEE Transactions on Computer, C-26(9)*, 917-922.

Ng, A.Y. (1997). Preventing 'Overfitting' of Cross-Validation Data. In *Proceedings of the Fourteenth Conference on Machine Learning*, 245-253.

Pelikan, M., Goldberg, D.E., & Cantú-Paz, E. (1999). *BOA: The Bayesian Optimization Algorithm*. Urbana-Champaign, ILL: IlliGAL Report 99003, University of Illinois at Urbana-Champaign, Illinois Genetic Algorithms Laboratory.

Pelikan, M., & Müehlenbein, H. (1999). The Bivariate Marginal Distribution Algorithm. In *Advances in Soft Computing-Engineering Design and Manufacturing* (pp. 521-535). London, England: Springer-Verlag.

Pudil, P., Novovicova, J., & Kittler, J. (1994). Floating Search Methods in Feature Selection. *Pattern Recognition Letters, 15(1)*, 1119-1125.

Sangüesa, R., Cortés, U., & Gisolfi, A. (1998). A parallel algorithms for building possibilistic causal networks. *International Journal of Approximate Reasoning, 18 (3-4)*, 251-270.

Siedelecky, W., & Sklansky, J. (1988). On automatic feature selection. *International Journal of Pattern Recognition and Artificial Intelligence, 2*, 197-220.

Syswerda, G. (1993). Simulated crossover in genetic algorithms. In Whitley, L.D. (Ed.), *Foundations of Genetic Algorithms*, Vol. 2 (pp. 239-255). San Mateo, CA: Morgan Kaufmann.

Thierens, D., & Goldberg, D.E. (1993). Mixing in Genetic Algorithms. In *Proceedings of the Fifth International Conference in Genetic Algorithms*, 38-45.

Vafaie, H., & De Jong, K. (1993). Robust feature selection algorithms. In *Proceedings of the Fifth International Conference on Tools with Artificial Intelligence* (pp. 356-363).

Yang, Y., & Pedersen, J.O. (1997). A Comparative Study on Feature Selection in Text-Categorization. In *Proceedings of the Fourteenth International Conference on Machine Learning*, 412-420.

Xiang, Y., & Chu, T. (1999). Parallel Learning of Belief Networks in Large and Difficult Domains. *Data Mining and Knowledge Discovery, 3 (3)*, 315-338.

Chapter VI

Towards the Cross-Fertilization of Multiple Heuristics: Evolving Teams of Local Bayesian Learners

Jorge Muruzábal
Universidad Rey Juan Carlos, Spain

Evolutionary algorithms are by now well-known and appreciated in a number of disciplines including the emerging field of data mining. In the last couple of decades, Bayesian learning has also experienced enormous growth in the statistical literature. An interesting question refers to the possible synergetic effects between Bayesian and evolutionary ideas, particularly with an eye to large-sample applications. This chapter presents a new approach to classification based on the integration of a simple local Bayesian engine within the learning classifier system rule-based architecture. The new algorithm maintains and evolves a population of classification rules which individually learn to make better predictions on the basis of the data they get to observe. Certain reinforcement policy ensures that adequate teams of these learning rules be available in the population for every single input of interest. Links with related algorithms are established, and experimental results suggesting the parsimony, stability and usefulness of the approach are discussed.

INTRODUCTION

Evolutionary algorithms (EAs) are characterized by the long-run simulation of a population of functional individuals which undergo processes of creation, selection, deployment, evaluation, recombination and deletion. There exists today a fairly wide variety of EAs that have been tested and theoretically investigated (see e.g., Banzhaf, Daida, Eiben, Garzon, Honavar, Jakiela & Smith, 1999). One of the most interesting and possibly least explored classes of EAs refers to the learning classifier system (LCS) architecture (Holland, 1986; Holland, Holyoak, Nisbett & Thagard, 1986). In this chapter we shall be concerned with a new LCS algorithm (called BYPASS) for rule-based classification. Classification is indeed a most relevant problem in the emerging data mining (DM) arena (Fayyad, Piatetsky-Shapiro, Smyth & Uthurusamy, 1996; Freitas, 1999), and many issues still require further investigation (Michie, Spiegelhalter & Taylor, 1994; Weiss & Indurkhya, 1998).

In recent years, the sustained growth and affordability of computing power has had a tremendous impact on the wide applicability of Bayesian learning (BL) methods and algorithms. As a result, a number of solid computational frameworks have already flourished in the statistics and DM literature (see for example, Buntine, 1996; Cheeseman & Stutz, 1996; Gilks, Richardson & Spiegelhalter, 1996; Heckerman, 1996). It seems fair to say that more are on their way (Chipman, George & McCulloch, 1998; Denison, Adams, Holmes & Hand, 2000; Tirri, Kontkanen, Lahtinen & Myllymäki, 2000; Tresp, 2000). BL approaches establish some prior distribution on a certain space of structures, and inferences are based on the posterior distribution arising from this prior distribution and the assumed likelihood for the training data. Predictive distributions for unseen cases can sometimes be computed on the fly, and all these distributions may be coherently updated as new data are collected.

Given the wide diversity of these paradigms, it is not surprising that synergetic effects between BL and EAs have been naturally explored along several directions. To begin with, and perhaps most obviously, many EAs are function optimizers, hence they can be used to tackle the direct maximization of the posterior distribution of interest (Franconi & Jennison, 1997). On the other hand, the Bayesian optimization algorithm (Pelikan, Goldberg & Cantú-Paz, 1999) and other *estimation of distribution algorithms*, see for example the rule-oriented approach in Sierra, Jiménez, Inza, Muruzábal & Larrañaga (2001), replace the traditional operators in EAs (crossover and mutation) with probabilistic structures capturing interdependencies among all problem variables. These structures are simulated to yield new individuals, some of which are used to build a more refined model for the next generation (see also Zhang, 2000).

By way of contrast, the BYPASS approach does not attempt to formulate any *global* model of either the variables or the population of classification rules. Examples of BL global models (and algorithms) for tree and Voronoi tessellation sets of rules are given in Chipman et al. (1998), Denison et al. (2000) and Paass and

Kindermann (1998). All these models are either anchored on non-overlapping rules, or maintain the familiar (exhaustive) tree-based interpretation, or both. The BL in BYPASS is essentially *local* in that it only affects individual rules in the population. As in other LCSs, the (self-)organization of the population relies entirely on the sequential reinforcement policy. In the case of BYPASS, however, reinforcement is in turn tightly linked to (individual) predictive *scoring*, which improves substantially when previous experience is adequately reflected via BL. This is the type of synergy or cross-fertilization explored in this chapter.

The attempted organization process in BYPASS is based as usual on *performance* by the LCS's *match set*, a subset (team or committee) of rules available for any given input. Organization of these teams may turn out to be relatively difficult depending on a variety of features including the shape and relative position of the input regions associated with output labels, as well as the appropriateness and complexity of the selected representation scheme and reinforcement policy. The dynamics of the LCS algorithm is typically quite rich: useful new rules have to find their place among other (partially overlapping) rules; tentative, poor rules add noise to the performance subsystem (which in turn affects the reinforcement process); the contribution of the typical rule discovery engine, a genetic algorithm, is hard to tune up, and so on.

These aspects make the BYPASS approach very different from other approaches based on committees of rules as, for example, Breiman's bagging trees (1996) (see also Domingos, 1997). Standard classification trees (Breiman, Friedman, Olshen & Stone, 1984) constitute a natural reference for BYPASS since they often provide rules which are essentially identical in structure. In the bagging trees algorithm, a basic tree learner is used repeatedly to provide a number of parallel, independently generated solutions, that is, no information between these solutions is *exchanged* during the building phase. These single-tree-based predictions are combined via majority voting to yield improved performance. The present LCS approach tries to extend this framework by letting the interactions between rules within teams be a critical part of the overall organization process.

Like other LCSs (Wilson, 2000), the BYPASS approach presents many appealing features from the DM perspective. The amount of memory required by the system depends on the size of the population, so huge data sets can be tentatively analyzed via reduced sets of general, long-reaching rules. LCSs are rather autonomous and can be left alone with the data for awhile; when performance is deemed appropriate, they can be halted and useful populations extracted and post-processed, or else populations can be merged and reinitialized. The induced probabilistic rules are easy to interpret and allow for characterization of broad regularities. LCSs can also benefit from parallel implementations facilitating faster learning when needed. Last but not least, the architecture is open-ended, so further heuristics can be incorporated in the future.

This chapter reviews the BYPASS algorithm and illustrates its performance in both artificial and real data sets of moderate dimensionality. It is shown that the system can indeed self-organize and thus synthesize populations of manageable size, notable generality, and reasonable predictive power. These empirical results are put in perspective with respect to the tree representation and bagging trees method. The organization is as follows. The second section reviews some relevant background covering LCSs and classification trees. A detailed description of the BYPASS algorithm is then provided, followed by the empirical evidence and a discussion of performance by other methods and prospects for future work. The chapter closes with some conclusions.

BACKGROUND

In this section we first review basic aspects of the LCS architecture; then we focus on the classification problem and discuss key differences between BYPASS and other LCSs for classification. Finally, we comment on the relationship with standard decision trees and the standard bagging trees approach.

While LCSs were introduced by John Holland, the father of genetic algorithms (Holland 1986, 1990; Holland et al., 1986), in recent years his original architecture has been progressively replaced by somewhat simpler variants that have nonetheless explored the main LCS tenets in certain detail (Booker, 1989; Butz, Goldberg & Stolzmann, 2000; De Jong, Spears & Gordon, 1993; Frey & Slate, 1991; Goldberg, 1990; Lanzi, Stolzmann & Wilson, 2000; Parodi & Bonelli, 1993; Robertson & Riolo, 1988; Wilson, 1987, 1998, 2000). Standard LCSs and BYPASS consist of an unstructured *population* of rules (or classifiers), all sharing the same syntax and reasoning, that evolves over time according to certain evolutionary principles. The rule population is typically initialized at random and evolves according to the interaction between rules and the environment (training sample). Training items are presented to the system on a one-at-a-time basis. The matching and performance subsystems determine how the system's response or prediction is built up from the current population. The success of this response determines how reward enters the system. Each individual rule is endowed with one or more numerical measures of its current worth, and these values are refined at each (relevant) step according to the reinforcement policy administering the reward. Rules may be removed if some of these indicators drop too low. Other indicators may guide the rule-discovery subsystem. Population size may or may not be fixed. An LCS is thus completely specified by the representation of individual rules and by the (representation-dependent) performance, reinforcement, rule discovery and rule deletion subsystems.

It is appropriate to focus now on the classification context relevant to BYPASS; for a general approach to the problem of classification, see for example Hand (1997). It is customary here to assume the availability of *training* data (x_i, y_i), $i = 1, ..., n$, where x is a numerical vector of predictors and y is the associated response, output label or known classification, $1 \leq y \leq k$. These data provide the crucial information on which some criterion to classify future x vectors (with unknown y) will be based. BYPASS classifiers are designed of course to meet the nature of these training data.

Thus, the present rules have the general structure $Q \rightarrow R$ (σ), where Q is called the receptive field, R is the rule's prediction and σ typically stores summaries of previous experience and possibly other objects of interest related to Q. Recall that, at each time step, a single item from the training file is selected and shown to the system. A first key observation is that either $x \in Q$ or $x \notin Q$ for all x and all Q. The subset of rules whose receptive fields *match* a given x (that is, $Q \ni x$) is called the *match set*, say $M = M(x)$ (as shown below, M may be empty, although this case tends to be less likely over time). The system makes a prediction $z = z(x)$ based solely on the information in M; in other words, all other rules are ignored at this time step. This prediction z is compared to the corresponding y (never used so far), and *reward* is passed along some members of M (whose σ buffers are updated). Hereafter, the current (x,y) is essentially "forgotten" and a new cycle begins.

While a wide variety of Rs and σs have been proposed in the literature, many design issues remain open to controversy. For classification tasks, LCSs typically rely on single-label predictions, say $R = \{j\}$ for some j (Holland et al., 1986; Wilson, 1998, 2000). Furthermore, once a rule is created, only σ changes, that is, both Q and R remain fixed throughout the rule's life. Thus, if a useful receptive field is discovered and happens to be attached to the wrong output label, it will most likely be discarded soon. However, in order to perform near-optimally, LCSs should be able to refine appropriately the predictive part of every single rule they consider.

The BYPASS approach provides precisely this ability by setting up a simple Multinomial-Dirichlet Bayesian model for each classifier. The Multinomial distribution is the natural choice for modeling the arrival of cases belonging to one of several categories, whereas the Dirichlet prior distribution is the standard *conjugate* family for the Multinomial choice (Denison et al., 2000). The idea behind this battery of individual models is to let R be the predictive probability distribution based on the corresponding model and all previously observed data $D(Q) = \{(x,y), x \in Q\}$. As R changes with D, all useful receptive fields have a chance to survive. Note that Q is not modified at all, yet R always presents the most up-to-date predictive distribution. The use of probability distributions in this context can be argued to enrich the knowledge representation in that classifiers measure routinely and coherently the level of uncertainty associated with their receptive fields (Muruzábal, 1995, 1999).

It is straightforward to see that this Bayesian scheme requires only the storage of the k output frequencies in $D(Q)$, say c_j, together with Dirichlet hyper-parameters $a_j, j = 1,...,k$. The classifier's predictive probability R_j becomes $R_j = (a_j + c_j)/(a_. + c_.)$, where $a_.$ and $c_.$ equal the sum of coordinates of the associated vectors. Hyper-parameters a_j are selected once and for all at birth and they can reflect different prior predictive preferences. What matters most is the sum $a_.$, which controls the prevalence of a_j in R_j as the classifier accumulates experience. That is, we can view $a_.$ as the degree of *endurance* assigned to the emerging classifier's prediction R and, as usual in BL, we can interpret it in terms of sample size supporting that particular prediction. For randomly initialized rules, $a_.$ is set to 1 (so that a is soon overridden by the incoming data).

As part of its σ structure, each classifier in BYPASS maintains also an *accuracy* measure ρ. This measure is seen to converge to the standard entropy measure of the conditional distribution of y given $x \in Q$. Thus, the rule with the best accuracy (providing the sharpest or least uncertain prediction) in each match set can be used as the *unique* rule determining the system's prediction or response. This single-winner policy is rather common in other LCSs (see, for example Butz et al., 2000), although the basic quantity on which selections are made may have nothing to do with™ the previous entropy measure. In BYPASS the accuracy measure ρ is not used to this end; rather, *all* matching rules are combined to determine the system's response and no rule plays any special role in this determination.

As noted by Butz et al. (2000), the fact that the previous LCS algorithms wish to also be useful in *navigation* problems somehow complicates the treatment of the classification problem. BYPASS does not extend trivially to navigation tasks because it is designed for *immediate* (rather than delayed) reinforcement. In any case, many LCSs have been shown to achieve optimal or near optimal performance in *both* navigation and classification tasks of some difficulty. These alternative algorithms highlight above all the richness of the LCS framework. While they vary substantially in their s objects, none includes anything comparable to the Bayesian memory records c_j.

On the other hand, Frey and Slate (1991) consider a "Holland-style" learning system to tackle a difficult letter classification task also using single-label predictions and the single-winner approach. Among other things, they showed that the introduction of *two* measures of classifier performance, respectively called *accuracy* and *utility*, led to an easier-to-optimize architecture while providing similar or even better performance figures than those based on the traditional *single* measure of strength (at the time advocated by Holland and others). The basic idea behind this duality is to distinguish the intrinsic value of a given classifier (accuracy) from its relative value given the remaining rules in the population (utility) (see Booker, 1989; Wilson, 1998) for similar divisions of classifier's value. For example, the present implementation of the accuracy measure r identifies the intrinsic value of a rule with its conditional entropy. Utility helps to prevent redundancy in that it becomes possible to remove highly accurate classifiers that are nonetheless useless as the system already possesses other, perhaps even better units to solve the same subtask.

BYPASS fully endorses this accuracy-utility paradigm pioneered by Frey and Slate (1991). In fact, their utility μ is also quite similar to that considered in BYPASS. Specifically, μ is expressed as $\mu = \kappa/\alpha$ where α is a simple age counter that increases with every datum presented to the system and κ is a raw utility counter that increases from time to time only. Overall, the BYPASS σ vector comprises four values $\sigma = (\rho, \kappa, \alpha, \lambda)$, where λ keeps track of the average size of the match sets to which the classifier belonged. As will be seen, however, only the κ scalar is crucially influential on the rule's survival: rules with small utility μ tend to be removed from the population.

This completes the description of the rule representation in BYPASS. Before we embark on the remaining aspects of the architecture, it is useful to revisit the issue of *generality*. Assume, for ease of exposition, that all predictors in x are Boolean. Then, receptive fields Q belong to $\{0,1,\#\}^n$, where # is the usual "don't care" or wildcard character. The *specificity* of a rule h is defined as the percentage of non-# in Q; it is always strictly positive (the trivial receptive field matching all inputs x is never allowed into the system). General rules have lower specificity. Too specific rules are matched rarely and tend to produce too fragmented (hence oversized) populations. On the other hand, over-general rules are too uncertain and may seriously confuse the system.

An extended debate is taking place in LCS research about the goal of achieving rules of *maximal* generality. In simulated work, these rules are usually understood as those exhibiting the *correct* level of generality, that is, the inferred rules must be specific enough to completely eliminate ambiguity yet, at the same time, general enough to disregard useless input information (Butz et al., 2000; Wilson, 1998). Both XCS and ACS present reinforcement biases and/or rule-discovery heuristics that explicitly implement both specialization and generalization pressures. These designs strike an interesting balance that reportedly helps to achieve maximal generality. However, the complex counteracting effects delivered by such heuristics may not always be easy to understand. After all, we already know that slight variations in the mutation rate alone are responsible for deep changes in many EAs (see, e.g.,Jennison & Sheehan, 1995). As shown below, BYPASS also incorporates biases towards generality, although an effort is made to keep them as implicit as possible.

The issue of generality is also closely related to classification trees. Assuming again Boolean predictors, each leaf in a tree can be seen as a single $Q \rightarrow R$ rule in BYPASS, and the number of leaves corresponds to population size. However, all receptive fields extracted from a tree constitute a *partition* of input space $\{0,1\}^n$, whereas in BYPASS no such constraint exists. A first direct implication is that just a single rule is available from each tree for any new x. Thus, it is impossible to consider a notion of rule utility as envisaged above. Rule specificity relates to tree depth: general rules are those extracted from shallow trees. The deeper a tree, the smaller the data subset at leaves and hence typically the sharper the associated R's. Deep or bushy trees have limited out-of-sample performance. For this reason, shallower trees are explicitly searched for during the usual *pruning* or generalization phase (Breiman et al., 1984).

Another way of improving single-tree performance is by forming committees of trees. Breiman's (1996) *bagging trees* approach is based on B bootstrapped samples of the original training data and proceeds by fitting a separate tree to each of them. Results from these trees are then combined via simple majority voting. It has been shown repeatedly that bagging yields a substantial improvement over single trees, although it is not entirely clear why (see for example, Domingos, 1997). Related approaches fit differential *weights* to trees prior to mixing (Hand, 1997); these alternative approaches will not be considered here.

THE BYPASS ALGORITHM

Now that we have seen basic aspects of LCSs and how the BYPASS representation relates to other learning systems, in this section we review the remaining aspects of the BYPASS algorithm, namely, its initialization, matching, performance, reinforcement, rule discovery and rule deletion policies. We will establish several further connections with other ideas in the literature. Experimental results are presented in the next section.

The initial population is always generated according to a simple extension of EXM, the exemplar-based generalization procedure, also known as the cover detector (Frey & Slate, 1991; Robertson & Riolo, 1988; Wilson, 1998). EXM randomly selects a single data item (x,y) and builds a single classifier from it. The receptive field Q is constructed by first setting $Q = x$ and then parsing through its coordinates $l = 1,...,n$: with some fixed generalization probability π, the current value x_l is switched to #, otherwise $Q_l = x_l$ is maintained. As regards R, the likelihood vector c is set to 0, whereas a places most of the mass, say a_0, at the current y and distributes $1-a_0$ evenly among the remaining labels. Naturally, $\alpha = \kappa = 0$; initial values for ρ and λ are set after the first match. This procedure is repeated until the user-input initial population size, say P_0, is obtained. No exact duplicated receptive fields are allowed into the system.

Typically only the case $\pi = .5$ is considered. When EXM is used with larger π, the system is forced to work with more general rules (unless specific rules are produced by the rule discovery heuristic *and* maintained by the system). Thus, larger π introduce a faster Bayesian learning rate (since rules become active more often) as well as a higher degree of overlap between receptive fields. However, match set size also increases steadily with decreasing specificity h. Some pilot runs are usually needed to select the most productive value for the π parameter. For DM applications, n is typically large and very large π is the only hope of achieving easy-to-interpret rules.

We now look at matching issues. A receptive field is matched if all its

Table 1: Summary of BYPASS main execution parameters. Other less important parameters (and associated values used below) are the initial population size P_0 (50 or 100); the updating constant τ (1/50); the prior hyperparameter a_0 (.7); and GA parameters, namely, type of crossover (uniform) and mutation probability β (5.0 10^{-5}). Most system parameters can be changed online.

Parameter	Description
π	Generalization bias
μ_0 (*grace*)	Utility thresholds
(p,γ)	Reward policy
θ	GA activity rate

coordinates are. For Boolean predictors l, exact matching is required: $|x_l - Q_l| < 1$. Real-valued predictors are linearly transformed and rounded to a 0-15 integer scale prior to training (see Table 2). For integer-valued predictors, matching requires only $|x_l - Q_l| < 2$. This window size seems to provide adequate flexibility and remains fixed for all predictors and all classifiers throughout all runs; for another approach to integer handling, see Wilson (2000). Eventually, the match set M may be empty for some x. Note that this becomes less likely as π increases (it will hardly be a problem below). In any case, whenever the empty M condition arises, it is immediately taken care of by a new call to EXM, after which a new input x is selected.

Once the (non-empty) M is ascertained, two system predictions are computed, namely, the single-winner (SW) and mixture-based (MIX) predictions. SW selects the classifier in M with the lowest uncertainty evaluation ρ as its best resource (and ignores the remaining classifiers; see the previous section). The maximum a posteriori (MAP) class label z_{SW} is then determined from this single R as

$$z_{SW} = \mathrm{argmax}_{1 \le j \le k} \{R_j\}.$$

On the other hand, MIX combines first the m matched Rs into the uniform mixture distribution

$$R_{MIX} = (1/m) \sum_{1 \le s \le m} R(s)$$

and then obtains the prediction z_{MIX} by MAP selection as before.

The MIX prediction is generally preferred over the SW alternative with regard to the system's reinforcement and general guidance. The MIX prediction combines multiple sources of information and it does so in a cooperative way. It can be argued that the SW predictive mode tends to favor relatively specific classifiers and therefore defeats to some extent the quest for generality. The bias towards the MIX mode of operation can be seen throughout the design of BYPASS: several system decisions are based on whether z_{MIX} is correct or not. For example, the rule-generation mechanism is always triggered by MIX failure (regardless of the success of z_{SW}).

The accuracy ρ is updated at each step (no entropy calculations are needed) according to the familiar discounting scheme

$$\rho \leftarrow (1 - \tau)\,\rho + \tau\, S_y,$$

Table 2: Artificial and real data sets used in the experiments below. n is the number of predictors and k is the number of output categories. Recall that real predictors are linearly transformed and rounded to a 0-15 integer scale prior to training; thus, in general, $Q \in \{0,1,2,...,9,A,B,C,D,E,F\}^n$. Uniform weights w_j are used in the first case. For the satellite data, output labels 1, 3 and 6 have higher frequencies f_j and therefore non-uniform weights w_j are used.

	n	k	predictors	training	test
jmultiplexer	33	8	Boolean	10,000	10,000
satellite	36	6	Real	4,435	2,000

where S_y is the well-known *score* of each individual classifier in M, namely,
$$S_y = - \log (R_y) > 0,$$
and τ is a small positive number. As noted earlier, the *SW* prediction is deemed of secondary interest only, so there would be no essential loss if ρ were omitted altogether from the current discussion of performance.

On the other hand, the individual scores S_y of matched rules are central quantities in BYPASS reinforcement policy. Clearly, the *lower* S_y, the better R at this particular x. Again, several decisions will be made depending on the absolute and relative magnitude of these S_y. Any upper bound set on S_y can be expressed equivalently as a lower bound for R_y. An important point regarding these bounds is that, no matter how they are expressed, they have an intrinsic meaning that can be cross-examined in a variety of related k-way classification problems (obviously, it

*Table 3: A single cycle based on the second multiplexer population (Figure 1). The first line is the input item (**x**,y). The second line simply places the eight output labels. Eight matched classifiers are listed next (only Q, R, and ρ are shown). Predictive distributions R are shown graphically by picking only some labels with the largest predicted probabilities. The SW mode of operation (involving the lowest accuracy) is shown to fail in the next few lines. Finally, the MIX mode is shown to succeed and the p = 3 rewarded units are reported. #s are replaced by dots (and subsets of 11 coordinates are mildly separated) for clarity.*

```
          01000111001 11011101010 11101010111          *
                                             ABCDEFGH
   0/  .......... .......... .11.......1     * *       1.911
   1/  ..0..1.1... .......... ..........     *    *    1.936
   2/  .......... 1.0....1... ..........     *      *  1.894
   3/  .......... .......... .1....1..1.     **        1.893
   4/  01...11.... .......... ..........     *       * 1.384
   5/  .......... 110......1. ..........        **     1.344
   6/  .......... 1.0....1.1. ..........        **     1.347
   7/  .......... .10..1...1. ..........        **     1.365

Single winner is:
                                             ABCDEFGH
       .......... 110......1. .......... ..         **  1.344

Predicted category is:     G
Single winner's score: 1.367

Combined prediction is:
                                             ABCDEFGH
                                                   **

Predicted category is:            H
Combined prediction's score: 1.494
Rewarded units: (5 6 7)
```

does not make sense to relate scores based on different k).

Reinforcement takes place every cycle and essentially involves the updating of each matched classifier's raw utility κ in light of the system's predicted label z_{MIX} and the current observation y. Two cases are distinguished, success or failure, and in each case different subsets of classifiers are selected from M for reward. If z_{MIX} succeeds, then classifiers with the lowest S_y should be the prime contributors. A simple idea is to reward the p lowest values. The κ counter of each of these units is updated as $\kappa \leftarrow \kappa + w_y$, where w_y depends in turn on whether all output labels are to be given the same weight or not. If so, then $w_j \equiv 1$, otherwise, $w_j = (k f_j)^{-1}$, where f_j denotes the relative frequency of the j-th output label in the training sample. The rationale is that widely different f_j make it unfair to reward all classifiers evenly. Even if all output labels show up equally often, we may have more interest in certain labels; an appropriate bias can then be introduced by appropriately chosen w_j.

In the case of z_{MIX} failure, it can be argued cogently that not all matched

Table 4: Selected classifiers by MAP label for the satellite data. All these classifiers belong to a single population obtained under ($p = 5$, $\gamma = 1.15$). The three best accuracies in each team are extracted. Receptive fields are shown first (see text for details). The last row shows predictive distributions and accuracies (in the same order). The total number of classifiers in each class is 12, 10 and 15 respectively. Again, #s are transformed into dots for ease of reference.

```
        Label j=4            Label j=5                 Label j=6

9..  ..9  ...  5..       ...  .4.  ...  ...       ...  ..7  ...  ...
...  9..  ..7  ...       .3.  ...  ...  ...       ...  ...  ...  4..
...  ...  ...  ...       .4.  ...  ...  ...       6..  ...  ..4  ...

...  ...  .7.  ...       ...  ...  ...  ...       ...  ...  .4.  3..
...  ...  ..7  ...       ...  .4.  .4.  ...       ...  ...  ...  4..
..9  ...  ...  ...       ...  5..  ...  ...       ...  ..7  ..4  ...

..8  .8.  ...  ...       .54  ...  ...  ...       ...  6..  ...  3..
.88  ...  .7.  ...       ...  4..  ...  ...       ...  .8.  ...  ...
...  ...  ...  ...       ...  .44  ...  ...       .6.  ...  ...  ...

ABCDEF                   ABCDEF                   ABCDEF
   *  *    0.817          *    *    0.256          **        0.113
   *  *    0.975          *    **   0.371          **        0.146
   *  *    0.776          *    **   0.113          *    *    0.222
```

classifiers are worth no reward at all. Taking again S_y as the key quantity, a *patient* reinforcement policy reinforces *all* rules with scores below certain system threshold $\gamma > 0$: their κ counters are increased just as if z_{MIX} had been successful. A potentially important distinction is therefore made between, say, classifiers whose second MAP class is correct and classifiers assigning very low probability to the observed output label. The main idea is to help rules with promising low scores to survive until a sufficient number of them are found and maintained. In this case they will hopefully begin to work together as a team and thus they will get their reward from correct z_{MIX}!

The resulting reward scheme is thus parameterized by $p > 0$ and $\gamma \geq 0$. Since the number of matched classifiers per cycle (m) may be rather large, a reward policy reinforcing a single classifier might appear rather "greedy". For this reason, higher values of p are typically tried out. The higher p, the easier the cooperation among classifiers (match sets are just provided as more resources to establish themselves). On the other hand, if p is too high then less useful units may begin to be rewarded and the population may become too large. Moderate values of p usually give good results in practice. Parameter γ must also be controlled by monitoring the actual number of units rewarded at a given γ. Again, too generous γ may inflate the population excessively. It appears that some data sets benefit more from $\gamma > 0$ than others, the reasons having to do with the degree of overlap among data categories (see table).

Table 5: Selected classifiers by MAP label as in Table 4.

```
Label j=1                 Label j=2                 Label j=3

... ... ... ...           ... ... ... ...           ... ... ... ...
.6. ... .. ...            ... ... ... ..D           .D. ... ... ...
... .C. ... ...           ... ... ... ...           ... ... ... ...


.6. ... .. ...            ... .0. ... ...           ... ... ... ...
.6. ... B.. ...           ... ... .. ...            ... ... .. ...
... ... .. ...            ... ... .. ...            C.D ... ... ...


.6. ... C.. ...           ... ... ... ...           .C. B.. ... ...
... ... ... ...           ... ... ... .B.           ..C ... ... ..7
... ... .. ...            ... ... .. ...            ..D ... ... ...


    ABCDEF                    ABCDEF                    ABCDEF
     *       0.116            *        0.000           **       0.112
     *       0.044            *        0.027           **       0.106
    **       0.018           **        0.005           **       0.029
```

BYPASS rule discovery sub-system includes a genetic algorithm (GA) and follows previous recommendations laid out in the literature. For example, it is important to restrict mating to rules that are known to be related in some way (Booker, 1989). A familiar solution is to use again the match set M as the basic *niche*: only rules that belong to the same M will ever be considered for mating (as opposed to a population-wide GA). To complement this idea, the GA is triggered by z_{MIX} failure. A further control is introduced: at each failure time either the GA itself or the EXM routine will act depending on the system's score threshold θ. Specifically, the procedure first checks whether there are at least two scores S_y in M lower than θ. If so, standard crossover and mutation are applied as usual over the set of matched receptive fields (Goldberg, 1989). Otherwise, a single classifier is generated by EXM (on the basis of the current datum). The rationale is to restrict further the mating process: no recombination occurs unless there are rules in the match set that have seen a substantial number of instances of the target label y. The θ parameter can be used to strike a balance between the purely random search carried out by EXM and the more focused alternative provided by the GA. This is useful because EXM provides useful variability for the GA to exploit. Since rules created by the GA tend to dominate and often sweep out other useful rules, best results are obtained when θ is relatively demanding (Muruzábal, 1999).

Both standard uniform and single-point crossover are implemented (Syswerda, 1989). In either case, a single receptive field is produced by crossover. Mutation acts on this offspring with some small coordinate-wise mutation probability β. The final Q is endowed with $\kappa = 0$, $c_j \equiv 0$ and a following y as in EXM above. Receptive fields are selected for mating according to the standard roulette-wheel procedure with weights given by the normalized inverses of their scores S_y. As before, exact copies of existing receptive fields are precluded.

Finally, consider the rule deletion policy. At the end of each cycle, all classifiers have their utility $\mu = \kappa/\alpha$ checked for "services rendered to date". Units

Table 6: Bagging performance on the jmultiplexer problem. First three lines: S-PLUS fitting parameters. Next three lines: single (bagged) tree size, test success rate and edge (net advantage of the bagged rate over the single-tree rate). Given figures are averages over five runs. A total of fifty bagging trees were used in all cases. Results are presented in decreasing order of rule generality. Note that no pruning was necessary since trees of the desired size were grown directly in each case.

	Series 1	Series 2	Series 3	Series 4
minsize	20	10	8	6
mincut	10	5	4	3
mindev	.05	.01	.005	.0025
size	32	120	212	365
success rate	25.2	44.4	51.6	53.2
edge	+8.1	+21.8	+27.6	+27.1

become candidates for deletion as soon as their utility μ drops below a given system threshold μ_0. This powerful parameter also helps to promote generality: if μ_0 is relatively high, specific classifiers will surely become extinct no matter how low their accuracy ρ. It is convenient to view μ_0 as $\mu_0=1/v$, with the interpretation (assuming $w_j \equiv 1$) that classifiers must be rewarded once every v cycles on average to survive. Early versions of the system simply deleted all classifiers with $\mu < \mu_0$ at once. It was later thought a good idea to avoid sudden shocks to the population as much as possible. Therefore, only one classifier is actually deleted per cycle, namely the one exhibiting the largest λ. The idea is to maintain all teams or match sets of about the same size. Also, because sometimes a relatively high μ_0 is used, a *mercy* period of guaranteed survival α_0 is granted to all classifiers; that is, no unit with $\alpha \leq \alpha_0$ is deleted, (Frey & Slate, 1991). This gives classifiers some time to refine their likelihood vectors before they can be safely discarded. Again, to aid interpretation, parameter α_0 is usually re-expressed as $\alpha_0 = mercy \times v$, so values of *mercy* are provided in turn.

Two major modes of training operation are distinguished: during *effective* training, the system can produce as many new units as it needs to. As noted above, effective training can be carried out at a variety of θ values. During *cooling*, the rule-discovery sub-system is turned off and no new rules are generated (except those due to empty match sets); all other system operations continue as usual. Since populations typically contain a body of tentative rules enjoying the *mercy* period, utility constraints often reduce the size of the population considerably during the cooling phase. This downsizing has often noticeable effects on performance, and therefore some cooling time is recommended in all runs. Once cooled, the final population is ready for deployment on new data. During this testing phase, it is customary to "freeze" the population: classifiers no longer evolve (no summaries are updated), and no new rules are injected into the system.

One or several cooled populations may be input again to the system for consolidation and further learning. In this case, the new prior vector a is taken as the old c vector plus a vector of ones (added to prevent zero entries). This seeks naturally that the behavior learned by the older rules demonstrates upon re-initialization from the very first match.

To summarize, BYPASS is a versatile system with just a few, readily interpretable parameters; Table 1 summarizes them. These quantities determine many different search strategies. As noted earlier, some pilot runs are typically conducted to determine suitable values for these quantities in light of the target goal and all previous domain knowledge. In this chapter, these pilot runs and related discussion are omitted for brevity; no justification for the configurations used is given (and no claim of optimality is made either). Experience confirms that the system is robust in that it can achieve sensible behavior under a broad set of execution parameters. In any case, a few specific situations that may cause system malfunctioning are singled out explicitly below.

EXPERIMENTAL WORK

This section presents performance results related to the *juxtaposed* multiplexer (or simply *jmultiplexer* for short) and satellite data sets. The main characteristics of these data sets are summarized in Table 2.

The satellite data can be found in the UCI repository (Blake & Merz, 1998; see also Michie et al., 1994). The jmultiplexer stems from the familiar multiplexer suite of problems, a standard benchmark for testing learning abilities in LCSs and other systems (Butz et al., 2000; Wilson, 1998). Experimental code (available from the author upon request) is written in LISP and runs within the XLISPSTAT environment developed by Tierney (1990).

Given the complex dynamics of LCSs, it is crucial to grasp as much detail as possible of their internal work. In particular, the use of monitoring summary plots during training is advocated. An example of such a summary screen is provided in Figure 1 (which will be discussed in depth later). Each of these screens consists of the following eight panels (top row first, from left to right). In all but the last panel, a trajectory is shown which is made up by collecting partial statistics every `wlc` training cycles.

(i)   *MIX* (training) success rate: percentage of correct predictions. This is the performance indicator of foremost interest (the related *SW* success rate is plotted indirectly in panel 4). Smoothed curves (provided by the LOWESS procedure) are drawn here and elsewhere to improve trend perception. Cooling periods are signaled by Xs; thus, we see that all but the last 40 are effective training periods.

(ii) Total number of classifiers and total number of classifiers that were produced by the GA (all units maintain an inert label to track down their origin).

(iii) Average specificity of the population, say h^*.

(iv) The edge or difference between *MIX* and *SW* success rates. If this drops below 0, the system is confused by mixing predictions.

(v)   The *aging* index of the population. This is computed as the ratio between the average α in the population and the total number of data presented so far. An increasing trend indicates proper aging. Non-increasing patterns reveal that new rules tend to replace older units over and over.

(vi) The average size of the match set, say m^*. Two symbols are actually plotted at each abscissa corresponding to separate averages for correct and wrong z_{MIX}. This size is an important indicator of system performance. Note that there should be some sort of agreement between the postulated p and the actual m^*.

(vii) The average (per cycle) number of rewarded units when z_{MIX} is wrong, say γ^*. This is of course 0 unless $\gamma > 0$. Lines are drawn at ordinates $\gamma^* = 1$ and $\gamma^* = 2$ for ease of reference.

(viii) Some run parameters and further statistics of interest. The latter include the average accuracy ρ^* in the final population and the total number of rules created by the system. For ease of reference, the run length is expressed as the product of the total number of periods (440 here) times wlc.

Multiplexer Data

The standard n-multiplexer is a binary classification problem where each input x consists of $n=L+2^L$ Boolean coordinates: the first L are the address bits, the rest are register bits. The address bits encode a particular register bit, and the associated response y is precisely the value stored there. The optimal, maximally general solution to the n-multiplexer consists of 2^{L+1} rules, all with specificity h equal to $100(L+1)/n$. These rules provide a complete partition of input space and never make mistakes.

The jmultiplexer merges several multiplexers into one. Specifically, the $s \times l$ jmultiplexer combines s independent l-multiplexers to yield input vectors x of length $n=sl$. The combination of these partial binary outputs o_i is taken as the encoding $o=o(y)=(o_s...o_3o_2o_1)$ of the output label $1 \leq y \leq 2^s = k$. We shall be concerned here with the 3×11 jmultiplexer. In this case, for example, $o = 001$ corresponds to output label 2. This data set is considered with the purpose of illustrating both the generality of BYPASS classifiers and the predictive power of the underlying team-based evolution of rules.

Figure 1: BYPASS follow-up screen showing a single run for the jmultiplexer data. Execution parameters are $\pi = .8, \mu_0 = 1/40$ (mercy = 6), p = 3, $\gamma = 1.7$ and $\theta = 1.62$. Window size is wlc = 2,500. From left to right, top down: MIX success rate, population size, specificity, edge, aging index, match set size, reward on failure and some run statistics; see text for details.

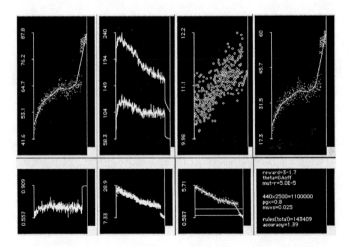

Just as the standard 11-multiplexer admits an optimal solution involving 16 rules, the obvious solution set for this 3×11 jmultiplexer consists of $16^3=4,096$ disjoint receptive fields, each having about 36% specificity. BYPASS definitely provides an alternative, more economical solution to this problem. Figure 2 shows a run executed under the configuration $\pi=.75$, $\mu_0 = 1/35$ (*mercy* = 6) and $p = 3$, $\gamma = 1.7$. This run involves three phases: $\theta = 0$ was used first for one million cycles, then the GA was let into play under $\theta = 1.62$ for a second million cycles; finally, the system was cooled for an additional .2 million cycles.

The final population consists of 173 classifiers with average specificity $h^* = 11\%$ and match sets of about $m^* = 12$ rules. It could still be reducing its size as suggested by the image. This population achieves an outstanding 77.8% success rate on the test sample. The *MIX* over-fit (difference between training and test rates) is about 2%. In both training and testing, the *MIX* edge over *SW* predictions is close to 55 percentage points. The proportion of genetic classifiers is also about 55%. Note the impact on h^* by the GA (implying a burst in m^* as well). Finally, note also the initial increasing trend in γ^*. This is partially curbed subsequently by the GA (again, after a sudden uprise), and ultimately resolved by cooling.

Let us now take a closer look at the individual classifiers in this final population. A natural way to split up the population is to extract units whose MAP predictions equal the various output labels. For each output label we find basically the same picture: two groups of rules of about the same size. Most (sometimes all) rules in the first group were created by the GA, and their accuracies ρ are close to

Figure 2: A single BYPASS run for the jmultiplexer data. Each dot reflects wlc = 25,000 cycles. From left to right, top down: MIX success rate, population size, average specificity, aging index, match set size and reward on failure. Three phases involving different execution parameters are clearly distinguished; see text for details.

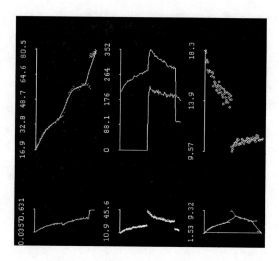

1.4. Each of these rules uses exactly four bits to perfectly capture a single bit o_i. Therefore, their predictive distributions are roughly uniform over a subset of four output labels, with corresponding entropy of about 1.386. For instance, for $j=1$, we find the receptive field 00#00#...# predicting {1,3,5,7}. Note that this rule does not even belong to the optimal solution set for the reduced 11-multiplexer problem: its receptive field covers indeed half of both optimal receptive fields 0000##...# and 001#0#...#. Yet, it has the same specificity and makes no mistakes either, so that, to the system's eyes, is undistinguishable from them. This phenomenon explains why it is so difficult to organize the collection of such "optimal" receptive fields.

The second group of rules consists of receptive fields with just *three* defined bits and accuracy ρ close to 1.9. These rules are nearly always created by EXM. For instance, 00#0#...# makes some mistakes but tends to be successful when $o_1 = 0$. Unlike rules in the previous group, its predictive distribution assigns mass to *all* eight output labels, but {1,3,5,7} concentrates about 3/4. We sometimes refer to these four-bit and three-bit regularities as *neat* and *blurred* respectively. Needless to say, both types of regularities require classifiers equipped with probabilistic predictions to be adequately described.

We note that not all output labels are equally covered: the number of mistakes (on the test sample) by category are 147, 135, 178, 224, 379, 269, 401 and 488 respectively. According to our MAP splitting, the last two categories include only 14 and four classifiers respectively (of course, there is some noise here due to sampling variation). Thus, it appears that further progress can be made in the

Figure 3: A single BYPASS run for the satellite data. Execution parameters are π = .9, μ_0 = 1/25 (mercy = 10), p = 5, γ = 1.15 and θ = 0. Window size is wlc = 250. From left to right, top down: MIX success rate, population size, specificity, edge, aging index, match set size, reward on failure and some run statistics; see text for details.

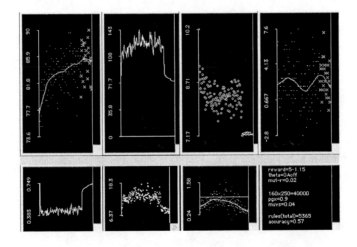

organization of the underlying population. This can be attempted by again executing the algorithm with this population as a starting point.

Figure 1 shows another run implementing precisely this strategy. The previous population was reinitialized as described earlier and then one million effective training cycles plus .1 million cooling cycles were conducted under the slightly different configuration $\pi = .8$, $\mu_0 = 1/40$ (*mercy* = 6, $p = 3$, $\gamma = 1.7$ and $\theta = 1.62$ as before). The resulting population includes only 105 rules, yet it achieves an even better test success rate of 83.3%. Again, the population is still decreasing at termination time, and it would appear that the smaller the population, the better the system works. Note how the proportion of genetic classifiers stabilizes at above the middle of the run, yet h^* increases all the time. We are witnessing indeed the takeover by the neat regularities as evidenced by the overall median accuracy ρ^* (read off the last panel). Under the new training regime, γ^* remains within better bounds than in Figure 2. Match sets average about $m^* = 8$ rules.

Table 3 illustrates a single learning cycle by this population: matching, predictions and reinforcement. In this case we find exactly 4 neat and 4 blurred regularities, and output bits $o_1 = 1$, $o_2 = 1$ and $o_3 = 1$ are supported by 2, 4 and 2 rules respectively. Although all these classifiers concentrate on subsets of 4 output labels (and have similar R_j for them), only two output labels are highlighted in each case. Exactly which two are shown is largely due to the underlying programming of the display. The important point is that it is the set of hidden probabilities that matters, not the simplified but nonetheless useful display. Note also that neat regularities will tend to produce better scores and hence accumulate reward.

Satellite Data

The satellite data is used primarily to provide some insights into the effect of adding $\gamma > 0$ over the alternative $\gamma = 0$ in the reinforcement policy. The benefits of allowing $\gamma > 0$ have been illustrated in other data sets considered previously (Muruzábal, 1999). It is shown here that $\gamma > 0$ does provide an increase in success rate, although it tends to use a relatively higher population size. It will follow that both $\gamma > 0$ and $\gamma = 0$ should be tried out and contrasted when tackling a fresh data set. In any case, the system is shown again to reach reasonable predictive power in terms of rather general rules.

With respect to the previous multiplexer runs, the following runs show a much faster learning horizon (a total of just 40,000 training cycles were considered in all cases), while describing basic behavior under integer-valued predictors, different utility weights w_j, greater π and no GA. Specifically, $\pi = .9$, $\mu_0 = 1/25$ (*mercy* = 10), $\theta = 0$ were fixed and the configurations ($p = 3$, $\gamma = 0$) and ($p = 5$, $\gamma = 1.15$) were each run ten times. Note that this γ value is rather conservative compared to the previous $\gamma = 1.7$ in the multiplexer runs; a greater π was used under $\gamma = 1.15$ in an attempt to facilitate the integration of rules thus reinforced.

Averaged results indicate a 3% advantage in MIX (test) performance by ($p = 5$, $\gamma = 1.15$), concretely from 80.0 to 83.0%, although population size approximately doubles from 36 to 77. The final average accuracy of rules r* also varies substantially: ($p = 3, \gamma = 0$) provides relatively sharper predictive distributions (from .34 to .65). Specificity $h*$ remains around 7% in both cases. On closer examination of performance, it is noted that the subset {1,2,3} is relatively easy for both variants, yet {4,5,6} is best learned by ($p = 5, \gamma = 1.15$) (see Michie et al., 1994). Hence, it appears that different labels may indeed be most suitable for different learning strategies.

To summarize, ($p = 3, \gamma = 0$) provides more concise populations and more accurate classifiers, whereas ($p = 5, \gamma = 1.15$) presents more robust learning and hence slightly better success rates. Figure 3 illustrates a single run by ($p = 5, \gamma = 1.15$). The final population contains 74 rules, and its success rate in the test sample is 83.1%. Note the steady learning during training and the nearly negligible edge over SW predictions in this case. It is likely that better results can be achieved by raising γ a bit (and perhaps lowering p to 4 or 3).

In an effort to separate out the tough classes {4,5,6}, some relevant classifiers from the previous population are singled-out and depicted in Table 4. Again, rules are split by MAP prediction, and the three most accurate rules in each case are shown in each column. In the satellite data, predictors x_i are naturally grouped into four blocks of nine sites each: blocks correspond to spectral frequencies and sites reflect standard grid neighborhoods of single target locations. Hence, the correlation structure among predictors is rather high. Table 4 displays receptive fields according to this interpretation. Several key differences among the three target labels stand out, and these differences can be exploited in terms of rather simple criteria as follows. To begin with, note the degree to which the within-block correlation is reflected: in the majority of cases (26 out of 36), a single number is sufficient to characterize the whole block. The first two spectral bands seem equally informative for separating purposes; for example, in terms of the first block, labels 4, 5 and 6 seem linearly separable as the HIGH, LOW and MEDIUM levels of the representative block value. Note that category 4 seems the most difficult as evidenced by its definitely higher ρ-values; it seems to blend much with category 6. Labels 5 and 6, however, allow sharper characterizations. In particular, output label 6 seems to make frequent use of the fourth spectral band to achieve its low accuracy (Michie et al., 1994).

This analysis is complemented by a similar analysis of the MAP rules for output labels {1,2,3} (see Table 5). Receptive fields together with accuracies and predictive distributions are shown again, and all 10 populations obtained under ($p = 3, \gamma = 0$) were examined for completeness. In Table 5, classifiers with simultaneously low accuracy and low specificity have been manually selected. Label 2 allows maximum generality and very low accuracy: lots of very sharp, very general rules are easily found for this category (a single defined bit seems sufficient). On the other hand, label 3 is somewhat confounded with label 4 (although the present smaller accuracies suggest that the situation is not as bad as in the case of labels 4 and 6 in Table 4). In any case, the difference between categories 3 and 4 is clear by looking at the receptive fields in Tables 4 and 5.

Performance by alternative algorithms on the satellite data is reported in Michie et al. (1994). Although the GA was not used and no special optimization of (p, γ) was carried out, BYPASS still surpasses some of such algorithms. In particular, the original CART algorithm (Breiman et al., 1984) achieves slightly better results (86%) using 66 rules. Under the $(p = 3, \gamma = 0)$ configuration, BYPASS is six points below in performance but reduces the number of rules by more than 50%.

DISCUSSION

In light of the previous results, several preliminary conclusions may be advanced. First, and most importantly, it is suggested that complex problems may hide a number of useful, broad regularities worth exploring in detail. This exploration has been typically neglected in the past because the pressure is fairly strong towards the lowest possible error rates, and these error rates are allegedly harder to obtain unless rather specific rules are used. However, it may well be the case that, by sacrificing a bit of predictive power, we can gain new insights into these complex problems.

Second, these broad regularities can be captured by appropriate classifiers that carefully monitor uncertainty in an interaction-rich environment. The system's self-organizational ability has been portrayed, and the joint activation of related classifiers has been shown to lead to a surprisingly high recognition rate based on a relatively small population. Interpretation of classifiers is straightforward, and the analysis of relevant subsets of receptive fields has led to strikingly simple classification rules.

Finally, the suspicion is strong that the GA performs an interesting fusion of information that leads to more focused populations (Muruzábal, 1999). The actual GA activity rate (controlled by θ) definitely makes a difference, and further research is needed to ascertain the most productive rate and tunable parameters (an issue that is not explored in this chapter).

While the jmultiplexer data illustrate basic system performance under controlled conditions, the satellite experiments above indicate that BYPASS is competitive with respect to other learning algorithms in benchmark real data sets. In the remainder of this section, the jmultiplexer results are first put in perspective by using the alternative bagging trees algorithm. Some pending issues and future trends in the area are pointed out next.

Bagging Trees

This section studies how the jmultiplexer problem is handled by Breiman's bagging approach as implemented via the S-PLUS *binary* tree-fitting facility (Breiman, 1996; Breiman et al., 1984; Venables & Ripley, 1997), that is, each split divides the data subset into *two* branches. All trees were fitted on the basis of the same training file as BYPASS (containing 10,000 items), but a different bootstrapped sample (of the same size) was used in each case. As regards testing, samples of size 250 were extracted from BYPASS test file for reasons of computational economy. Performance on this smaller (and more manageable) sample is seen to correlate highly with full-sample figures.

Trees are fitted using four different configurations pursuing four target sizes (see Table 6). The total number of leaves (or tree size) is controlled by S-PLUS fitting parameters minsize, mincut and mindev. By tuning these parameters appropriately, we can attempt to emulate BYPASS performance using either rules that match the average specificity found there (10-11%) or else more specific rules. The other free parameter of the procedure is B, the number of bagged trees; in all cases Breiman's (1996) suggestion for classification problems (namely, $B=50$) was used. Note that this value is much higher than BYPASS match set size m^* (ranging between 8 and 12); it is thus clear that alternative suites of comparisons may be carried out as well.

As Breiman (1996) points out, procedures that compute predicted probabilities (like BYPASS and classification trees) have a choice when it comes to bagging. For any given input x, single trees can provide either the full (conditional) predictive distribution at the relevant leaf or simply the corresponding MAP label. In the former case, such distributions would be averaged and the resulting MAP label would be output; this is the approach pursued in BYPASS. In the latter case, the B labels are simply scanned for the mode. Note that this alternative approach is obviously also possible in BYPASS. In his extended series of experiments, Breiman (1996) reports that no noticeable advantage is provided by mixing, so he does not advocate this procedure. For this reason, our bagging results are also based on plain majority voting.

Table 6 shows that the bagging approach cannot really reach BYPASS performance in this problem. The highest level of generality (lowest size, series 1) is the closest to BYPASS but it proves clearly insufficient. Success rates do increase with tree size, but even in the case of the largest trees (series 4), performance is far behind the previous 83.3%. In this case, the bagging tree procedure is based on 50×365=18,250 rules, or about 200 times the population size in BYPASS! Moreover, Table 6 suggests that not much will be gained by growing larger trees: both success rate and edge seem close to their asymptotic levels already (Breiman, 1996). It thus seems likely that the training procedure makes a substantial difference: for complex datasets, rules may need to communicate with each other in some way to get the population and its various performing teams well organized.

The Future

Since LCSs are extremely interesting and versatile architectures for various learning problems and new approaches to classification continue to be uncovered, the intersection of these fields is expected to have a large and productive life. LCSs provide a flexible framework for the incorporation of further heuristic knowledge, so their potential in the nascent DM field is just beginning to be explored. For example, the traditional bit string representation has been enlarged to allow the encoding of more complex structures, so LCS classifiers may end up performing less trivial computations than the plain bookkeeping illustrated in BYPASS.

More specifically, in the context of BYPASS, a number of design issues deserve additional analysis and possible enhancement. To begin with, the landscape of reinforcement parameters (p, γ) should be clarified to a higher degree, and more sophisticated reinforcement procedures may be designed in the future. As we have seen, the γ parameter is rather influential on population size; as populations grow, execution time slows down and predictions may be corrupted. Practical guidelines to select the value of γ on the basis of training data features remain to be established. Also, for DM purposes (involving typically a huge number of predictors n), the limit of generality is worth exploring in detail by experimenting with even higher π and greater μ_0. Likewise, emergent cooperation among relatively vague, less accurate rules seems a very promising exercise to pursue simplicity and conciseness. Given the transparency of the present rule representation, automated analyses may perhaps be carried out in the future with the idea of providing *online* insights about teams (or output labels) as those uncovered manually in Tables 4 and 5. Finally, the full scope of the strategy should be ascertained by continuing the analysis of its noise tolerance levels (Muruzábal & Muñoz, 1994).

Other inferential problems, including regression (that is, continuous y), should be amenable to a similar treatment as well. As noted earlier, BYPASS preference for output labels can be either offset or primed by suitable choice of the output label weights w_j; it is thus possible to focus the analysis on selected categories of interest. Finally, predictive scores provide a natural probabilistic interpretation for the degree of "surprise" associated with incoming data. Applications concerned with *deviation detection* may thus be engineered in the future as well.

CONCLUSION

A new evolutionary architecture for large data set analysis has been presented. The BYPASS algorithm has been shown to exploit a simple probabilistic representation supplemented with Bayesian learning to support its decisions and achieve satisfactory performance in both synthetic and real data. A central issue refers to the generality and accuracy of the inferred rules: the present results suggest that much can be gained by pressing the system to work with less certain rules. The resulting framework seems capable of incorporating additional heuristic methods. These are particularly welcome as regards the rule-discovery task, which makes the framework even more attractive for future developments.

ACKNOWLEDGMENT

The author is supported by grants HID98-0379-C02-01 and TIC98-0272-C02-01 from the Spanish CICYT agency, and by grant SUPCOM98-Lot 8 from the European Community. Thanks are due to the anonymous reviewers for their constructive comments.

REFERENCES

Banzhaf, W., Daida, J., Eiben, A. E., Garzon, M. H., Honavar, V., Jakiela, M. & Smith, R. E. (Eds.) (1999). *Proceedings of the Genetic and Evolutionary Computation Conference.* Morgan Kaufmann.

Blake, C. L. & Merz, C. J. (1998). UCI Repository of machine learning databases. [http://www.ics.uci.edu/~mlearn/MLRepository.html]. Department of Information and Computer Science, University of California at Irvine.

Booker, L. B. (1989). Triggered Rule Discovery in Classifier Systems. In Schaffer, J. D. (Ed.), *Proceedings of the Third International Conference on Genetic Algorithms* (pp. 265-274). Morgan Kaufmann.

Breiman, L. (1996). Bagging Predictors. *Machine Learning, 24,* 123-140.

Breiman, L., Friedman, J. H., Olshen, R. A. & Stone, C. J. (1984). Classification and Regression Trees. Wadsworth.

Buntine, W. (1996). Graphical Models for Discovering Knowledge. In Fayyad et al. (Eds.), *Advances in Knowledge Discovery and Data Mining* (pp. 59-82). AAAI Press and MIT Press.

Butz, M. V., Goldberg, D. E. & Stolzmann, W. (2000). *The Anticipatory Classifier System and Genetic Generalization.* (Report No. 2000032). Urbana-Champaign, IL: University of Illinois, Illinois Genetic Algorithms Laboratory.

Cheeseman, P. & Stutz, J. (1996). Bayesian Classification (AUTOCLASS): Theory and Results. In Fayyad et al. (Eds.), Advances in Knowledge Discovery and Data Mining (pp. 153-178). AAAI Press and MIT Press.

Chipman, H., George, E. & McCulloch, R. (1998). Bayesian CART Model Search. *Journal of the American Statistical Association, 93,* 935-960.

De Jong, K. A., Spears, W. M. & Gordon, D. F. (1993). Using Genetic Algorithms for Concept Learning. *Machine Learning, 13,* 161-188.

Denison, D. G. T., Adams, N. M., Holmes, C. C. & Hand, D. J. (2000). Bayesian Partition Modelling. Retrieved November 18, 2000 from the World Wide Web: http://stats.ma.ic.ac.uk/~dgtd/tech.html.

Domingos, P. (1997). Why Does Bagging Work? A Bayesian Account and its Implications. In D. Heckerman, H. Mannila, and D. Pregibon (Eds.), *Proceedings of the Third International Conference on Knowledge Discovery and Data Mining* (pp. 155-158). AAAI Press.

Fayyad, U. M., Piatetsky-Shapiro, G., Smyth, P. & Uthurusamy, R. (Eds.) (1996). Advances in Knowledge Discovery and Data Mining. AAAI Press and MIT Press.

Franconi, L. & Jennison, C. (1997). Comparison of a Genetic Algorithm and Simulated Annealing in an Application to Statistical Image Reconstruction. *Statistics and Computing, 7,* 193-207.

Freitas, A. A. (Ed.) (1999). Data Mining with Evolutionary Algorithms: Research Directions. Proceedings of the AAAI-99 and GECCO-99 Workshop on Data Mining with Evolutionary Algorithms. AAAI Press.

Frey, P. W. & Slate, D. J. (1991). Letter Recognition Using Holland-style Adaptive Classifiers. *Machine Learning, 6,* 161-182.

Gilks, W. R., Richardson, S. & Spiegelhalter, D. J. (1996). Markov Chain Monte Carlo in Practice. Chapman and Hall.

Goldberg, D. E. (1989). Genetic Algorithms in Search, Optimization, and Machine Learning. Addison-Wesley.

Goldberg, D. E. (1990). Probability Matching, the Magnitude of Reinforcement, and Classifier System Bidding. *Machine Learning, 5*, 407-425.

Hand, D. J. (1997). Construction and Assessment of Classification Rules. John Wiley & Sons.

Heckerman, D. (1996). Bayesian Networks for Knowledge Discovery. In Fayyad et al. (Eds.), Advances in Knowledge Discovery and Data Mining (pp. 273-305). AAAI Press and MIT Press.

Holland, J. H. (1986). Escaping Brittleness: The Possibilities of General-Purpose Learning Algorithms Applied to Parallel Rule-Based Systems. In Michalski, R. S., Carbonell, J. G. & Mitchell, T. M. (Eds.), Machine Learning: An Artificial Intelligence Approach II. Morgan Kaufmann.

Holland, J. H. (1990). Concerning the Emergence of Tag-Mediated Lookahead. *Physica D, 42*.

Holland, J. H., Holyoak, K. J., Nisbett, R. E. & Thagard, P. R. (1986). Induction: Processes of Inference, Learning and Discovery. MIT Press.

Jennison, C. & Sheehan, N. A. (1995). Theoretical and Empirical Properties of the Genetic Algorithm as a Numerical Optimizer. *Journal of Computational and Graphical Statistics, 4*, 296-318.

Lanzi, P. L., Stolzmann, W. & Wilson, S. W. (Eds.) (2000). Learning Classifier Systems. From Foundations to Applications. Springer-Verlag.

Michie, D., Spiegelhalter, D. J. & Taylor, C. C. (1994). Machine Learning, Neural and Statistical Classification. Ellis Horwood.

Muruzábal, J. (1995). Fuzzy and Probabilistic Reasoning in Simple Learning Classifier Systems. In D. B. Fogel (Ed.), *Proceedings of the 2nd IEEE International Conference on Evolutionary Computation* (pp. 262-266). IEEE Press.

Muruzábal, J. (1999). Mining the Space of Generality with Uncertainty-Concerned, Cooperative Classifiers. In Banzhaf et al. (Eds.), *Proceedings of the Genetic and Evolutionary Computation Conference* (pp. 449-457). Morgan Kaufmann.

Muruzábal, J. & Muñoz, A. (1994). Diffuse pattern learning with Fuzzy ARTMAP and PASS. *Lecture Notes in Computer Science, 866* (pp. 376-385). Springer-Verlag.

Paass, G. & Kindermann, J. (1998). Bayesian Classification Trees with Overlapping Leaves Applied to Credit-Scoring. *Lecture Notes in Computer Science, 1394* (pp. 234-245). Springer-Verlag.

Parodi, A. & Bonelli, P. (1993). A New Approach to Fuzzy Classifier Systems. In S. Forrest (Ed.), *Proceedings of the Fifth International Conference on Genetic Algorithms* (pp. 223-230). Morgan Kaufmann.

Pelikan, M., Goldberg, D. E. & Cantú-Paz, E.(1999). BOA: The Bayesian Optimization Algorithm. In Banzhaf et al. (Eds.), *Proceedings of the Genetic and Evolutionary Computation Conference* (pp. 525-532). Morgan Kaufmann.

Robertson, G.G. & Riolo, R.L. (1988). A Tale of Two Classifier Systems. *Machine Learning, 3*, 139-159.

Sierra, B., Jiménez, E. A., Inza, I., Muruzábal, J. & Larrañaga, P. (2001). Rule induction by means of EDAs. In Larrañaga, P. & Lozano, J. A. (Eds.), *Estimation of Distribution Algorithms. A new tool for Evolutionary Computation*. Kluwer Academic Publishers.

Syswerda, G. (1989). Uniform Crossover in Genetic Algorithms. In Schaffer J. D. (Ed.), *Proceedings of the Third International Conference on Genetic Algorithms* (pp. 2-9).

Morgan Kaufmann.

Tierney, L. (1990). LISP-STAT. An Object-oriented Environment for Statistical Comput-ing and Dynamic Graphics. John Wiley & Sons.

Tirri, H., Kontkanen, P., Lahtinen, J. & Myllymäki, P. (2000). *Unsupervised Bayesian Visualization of High-Dimensional Data*. Paper presented at the Sixth ACM SIGKDD International Conference on Knowledge Discovery and Data Mining, Boston, MA.

Tresp, V. (2000). *The Generalized Bayesian Committee Machine*. Paper presented at the Sixth ACM SIGKDD International Conference on Knowledge Discovery and Data Mining, Boston, MA.

Venables, W. N. & Ripley, B. D. (1997). Modern Applied Statistics with S-PLUS. Springer-Verlag.

Weiss, S. M. & Indurkhya, N. (1998). Predictive Data Mining. A Practical Guide. Morgan Kaufmann.

Wilson, S. W. (1987). Classifier Systems and the Animat Problem. *Machine Learning, 2*, 199-228.

Wilson, S. W. (1998). Generalization in the XCS Classifier System. In Koza, J.R., Banzhaf, W., Chellapilla, K., Deb, K., Dorigo, M., Fogel, D. B., Garzon, M. H., Goldberg, D. E., Iba, H., and Riolo, R. (Eds.), *Proceedings of the Third Genetic Programming Conference* (pp. 665-674). Morgan Kaufmann.

Wilson, S. W. (2000). Mining Oblique Data with XCS. In Lanzi, P. L., Stolzmann, W., and Wilson, S. W. (Eds.), *Lecture Notes in Artificial Intelligence, 1996*. Springer-Verlag.

Zhang, B.-T. (2000). Bayesian Methods for Efficient Genetic Programming. *Genetic Programming and Evolvable Machines, 1(3)*, 217-242.

Chapter VII

Evolution of Spatial Data Templates for Object Classification

Neil Dunstan
University of New England, Australia

Michael de Raadt
University of Southern Queensland, Australia

Sensing devices are commonly used for the detection and classification of subsurface objects, particularly for the purpose of eradicating Unexploded Ordnance (UXO) from military sites. UXO detection and classification is inherently different to pattern recognition in image processing in that signal responses for the same object will differ greatly when the object is at different depths and orientations. That is, subsurface objects span a multidimensional space with dimensions including depth, azimuth and declination. Thus the search space for identifying an instance of an object is extremely large. Our approach is to use templates of actual responses from scans of known objects to model object categories. We intend to justify a method whereby Genetic Algorithms are used to improve the template libraries with respect to their classification characteristics. This chapter describes the application, key features of the Genetic Algorithms tested and the results achieved.

There has been increased interest in the use of sensing devices in the detection and classification of subsurface objects, particularly for the purpose of eradicating Unexploded Ordnance (UXO) from military sites (Putnam, 2001). A variety of sensor technologies have been used including magnetic, electromagnetic, thermal and ground penetrating radar devices. Depending on the technology and terrain, devices may be handheld or vehicular-borne. Scanning of a section of ground produces a two-dimensional data set representing the impulse response at each spatial location. Classifying subsurface objects involves matching a representation or model of each known object against that of an unknown object. Previous classification techniques have attempted to model objects in ways that are independent of depth and orientation. At the recent Jefferson Proving Ground Trials, it was found that current techniques do not provide adequate discrimination between UXO and non-UXO objects for cost-effective remediation of military sites (US Army Environment Center, 1999). Our approach (Dunstan and Clark, 1999) is to use templates of actual responses from known object scans to model objects. Template matching was used by Damarla and Ressler (2000) for airborne detection of UXO from Synthetic Aperture Radar data sets. Their results showed that a single template could correlate well against a range of large ordnance categories for the purpose of identifying sites requiring remediation. Hill et al. (1992) used Genetic Algorithms to match medical ultrasound images against derived templates of the human heart. The Genetic Algorithm was used to find the best match of an unknown ultrasound and a derived template. Our goal is primarily to achieve the capability of discriminating between UXO and non-UXO objects and, if possible, between the various categories of UXO. Our approach to classification of scans of unknown objects is to match the scan data against a model of each known object. Each model consists of a set of templates of scans of objects known to be of that category. A match is based on correlations of each template against the scan data. Two measures are calculated: the Normalized Cross Correlation Value (NCV) —this is the Normalized Cross Correlation as a percentage of the optimum score; and Fitness Error Factor (FEF)—the absolute difference between the area of the object signal response and the area of the template as a percentage. FEF helps to invalidate correlations with good NCV but with templates significantly larger or smaller than the object's response area. We define a Positive Correlation between a template and a scanned object to exist when the $NCV > MinNCV$ and the $FEF < MaxFEF$. That is, the NCV correlation is sufficiently large and the FEF is sufficiently small. A classification function will then use correlation results from all templates from all categories to return a category type for the unknown object. Therefore, we would wish our template sets for each category to be truly representative of that category, and able to distinguish between objects of its own and other categories. Sadly, our template library is small and not systematic in its coverage of the depth/orientation spectrum. Nevertheless, our existing templates show some promise in ability and we seek to maximize their effect.

The background to this research is the Jefferson IV Field Trials, conducted by U.S. military agencies in 1998 to assess the abilities of current detection technologies to discriminate between buried Unexploded Ordnance (UXO) and non-UXO. Ten companies using a variety of sensors were allowed trial scans of the UXO and non-UXO objects to be used. In all there were 10 categories of UXO and about 40 categories of non-UXO. Participants had to classify each of the subsurface objects located out in the field as either UXO or non-UXO. They were assessed according to these measures:

- TruePositive (TP) - number of UXO objects declared UXO
- FalsePositive (FP) - number of non-UXO objects declared UXO
- TrueNegative (TN) - number of non-UXO objects declared non-UXO
- FalseNegative (FN) - number of UXO objects declared non-UXO

An accuracy figure was calculated as (%TP + %TN) / 2, and 50% accuracy was deemed the "line of no discrimination", that is, inability to discriminate between UXO and non-UXO. Only one company performed marginally better than 50% accuracy. In site remediation, the FalseNegatives (FNs) are the bombs missed because they are identified as non-UXO, and the FalsePositives (FP's) are the junk dug up because they are incorrectly identified as a bomb. FNs and FPs can also be referred to as the "risk" and the "cost" respectively. Nominal figures of 5% risk and 25% cost were suggested as benchmarks. No technology presented at the Jefferson IV Field Trials was deemed "cost-effective".

Our data set is trial scans from the Jefferson IV trial, which were generated using an electromagnetic sensor. They consist of 10 scans of each of the UXO categories and one to four scans of each of the non-UXO categories. Each scan is a file representing the signal response from the object over a spatial grid. Typical feature selection and category modeling consists of attempting to parameterize the response of a typical object independently of depth and orientation, that is, to look for common features. Our approach is to use a library of 2-D templates of the object scanned over the depth/orientation spectrum as a model of each UXO category. A template is the largest rectangular chunk of the data that we know to be part of the object's response area. A close match of the data of an unknown object against any template will be a positive indication that this object belongs to the template's category. The problem is that no such library of templates exists, though future research may develop such a library using empirical or algorithmic methods. Nevertheless we can construct a pilot system to investigate the feasibility of our approach using the data available. In order to develop a classifier function, the data set is divided into Training and Test sets, and the UXO categories are limited to just the largest five. The sixth category will be "unclassified," meaning not any of the UXO categories. Models for each of the UXO categories will be sets of templates taken from the training set of those categories. Classification will be based on the match results of an unknown object against all templates from all models.

Genetic Algorithms have proven their worth in optimisation and search problems of a non-linear nature. Since their inception by Holland (1992), Genetic Algorithms have become widely used and their effectiveness has improved (Baker, 1985; Fogart, 1989; Goldberg, Deb & Clark, 1992). They are now being applied to varying problem domains including Data Mining. An example is Hill et al, (1992).

A simple Genetic Algorithm is described as follows. A set of possible solutions is generated to form a population of 'individuals'. The individuals are assessed for their 'fitness'. According to fitness values, individuals are selected to form a successive population. After crossing-over data within individuals (to focus the strengths that made them more 'fit') and adding mutations (to introduce variety into the population), this new population is then subjected to a fitness test, and the cycle continues.

We split our data into a training set and a test set (used for independent assessment of accuracy), and attempted to optimise a template set for each category using a Genetic Algorithm and the training set. Improved performance simplifies the final classification function by reducing conflicts arising when templates from more than one category register positive correlations for the same unknown object. In the context of UXO detection, it is sufficient to distinguish between UXO and non-UXO rather than between categories of objects. The Genetic Algorithm involved a population of 20 individual template sets. Each individual consisted of five templates from each category. The fitness of each individual was assessed on the basis of how well its set of templates identified membership within categories. The Genetic Algorithms succeeded in significantly increasing the accuracy of all template categories by around 10%.

SPATIAL DATA SETS
AND TEMPLATE MATCHING

The data set contains signal responses for different ordnance objects used in the Jefferson IV trial (U.S. Army Environment Center, 1999). Each object was scanned at different depths (from 0.326 metres to 1.68 metres), azimuth (horizontal displacement from 0 to 335 degrees in 45-degree increments) and declination (vertical displacement of 0, +45 degrees being nose down and –45 degrees being nose up). While a variety of depths and orientations were covered, the scanning set does not constitute a systematic set of all combinations for each object. There were only ten scans of each ordnance category. For each scan, the object was placed in the centre of a 10-metre by 5-metre area. Signal responses were recorded from scanlines at the rate of 20 responses per metre with scanlines 0.5 metres apart.

Each scan produced a file of numbers in the range -5000 to +5000. The file format consists of nine lines of numbers separated by whitespace. Each line has 200 numbers representing one scanline. Files were given the generic name *Xnht.dat* where *X* is:

- *A* for North-South scan of a UXO object;
- *B* for East-West scan of a UXO object;
- *C* for a North-South scan of a non-UXO object; or
- *D* for a North-South scan of a non-UXO object;
- *n* is the diameter in millimetres of the object; and

- *t* is the trial target number.
- *n* denotes the object category.

The scanned object may be considered as a two-dimensional matrix of integer values

$$X^{i,j}, \ 0<i<I\text{-}1, \ 0<j<J\text{-}1$$

Since it was known that the object was centred during scanning, the template extraction process first identified a peak value at a central location in the file. A central location was defined to be on scanlines 3, 4 or 5 and within samples 80 to 120. The template was defined to be the largest rectangular contiguous sequence of positive samples over a fixed threshold value that contained the peak value. The template extraction process therefore takes a significant area of response data from the raw data set that is known to be a response from the object. The template is stored in a file of similar format to the spatial data set files. The template may be considered as a two-dimensional matrix of integer values

$$H^{k,l}, \ 0<k<K\text{-}1, \ 0<l<L\text{-}1$$

The basic tool used for correlation was Normalised Cross Correlation (NCC) which produces a correlation value $Y^{i,j}$ for each possible location of the template $H^{k,l}$ in the data set $X^{i,j}$

$$Y^{i,j} = \frac{\left(\sum_{k=0}^{K-1}\sum_{l=0}^{L-1} H^{k,l} \times X^{i+k,j+1}\right)^2}{\sum_{k=0}^{K-1}\sum_{l=0}^{L-1}\left(X^{i+k,j+1}\right)^2}, \quad 0<i<I-1, \quad 0<j<J-1$$

The best match using NCC is the value closest to

$$p = \sum_{k=0}^{K-1}\sum_{l=0}^{L-1}\left(H^{k,l}\right)^2$$

being the perfect match. NCC is converted to NCV by dividing it by *p* to produce a value between 0 and 1 where an NCV value of 1 is the perfect match.

Table 1 shows NCV correlations of a 155 millimeter object (*A155h056.dat*) against templates from 155, 152 and 90 millimeter categories. Note that a perfect

Table 1. NCV Correlation of various templates with the object represented in the file A155h056.dat

Template	NCV	Template	NCV	Template	NCV
A155h056.dat.plate	1.0000	A152h027.dat.plate	0.8719	A090h031.dat.plate	0.8933
B155h056.dat.plate	0.9390	B152h027.dat.plate	0.9151	B090h031.dat.plate	0.8766
A155h117.dat.plate	0.8072	A152h114.dat.plate	0.9336	A090h141.dat.plate	0.8991
B155h117.dat.plate	0.8851	B152h114.dat.plate	0.8789	B090h141.dat.plate	0.8948
A155h090.dat.plate	0.9600	A152h092.dat.plate	0.9121	A090h104.dat.plate	0.9149
B155h090.dat.plate	0.7795	B152h092.dat.plate	0.9486	B090h104.dat.plate	0.9258
A155h108.dat.plate	0.9550	A152h051.dat.plate	0.7697	A090h079.dat.plate	0.7540
B155h108.dat.plate	0.9348	B152h051.dat.plate	0.8651	B090h079.dat.plate	0.8223
A155h008.dat.plate	0.9235	A152h105.dat.plate	0.9210	A090h138.dat.plate	0.8906
B155h008.dat.plate	0.9252	B152h105.dat.plate	0.9051	B090h138.dat.plate	0.8328

match is obtained when the object was matched against its own template and good results are obtained with templates from other 155 millimeter object templates. However, there are also good correlations with templates of objects from the other (smaller) categories.

The Fitness Error Factor (FEF) is a measure of how well the template fits the object signal response in terms of size. FEF could be considered a correlation measure in its own right but is used here to highlight certain problems with oversized and undersized templates recording good NCV scores that need to be disqualified. The FEF is calculated as the absolute difference between the largest contiguous rectangular area of samples above a threshold in the data set that includes the area under the template and the template size, divided by the template size. That is, let K and L be the template dimensions and K' and L' be the data set response area, then

$$FEF = \frac{|K \times L - K' \times L'|}{K \times L}$$

An FEF of 0 indicates a perfect fit. An FEF of 1 indicates that there was a mismatch in size equivalent to the size of the template. A "valid" correlation is a match with NCV > 0.9 and FEF < 0.1 (though different thresholds are investigated). To use these correlations in the context of a classification system, we use a simple classification method as follows: Should any template from a UXO category library record a valid correlation with an object, that object is classified as UXO. This method implies that "risk" is more significant than "cost", that is, the method is biased towards the identification of UXO rather than non-UXO.

The conflict situation occurs when valid correlations occur with the unknown object and templates from more than one category. Clearly we would like to minimize conflicts, as our secondary goal is to be able to identify the UXO category.

GENETIC ALGORITHMS

Preliminary tests show that data and templates from the same category often do have valid correlations, but also that there is a lot of potential conflict. We would like to manipulate the templates in each model (or library) to improve the model's ability to identify its own category and not positively identify other categories.

We introduce new assessment measures to cater for the twin goals of discrimination between categories and between UXO and non-UXO.

TMC "True My Category" is the number of positive correlations with objects of one's own category.

TOC "True Other Categories" is the number of negative correlations with objects of other categories.

TUXO "True UXO" is the number of positive correlations with UXO objects.

TNUXO "True Non-UXO" is the number of negative correlations with non-UXO objects.

FUXO "False UXO" is the number of incorrect positive correlations with UXO objects.

FNUXO "False Non-UXO" is the number of incorrect positive correlations with non-UXO objects.

These measures are used to assess the performance of an entire category library. Any positive correlation by any template in the library results in a positive correlation for that object. We chose the "B" and "C" data sets as our training set and the "A" and "D" data sets as the test set. As a starting point for the template libraries we chose the "A" templates, thus avoiding perfect matches with the training set. Perfect matches are a possibility when comparing original templates against the test set before alteration by the genetic algorithm, thus validating the correlation method. Table 2 shows the results of using the original, unimproved templates against the training set.

There were 5 A and 5 B scans for each of the 5 UXO categories. There were 110 C and 110 D scans of non-UXO objects. Hence TUXO = 25 – FUXO and TNUXO = 110 – FNUXO. When used with the original template libraries, the classification function records an UXO/non-UXO discrimination accuracy of *(72+45)/2 = 58.5%* against the training set data. Risk is *100 – 72 = 28%* and Cost is 100 – 45 = 55%.

The problem was approached by using two similar Genetic Algorithms that ran concurrently. An algorithm was created by each of the authors, according to their GA design experience. The mechanism of a Genetic Algorithm which determines which individuals in the population should be used as the basis for forming the successive population (the next generation if you like) is known as the selection mechanism. The two algorithms in this study differed by the method used in implementing the selection mechanism. One used a deterministic method to control selection, and the other, a probabilistic method. A deterministic method is defined by sorting the population according to fitness, a 'least fit' proportion of the population is dropped, while the remainder is used for duplication (to maintain a population size) then crossover and mutation. In a probabilistic method, each individual is assigned a relative fitness (relative to the entire population). The sum of all individuals' relative fitness is then one. Individuals are then selected for the successive population as follows. A random number between 0.0 and 1.0 is generated. Individuals' relative fitness values are accumulated until the value of the random number is exceeded. The current individual at that point is then added to the next generation. This method is often illustrated by a roulette wheel where each individual occupies a segment of the wheel proportional to their relative fitness. The

Table 2. Unimproved template libraries against training set data

Library	TMC	%	TOC	%	TUXO	%	TNUXO	%
155	4	80	98	75	9	36	83	75
152	0	0	119	91	3	12	102	92
107	2	40	88	67	12	24	78	70
105	4	80	110	84	8	32	94	85
90	2	40	111	85	4	16	93	84
Classification					18	72	52	45

Table 3. Improved template libraries against the training set data

Library	TMC	%	TOC	%	TUXO	%	TNUXO	%
155	4	80	104	80	11	44	91	82
152	0	0	124	95	3	12	107	97
107	2	40	99	76	12	48	89	80
105	4	80	113	86	9	36	98	89
90	3	60	119	91	5	20	101	91
Classification					20	80	72	65

Table 4. Improved template libraries against the test set data

Library	TMC	%	TOC	%	TUXO	%	TNUXO	%
155	5	100	102	78	8	32	85	77
152	5	100	118	90	6	24	99	90
107	5	100	105	80	11	44	91	82
105	5	100	119	91	8	32	102	92
90	5	100	119	91	9	36	103	93
Classification					25	100	64	58

individual is selected when a ball falls in their segment.

The focus of the Deterministic Algorithm was to improve templates on a per-library basis, while the Probabilistic Algorithm aimed to improve all libraries simultaneously. It was hoped that the evolution of these two approaches would converge toward an optimal point in the search space, thus validating results gained.

As described above, a template is a matrix of numbers extracted from the scan file of an object. This structure was maintained in the 'genome' representation of a template, a set of which forms an individual. Multi-Point Crossover was applied so that templates crossed-over with relative templates from another individual. Mutation at random points in templates was used to introduce variation into the population in both algorithms.

Deterministic Algorithm

A deterministic algorithm was used on a per-library basis. Each library of templates was improved according to its performance against the training set data. Each individual library in the population was assessed according to a fitness function as follows:

$$Fitness = 10{\times}TMC + 5{\times}TUXO + 1{\times}TNUXO$$

Selection identified the worst 25% and second worst 25% of the individuals. The worst 25% was replaced by crossover data from the best 25% of individuals. The second worst 25% received mutated data from the second best 25% of individuals. Table 3 shows the results of the improved template libraries against the training data set. Table 4 shows the results of the improved template libraries against the test data set. Note that the 100% TMC and TUXO results are due to the fact that

Table 5. Improved group of template libraries against the training set data

Library	TMC	%	TOC	%	TUXO	%	TNUXO	%
155	4	80	99	76	9	36	84	76
152	0	0	120	92	2	8	102	92
107	2	40	89	68	11	44	78	70
105	3	60	109	83	8	32	94	85
90	3	60	111	85	5	20	93	84
Classification					18	72	55	50

Table 6. Improved group of template libraries against the test set data.

Library	TMC	%	TOC	%	TUXO	%	TNUXO	%
155	5	100	105	80	6	24	86	78
152	5	100	119	91	6	24	100	90
107	5	100	96	73	11	44	82	74
105	5	100	116	89	8	32	99	90
90	5	100	111	85	10	40	96	87
Classification					25	100	60	54

initial template libraries were sourced from the test set, even though they were subsequently modified by the genetic algorithm.

Probabilistic Algorithm

A non-deterministic algorithm was used on all libraries. Each library of templates was improved according to its performance against the training set data. Each template set in the individual was assessed according to a sub-fitness function as follows:

$$Fitness^i = 2{\times}TOC + -5{\times}FUXO + -2{\times}FNUXO$$

The fitness value for the individual is then:

$$Fitness = \sum_{i=0}^{i<l} Fitness^i + \sum_{i=0}^{i<l}\left(10{\times}TMC^i\right)$$

where TMC^i is considered true if one or more of the templates within set i correctly identified an object of its own category. In this way, fitness was assessed for the entire combined group of libraries rather than for each library separately. This figure was then scaled down to a figure between zero and one.

Selection was based on a probabilistic Roulette Wheel selection mechanism with Fitness Scaling (Ladd, 1996) and Elitism to preserve the fittest individual from each generation to the next. Table 5 shows the results of the improved group of template libraries against the training data set. Table 6 shows the results of the improved group of template libraries against the test data set.

The fitness values of the best and worst individuals, from one GA run, are displayed in the graph in Figure 1 as the population evolves over 600 generations.

Varying Correlation Thresholds

It was also possible for us to model the effect of altering the thresholds of NCV and FEF correlations, and in doing so observe the effect on the improvement of the template sets in the Genetic Algorithm. Results were achieved using the Probabilistic Algorithm as described above with different settings for MinNCV and MaxFEF that together define a positive correlation.

By altering the thresholds to 0.8 for the minimum acceptable NCV and 0.2 for the maximum allowable FEF value, improvement occurred more rapidly as shown in Figure 2. Table 7 shows the results of the improved group of template libraries

Figure 1 Improvement of fitness over 600 generations

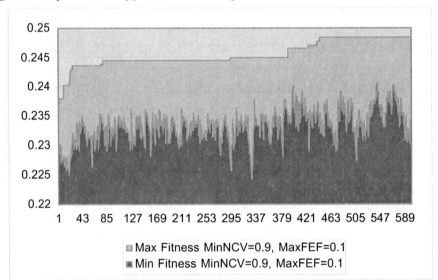

Figure 2 Improvement with altered thresholds

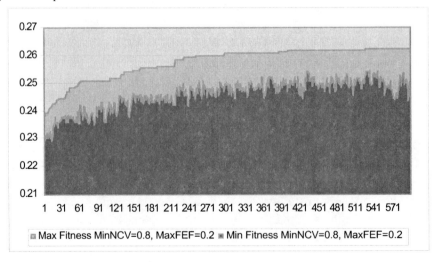

Table 7. Improved group template libraries with reduced thresholds against the training set data.

Library	TMC	%	TOC	%	TUXO	%	TNUXO	%
155	5	100	76	58	11	44	62	56
152	1	20	70	53	9	36	58	52
107	4	80	56	43	18	72	50	45
105	4	80	89	68	10	40	75	68
90	5	100	80	61	13	52	68	61
Classification					23	92	32	29

Table 8. Improved group of template libraries with reduced thresholds against the test set data.

Library	TMC	%	TOC	%	TUXO	%	TNUXO	%
155	5	100	67	51	11	44	53	48
152	5	100	68	52	15	60	58	52
107	5	100	61	47	16	64	52	47
105	5	100	93	71	14	56	82	74
90	5	100	84	64	15	60	74	54
Classification					25	100	30	27

against the training data set using the reduced threshold values. Table 8 shows the results of the improved group of template libraries against the test data set using the reduced threshold values. The fitness of the best and worst individuals are displayed in the graph in Figure 2 as the population evolves over 600 generations.

Summary of Results

The accuracy of the original and three derived sets of template libraries are summarised in Figure 3 and Table 9.

Figure 3 indicates the improvement of the three sets of template libraries in their ability to discriminate UXO and non-UXO. The libraries produced by the Deterministic GA, which improved on a per-library basis, showed improved discrimination ability against UXO and non-UXO. The Probabilistic GA showed lesser improvement against non-UXO. When the same algorithm was used with altered thresholds, a bias was generated that forced an improvement of discrimination of UXO objects at the expense of non-UXO objects. These effects are combined to give an overall improvement value as shown in Table 9.

CONCLUSIONS AND DISCUSSION

Spatial data templates from subsurface object scans can be used in an object recognition system using a combination of correlation measures. We have success-

Figure 3 Improvement over the different algorithms

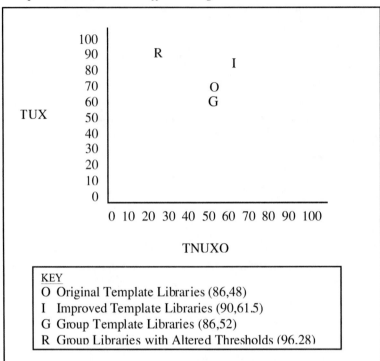

fully used Normalized Cross Correlation with Fitness Error Factor (a size correlation measure) to define valid correlations between templates and unknown objects. Even unimproved templates taken from real scans of known objects performed reasonably well in discriminating between UXO and non-UXO categories.

A variety of evolution procedures were used in attempts to improve the performance of the template libraries in a classification system. A deterministic Genetic Algorithm applied separately to libraries modeling each UXO category succeeded in achieving over 75% accuracy over the whole data set. A Probabilistic Genetic Algorithm was applied to the group of libraries with suitable fitness, and selection techniques also resulted in improved accuracy when compared to the original libraries. These results obtained by these methods give validity to their use.

Reducing the threshold criteria for valid correlations achieved faster convergence under the algorithm but led to less accurate discrimination between UXO and non-UXO, as too many non-UXO objects then correlated well against UXO templates. A possible explanation for this effect may be due to the reduced threshold accentuating the fitness function favouring "risk" over "cost."

Despite setting fitness criteria in order to discourage conflict arising from templates from more than one UXO category recording valid correlations with the same objects, the libraries produced were not good at discriminating between categories of UXO. It is expected that a more sophisticated classification system with mechanisms for dealing with such conflict are required for this level of

Table 9. Summary of accuracies of original and improved template libraries.

Accuracy	Training Set	Test Set	All Data Sets
Original Libraries	58.5%	75.5%	67%
Improved Libraries	72.5%	79%	75.5%
Group Libraries	61%	77.5%	69%
Group Libraries with Reduced Threshold	60.5%	63.5%	62%

classification. From the point shown in the results presented here, further improvement is possible where genetic algorithms are run over longer periods, however, as shown in Figures 1 and 2, the rate of improvement decreases over time.

We were able to identify a number of parameters in the evolution process that may be investigated in future work. These include the weightings applied to successful and unsuccessful correlations in various categories and correlation measure thresholds, when calculating fitness. Population resizing and parellelizing fitness testing within the Genetic Algorithm in order to increase the rate of improvement are possible avenues.

ACKNOWLEDGMENTS

This research is supported by the Australian Research Council and Geophysical Technology Limited.

REFERENCES

Baker, J.E. (1985). Adaptive Selection Method For Genetic Algorithms. In *Proceedings of the International Conference on Genetic Algorithms (ICGA'85)*.

Damarla, T. & Ressler, M. (2000). Issues in UXO Detection using Template Matching. *Proceedings of the UXO Countermine Forum, Anaheim, USA*.

Dunstan, N. & Clark, P. (1999). Parallel Processing of Electromagnetic and Magnetic Data Sets for UXO Detection. *Proceedings of the UXO Forum 99, Atlanta, USA, May, 1999*.

Fogarty, T.C. (1989). Varying the Probability of Mutation in the Genetic Algorithm. In *Proceedings of the Third International Conference on Genetic Algorithms (ICGA'89)*.

Goldberg, D.E., Deb, K. & Clark, J.H. (1992) Genetic Algorithms, Noise, and the Sizing of Populations. *Complex Systems, 6(4)*.

Hill, A., Taylor, C. J. & Cootes, T. (1992). Object Recognition by Flexible Template Matching Using Genetic Algorithms. *Lecture Notes in Computer Science 588*. Springer-Verlag, 852-856.

Holland, J.H.. (1992). *Adaptation in Natural and Artificial Systems: An Introductory Analysis with Applications to Biology, Control, and Artificial Intelligence*. USA: MIT Press.

Ladd, R.S. (1996). *Genetic Algorithms in C++*. USA: M&T Books.

Putnam, J.D. (2001). Field Developed Technologies for Unexploded Ordnance Detection, *Second Australian-American Joint Conference on the Technologies of Mine Countermeasures*, Sydney, Australia.

US Army Environment Center and US Armed Forces Research and Development, *Jefferson Proving Ground Technology Demonstration Program Summary*, 1999.

PART THREE:

GENETIC PROGRAMMING

Chapter VIII

Genetic Programming as a Data-Mining Tool

Peter W.H. Smith
City University, London, UK

INTRODUCTION

Genetic Programming (GP) has increasingly been used as a data-mining tool. For example, it has successfully been used for decision tree induction (Marmelstein and Lamont, 1998; Choenni, 1999), data fusion (Langdon, 2001) and has also been used for the closely related problem of intelligent text retrieval on the Internet (Bergstrom, Jaksetic and Nordin, 2000). Indeed its ability to induce a program from data makes it a very promising tool for data mining applications. It has been successfully applied in many different fields and has even produced results that have exceeded those produced by other means. For example it has been used to evolve chemical structures (Nachbar, 2000) using a quantitative structure activity relationship model. It has also had success in spacecraft attitude control (Howley, 1996) where near-minimum spacecraft attitude manoeuvres were evolved which outperformed previous hand-coded solutions. It has also been used in quantum computing, where it was used to evolve quantum algorithms (Barnum, Bernstein and Spector, 2000). In this work, it rediscovered known algorithms such as Deutsch's Early Promise Problem and discovered quantum results that experts did not think could exist, for example, AND-OR query problem. These examples demonstrate the versatility and potential of GP.

Despite its many successes, some potential users of GP sometimes discover when using it that the programs created during a run tend to grow, often exponentially in size leading to stagnation in the search process. Alternatively, they may discover that GP simply gets nowhere with their application. The aim of this chapter is to explain what to do when these difficulties occur, with particular relevance to data mining applications.

In this chapter, we briefly describe how GP works and the design decisions that have to be made in setting it up. Its potential uses in data mining are then discussed.

The problem of code growth is then described in detail and the reasons why it happens are explored. Strategies for improving search and overcoming the problems caused by code growth are then examined.

AN INTRODUCTION TO GENETIC PROGRAMMING

This section provides a brief description of GP, primarily the decisions that have to be made in setting it up to make it work successfully. A more complete description of what GP is may be found in Koza (1992) or Banzhaf et al. (1998).

GP is a method of program induction that can be used to evolve functions or even whole programs to solve complex tasks. It is ideally suited to problems that are difficult to solve by more conventional methods or for the recognition of complex patterns in data.

GP can be defined as the application of genetic algorithms to programs, or alternatively it may be described as program induction by evolution. These programs are typically represented as trees. It can then be used to evolve a regression function, or perhaps a program that can be used to explain a complex pattern in data. The trees are made up of functions and terminals that together make executable programs. Programs are selected from the population by means of a fitness function and recombined to form a new generation of programs. Figure 1 illustrates standard crossover on trees, which is the most common method of recombination used in GP. The whole process is repeated until (hopefully) a solution is found.

Figure 1: Standard Crossover in Genetic Programming

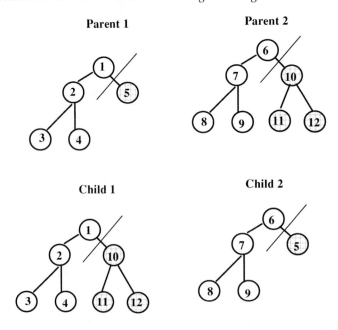

Producing a GP solution to a problem typically involves the following steps:
- Determination of initial parameters.
- Decide on the function and terminal set.
- Determine the fitness function to be used.
- Decide on the population size and population model to be used.
- Determine the tree parameters to be used.
- Decide on the method of initial population creation.
- Determine the recombination operator and method of selection.
- Determine the dataset to be used (if any).
- Run the GP system and if necessary, repeat or change some of the above steps.

Function Sets and Terminals

The function and terminal set is dependent upon the type of problem to be solved. The functions make up the internal nodes of the tree. The terminal set normally consists of a set of variables and possibly constants. For example, if we are trying to determine the relationship between a dependent variable **y** and two independent variables **a** and **b**, then the terminal set will consist of **a** and **b** and possibly some constant values (referred to as ephemeral random constants); the value of y is then obtained by evaluating the tree.

To determine the composition of the function set involves looking at the domain of the problem. The function set may be nothing more than the basic arithmetic operators {+,-,*,/}; if the relationship between the two independent variables and the dependent variable is clearly non-linear, then it may be useful to include {**exp** and **log**}. If the relationship appears to be cyclical, then the addition of {**sine**} would be advantageous.

If the aim of the GP run is to produce a boolean function, then the function set will need to contain boolean functions {AND, OR, NAND, etc.} The creation of a decision tree would have to include relational operators and predicates. Unfortunately, there are as yet no infallible guidelines for the decision about the composition of the function set, and the performance of a GP system on a particular problem can depend critically on the functions that it has been given to work with.

The Fitness Function

The fitness function is also vitally important for the success of GP. It is used to drive evolution towards the best solution. If it fails to adequately discriminate between solutions, then the GP search will be severely hampered. One common failing of fitness functions is that they often fail to distinguish between solutions that are adequate and those that are optimum. Sometimes, it needs to be designed to get the GP system started by rewarding even a minute improvement in performance. All too often, with a poorly designed fitness function, the population achieves a uniformly depressing fitness of 0 (i.e., no fitness at all).

Consider the problem of classification: a simple method of creating a fitness function for a classification problem is to use a set of say 100 data items that have been classified by hand (or by some other means). The aim is to accurately classify all 100 data items, and any item that is not classified correctly is subtracted from 100. Thus, members of the population will have a fitness ranging from 0 to the perfect score of 100. However, even if a GP program produces a fitness value of 100 on the data presented to it, it may then fail miserably on a data set that it has never seen before due to overfitting or a lack of generality in its solutions.

Fitness values are usually normalised by computing an error **e** (in the above example, this would be the number of data items that are incorrectly classified) and computing fitness in the range 0 to 1 by the following formula:

$$\text{Fitness} = 1/(1+e)$$

The normalization of fitness values allows us to standardize fitness measures so that the same scale is used for all kinds of problems.

Population Sizes and Population Models

GP uses large populations; sizes between 1,000-5,000 are not untypical. Large population sizes can be computationally expensive and hence slow, thus for exploratory work, smaller populations can be used to good effect. Generally speaking, the larger the population size, the greater the chances are that GP will find a good solution. However, it is always possible that something else may be adversely affecting the performance of the GP system. For example, improving the fitness function is always likely to produce more fruitful results than simply increasing the population size in the hope that it will enhance performance. There are two population models that are commonly used in GP: steady state and generational. Steady state allows members of the population to survive from one generation to the next. It works by weeding out less fit members of the population—the fitter ones survive to the next generation. The advantage of this method is that it enables fit specimens to be preserved. The generational model involves creating a totally new population with every generation and throwing away all members of the previous generation.

Tree Depth Parameters

Of the tree parameters, the most important is the one that limits the depth of the trees. Most GP systems will allow the user to set a limit on the maximum depth of the trees to be created. Very large trees result in very slow GP runs, so for experimental work it is often useful to set a very low maximum tree depth. Furthermore, it is particularly important for data mining solutions that they are relevant and meaningful. Very large trees do not usually produce easy-to-understand solutions.

The Initial Population

Creating an initial population involves the generation of a random population of trees.

The most common form of tree generation is called ramped half and half (Koza, 1992) in which half of the trees are full trees and the other half are grown down to a predetermined depth. This process is repeated until a complete population has been created. Whenever a population is to be created for a new problem, it is always worth considering the tree structure. Is there anything inherent in the problem itself that might determine the structure of the final tree? For example, decision trees will sometimes be symmetrical. It may be worth considering starting the population with full trees when the trees are likely to be symmetrical. Even the method used to determine the initial population can have a significant effect on the performance of the GP system. Additionally, it is always worth considering whether it might be beneficial to seed the initial population by planting certain types of trees in it. This will always tend to bias the search in one particular direction and if intuitions about the problem are wrong, then it will impede the search.

Recombination Operators

After all these decisions have been made, it is finally time to start running the GP system, but not before a decision has been made about the method of recombination to be used and the method of selection. The recombination operator determines how the trees are altered genetically. By far the most common method of recombination is crossover (generally referred to as standard crossover) in which two parents are selected, a crossover point is determined and the trees are recombined to produce two children. Crossover is achieved in tree-based structures in the following manner: two parents are chosen for recombination, a crossover point is chosen randomly in each tree (any edge between the nodes is a potential crossover point). The two parents are now split into two sub-trees. Each parent yields one sub-tree that contains the original root node. The sub-tree containing the root node from parent 1 is recombined with the sub-tree from parent 2 that does not contain the root and vice versa. Although standard crossover is commonly used, it may come as a surprise that it is now the subject of a lot of debate in the GP community (Angeline, 1997). The future of crossover in GP is by no means certain.

Selection

Selection is the method by which members of the population are selected for recombination (i.e., the method of determining which members of the population are permitted to "breed"). The two most common forms of fitness selection are fitness proportionate selection and tournament selection. Fitness proportionate selection allows each member of the population a chance of being selected in proportion to its fitness. Tournament selection involves choosing a small number of members of the population and holding a tournament to decide on the fittest two members that are then used for recombination. A typical tournament size is 7; increasing the tournament size tends to increase the selection pressure, i.e., forces the population to evolve in a certain direction. A high selection pressure may produce results when the search doesn't appear to be getting started, but it can also cause premature convergence to a local optimum with a largely homogeneous population, dominated by a small number of program structures. The run continues until either no improvement in the fitness of the population is detected or until a solution emerges. It is generally true that once the fitness of the population levels off, then it is unlikely to show any further improvement.

THE USE OF GENETIC PROGRAMMING IN DATA MINING

The Stages of Data Mining

Fayyad, Piatetsky-Shapiro and Smyth (1996) identify nine stages in the process of knowledge discovery in databases (KDD). The first stage is to understand the knowledge domain and establish the goals of the KDD process. Secondly, a target dataset or a sample needs to be chosen. The third stage is to clean and preprocess the data. This process involves deciding what to do about missing or inaccurate data. Genetic Programming has been successfully applied to applications that involve noisy data (Reynolds, 1994) and from this perspective can be seen as a robust technique. The next step is data projection and reduction, which may involve dimensionality reduction. The fifth stage is to match the aims of the KDD to a particular data-mining method. The sixth stage is exploratory analysis, hypothesis and model selection: that is choosing the data mining techniques and selecting methods to be used in searching for patterns in data. It is at this stage that the decision must be made whether to use GP or not. The seventh stage is the data mining process itself, and this involves the use of a particular representation that may be decision trees or clustering. The eighth stage of KDD is the interpretation of the results. The final stage consists of acting on the results produced.

Genetic Programming and Data Mining Methods

The principal data-mining methods are: classification, clustering, regression, summarization, change and deviation detection and dependency modelling. The first three methods will be discussed in some detail, as they are most amenable to solution using GP.

Classification

Data classification can be carried out using black box methods such as neural networks. These may provide accurate classifiers but might provide no explanation of how they classify the data. Classification algorithms such as C4.5 (Ross Quinlan, 1993) also generate decision trees but tend to produce overly complex decision trees. GP is potentially capable of providing a compromise between these two rather extreme positions. Classification is a way of partitioning the dataset into one of many *predefined* classes. For example we want to categorise a set of bank loan applications into good/bad credit risks. We are not interested in any other form of partition. The easiest way of creating a GP solution is to use a pre-classified dataset that GP can be evolved against. Any potential solution must be tested for generality and robustness by applying it to a completely different dataset.

The fitness function for this application might consist of a set of existing loan applications along with their outcomes (i.e., was the loan repaid or defaulted). The more cases that are correctly categorized, the better the fitness of the proposed solution. Other factors can be included in the fitness function, for example the simplicity of the rule used for classification.

Consider the problem of classifying bank loan requests: the requisite fields might be: *Age*, *Loan-amount*, *Occupation* and *Income*. Then a GP tree may consist of terminals {: *Age*, *Loan-amount*, *Occupation*, *Income*, constants} with a function set {IF, <,>,=}. However this setup will almost certainly result in large unwieldy trees. A more controlled approach is to use a tuple-set descriptor (TSD) (Freitas, 1997). A TSD might be (Age<25,loan-amount<10000,occupation=professional, income>20000). Each member of the GP population may be described as a TSD (i.e., the structure of the tree is controlled by the TSD). This means that the terminal set will consist of the names of the predicting attributes of the TSD. The function set will then consist of comparison operators (>,<,=, ≠, ≤, ≥) and logical connectives (AND,OR,NOT). The TSD given above will then become: ((Age <25) AND (loan-amount<10000) AND (occupation=professional) AND (income>20000)). A structure preserving crossover operator is then used to ensure that all trees represent valid TSDs and the run continues until a useful decision tree has evolved.

Figure 2a: A Freely Evolved GP Decision Tree

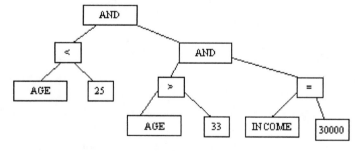

Figure 2b: A Tuple Set Descriptor as a GP Tree

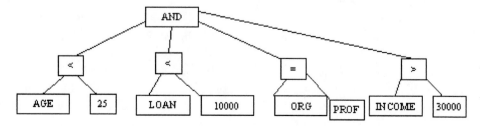

Figures 2a and 2b illustrate the difference between using standard GP to evolve a decision tree and using a TSD. The TSD is a template tree that ensures that a feasible decision will be evolved. If the attributes of the TSD are not clearly established, then this method can prevent GP from finding a suitable decision tree.

Clustering

Clustering involves the identification of a finite set of categories or clusters from a dataset in which the categories are not known beforehand. The categories can be mutually exclusive, or they may be more complex, for example they could be overlapping or even hierarchical. A major problem with clustering is being able to distinguish interesting partitions from the many other ways of partitioning a data set that are unimportant. The difficulty with clustering is to establish which partitions are interesting and which are not.

One way of ensuring that a GP solution concentrates on relevant partitions of the dataset is to introduce some form of relevance measure into the fitness function, though it is far from clear how this can be achieved in practice. One metric may be rule simplicity – the application of Occam's Razor. Silberschatz and Tuzhilin (1995) and Piatestky-Shapiro and Matheus (1994) suggested an interestingness metric that in practical terms is a measure that combines validity, novelty, usefulness and simplicity.

The principal difficulty with the use of GP for clustering appears to be the design of the fitness function. In this respect GP is neither better nor worse placed than many other clustering techniques. One point that it has in its favour is its ability to provide some form of explanation as to why it has produced the clusters that it has found. Some of the metrics described (validity and novelty especially) may be difficult to measure without human intervention, and for GP this idea is highly impractical if only for the sheer impracticality. Human assessment can be notoriously subjective and variable.

Regression

The primary purpose of regression is to estimate the value of a dependent variable given a known value of one or more independent variables. Good techniques already exist for both bivariate and multivariate linear regression. Linear regression can be quickly and easily carried out by a statistical package such as SPSS. However GP performs symbolic regression, without the need for data transformations and is also capable of regression analysis on variables that exhibit non-linear relationships. Whenever a regression analysis is required for a data mining application, a more conventional form should always be considered first. Most data is linear and standard regression will almost always outperform GP on linear data.

However, for regression analysis of non-linear data, GP should be considered as a potentially useful technique. Regression problems are solved by fitting a computed function on the tree to the dataset using a fitness function that minimizes the error between them. GP regression is symbolic, i.e., it involves attempting to find a function that provides the closest fit to the data. A GP regression analysis typically uses a terminal set consisting of constants, plus the independent variables. For example a multi-variate regression problem with five independent variables and one dependent variable will use a terminal set consisting of the five variables plus constants. The GP tree will compute the dependent variable. The function set may be as simple as the four arithmetic operators {+,-,*,/}; if it is clearly exponential, then it may be advantageous to add {log, exp} to the function set.

If it is sinusoidal in shape, then the addition of {sine} may be useful. Data is divided up into a training and test set. Then GP is run to see whether a function evolves that fits the data. The fitness function typically used is the absolute value of the error. Figure 3 provides a pretty printed example of an evolved GP tree for a regression problem. It is a univariate regression problem using only the standard arithmetic operators. Note the prevalence of constant values. Care should be taken to validate the regression function as GP sometimes has a tendency to overfit (Langdon, 2001).

The constants used in the GP run are called ephemeral random constants and are an Achilles' Heel of GP. When the initial population is set up, the population is liberally scattered with constants randomly chosen from a preset range of real numbers (usually $-1 \leq E \leq +1$). The implication of this is that it is much more difficult for GP to evolve for example, the polynomial $x^2 - 678.3x$ than it would be to evolve $x^2 - 0.3x$. The evolution of large constants can cause excessive bloat, and even recent research in GP regression has failed to recognize this problem. For example (Eggermont and Van Hemert 2001) attempted to boost GP regression by stepwise adaptation of weights. The polynomial function set chosen was generated using two

Figure 3 : A Sample GP Tree For A Regression Problem

```
(-  (*  (/  (/  0.35398 (*  0.38705 0.06134))
          (/  (-  (*  (-  (-  (+  0.26742 X)
                          (-  (*  0.38705 0.06134)
                              (/  (+  0.26742 X)
                                  (*  0.38705 0.06134)))) X)
                      (/  (+  (+  (*  0.98588 0.44788)
                              (*  0.38705 0.06134)) 0.35398)
                          (/  (*  (*  0.38705 0.06134) X)
                              (*  X 0.02914))))
                  (/  (+  0.26742 X)
                      (*  0.38705 0.06134)))
              (* 0.38705 (/  (+  0.26742 X)
                          (*  0.38705 0.06134)))))
      (/  (*  0.38705 0.06134)
          (-  X -0.28017)))
  (- X (/  (+  0.26742 X)
          (*  0.38705 0.06134))))
```

variables {**w,b**}, where **w** was the degree of the polynomial and **b** was the maximum coefficient size of each polynomial term. However, the ephemeral random constants were then chosen from the set {Z: $-b \leq Z \leq +b$}, thus prior knowledge of the coefficients was used to find a regression function for the polynomials. For real regression problems however, **b** would be unknown and the authors of this study would then encounter far more uncertain results.

There have been attempts to solve this problem, for example, Evett and Fernandez (1998) tried to evolve constants, using a form of simulated annealing that adapted the constants according to the amount of error and reported some success with this approach.

GP can be used for bivariate or multivariate regression. The purpose of carrying out a regression analysis on a dataset is to eliminate or predict a characteristic of one variable from others. Koza (1992) contains several examples of regression using GP; including the discovery of trigonometric identities, econometric modeling and forecasting and the empirical discovery of Kepler's Law. Symbolic GP regression has been applied to a wide range of applications with varying degrees of success. It has been used for business strategies and economic forecasting (Duffy and Engle-Warnick, 1999; Kaboudan, 1999), chaotic time series (Geum, 1999) and chemical process modeling (McKay, Willis and Barton, 1997). Taylor et al. (1998) report better results with GP than with conventional regression techniques on infrared spectroscopy data, which clearly indicates that GP should be considered as a serious method for problems requiring regression analysis.

Challenges Confronting Genetic Programming in Data-Mining

Summarization is a method of finding a compact description for a subset of data. One particularly important application of summarization is text summarization. It is difficult to see how GP may be usefully employed for summarization tasks although it has been used for the closely related task of intelligent text retrieval (Choenni,1999). Change and deviation detection is a method of discovering the most significant changes in the data from previously measured or normative values. Once again, it is difficult to see how GP can be employed on this task. Dependency Modelling involves finding a model that describes significant dependencies between variables. GP has potential for dependency modelling though it appears to be relatively unexplored so far.

SCALING UP GENETIC PROGRAMMING

GP has shown considerable promise in its problem-solving capability over a wide range of applications and problem domains, but there are problems with scaling it up to solve harder problems. Many of the difficulties in scaling it are neatly summarised in Marmelstein and Lamont, 1998:

- GP performance is very dependent on the composition of the function and terminal sets.
- There is a performance tradeoff between GP's ability to produce good solutions and parsimony—particularly pertinent to data mining applications.
- The size and complexity of GP solutions can make it difficult to understand. Furthermore, solutions can become bloated with extraneous code (introns).

Some of these issues have already been tackled by the GP research community, but many of the results are not easily accessible outside. Data mining presents compelling reasons for restricting code growth; solutions need to be small in order that they are firstly plausible and secondly easy to understand. However there is an even more fundamental reason for restricting code growth: it can cause the whole search process to stagnate and flounder, a very good reason to look for a cure to this problem.

In order to explain why code growth happens, we need to look at its causes. The tendency of GP trees to grow in size is called "bloat". Bloat is not caused by one single phenomenon, but rather there appear to be several different causes. Firstly, bloat may be caused simply by inefficient representations, for example

$$(+ \ x \ (+ \ 1 \ (+ \ 1 \ (+ \ 1 \ (+1 \ 1)))))$$

which could be represented more compactly as (+x 5).

However the most important and pernicious cause of code growth can be explained by the presence of "introns". Intron is a term that has been borrowed from genetics in which it describes regions of DNA that appear to have no function.

They often arise because of redundant predicates in trees: for example in the artificial ant problem, a predicate is used to test whether there is food in the next square immediately ahead of the ant. This predicate conditionally executes the first or second parameter depending on whether it returns true or false. The nested predicate

(IF-FOOD-AHEAD MOVE (IF-FOOD-AHEAD (...) LEFT))

has the potential to create an intron. **IF-FOOD-AHEAD** tests the square to see whether it contains food; if true, the move operator is executed, otherwise the inner predicate is executed and consequently, the section (...) will never be executed because the predicate has already been tested and found to be false. This is a major source of code growth.

Introns can also arise in arithmetic trees for example,

$$(* \ 0 \ (+ \ (- \ X \ 2) \ 2)).$$

The highlighted section is nonfunctional because it is multiplied by 0. Other forms of introns have also been identified (Smith and Harries, 1998; Luke, 2000).

Having identified what causes code growth in GP, the next question is why introns cause runaway code growth? If we consider this in evolutionary terms, as a GP run progresses, it becomes increasingly difficult to produce offspring that are fitter than their parents, then it becomes an effective survival strategy for an offspring to have the same fitness as their parents. Also, as the run proceeds, crossover is more likely to have a destructive effect producing offspring that are less fit than their parents. The growth of introns forms a defense mechanism against the effects of destructive crossover.

Smith (1999) identified four methods for controlling code growth and these will be described in turn.

Code Growth Prevention by Physical Means

The earliest attempt to control code growth by the physical removal of nonfunctional sections of code was reported in Koza (1992). An editor was used to remove nonfunctional code that included both domain independent and domain-specific editing rules. However, he noted that the use of an editor appeared to impede the search. It was suggested that this might have occurred because the physical removal of code resulted in the reduction of genetic diversity from the population as a whole. Soule, Foster and Dickinson (1996) also raised a note of caution about the use of editing, pointing out that it is very difficult to ensure that an editor would remove everything that wasn't useful allowing what remains to grow exponentially. Davidson, Savic and Walters (2000) demonstrated that arithmetic trees can be simplified dynamically in regression problems and it seems likely that other GP applications might be susceptible to this treatment also.

Another form of physical prevention is to impose a hard limit on tree depth. Although Gathercole and Ross (1996) and Langdon and Poli (1997) reported problems caused by the interaction between the physical limits imposed, crossover and the ability of GP to find solutions, it might be of interest in data-mining applications for the following reasons:

- For decision tree induction, it is important that the decision trees are meaning-ful and easy to understand and this almost invariably means small in size. The principal argument ranged against restricting the maximum tree depth is that it might fail to find a solution. However, this doesn't apply to decision tree induction where the tree size is required to be small.
- Restricting the maximum tree depth on a GP system is trivial as it simply means setting a parameter. Writing a domain specific tree editor is a nontrivial task.

On running GP for classification problems, particularly when the aim is decision tree induction, it is always worth considering imposing a tree-depth limit.

Code Growth Prevention by Parsimony Pressure

Parsimony pressure is a form of code growth restriction in which large trees are penalised by incorporating size as a factor in the fitness function. If fitness is determined by a function f then $f=(h,s)$ where h is the fitness heuristic and s is the size of the solution obtained. Parsimony was first used by Koza (1992) in the block-stacking problem. It was subsequently refined and used by Kinnear (1993), Zhang and Muhlbein (1995), and Iba, De Garis and Sato (1994). Kinnear (1993) used parsimony in the evolution of sorting algorithms and observed that the introduction of parsimony pressure not only decreases the size of potential solutions but also increases their generality considerably. Generality is particularly important for data mining where the emphasis is on utility and understandability.

Parsimony pressure is not without problems of its own however. In its simplest form, parsimony is applied as a factor to determine fitness from the start of the GP run. This tends to favour small solutions disproportionately over larger solutions and this problem is particularly acute in the early stages of search when all trees tend to have a very low performance fitness value, hence magnifying the effect that parsimony pressure has, and putting a break on any code growth at all. In the early stages of a GP run, all potential solutions tend to have a very low fitness value and size could have an effect out of all proportion. This can seriously impede the search and sometimes prevents it from even getting started. Koza (1992) noted that use of parsimony pressure resulted in a 6-fold increase in the number of solutions generated and processed for the multiplexer problem. Nordin and Banzhaf (1995) also note that constant application of parsimony pressure produces worse results. However, Zhang and Muhlbein (1995) introduced a form of adaptive parsimony pressure that is responsive to the size and fitness of individuals. This appeared to get round the difficulty of the search getting started because of the excessive influence of parsimony in the early stages.

Some GP systems allow access to the tree size of individuals. Using this in the fitness functions allows parsimony pressure to be implemented simply and effectively.

Code Growth Prevention by Alternative Selection

A more recent method of code growth control is alternative selection. Standard selection allows all potential offspring through to the next generation regardless of their fitness. However, introns have been identified as a major cause of code growth. The consequence of a tree containing a large section of nonfunctional code is that crossover within that section has no effect on the fitness of any offspring produced. Using this observation, we can then change the selection mechanism so that it forbids any offspring that has the same fitness as its parents. This is the basis of the alternative selection schemes described in Smith and Harries (1998). One method of alternative selection that has received considerable attention is Improved Fitness Selection (IFS) (Smith and Harries, 1998), first described as nondestructive crossover by Altenburg (1994).

Although IFS discouraged the growth of introns, it still allowed another form of code growth. We discovered that this was caused by a phenomenon that we called the incremental fitness intron. An incremental fitness intron is one that contributes only a small amount to the overall fitness value of the tree. An example of where an incremental fitness intron might arise is where a subtree is evolving towards a 0 by, for example dividing 1 by an ever-larger value. Because the fitness function ensures that the closer the specimen gets to 0, the fitter it is, incremental fitness introns flourish under the regime of IFS.

In order to remove incremental fitness introns, we introduced fitness bands. A 1% fitness band only allows an offspring to survive if its fitness is at least 1%

different to its parents. Under this regime, we were able to prevent code growth, even that caused by incremental fitness introns, and at the same time extend GP search and thus enable it to solve problems that were out of reach of standard GP (Smith and Harries, 1998). Using alternative selection strategies may be particularly important in data mining applications where there is a need to work with data of a higher dimensionality.

Code Growth Control Using Alternative Crossover Mechanisms

It has been recognised from the early stages in GP that the choice of genetic recombination operator can influence the growth in code size. Sims (1993) was an early attempt to limit code growth using a set of mutation operators that were designed to bias against an increase in code size. Rosca and Ballard (1996) approached the problem from a different angle, suggesting that the genetic operators themselves change dynamically to deal with increases in the size of members of the population selected for recombination. Their approach focuses on the effect of varying the probability of destructive genetic operators relative to the complexity of structures present in the population.

Standard crossover should not be regarded as the best method of genetic recombination simply because it is the most widely used. Alternate forms are possible, but existing off-the-shelf GP systems may only provide standard crossover (or perhaps also mutation), and implementing nonstandard forms of crossover can be time consuming and may produce no extra benefits for a data mining project. However, research is taking crossover in the direction of domain-specific forms of crossover (Langdon, 2000) and it is likely that in the future crossover may be more directed to the domain of the problem.

SUMMARY

This chapter has outlined areas in which GP may be successfully applied to data mining including clustering and categorisation. GP has faced problems with scaling and these have been investigated. Some of the recent research into identifying why the scaling problem exists and what can be done to improve the performance of GP on harder problems has also been described.

GP can be a potentially useful tool for data mining applications, but its strengths and weaknesses need to be clearly understood. This chapter describes some of the common problems that are encountered in using GP and suggests potential solutions.

Code growth is identified as a major problem GP and four methods of attack are described in increasing order of difficulty. In trying to apply GP to any problem, it is important to identify the method that is most likely to lead to an enhanced search capability and apply it. However, it is important also to recognise that some methods of enhancing search are easier to implement than others and it is useful to try easy methods first. In the future many of these methods are almost certain to be provided without any explicit effort by the user.

REFERENCES

Altenberg, L. (1994). The evolution of evolvability in genetic programming. In Kinnear K.J. (ed.) *Advances in genetic programming*, pp. 47-74. MIT Press, Cambridge, Mass.

Angeline P.J.(1997). Subtree Crossover: Building Block Engine or Macromutation? *Genetic Programming 1997: Proceedings of the Second Annual Conference*, pp. 9-17, Morgan Kaufmann, San Francisco.

Banzhaf W. ,Nordin P., Keller R. E. and Francone, F. D. (1998). *Genetic Programming: An Iintroduction*. Morgan Kaufmann, San Francisco.

Barnum, H., Bernstein H.J. and Spector L. (2000). Quantum circuits for OR and AND of Ors *Journal of Physics A: Mathematical and General*, 33(45), 8047-8057.

Bergstrom, A., Jaksetic, P. and Nordin P. (2000). Acquiring textual relations automatically on the web using genetic programming. *Genetic Programming: Proceedings of EuroGP'2000*, LNCS, Vol. 1802, pp. 237-246, Springer-Verlag, 2000.

Choenni, S. (1999) On the suitability of genetic-based algorithms for data mining *Advances in Database Technologies*, LNCS, Vol. 1552, pp. 55-67, Springer-Verlag, 1999.

Davidson, J.W., Savic, D.A. and Walters, G.A. (2000). Rainfall runoff modelling using a new polynomial regression method. *Proceedings of the 4th International Conference on HydroInformatics*.

Duffy, J. and Engle-Warnick, J. (1999). Using symbolic regression to infer strategies from experimental data. *Proceedings of the fifth International Conference: Computing in Economics and Finance,* 150-155.

Eggermont, J. and Van Hemert, J.I. (2001). *Adaptive Genetic Programming Applied to New and Existing Simple Regression Problems*. In Miller J. et al. (Eds.) *Genetic Programming: Proceedings of the 4th European Conference on Genetic Programming, EUROGP2001,* Lake Como, Italy. pp. 23-35. Lecture Notes in Computer Science Number 2038. Springer-Verlag, Berlin.

Evett, M. and Fernandez, T. (1998). Numeric Mutation Improves the discovery of Numeric Constants by Genetic Programming. In Koza, J.R. et al. (Eds.) *Genetic Programming 98: Proceedings of the Third International Conference*, pp. 223-231. Morgan Kaufmann.

Fayyad, U., Piatetsky-Shapiro, G. and Smyth, P. (1996). From data mining to knowledge discovery: an overview. In Fayyad U., Piatetsky-Shapiro G., Smyth P. and Uthurusamy R. (eds.) *Advances in Knowledge Discovery and Data Mining*. pp. 1-32. AAAI Press, Cambridge, Mass. Regression in GP. Evolutionary Programming VII. Proceedings of the 7th Annual Conference.

Freitas, A. (1997). A genetic programming framework for two data mining tasks: classification and generalised rule induction. In Koza J.R. et al. (eds.) *Genetic Programming 1997: Proceedings of the second International Conference*, pp. 96-101, Morgan Kaufmann.

Gathercole, C. and Ross, P. (1996). An adverse interaction between crossover and restricted tree depth in genetic programming. In Koza J.R. et al. (eds.) *Proceedings of the First International Conference on Genetic Programming.* pp. 291-296. MIT Press, Cambridge, Mass.

Geum, Yong Lee (1999). Genetic recursive regression for modelling and forecasting real-world chaotic time series. In Spector L. (ed.) *Advances in Genetic Programming 3*, pp. 401-423, MIT Press, 1999.

Howley, B. (1996) Genetic programming of near-minimum-time spacecraft attitude maneuvers *Genetic Programming 1996: Proceedings of the First Annual Conference*, pp. 98-106, MIT Press, Cambridge, Mass.

Iba, H., de Garis, H. and Sato, T. (1994) Genetic programming using a minimum description length principle. In Kinnear K.E. (ed.) *Advances in Genetic Programming*, pp. 265-284 MIT Press, Cambridge, Mass.

Kaboudan, M.A. (1999) Genetic evolution of regression models for business and economic forecasting. *Proceedings of the Congress on Evolutionary Computation*, Vol. 2, pp. 1260-1268. IEEE Press.

Kinnear, K.E. (1993) Generality and difficulty in genetic programming: Evolving a sort. In Forrest S. (ed.) *Proceedings of the Fifth International Conference on Genetic Algorithms*, pp. 287-294. University of Illinois at Urbana-Champaign. Morgan Kaufmann, San Francisco, CA.

Koza, J.R. (1992). *Genetic programming: on the programming of computers by means of natural selection*. MIT Press, Cambridge, Mass.

Langdon, W.B. (2000) Size fair and homologous tree genetic programming crossovers. *Genetic Programming and Evolvable Machines*, 1,2, pp. 95-119.

Langdon, W.B. and Poli, R. (1997b). Fitness causes bloat. *Technical Report CSRP-97-09* University of Birmingham, School of Computer Science.

Langdon, W.B. and Buxton, B.F. (2001). Evolving Receiver Operating Characteristics for Data Fusion. In Miller, J. et al. (Eds.) *Genetic Programming: Proceedings of the 4th European Conference on Genetic Programming, EUROGP2001, Lake Como, Italy*. pp. 23-35. Lecture Notes in Computer Science Number 2038. Springer-Verlag, Berlin.

Luke, S. (2000). *Issues in Scaling Genetic Programming: Breeding Strategies, Tree Generation, and Code Bloat*. PhD Thesis, Department of Computer Science, University of Maryland.

Marmelstein, R.E. and Lamont, G. (1998). Pattern classification using a hybrid genetic program-decision tree approach. In Koza J.R. et al. (Eds.) *Genetic Programming 98: Proceedings of the Third International Conference*, pp. 223-231. Morgan Kaufmann.

McKay, B., Willis, M.J. and Barton, G.W. (1997). Steady-state modelling of chemical process systems using genetic programming. *Computers and Chemical Engineering*, 21(9), 981-996.

Nachbar, R.B. (2000). Molecular evolution: automated manipulation of hierarchical chemical topology and its application to average molecular structures *Genetic Programming And Evolvable Machines*, 1(1/2), 57-94.

Nordin, P. and Banzhaf, W. (1995). Complexity compression and evolution. In Eshelman L.J. (Ed.) *Proceedings of the Sixth International Conference on Genetic Algorithms*, pp. 310-317. Morgan Kaufmann.

Piatetsky-Shapiro, G. and Matheus, C. (1994). The interestingness of deviations. In *Proceedings of KDD-1994*. Fayyad U. and Uthurusamy R. (eds.) Technical Report WS-03. Menlo Park Ca, AAAI Press.

Reynolds, C.W. (1994). Evolution of Obstacle Avoidance Behaviour: Using Noise to Promote Robust Solutions. In Kinnear K.E. (ed.) *Advances in Genetic Programming*, pp. 221-242 MIT Press, Cambridge, Mass.

Rosca, J.P. and Ballard, D.H. (1996). Complexity drift in evolutionary computation with tree representations. *Technical Report NRL5*, University of Rochester.

Ross, Q. J. (1993). *C4.5 – Programs for machine learning.* Morgan Kaufmann, 1993.

Silberschatz, A. and Tuzhilin, A. (1995) On subjective measures of interestingness in knowledge discovery. In *Proceedings of KDD-95: First International Conference on Knowledge Discovery and Data Mining,* pp. 275-281. Menlo Park, Ca: AAAI.

Sims, K. (1993) Interactive evolution of equations for procedural models. *The Visual Computer,*9 pp. 466-476, 1993.

Smith, P.W.H. and Harries, K. (1998). Code growth, introns and alternative selection schemes. *In Evolutionary Computation.* Cambridge: MIT Press. 6(4), 339-360.

Smith, P.W.H. (1999) Controlling code growth in genetic programming. In John R. and Birkenhead R. (eds.) *Advances In Soft Computing,* pp. 166-171. Physica-Verlag, 1999.

Soule, T. and Foster, J.A. (1997). Code size and depth flows in genetic programming. In Koza J.R. et al. (eds.) *Genetic Programming 1997: Proceedings of the Second International Conference,* pp. 313-320, Morgan Kaufmann.

Soule, T., Foster, J.A. and Dickinson, J. (1996). Code growth in genetic programming. In John R. Koza et al. (eds.) *Genetic Programming 1996: Proceedings of the First International Conference,* pp. 215-223, Stanford Unversity. MIT Press, Camb, Mass.

Taylor, J., Goodacre, R., Winson, M.K., Rowland, J.J., Gilbert ,R.J. and Kell, D.B. (1998). Genetic programming in the interpretation of fourier transform infrared spectra: quantification of metabolites of pharmaceutical importance. In *Koza J.R. et al. (eds.)Genetic Programming 98: Proceedings of the Third International Conference,* 377-380. Morgan Kaufmann.

Zhang, B. T. and Mühlenbein, H. (1995). Balancing accuracy and parsimony in genetic programming. *Evolutionary Computation.* Cambridge: MIT Press. 3(1), 17-38.

Chapter IX

A Building Block Approach to Genetic Programming for Rule Discovery

A.P. Engelbrecht and L. Schoeman
University of Pretoria, South Africa

Sonja Rouwhorst
Vrije Universiteit Amsterdam, The Netherlands

Genetic programming has recently been used successfully to extract knowledge in the form of IF-THEN rules. For these genetic programming approaches to knowledge extraction from data, individuals represent decision trees. The main objective of the evolutionary process is therefore to evolve the best decision tree, or classifier, to describe the data. Rules are then extracted, after convergence, from the best individual. The current genetic programming approaches to evolve decision trees are computationally complex, since individuals are initialized to complete decision trees.

This chapter discusses a new approach to genetic programming for rule extraction, namely the building block approach. This approach starts with individuals consisting of only one building block, and adds new building blocks during the evolutionary process when the simplicity of the individuals cannot account for the complexity in the underlying data.

Experimental results are presented and compared with that of C4.5 and CN2. The chapter shows that the building block approach achieves very good accuracies compared to that of C4.5 and CN2. It is also shown that the building block approach extracts substantially less rules.

A BUILDING BLOCK APPROACH TO GENETIC PROGRAMMING FOR RULE DISCOVERY

Recently developed knowledge extraction tools have their origins in artificial intelligence. These new tools combine and refine approaches such as artificial neural networks, genetic algorithms, genetic programming, fuzzy logic, clustering and statistics. While several tools have been developed, this chapter concentrates on a specific evolutionary computing approach, namely genetic programming (GP).

Evolutionary computing approaches to knowledge discovery have shown to be successful in knowledge extraction applications. They are, however, computationally expensive in their nature by starting evolution on large, complex structured individuals. This is especially true in the case of genetic programming where complex decision trees are evolved. This chapter presents a building-block approach to genetic programming, where conditions (or conjuncts) and sub-trees are only added to the tree when needed. The building-block approach to genetic programming (BGP) starts evolution with a population of the simplest individuals. That is, each individual consists of only one condition (the root of the tree), and the associated binary outcomes – thus representing two simple rules. These simple individuals evolve in the same way as for standard GP. When the simplicity of the BGP individuals fails to account for the complexity of the data, a new building block (condition) is added to individuals in the current population, thereby increasing their representation complexity. This building-block approach differs from standard GP mainly in the sense that standard GP starts with an initial population of individuals with various complexities.

The remainder of the chapter is organized as follows: the next section offers background on current knowledge extraction tools, and gives a motivation for the building-block approach. A short overview of standard GP is also given. The section that follows discusses the building-block approach in detail, with experimental results in the last section.

BACKGROUND

This section gives a short overview of well-known knowledge extraction tools, motivates the building-block approach and presents a summary of standard GP.

Knowledge Extraction Tools

The first knowledge extraction tools came from the machine learning community, grouped in two main categories based on the way that a classifier is constructed: decision tree approaches and rule induction approaches. The most popular decision tree algorithm was developed by Quinlan (1992), namely ID3. Subsequent improvement of ID3 resulted in C4.5 (Quinlan, 1993), which was later further extended, with the improved version called C5 (Quinlan, 1998). These decision tree approaches construct a decision tree, from which if-then rules are extracted (using e.g.,

C4.5rules (Quinlan, 1993)). The AQ family of rule induction algorithms included some of the first algorithms to induce rules directly from data (Michalski, Mozetic, Hong & Lavrae, 1986). CN2 (Clarke & Niblett, 1989), which uses a beam strategy to induce rules, is one of the most popular algorithms in this class, still in use by many data mining experts.

Recently the development of new data mining tools concentrated on neural networks (NN) and evolutionary computing (EC). The use of NNs in data mining requires that a NN classifier be built first. That is, an NN has to be trained to an acceptable accuracy. After training, a rule extraction algorithm is applied in a post-processing phase to convert the numerically encoded knowledge of the NN (as encapsulated by the weights of the network) into a symbolic form. Several rule extraction algorithms for NNs have been developed, of which the KT-algorithm of Fu (1994) and the N-of-M algorithm of Craven and Shavlik (1994) are popular.

Several evolutionary computing algorithms have also been developed to evolve decision structures. One way of using a genetic algorithm (GA) in data mining is to use the GA to select the most relevant features to be used as input to other data mining algorithms such as C4.5 or CN2. Studies showed that the combination of GA plus a traditional induction algorithm gives better results in terms of accuracy and reducing the dimension of feature space, than using only the traditional induction algorithm (Cherkauer & Shavlik, 1996). Alternatively, GAs can be used to search for optimal rule sets. For example, GABIL (De Jong, Spears & Gordon, 1991) performs an incremental search for a set of classification rules, represented by fixed-length bit-strings, using only features with nominal values. The bit-strings used by the GA represent a rule using $nk_i + 1$ bits, where n is the total number of features and k_i is the number of values of feature i, $i \leq n$. The last bit of the string is used to store the classification. GABIL initially accepts a single instance from a pool of instances and searches for as perfect a rule set as possible for this example within the time/space constraints given. This rule set is then used to predict the classification of the next instance. If the prediction is incorrect, the GA is invoked to evolve a new rule set using the two instances. If the prediction is correct, the instance is simply stored with the previous instance and the rule set remains unchanged.

Other GA-based knowledge discovery tools include SET-Gen (Cherkauer et al., 1996), REGAL (Giordana, Saitta & Zini, 1994) and GA-MINER (Flockhart & Radcliffe, 1995).

A genetic programming (GP) approach to rule discovery involves the evolution of a decision tree that forms an accurate classifier. After convergence, rules are extracted from the decision tree as represented by the best individual. Research in applying GP for data mining is fairly new, including the work of Marmelstein and Lamont (1998), Bojarczuk, Lopes and Freitas (1999), Eggermont, Eiben and Hemert (1999), Bot (1999), Folino, Pizzyti and Spezzano (2000), and Wong and Leung (2000). Where Marmelstein et al. (1998) and Bojarczuk et al. (1999) used standard GP operators to evolve decision trees, Folino et al. used a hybrid GP and simulated annealing strategy to evolve decision trees. Eggermont et al. (1999) used a stepwise adaptation of weights (SAW) strategy to repeatedly redefine the fitness function during evolution. LOGENPRO (Wong et al., 2000) combines the parallel search power of GP and the knowledge representation power of first-order logic. It takes advantage of existing inductive logic programming and GP systems, while avoiding their disadvantages. A suitable grammar to represent rules has been designed and modifications of the grammar to learn rules with different format have been studied, having the advantage that domain knowledge is used and the need for a closed function set is avoided. Bot (1999) uses GP to evolve oblique decision trees, where the functions in the nodes of the trees use one or more variables. The building-block approach to GP differs from the above GP approaches in that standard decision trees are evolved, from simple trees to complex trees.

Ockham's Razor and Building Blocks

William of Ockham (1285-1347/49) was a leading figure in the fourteenth-century golden age of Oxford scholasticism (McGrade, 1992). He became well-known for his work in theology and philosophy. Currently, his name is mostly associated with the so-called 'principle of parsimony' or 'law of economy' (Hoffmann, Minkin and Carpenter, 1997). Although versions of this principle are to be found in Aristotle and works of various other philosophers preceding Ockham, he employed it so frequently and judiciously that it came to be associated with his name. Some centuries were to elapse before the principle of parsimony became known as 'Ockham's razor' (the earliest reference appears to be in 1746). The metaphor of a razor cutting through complicated scholastic and theological arguments to reach the core of truth is probably responsible for the general appeal of the principle and for associating it with Ockham's name.

The principle of parsimony can be stated in several ways, for example:

- It is futile to do with more what can be done with fewer. [*Frustra fit per plura quod potest fieri per pauciora.*]
- Plurality should not be assumed without necessity. [*Pluralitas non est ponenda sine necessitate.*]
- Entities are not to be multiplied beyond necessity. [*Non sunt multiplicanda entia praeter necessitatem.*]

Although the principle of parsimony was formulated to guide the evaluation of symbolic reasoning systems, it is frequently quoted in scientific disciplines. Ockham's razor has, among others, inspired the generalization of neural networks with as few as possible connections (Thodberg, 1991), and fitness evaluation based on a simplicity criterion (Bäck, Fogel & Michalewicz, 2000b, p. 15).

In evolutionary computation the idea of building blocks is primarily associated with genetic algorithms. The building-block hypothesis states that GAs produce fitter partial solutions by combining building blocks comprising short, low-order highly fit schemas into more highly fit higher-order schemas (Hoffmann et al., 1997). In this chapter building blocks are used with genetic programming where the population is a set of possible decision trees, consisting of conditions.

In keeping with the economy principle or principle of parsimony as embodied by Ockham's razor, the building-block approach to genetic programming starts with an initial population of very simple programs of one node each. Building blocks, like decisions, are added gradually to increase representation complexity. At no stage the population of programs will be more complex than what is absolutely necessary, thus no plurality is assumed without necessity.

GENETIC PROGRAMMING FOR DECISION TREES

Genetic programming (GP) is viewed as a specialization of genetic algorithms (Bäck et al., 2000a, 2000b). Similar to GAs, GP concentrates on the evolution of genotypes. The main difference is in the representation scheme used. Where GAs use string representations, GP represents individuals as executable programs (represented as trees). The objective of GP is therefore to evolve computer programs to solve problems. For each generation, each evolved program (individual) is executed to measure its performance, which is then used to quantify the fitness of that program.

In order to design a GP, a grammar needs to be defined that accurately reflects the problem and all constraints. Within this grammar, a terminal set and function set are defined. The terminal set specifies all the variables and constants, while the function set contains all the functions that can be applied to the elements of the set. These functions may include mathematical, arithmetic and/or boolean functions. Decision structures such as if-then-else can also be included within the function set. Using tree terminology, elements of the terminal set form the leaf nodes of the evolved tree, and elements of the function set form the non-leaf nodes.

In terms of data mining, an individual represents a decision tree. Each non-leaf node represents a condition, and a leaf node represents a class. Thus, the terminal set specifies all the classes, while the non-terminal set specifies the relational operators and attributes of the problem. Rules are extracted from the decision tree by following all the paths from the root to leaf nodes, taking the conjunction of the condition of each level. The fitness of a decision tree is usually expressed as the accuracy of that tree, i.e., the number of instances correctly covered. Crossover occurs by swapping randomly selected sub-trees of the parent trees. Several mutation strategies can be implemented:

- *Prune mutation*: A non-leaf node is selected randomly and replaced by a leaf node reflecting the class that occurs most frequently.
- *Grow mutation*: A node is randomly selected and replaced by a randomly generated sub-tree.
- *Node mutation*: The content of nodes are mutated, in any of the following ways: (1) the attribute is replaced with a randomly selected one from the set of attributes; (2) the relational operator is replaced with a randomly selected one; and (3) perturb the threshold values with Gaussian noise in the case of

continuous-valued attributes, or replace with a randomly selected value for discrete-valued attributes.

Usually, for standard genetic programming the initial population is created to consist of complete decision trees, randomly created. It is however possible that the initial population can consist of decision trees of varying sizes.

BUILDING BLOCK APPROACH TO GENETIC PROGRAMMING (BGP)

This section describes the building-block approach to genetic programming for evolving decision trees. The assumptions of BGP are first given, after which the elements of BGP are discussed. A complete pseudo-code algorithm is given.

Assumptions

BGP assumes complete data, meaning that instances should not contain missing or unknown values. Also, each instance must have a target classification, making BGP a supervised learner. BGP assumes attributes to be one of four data types:

- Numerical and discreet (which implies an ordered attribute), for example the age of a patient.
- Numerical and continuous, for example length.
- Nominal (not ordered), for example the attribute colour.
- Boolean, which allows an attribute to have a value of either true or false.

Elements of BGP

The proposed knowledge discovery tool is based on the concept of a building block. A building block represents one condition, or node in the tree. Each building block consists of three parts: <attribute> <relational operator> <threshold>. An <attribute> can be any of the attributes of the database. The <relational operator> can be any of the set $\{=, \neq, <, \leq, >, \geq\}$ for numerical attributes, or $\{=, \neq\}$ for nominal and boolean attributes. The <threshold> can be a value or another attribute. Allowing the threshold to be an attribute makes it possible to extract rules such as 'IF Income > Expenditure THEN outcome'. It is however possible that the decision tree contain nodes where incompatible attributes are compared, for example 'Sex > Expenditure'. This problem can, however, be solved easily by including semantic rules to prevent such comparisons, either by penalizing such trees, or by preventing any operation to create such comparisons.

The initial population is constructed such that each individual consists of only one node and two leaf nodes corresponding to the two outcomes of the condition. The class of a leaf node depends on the distribution of the training instances over the classes in the training set and the training instances over the classes, propagated to the leaf node. To illustrate this, consider a training set consisting of 100 instances which are classified into four classes *A*, *B*, *C* and *D*. Of these instances, 10 belong to class *A*, 20 to class *B*, 30 to class *C* and 40 to class *D*. Thus, the distribution of the classes in this example is skewed [10,20,30,40]. If the classes were evenly distributed, there would be 25 instances belonging to class *A*, also 25 belonging to class *B*, etc. Now let's say there are 10 out of the 100 instances, which are propagated to the leaf node, for which we want to determine the classification. Suppose these 10 instances are distributed in the following way: [1,2,3,4]. Which class should be put into the leaf node when the distribution of training instances over the classes in the training set is the same as the distribution in the leaf node? In this case we chose to put the class with the highest number of instances into the leaf node, which is class *D*. What happens if the two distributions are dissimilar to each other? Let's say the overall class distribution is again [10,20,30,40] and the distribution of the instances over the classes propagated to the leaf node this time is [2,2,2,2]. A correction factor that accounts for the overall distribution will be determined for each class first. The correction factors are 25/10, 25/20, 25/30 and 25/40 for classes *A, B, C* and *D* respectively, where 25 is the number of instances per class in case of an equal distribution. After this, the correction factors are combined with the distribution of the instances in the leaf node and the class corresponding to the highest number is chosen ([(25/10)*2, (25/20)*2, (25/30)*2, (25/40)*2] which equals [5, 1.25, 3.33, 1.88] and means class *A* will be chosen).

A first choice for the fitness function could be the classification accuracy of the decision tree represented by an individual. However, taking classification accuracy as a measure of fitness, for a set of rules when the distribution of the classes among the instances is skewed, does not account for the significance of rules that predict a class that is poorly represented. Instead of using the accuracy of the complete set of rules, BGP uses the accuracy of the rules independently and determines which rule has the lowest accuracy on the instances of the training set that are covered by this rule. In other words, the fitness of the complete set of rules is determined by the weakest element in the set.

In the equation below, the function $C(i)$ returns 1 if the instance i is correctly classified by rule R and 0 if not. If rule R covers P instances of the training set, then

$$Accuracy(R) = \sum_{i=1}^{P} C(i)/P$$

In short, the function above calculates the accuracy of a rule over the instances that are covered by this rule. Let S be a set of rules. Then, the fitness of an individual is expressed as

Fitness (S) = *MIN (Accuracy(R))*   *for all R ∈ S*

Tournament selection is used to select parents for crossover. Before crossover is applied, the crossover probability P_C and a random number r between 0 and 1 determine whether the crossover operation will be applied: if $r < P_C$ then crossover is applied, otherwise not. Crossover of two parent trees is achieved by creating two copies of the trees that form two intermediate offspring. Then one crossover point is selected randomly in each copy. The final offspring is obtained by exchanging sub-trees under the selected crossover points.

The current BGP implementation uses three types of mutation, namely mutation on the relational operator, mutation on the threshold and prune mutation. Each of these mutations occurs at a user-specified probability. Given the probability on a relational operator, M_{RO}, between 0 and 1, a random number r between 0 and 1 is generated for every condition in the tree. If $r < M_{RO}$, then the relational operator in the particular condition will be changed into a new relational operator. If the attribute on the left-hand side in the condition is numerical, then the new relational operator will be one of the set $\{=, \neq, <, \leq, >, \geq\}$. If the attribute on the left-hand side is not numerical, the new relational operator will either be = or $\neq$.

A parameter M_{RHS} determines the chance that the threshold of a condition in the decision tree will be mutated. Like the previous mutation operator, a random number r between 0 and 1 is generated, and if $r < M_{RHS}$ then the right-hand side of the particular condition will be changed into a new right-hand side. This new right-hand side can be either a value of the attribute on the left-hand side, or a different attribute. The probability that the right-hand side is an attribute is determined by yet another parameter P_A. The new value of the right-hand side is determined randomly.

A parameter P_P is used to determine whether the selected tree should be pruned, in the same way as the parameter P_C does for the crossover operator. If the pruning operation is allowed, a random internal node of the decision tree is chosen and its sub-tree is deleted. Two leaf nodes classifying the instances, that are propagated to these leaf nodes, replace the selected internal node.

The Algorithm

Algorithm BGP

    T := 0

    Select initial population

    Evaluate population P(T)

    while not 'termination-condition' **do**

        T := T + 1

        if 'add_conditions_criterion' **then**

          add condition to trees in population

        end if

        Select subpopulation P(T) from P(T-1)

        Apply recombination operators on individuals of P(T)

        Evaluate P(T)

        if 'found_new_best_tree' **then**

          store copy of new best tree

        end if

    end while

  end algorithm

Two aspects of the BGP algorithm still need to be explained. The first is the condition which determines if a new building block should be added to each of the individuals in the current population. The following rule is used for this purpose:

IF ($(ad_{(t)} + aw_{(t)}) - (ad_{(t-1)} + aw_{(t-1)}) < L$) THEN 'add_conditions'

where $ad_{(t)}$ means the average depth of the trees in the current generation t, $aw_{(t)}$ means the average width in the current generation, $ad_{(t-1)}$ is the average depth of the trees in the previous generation and $aw_{(t-1)}$ is the average width in the previous generation. L is a parameter of the algorithm and is usually set to 0. In short, if $L = 0$, this rule determines if the sum of the average depth and width of the trees in a generation decreases and adds conditions to the trees if this is the case. If the criterion for adding a condition to the decision trees is met, then all the trees in the population receive one randomly generated new condition. The newly generated condition replaces a randomly chosen leaf node of the decision tree. Since the new condition to be added to a tree is generated randomly, there is a small probability that the newly generated node is a duplicate. Such duplicates are accepted within the tree; however, when rules are extracted from the best individual after convergence, a simplification step is used to remove redundant conditions from the extracted rules. A different approach could be to prevent adding a node to the tree which already exists within that tree. The same applies to mutation and cross-over operators. Furthermore, it is possible that a node added to a tree (by means of the growth operator, mutation or cross-over) represents a condition that contradicts that of another node within the tree. This is not a problem, since such contradictions will result in a low accuracy of the tree, hence a low fitness value.

Finally, the evolutionary process stops when a satisfactory decision tree has been evolved. BGP uses a termination criterion similar to the temperature function used in simulated annealing (Aarts & Korst, 1989). It uses a function that calculates a goal for the fitness of the best rule set that depends on the *temperature* at that stage of the run. At the start of the algorithm, the temperature is very high and so is the goal for the fitness of the best rule set. With time, the temperature drops, which in turn makes the goal for the fitness of the best rule set easier to obtain. $T(t)$ is the temperature at generation t defined by a very simple function: $T(t) = T_0 - t$. T_0 is the initial temperature, a parameter of the algorithm. Whether a rule set S (as represented by an individual) at generation t is *satisfactory* is determined by the following rule:

$$IF \left(Fitness(S) > e^{\left(c\left(\frac{trainsize}{T_0}\right) - c\left(\frac{trainsize}{T(i)}\right) \right)} \right) \quad THEN \quad satisfactory$$

where c is a parameter of the algorithm (usually set to 0.1 for our experiments), and *trainsize* is the number of training instances. When the temperature gets close to zero, the criterion for the fitness of the best tree quickly drops to zero too. This ensures that the algorithm will always terminate within T_0 generations.

EXPERIMENTAL RESULTS

This section compares the building-block approach to genetic programming for data mining with well-known data mining tools, namely C4.5 and CN2.

Database Characteristics

The three data mining tools BGP, CN2 and CN4.5 were tested on three real-world databases, namely ionosphere, iris and pima-diabetes, and one artificial database, the three monks problems. None of the databases had missing values, two databases use only continuous attributes, while the other uses a combination of nominal, boolean or numerical attributes.

The ionosphere database contains radar data collected by a system consisting of a phased array of 16 high-frequency antennas with a total transmitted power in the order of 6.4 kilowatts. The targets were free electrons in the ionosphere. 'Good' radar returns are those showing evidence of some type of structure in the ionosphere. 'Bad' returns are those that do not; their signals pass through the ionosphere. Received signals were processed using an auto-correlation function whose arguments are the time of a pulse and the pulse number. Seventeen pulse numbers were used for the system. Instances in this database are described by two attributes per pulse number, corresponding to the complex values returned by the function resulting from the complex electromagnetic signal. This resulted in a data set consisting of 351 instances, of which 126 are 'bad' and 225 are 'good'. The instances use 34 continuous attributes in the range [0,1]. The 351 instances were divided into a training and a test set by randomly choosing 51 instances for the test set and the remaining 300 instances for the training set.

The iris database is possibly one of the most frequently used benchmarks for evaluating data mining tools. It is a well-defined problem with clear separating class boundaries. The data set contains 150 instances using three classes, where each class refers to a type of iris plant, namely *Setosa, Versicolour* and *Virginica*. The database uses four continuous attributes: *sepal length*, *sepal width*, *petal length* and *petal width* all measured in centimeters. Two attributes, *petal length* and *petal width*, both have high correlation with the classification. *Sepal width* has no correlation at all with the classification of the instances. To obtain a training and test set, the 150 instances were divided randomly into a set of 100 instances for the training and 50 instances for the test set.

The Monks task has three artificial data sets that use the same attributes and values. All three data sets use two classes: *Monk* and *Not Monk*. The instances for the first domain were generated using the rule: IF $(A1 = A2)$ OR $(A5 = 1)$ THEN *Monk*. For the second domain the following rule was used: IF TWO OF $A1 = 1, A2 = 1, A3 = 1, A4 = 1, A5 = 1, A6 = 1$ THEN *Monk*. The third domain was generated using the rule: IF $(A5 = 3$ AND $A4 = 1)$ OR $(A5 \neq 4$ AND $A2 \neq 3)$ THEN *Monk*. Five percent class noise was added to the training instances of the third data set. Of the 432 instances of the Monks-1 and Monks-2 subsets, 300 instances were randomly chosen for the training set and the 132 remaining instances were set aside for the test set.

The Pima-diabetes database consists of 768 patients who were tested for signs of diabetes. Out of the 768 patients, 268 were diagnosed with diabetes. All eight attributes are numerical; 268 instances were chosen randomly for the test set and the 500 remaining instances made up the training set.

Performance Criteria and Statistics

The three data mining tools were compared using four performance criteria, namely:

1. the classification accuracy of the rule set on training instances;
2. the generalization ability, measured as the classification accuracy on a test set;
3. the number of rules in the rule set; and
4. the average number of conditions per rule.

While the first two criteria quantify the accuracy of rule sets, the last two express the complexity, hence comprehensibility, of rule sets.

For each database, each of the three tools was applied 30 times on 30 randomly constructed training and test sets. Each triple of simulations (i.e., BGP, C4.5 and CN2) was done on the same training and test sets. Results reported for each of the performance criteria are averages over the 30 simulations, together with 95% confidence intervals. Paired t-tests were used to compare the results of each two algorithms in order to determine if there is a significant difference in performance. For each of the datasets used for experimentation, the optimal values for the BGP parameters, as summarized in Table 1, were first determined through cross-validation.

Results

Tables 2 and 3 show the mean accuracy on training and test sets over 30 runs for each algorithm. The confidence intervals and the standard deviations of the

Table 1: BGP system parameters

Parameter	Data Set					
	Ionosphere	Iris	Monks1	Monks2	Monks3	Pima-diabetes
c	0.1	0.1	0.1	0.1	0.1	0.1
L	0.0	0.0	0.0	0.0	0.0	0.0
Tournament Size, k	20	10	10	10	10	20
Initial temperature, T_0	2000	300	200	1500	500	2000
Prob. RHS is Attribute, P_A	0.1	0.2	0.7	0.2	0.1	0.1
Mut. On RHS, M_{RHS}	0.2	0.7	0.7	0.4	0.3	0.2
Mut. On Rel. Op., M_{RO}	0.4	0.2	0.2	0.2	0.3	0.4
Probability Pruning, P_P	0.5	0.2	0.2	0.5	0.5	0.5
Probability Crossover, P_C	0.5	0.5	0.8	0.5	0.5	0.5

accuracies are also given. The stars in the table indicate for each task which algorithm has the highest accuracy. Table 2 shows the accuracies on the training set. This table consistently shows that CN2 has the highest training accuracy on each task. Table 3, which summarizes the accuracies on the test set, shows that CN2 overfits the training data, since it does not perform well on the test set. The accuracies obtained by CN2 and C4.5 on the Monks1 task were very consistent. Each run resulted in perfect classification. When the data set of a task does not contain any noise, the two algorithms CN2 and C4.5 will most probably find a perfect classifier. The Monks2 problem is one of the exceptions to this rule, because it does not contain any noise and still has an accuracy of about 63% for CN2 and C4.5. For Monks3 there was only one available data set, so it was not possible to perform several runs of the algorithms. Therefore, for this task no confidence intervals, standard deviation or t-test were calculated.

The results of the t-tests are given in Table 4. For the Iono task, both CN2 and C4.5 obtained significantly better results than BGP. On the other hand, BGP performed significantly better than both CN2 and C4.5 on the Monks2 data set. On the remaining tasks the differences in mean accuracies were not found to be of significant size. BGP lacks the exploration power to find a classifier in a search that involves many continuous attributes, like the Iono task. This could be improved by adding a local search on the threshold level.

Table 2: Accuracy on training set, including confidence levels at 95% probability and standard deviation of accuracy. The star indicates the best accuracy on the given task.

Task	BGP		CN2		C4.5	
	Training Accuracy	Standard Deviation	Training Accuracy	Standard Deviation	Training Accuracy	Standard Deviation
Iono	0.895 ± 0.120	0.013	0.989 ± 0.038*	0.003	0.979 ± 0.051	0.007
Iris	0.967 ± 0.064	0.012	0.987 ± 0.040*	0.012	0.982 ± 0.047	0.010
Monks1	0.994 ± 0.026	0.022	1.000 ± 0.000*	0.000	0.999 ± 0.008	0.003
Monks2	0.715 ± 0.161	0.012	0.992 ± 0.030*	0.004	0.769 ± 0.150	0.049
Monks3	0.934	n/a	1.000*	n/a	0.951	n/a
Pima	0.766 ± 0.152	0.010	0.887 ± 0.113*	0.028	0.855 ± 0.126	0.025

Table 3: Accuracy on test set, including confidence levels at 95% probability and standard deviation of accuracy. The star indicates the best accuracy on the given task.

Task	BGP		CN2		C4.5	
	Test Accuracy	Standard Deviation	Test Accuracy	Standard Deviation	Test Accuracy	Standard Deviation
Iono	0.892 ± 0.111	0.037	0.921 ± 0.097	0.040	0.979 ± 0.051*	0.007
Iris	0.941 ± 0.085	0.027	0.943 ± 0.083	0.034	0.945 ± 0.082*	0.030
Monks1	0.993 ± 0.029	0.025	1.000 ± 0.000*	0.000	1.000 ± 0.000*	0.000
Monks2	0.684 ± 0.166*	0.040	0.626 ± 0.173	0.039	0.635 ± 0.172	0.051
Monks3	0.972*	n/a	0.907	n/a	0.963	n/a
Pima	0.725 ± 0.160	0.031	0.739 ± 0.157*	0.024	0.734 ± 0.158	0.025

In comparing the three algorithms, the biggest difference was not in the resulting accuracies, but in the mean number of rules extracted. As shown in Table 5, the classifier of the BGP algorithm used consistently less rules than the classifiers that resulted from CN2 and C4.5. What is especially striking in these results is that the BGP algorithm performs no tree or rule pruning of the best individual, in contrast to both C4.5 and CN2. The difference in the number of rules extracted is nicely illustrated on the Monks2 task, where BGP extracted on average six rules, while CN2 extracted 122.8 rules, and C4.5 extracted 13.9 rules. The mean number of conditions per rule for BGP is slightly larger in the Iono and Iris task, but smaller in the remaining tasks, showing that BGP managed to extract more crisp rules for most of the tasks.

The running time of the algorithms was not mentioned among the performance criteria in comparing the algorithms, but since big differences in running time for BGP versus CN2 and C4.5 were observed, it seems apt to discuss this topic here. Every time a recombination operator, like crossover, is applied to a decision tree, the training instances need to be redivided to the leaf nodes of the decision tree. Thus, the time complexity of one generation of BGP is in the order of $R * (N * P)$, where

Table 4: Comparison between BGP and CN2, and BGP and C4.5 using t-tests over 30 training and test sets to determine confidence intervals at 95%. A '+' means that BGP showed better results than the algorithm it is compared to and '-' means BGP's results wore worse. The bold font indicates that one method is significantly better than the other methods.

Task	BGP vs. CN2	BGP vs. C4.5
Iono	**-0.0286 ± 0.0263**	**-0.0385 ± 0.0142**
Iris	-0.0237 ± 0.0267	-0.00400 ± 0.0115
Monks1	0.00657 ± 0.00933	-0.00657 ± 0.00933
Monks2	**+0.0576 ± 0.0165**	**+0.0485 ± 0.0154**
Pima	-0.0132 ± 0.0160	-0.00844 ± 0.0190

Table 5: Mean number of rules per run and mean number of conditions per rule for each of the tasks and each of the algorithms. The star indicates for each row the smallest number of rules.

Task	BGP		CN2		C4.5	
	Average nr. Rules	Average nr. conditions	Average nr. rules	Average nr. conditions	Average nr. Rules	Average nr. conditions
Iono	4.70*	2.39	17.07	2.35	8.57	2.15
Iris	3.37*	2.02	5.33	1.64	4.10	1.60
Monks1	4.37*	2.22	18.0	2.37	21.5	2.73
Monks2	6.00*	2.96	122.8	4.53	13.9	3.01
Monks3	3*	1.67	22	2.17	12	2.77
Pima	3.70*	1.97	35.8	2.92	12.73	3.90

R is the number of recombination operators, N is the number of training instances and P is the number of individuals in a population. For k generations the time complexity is linear, of the order $O(k * (R * (N * P)))$. BGP has a much longer running time than the other two algorithms CN2 and C4.5 (in the order of hours versus minutes). This is a serious disadvantage of BGP. The computationally complexity of BGP limits the application of this tool to databases of small sizes. However, strategies such as local search and windowing (as employed in C4.5) can be used to decrease the computational complexity of BGP.

Conclusions and Future Work

A new approach was introduced, called 'Building block approach to Genetic Programming' (BGP), to find a good classifier for classification tasks in data mining. It is an evolutionary search method based on genetic programming, but differs in that it starts searching on the smallest possible individuals in the population, and gradually increases the complexity of the individuals. The individuals in the population are decision trees, using relational functions in the internal nodes of the tree. Selection of individuals for recombination is done using tournament selection. Four different recombination operators were applied to the decision trees: crossover, pruning and two types of mutation. BGP was compared to two standard machine learning algorithms, CN2 and C4.5, on four benchmark tasks: Iris, Ionosphere, Monks and Pima-diabetes. The accuracies of BGP were similar to or better than the accuracies of CN2 and C4.5, except on the Ionosphere task. The main difference with the C4.5 and especially CN2 is that BGP produced these accuracies consistently using less rules.

Two disadvantages of BGP are the time-complexity and problems with many continuous attributes. The development of scaling algorithms for BGP and GP for data mining to be suitable for handling large databases is an interesting topic for future research. Continuous-valued attributes enlarge the search space substantially, since there are an infinite number of threshold values to be tested. Currently the search for the best threshold is done through a mutation operator which adds a Gaussian value to the current threshold, thus doing a random search. Future extensions of BGP will include a mutation operator on thresholds that performs a local search for the best value of that threshold.

Other research directions to improve the performance of the current building block approach may include the following:
- adding a local search phase to optimize the threshold value of a condition,
- adding semantic rules to the grammar of the GP to prevent the comparison of incompatible attributes in the nodes of the decision tree,
- investigating new criteria, that also depends on classification accuracy, to test when new building blocks should be added, and
- implementing techniques to select the best building block to be added to individuals.

REFERENCES

Aarts, E.H.L., & Korst, J. (1989). *Simulated Annealing and Boltzmann Machines.* John Wiley & Sons.

Bäck, T., Fogel, D.B., & Michalewicz, Z. (Eds.). (2000a). *Evolutionary Computation 1.* Institute of Physics Publishers.

Bäck, T., Fogel, D.B., & Michalewicz, Z. (Eds.). (2000b). *Evolutionary Computation 2.* Institute of Physics Publishers.

Bojarczuk, C.C., Lopes, H.S., & Freitas, A.A. (1999). Discovering Comprehensible Classification Rules using Genetic Programming: A Case Study in a Medical Domain. *Proceedings of the Genetic and Evolutionary Computation Conference* (pp. 953-958). Morgan Kaufmann.

Bot, M. (1999). *Application of Genetic Programming to Induction of Linear Classification Trees. Final Term Project Report.* Faculty of Exact Sciences. Vrije Universiteit, Amsterdam.

Cherkauer, K.J., & Shavlik, J.W. (1996). Growing Simpler Decision Trees to Facilitate Knowledge Discovery. *Proceedings of the 2nd International Conference on Knowledge Discovery and Data Mining.*

Clarke, P., & Niblett, T. (1989). The CN2 Induction Algorithm. *Machine Learning. 3*, 261-284.

Craven, M.W., & Shavlik, J.W. (1994). Using Sampling and Queries to Extract Rules from Trained Neural Networks. *Proceedings of the 11th International Conference on Machine Learning.*

De Jong, K.A., Spears, W.M., & Gordon, D.F. (1991). Using Genetic Algorithms for Concept Learning. *Proceedings of International Joint Conference on Artificial Intelligence* (pp. 651-656). IEEE Press.

Eggermont, J., Eiben, A.E., & Van Hemert, J.I. (1999). Adapting the Fitness Function in GP for Data Mining. *Proceedings of the European Conference on Genetic Programming.*

Flockhart, I.W., & Radcliffe, N.J. (1995). *GA-MINER: Parallel Data Mining with Hierarchical Genetic Algorithms Final Report.* EPCC-AIKMS-GA-MINER-REPORT 1.0. University of Edenburgh.

Folino, G., Pizzyti C., & Spezzano, G. (2000). Genetic Programming and Simulated Annealing: A Hybrid Method to Evolve Decision Trees. *Proceedings of the European Conference on Genetic Programming.*

Fu, L.M. (1994). *Neural Networks in Computer Intelligence.* McGraw Hill.

Giordana, A., Saitta, L., & Zini, F. (1994). Learning Disjunctive Concepts by Means of Genetic Algorithms. *Proceedings of the 11th International Conference on Machine Learning* (pp. 96-104).

Hoffmann, R., Minkin, V.I., & Carpenter, B.K. (1997). Ockham's razor and Chemistry. *International Journal for the Philosophy of Chemistry. 3*, 3-28.

Marmelstein, R.E., & Lamont, G.B. (1998). Pattern Classification using a Hybrid Genetic Program – Decision Tree Approach. *Proceedings of the Third Annual Conference of Genetic Programming* (pp. 223-231). Morgan Kaufmann.

McGrade, A.S. (Eds.). (1992). *William of Ockham – A short Discourse on Tyrannical Government.* Cambridge University Press.

Michalski, R., Mozetic, I., Hong, J., Lavrae, N. (1986). The AQ15 Inductive Learning System: an Overview and Experiments. *Proceedings of IMAL.*

Quinlan, R. (1992). *Machine Learning and ID3*. Morgan Kauffmann Publishers.

Quinlan, R. (1993). *C4.5: Programs for Machine Learning*. Morgan Kaufmann Publishers.

Quinlan, R. (1998). C5.0.   Retrieved March 2001 from the World Wide Web: www.rulequest.com.

Thodberg, H.H. (1991). Improving Generalization of Neural Networks through Pruning. *International Journal of Neural Systems. 1*(4), 317 – 326.

Wong, M.L., & Leung, K.S. (2000). *Data Mining using Grammar Based Genetic Programming and Applications*. Kluwer Academic Publishers.

PART FOUR:

ANT COLONY OPTIMIZATION
AND IMMUNE SYSTEMS

Chapter X

An Ant Colony Algorithm for Classification Rule Discovery

Rafael S. Parpinelli and Heitor S. Lopes
Centro Federal de Educacao Tecnologica do Parana-Curitiba, Brazil

Alex A. Freitas
Pontificia Universidade Catolica do Parana, Brazil

This work proposes an algorithm for rule discovery called Ant-Miner (Ant Colony-Based Data Miner). The goal of Ant-Miner is to extract classification rules from data. The algorithm is based on recent research on the behavior of real ant colonies as well as in some data mining concepts. We compare the performance of Ant-Miner with the performance of the well-known C4.5 algorithm on six public domain data sets. The results provide evidence that: (a) Ant-Miner is competitive with C4.5 with respect to predictive accuracy; and (b) the rule sets discovered by Ant-Miner are simpler (smaller) than the rule sets discovered by C4.5.

INTRODUCTION

In essence, the classification task consists of associating each case (object or record) to one class, out of a set of predefined classes, based on the values of some attributes (called predictor attributes) for the case.

There has been a great interest in the area of data mining, in which the general goal is to discover knowledge that is not only correct, but also comprehensible and interesting for the user (Fayyad, Piatetsky-Shapiro, & Smyth, 1996; Freitas &

Lavington, 1998). Hence, the user can understand the results produced by the system and combine them with her own knowledge to make a well-informed decision, rather than blindly trusting a system producing incomprehensible results.

In data mining, discovered knowledge is often represented in the form of IF-THEN prediction (or classification) rules, as follows: *IF <conditions> THEN <class>*. The *<conditions>* part (antecedent) of the rule contains a logical combination of predictor attributes, in the form: *term1* AND *term2* AND ... . Each term is a triple *<attribute, operator, value>*, such as <Gender = female>.

The *<class>* part (consequent) of the rule contains the class predicted for cases (objects or records) whose predictor attributes satisfy the *<conditions>* part of the rule.

To the best of our knowledge the use of Ant Colony algorithms (Dorigo, Colorni, & Maniezzo, 1996) as a method for discovering classification rules, in the context of data mining, is a research area still unexplored by other researchers. Actually, the only Ant Colony algorithm developed for data mining that we are aware of is an algorithm for clustering (Monmarche, 1999), which is, of course, a data mining task very different from the classification task addressed in this chapter. Also, Cordón, Castillas and Herrera (2000) have proposed another kind of Ant Colony Optimization application that learns fuzzy control rules, but it is outside the scope of data mining.

We believe the development of Ant Colony algorithms for data mining is a promising research area, due to the following rationale. An Ant Colony system involves simple agents (ants) that cooperate with one another to achieve an emergent, unified behavior for the system as a whole, producing a robust system capable of finding high-quality solutions for problems with a large search space. In the context of rule discovery, an Ant Colony system has the ability to perform a flexible, robust search for a good combination of logical conditions involving values of the predictor attributes.

This chapter is organized as follows. The second section presents an overview of real Ant Colony systems. The third section describes in detail artificial Ant Colony systems. The fourth section introduces the Ant Colony system for discovering classification rules proposed in this work. The fifth section reports on computational results evaluating the performance of the proposed system. Finally, the sixth section concludes the chapter.

SOCIAL INSECTS AND REAL ANT COLONIES

Insects that live in colonies, such as ants, bees, wasps and termites, follow their own agenda of tasks independent from one another. However, when these insects act as a whole community, they are capable of solving complex problems in their daily lives, through mutual cooperation (Bonabeau, Dorigo, & Theraulaz, 1999). Problems such as selecting and picking up materials, and finding and storing foods, which require sophisticated planning, are solved by insect colonies without any kind of supervisor or controller. This collective behavior which emerges from a group of social insects has been called "swarm intelligence".

Ants are capable of finding the shortest route between a food source and the nest without the use of visual information, and they are also capable of adapting to changes in the environment (Dorigo, Colorni & Maniezzo, 1996).

One of the main problems studied by ethnologists is to understand how almost-blind animals, such as ants, manage to find the shortest route between their colony and a food source. It was discovered that, in order to exchange information about which path should be followed, ants communicate with one another by means of pheromone trails. The movement of ants leaves a certain amount of pheromone (a chemical substance) on the ground, marking the path with a trail of this substance. The collective behavior which emerges is a form of autocatalytic behavior, i.e. the more ants follow a trail, the more attractive this trail becomes to be followed by other ants. This process can be described as a loop of positive feedback, where the probability of an ant choosing a path increases as the number of ants that already passed by that path increases (Bonabeau, Dorigo & Theraulaz, 1999; Dorigo, Colorni & Maniezzo, 1996; Stutzle & Dorigo, 1999; Dorigo, Di Caro, & Gambardella, 1999).

The basic idea of this process is illustrated in Figure 1. In the left picture the ants move in a straight line to the food. The middle picture illustrates what happens soon after an obstacle is put in the path between the nest and the food. In order to go around the obstacle, at first each ant chooses to turn left or right at random (with a 50%-50% probability distribution). All ants move roughly at the same speed and deposit pheromone in the trail at roughly the same rate. However, the ants that, by chance, choose to turn left will reach the food sooner, whereas the ants that go around the obstacle turning right will follow a longer path, and so will take longer to circumvent the obstacle. As a result, pheromone accumulates faster in the shorter path around the obstacle. Since ants prefer to follow trails with larger amounts of pheromone, eventually all the ants converge to the shorter path around the obstacle, as shown in the right picture.

Figure 1: Ants finding the shortest path around an obstacle

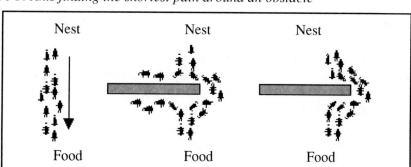

Artificial Ant Colony Systems

An artificial Ant Colony System (ACS) is an agent-based system which simulates the natural behavior of ants and develops mechanisms of cooperation and learning. ACS was proposed by Dorigo et al. (1996) as a new heuristic to solve combinatorial-optimization problems. This new heuristic, called Ant Colony Optimization (ACO), has been shown to be both robust and versatile – in the sense that it can be applied to a range of different combinatorial optimization problems. In addition, ACO is a population-based heuristic. This is advantageous because it allows the system to use a mechanism of positive feedback between agents as a search mechanism. Recently there has been a growing interest in developing rule discovery algorithms based on other kinds of population-based heuristics–mainly evolutionary algorithms (Freitas, 2001).

Artificial ants are characterized as agents that imitate the behavior of real ants. However, it should be noted that an artificial ACS has some differences in comparison with a real ACS, as follows (Dorigo et al., 1996):
- Artificial ants have memory;
- They are not completely blind;
- They live in an environment where time is discrete.

On the other hand, an artificial ACS has several characteristics adopted from real ACS:
- Artificial ants have a probabilistic preference for paths with a larger amount of pheromone;
- Shorter paths tend to have larger rates of growth in their amount of pheromone;
- The ants use an indirect communication system based on the amount of pheromone deposited in each path.

The key idea is that, when a given ant has to choose between two or more paths, the path that was more frequently chosen by other ants in the past will have a greater probability of being chosen by the ant. Therefore, trails with greater amount of pheromone are synonyms of shorter paths.

In essence, an ACS iteratively performs a loop containing two basic procedures, namely:
- i) a procedure specifying how the ants construct/modify solutions of the problem being solved; and
- ii) a procedure to update the pheromone trails.

The construction/modification of a solution is performed in a probabilistic way. The probability of adding a new item to the current partial solution is given by a function that depends on a problem-dependent heuristic (η) and on the amount of pheromone (τ) deposited by ants on this trail in the past. The updates in the pheromone trail are implemented as a function that depends on the rate of pheromone evaporation and on the quality of the produced solution. To realize an ACS one must define (Bonabeau et al., 1999):
- An appropriate representation of the problem, which allows the ants to incrementally construct/modify solutions through the use of a probabilistic

transition rule based on the amount of pheromone in the trail and on a local heuristic;

- A heuristic function (η) that measures the quality of items that can be added to the current partial solution;
- A method to enforce the construction of valid solutions, i.e. solutions that are legal in the real-world situation corresponding to the problem definition;
- A rule for pheromone updating, which specifies how to modify the pheromone trail (τ);
- A probabilistic rule of transition based on the value of the heuristic function (η) and on the contents of the pheromone trail (τ).

ANT-MINER – A NEW ANT COLONY SYSTEM FOR DISCOVERY OF CLASSIFICATIONS RULES

In this section we discuss in detail our proposed Ant Colony System for discovery of classification rules, called Ant-Miner (Ant Colony-Based Data Miner). This section is divided into six parts, namely: an overview of Ant-Miner, rule construction, heuristic function, pheromone updating, rule pruning, and system parameters.

An Overview of Ant-Miner

Recall that each ant can be regarded as an agent that incrementally constructs/modifies a solution for the target problem. In our case the target problem is the discovery of classification rules. As mentioned in the Introduction, the rules are expressed in the form:

IF <conditions> THEN <class> .

The *<conditions>* part (antecedent) of the rule contains a logical combination of predictor attributes, in the form: *term1* AND *term2* AND ... . Each term is a triple *<attribute, operator, value>*, where *value* is a value belonging to the domain of *attribute*. The operator element in the triple is a relational operator. The current version of Ant-Miner can cope only with categorical attributes, so that the operator element in the triple is always "=". Continuous (real-valued) attributes are discretized as a preprocessing step. The *<class>* part (consequent) of the rule contains the class predicted for cases (objects or records) whose predictor attributes satisfy the *<conditions>* part of the rule.

Each ant starts with an empty rule, i.e., a rule with no term in its antecedent, and adds one term at a time to its current partial rule. The current partial rule constructed by an ant corresponds to the current partial path followed by that ant. Similarly, the choice of a term to be added to the current partial rule corresponds to the choice of the direction to which the current path will be extended, among all the possible directions (all terms that could be added to the current partial rule).

The choice of the term to be added to the current partial rule depends on both a problem-dependent heuristic function and on the amount of pheromone associated with each term, as will be discussed in detail in the next subsections.

An ant keeps adding terms one at a time to its current partial rule until the ant is unable to continue constructing its rule. This situation can arise in two cases, namely: (a) when whichever term that could be added to the rule would make the rule cover a number of cases smaller than a user-specified threshold, called *Min_cases_per_rule* (minimum number of cases covered per rule); (b) when all attributes have already been used by the ant, so that there are no more attributes to be added to the rule antecedent.

When one of these two stopping criteria is satisfied, the ant has built a rule (i.e., it has completed its path), and in principle we could use the discovered rule for classification. In practice, however, it is desirable to prune the discovered rules in a post-processing step, to remove irrelevant terms that might have been unduly included in the rule. These irrelevant terms may have been included in the rule due to stochastic variations in the term selection procedure and/or due to the use of a shortsighted, local heuristic function—which considers only one attribute at a time, ignoring attribute interactions. The pruning method used in Ant-Miner will be described in a separate subsection later.

When an ant completes its rule and the amount of pheromone in each trail is updated, another ant starts to construct its rule, using the new amounts of pheromone to guide its search. This process is repeated for at most a predefined number of ants. This number is specified as a parameter of the system, called *No_of_ants*. However, this iterative process can be interrupted earlier, when the current ant has constructed a rule that is exactly the same as the rule constructed by the previous *No_Rules_Converg* – 1 ants. *No_Rules_Converg* (number of rules used to test convergence of the ants) is also a system parameter. This second stopping criterion detects that the ants have already converged to the same constructed rule, which is

Figure 2: Overview of Ant-Miner

```
Training Set = all training cases;
WHILE (No. of uncovered cases in the Training Set >
        Max_Uncovered_Cases)
    i = 0;
    REPEAT
        i=i+1;
        Ant_i incrementally constructs a classification rule;
        Prune the just-constructed rule;
        Update the pheromone of the trail followed by Ant_i;
    UNTIL (i ≥ No_of_Ants) OR
            (Ant_i constructed the same rule than the previous
            No_Rules_Converg – 1 Ants)
    Select the best rule among all constructed rules;
    Remove the cases correctly covered by the selected rule
    from the Training Set;
END WHILE
```

equivalent to converging to the same path in real Ant Colony Systems.

The best rule among the rules constructed by all ants is considered a discovered rule. The other rules are discarded. This completes one iteration of the system.

Then all cases correctly covered by the discovered rule are removed from the training set, and another iteration is started. Hence, the Ant-Miner algorithm is called again to find a rule in the reduced training set. This process is repeated for as many iterations as necessary to find rules covering almost all cases of the training set. More precisely, the above process is repeated until the number of uncovered cases in the training set is less than a predefined threshold, called *Max_uncovered_cases* (maximum number of uncovered cases in the training set).

A summarized description of the above-discussed iterative process is shown in the algorithm of Figure 2.

When the number of cases left in the training set is less than *Max_uncovered_cases,* the search for rules stops. At this point the system has discovered several rules. The discovered rules are stored in an ordered rule list (in order of discovery), which will be used to classify new cases, unseen during training. The system also adds a default rule to the last position of the rule list. The default rule has an empty antecedent (i.e., no condition) and has a consequent predicting the majority class in the set of training cases that are not covered by any rule. This default rule is automatically applied if none of the previous rules in the list cover a new case to be classified.

Once the rule list is complete, the system is finally ready to classify a new test case, unseen during training. In order to do this, the system tries to apply the discovered rules, in order. The first rule that covers the new case is applied – i.e., the case is assigned the class predicted by that rule's consequent.

Rule Construction

Let $term_{ij}$ be a rule condition of the form $A_i = V_{ij}$, where A_i is the i-th attribute and V_{ij} is the j-th value of the domain of A_i. The probability that $term_{ij}$ is chosen to be added to the current partial rule is given by equation (1).

$$P_{ij}(t) = \frac{\tau_{ij}(t) . \eta_{ij}}{\sum\limits_{i}^{a} \sum\limits_{j}^{b_i} \tau_{ij}(t) . \eta_{ij}}, \forall \, i \in I \qquad (1)$$

where:
- η_{ij} is the value of a problem-dependent heuristic function for $term_{ij}$;
- $\tau_{ij}(t)$ is the amount of pheromone currently available (at time t) in the position i,j of the trail being followed by the ant;
- a is the total number of attributes;
- b_i is the total number of values on the domain of attribute i;
- I are the attributes i not yet used by the ant.

The problem-dependent heuristic function η_{ij} is a measure of the predictive power of $term_{ij}$. The higher the value of η_{ij} the more relevant for classification the $term_{ij}$ is, and so the higher its probability of being chosen. This heuristic function will be explained in detail in the next subsection. For now we just mention that the value of this function is always the same for a given term, regardless of which terms already occur in the current partial rule and regardless of the path followed by previous ants.

The amount of pheromone $\tau_{ij}(t)$ is also independent of the terms which already occur in the current partial rule, but is entirely dependent on the paths followed by previous ants. Hence, $\tau_{ij}(t)$ incorporates an indirect form of communication between ants, where successful ants leave a "clue" (pheromone) suggesting the best path to be followed by other ants, as discussed earlier. When the first ant starts to build its rule, all trail positions i,j – i.e., all $term_{ij}$, $\forall i,j$ – have the same amount of pheromone. However, as soon as an ant finishes its path, the amounts of pheromone in each position i,j visited by the ant is updated, as will be explained in detail in a separate subsection later. Here we just mention the basic idea: the better the quality of the rule constructed by the ant, the higher the amount of pheromone added to the trail positions visited by the ant. Hence, with time the "best" trail positions to be followed – i.e., the best terms (attribute-value pairs) to be added to a rule – will have greater and greater amounts of pheromone, increasing their probability of being chosen.

The $term_{ij}$ chosen to be added to the current partial rule is the term with the highest value of equation (1) subject to two restrictions. The first restriction is that the attribute i cannot occur yet in the current partial rule. Note that to satisfy this restriction the ants must "remember" which terms (attribute-value pairs) are contained in the current partial rule. This small amount of "memory" is one of the differences between artificial ants and natural ants, as discussed earlier.

The second restriction is that a $term_{ij}$ cannot be added to the current partial rule if this makes the extended partial rule cover less than a predefined minimum number of cases, called the *Min_cases_per_rule* threshold, as mentioned above.

Note that the above procedure constructs a rule antecedent, but it does not specify which rule consequent will be assigned to the rule. This decision is made only after the rule antecedent is completed. More precisely, once the rule antecedent is completed, the system chooses the rule consequent (i.e., the predicted class) that maximizes the quality of the rule. This is done by assigning to the rule consequent the majority class among the cases covered by the rule.

In the next two subsections, we discuss in detail the heuristic function and the pheromone updating procedure.

Heuristic Function

For each term that can be added to the current rule, Ant-Miner computes a heuristic function that is an estimate of the quality of this term, with respect to its ability to improve the predictive accuracy of the rule. This heuristic function is based on information theory (Cover & Thomas, 1991). More precisely, the value of the heuristic function for a term involves a measure of the entropy (or amount of information) associated with that term. For each $term_{ij}$ of the form $A_i = V_{ij}$ – where A_i is the i-th attribute and V_{ij} is the j-th value belonging to the domain of A_i – its entropy is given by equation (2).

$$\text{infoT}_{ij} = - \sum_{w=1}^{k} \left(\frac{freqT_{ij}^{w}}{|T_{ij}|} \right) * \log_2 \left(\frac{freqT_{ij}^{w}}{|T_{ij}|} \right) \qquad (2)$$

where:
- k is the number of classes;
- $|T_{ij}|$ is the total number of cases in partition T_{ij} (partition containing the cases where attribute A_i has value V_{ij});
- $freqT_{ij}^{w}$ is the number of cases in partition T_{ij} that have class w.

The higher the value of $infoT_{ij}$, the more uniformly distributed the classes are, and so the lower the predictive power of $term_{ij}$. We obviously want to choose terms with a high predictive power to be added to the current partial rule. Therefore, the value of $infoT_{ij}$ has the following role in Ant-Miner: the higher the value of $infoT_{ij}$, the smaller the probability of an ant choosing $term_{ij}$ to be added to its partial rule. Before we map this basic idea into a heuristic function, one more point must be considered. It is desirable to normalize the value of the heuristic function, to facilitate its use in a single equation – more precisely, equation (1) – combining both this function and the amount of pheromone. In order to implement this normalization, we use the fact that the value of $infoT_{ij}$ varies in the range:
$$0 \le infoT_{ij} \le \log_2(k)$$
where k is the number of classes.

Therefore, we propose the normalized, information-theoretic heuristic function given by equation (3).

$$\eta_{ij} = \frac{\log_2(k) - \text{infoT}_{ij}}{\sum_{i}^{a} \sum_{j}^{b_i} \log_2(k) - \text{infoT}_{ij}} \qquad (3)$$

where:
- a is the total number of attributes;
- b_i is the number of values in the domain of attribute i.

Note that the $infoT_{ij}$ of $term_{ij}$ is always the same, regardless of the contents of the rule in which the term occurs. Therefore, in order to save computational time, we compute the $infoT_{ij}$ of all $term_{ij}$, $\forall i, j$, as a preprocessing step.

In order to use the above heuristic function, there are just two minor caveats. First, if the partition T_{ij} is empty, i.e., the value V_{ij} of attribute A_i does not occur in the training set, then we set $infoT_{ij}$ to its maximum value, i.e., $infoT_{ij} = \log_2(k)$. This corresponds to assigning to $term_{ij}$ the lowest possible predictive power.

Second, if all the cases in the partition T_{ij} belong to the same class, then $infoT_{ij}$

$= 0$. This corresponds to assigning to $term_{ij}$ the highest possible predictive power.

Rule Pruning

Rule pruning is a commonplace technique in rule induction. As mentioned above, the main goal of rule pruning is to remove irrelevant terms that might have been unduly included in the rule. Rule pruning potentially increases the predictive power of the rule, helping to avoid its over-fitting to the training data. Another motivation for rule pruning is that it improves the simplicity of the rule, since a shorter rule is in general more easily interpretable by the user than a long rule.

The rule pruning procedure is performed for each ant as soon as the ant completes the construction of its rule. The search strategy of our rule pruning procedure is very similar to the rule pruning procedure suggested by Quinlan (1987), although the rule quality criterion used in the two procedures are very different from each other.

The basic idea is to iteratively remove one term at a time from the rule while this process improves the quality of the rule. A more detailed description is as follows.

In the first iteration one starts with the full rule. Then one tentatively tries to remove each of the terms of the rule, each one in turn, and computes the quality of the resulting rule, using the quality function defined by formula (5) to be explained later. (This step may involve reassigning another class to the rule, since a pruned rule can have a different majority class in its covered cases.) The term whose removal most improves the quality of the rule is effectively removed from the rule, completing the first iteration. In the next iteration one removes again the term whose removal most improves the quality of the rule, and so on. This process is repeated until the rule has just one term or until there is no term whose removal will improve the quality of the rule.

Pheromone Updating

Recall that each $term_{ij}$ corresponds to a position in some path that can be followed by an ant. All $term_{ij}$, $\forall i, j$, are initialized with the same amount of pheromone. In other words, when the system is initialized and the first ant starts its search all paths have the same amount of pheromone.

The initial amount of pheromone deposited at each path position is inversely proportional to the number of values of all attributes, as given by equation (4).

$$\tau_{ij}(t = 0) = \frac{1}{(\sum_{i=1}^{a} b_i)} \qquad (4)$$

where:

- a is the total number of attributes;

- b_i is the number of values in the domain of attribute i.

The value returned by this equation is already normalized, which facilitates its use in a single equation, more precisely, equation (1) combining both this value and the value of the heuristic function.

Each time an ant completes the construction of a rule (i.e., an ant completes its path) the amount of pheromone in all positions of all paths must be updated. This pheromone updating has two basic ideas, namely:

(a) The amount of pheromone associated with each $term_{ij}$ occurring in the constructed rule is increased;

(b) The amount of pheromone associated with each $term_{ij}$ that does not occur in the constructed rule is decreased, corresponding to the phenomenon of pheromone evaporation in real Ant Colony Systems.

Let us elaborate each of these two ideas in turn.

Increasing the Pheromone of Used Terms

Increasing the amount of pheromone associated with each $term_{ij}$ occurring in the constructed rule corresponds to increasing the amount of pheromone along the path completed by the ant. In a rule discovery context, this corresponds to increasing the probability of $term_{ij}$ being chosen by other ants in the future, since that term was beneficial for the current ant. This increase is proportional to the quality of the rule constructed by the ant – i.e. the better the rule, the higher the increase in the amount of pheromone for each $term_{ij}$ occurring in the rule.

The quality of the rule constructed by an ant, denoted by Q, is computed by the formula: $Q = sensitivity \times specificity$ (Lopes, Coutinho, & Lima, 1997), as defined in equation (5).

$$Q = (\frac{TruePos}{TruePos + FalseNeg}) \times (\frac{TrueNeg}{FalsePos + TrueNeg}) \qquad (5)$$

where

- *TruePos* (true positives) is the number of cases covered by the rule that have the class predicted by the rule;
- *FalsePos* (false positives) is the number of cases covered by the rule that have a class different from the class predicted by the rule;
- *FalseNeg* (false negatives) is the number of cases that are not covered by the rule but that have the class predicted by the rule;
- *TrueNeg* (true negatives) is the number of cases that are not covered by the rule and that do not have the class predicted by the rule.

The larger the value of Q, the higher the quality of the rule. Note that Q varies in the range: $0 \leq Q \leq 1$. Pheromone update for a $term_{ij}$ is performed according to equation (6), $\forall i, j$.

$$\tau_{ij}(t+1) = \tau_{ij}(t) + \tau_{ij}(t) . Q, \forall\ i,j \in\ to\ the\ rule \qquad (6)$$

Hence, for all $term_{ij}$ occurring in the rule constructed by the ant, the amount of pheromone is increased by a fraction of the current amount of pheromone, and this fraction is directly proportional to Q.

Decreasing the Pheromone of Unused Terms

As mentioned above, the amount of pheromone associated with each $term_{ij}$ that does not occur in the constructed rule has to be decreased, to simulate the phenomenon of pheromone evaporation in real ant colony systems.

In our system the effect of pheromone evaporation is obtained by an indirect strategy. More precisely, the effect of pheromone evaporation for unused terms is achieved by normalizing the value of each pheromone τ_{ij}. This normalization is performed by dividing the value of each τ_{ij} by the summation of all τ_{ij}, $\forall i, j$. To see how this achieves the same effect as pheromone evaporation, note that when a rule is constructed only the terms used by an ant in the constructed rule have their amount of pheromone increased by equation (6). Hence, at normalization time the amount of pheromone of an *unused* term will be computed by dividing its current value (not modified by equation (6)) by the total summation of pheromone for all terms (which was increased as a result of applying equation (6) to the *used* terms). The final effect will be to reduce the normalized amount of pheromone for each *unused* term.

Used terms will, of course, have their normalized amount of pheromone increased due to application of equation (6).

System Parameters

Our Ant Colony System has the following four user-defined parameters:
- Number of Ants (*No_of_ants*) → This is also the maximum number of complete candidate rules constructed during a single iteration of the system, since each ant constructs a single rule (see Figure 2). In each iteration, the best candidate rule constructed in that iteration is considered a discovered rule. Note that the larger the *No_of_ants*, the more candidate rules are evaluated per iteration, but the slower the system is;
- Minimum number of cases per rule (*Min_cases_per_rule*) → Each rule must cover at least *Min_cases_per_rule*, to enforce at least a certain degree of generality in the discovered rules. This helps avoiding over-fitting to the training data;
- Maximum number of uncovered cases in the training set (*Max_uncovered_cases*) → The process of rule discovery is iteratively performed until the number of training cases that are not covered by any discovered rule is smaller than this threshold (see Figure 2);
- Number of rules used to test convergence of the ants (*No_Rules_Converg*) → If the current ant has constructed a rule that is exactly the same as the rule constructed by the previous *No_Rules_Converg* –1 ants, then the system concludes that the ants have converged to a single rule (path). The current iteration is therefore stopped, and another iteration is started (see Figure 2).

In all the experiments reported in this chapter these parameters were set as follows:

- Number of Ants (*No_of_ants*) = 3000;
- Minimum number of cases per rule (*Min_cases_per_rule*) = 10;
- Maximum number of uncovered cases in the training set (*Max_uncovered_cases*) = 10;
- Number of rules used to test convergence of the ants (*No_Rules_Converg*) = 10.

We have made no serious attempt to optimize these parameter values. Such an optimization will be tried in future research. It is interesting to notice that even the above non-optimized parameters' setting has produced quite good results, as will be seen in the next section.

There is one caveat in the interpretation of the value of *No_of_ants*. Recall that this parameter defines the *maximum* number of ants per iteration of the system. In our experiments the actual number of ants per iteration was on the order of 1500, rather than 3000. The reason why in practice much fewer ants are necessary to complete an iteration of the system is that an iteration is considered finished when *No_Rules_Converg* successive ants converge to the same path (rule).

COMPUTATIONAL RESULTS

We have evaluated Ant-Miner across six public-domain data sets from the UCI (University of California at Irvine) data set repository (Aha & Murphy, 2000). The main characteristics of the data sets used in our experiment are summarized in Table 1. The first column of this table identifies the data set, whereas the other columns indicate, respectively, the number of cases, number of categorical attributes, number of continuous attributes, and number of classes of the data set.

As mentioned earlier, Ant-Miner discovers rules referring only to categorical attributes. Therefore, continuous attributes have to be discretized as a preprocessing step. This discretization was performed by the C4.5-Disc discretization algorithm, described in Kohavi and Sahami (1996). This algorithm simply uses the C4.5 algorithm for discretizing continuous attributes. In essence, for each attribute to be discretized, we extract from the training set, a reduced data set containing only two attributes: the attribute to be discretized and the goal (class) attribute. C4.5 is then applied to this reduced data set. Therefore, C4.5 constructs a decision tree in which

Table 1: Data Sets Used in Our Experiments

Data set	#cases	#categ. attrib.	#contin. attrib.	#classes
breast cancer (Ljubljana)	282	9	0	2
breast cancer (Wisconsin)	683	0	9	2
Tic-tac-toe	958	9	0	2
Dermatology	358	33	1	6
Hepatitis	155	13	6	2
Heart disease (Cleveland)	303	8	5	5

all internal nodes refer to the attribute being discretized. Each path from the root to a leaf node in the constructed decision tree corresponds to the definition of a categorical interval produced by C4.5. See the above-mentioned paper for details.

We have evaluated the performance of Ant-Miner by comparing it with C4.5 (Quinlan, 1993), a well-known rule induction algorithm. Both algorithms were trained on data discretized by the C4.5-Disc algorithm, to make the comparison between Ant-Miner and C4.5 fair.

The comparison was carried out across two criteria, namely the predictive accuracy of the discovered rule sets and their simplicity, as discussed in the following.

Predictive accuracy was measured by a 10-fold cross-validation procedure (Weiss & Kulikowski, 1991). In essence, the data set is divided into 10 mutually exclusive and exhaustive partitions. Then a classification algorithm is run 10 times. Each time a different partition is used as the test set and the other nine partitions are used as the training set. The results of the 10 runs (accuracy rate on the test set) are then averaged and reported as the accuracy rate of the discovered rule set.

The results comparing the accuracy rate of Ant-Miner and C4.5 are reported in Table 2. The numbers after the "$\pm$" symbol are the standard deviations of the corresponding accuracy rates. As shown in this table, Ant-Miner discovered rules with a better accuracy rate than C4.5 in four data sets, namely Ljubljana breast cancer, Wisconsin breast cancer, Hepatitis and Heart disease. In two data sets, Ljubljana breast cancer and Heart disease, the difference was quite small. In the other two data sets, Wisconsin breast cancer and Hepatitis, the difference was more relevant. Note that although the difference of accuracy rate in Wisconsin breast cancer seems very small at first glance, this holds only for the absolute value of this difference. In reality the relative value of this difference can be considered relevant, since it represents a reduction of 20% in the error rate of C4.5 $((96.04 - 95.02)/(100 - 95.02) = 0.20)$.

On the other hand, C4.5 discovered rules with a better accuracy rate than Ant-Miner in the other two data sets. In one data set, Dermatology, the difference was quite small, whereas in the Tic-tac-toe the difference was relatively large. (This result will be revisited later.) Overall one can conclude that Ant-Miner is competitive with C4.5 in terms of accuracy rate, but it should be noted that Ant-Miner's

Table 2: Accuracy Rate of Ant-Miner vs. C4.5

Data Set	Ant-Miner's accuracy rate (%)	C4.5's accuracy rate (%)
Breast cancer (Ljubljana)	75.42 $\pm$ 10.99	73.34 $\pm$ 3.21
Breast cancer (Wisconsin)	96.04 $\pm$ 2.80	95.02 $\pm$ 0.31
Tic-tac-toe	73.04 $\pm$ 7.60	83.18 $\pm$ 1.71
Dermatology	86.55 $\pm$ 6.13	89.05 $\pm$ 0.62
Hepatitis	90.00 $\pm$ 9.35	85.96 $\pm$ 1.07
Heart disease (Cleveland)	59.67 $\pm$ 7.52	58.33 $\pm$ 0.72

accuracy rate has a larger standard deviation than C4.5's.

We now turn to the results concerning the simplicity of the discovered rule set. This simplicity was measured, as usual in the literature, by the number of discovered rules and the total number of terms (conditions) in the antecedents of all discovered rules.

The results comparing the simplicity of the rule set discovered by Ant-Miner and by C4.5 are reported in Table 3. Again, the numbers after the "±" symbol denote standard deviations. As shown in this table, in five data sets the rule set discovered by Ant-Miner was simpler – i.e., it had a smaller number of rules and terms – than the rule set discovered by C4.5. In one data set, Ljubljana breast cancer, the number of rules discovered by C4.5 was somewhat smaller than the rules discovered by Ant-Miner, but the rules discovered by Ant-Miner were simpler (shorter) than the C4.5 rules. To simplify the analysis of the table, let us focus on the number of rules only, since the results for the number of terms are roughly analogous. In three data sets the difference between the number of rules discovered by Ant-Miner and C4.5 is quite large, as follows.

In the Tic-tac-toe and Dermatology data sets, Ant-Miner discovered 8.5 and 7.0 rules, respectively, whereas C4.5 discovered 83 and 23.2 rules, respectively. In both data sets C4.5 achieved a better accuracy rate. So, in these two data sets Ant-Miner sacrificed accuracy rate to improve rule set simplicity. This seems a reasonable trade-off, since in many data mining applications the simplicity of a rule set tends to be even more important than its accuracy rate. Actually, there are several rule induction algorithms that were explicitly designed to improve rule set simplicity, even at the expense of reducing accuracy rate (Bohanec & Bratko, 1994; Brewlow & Aha, 1997; Catlett, 1991).

In the Heart disease data set, Ant-Miner discovered 9.5 rules, whereas C4.5 discovered 49 rules. In this case the greater simplicity of the rule set discovered by Ant-Miner was achieved without unduly sacrificing accuracy rate – both algorithms have similar accuracy rates, as can be seen in the last row of Table 1.

There is, however, a caveat in the interpretation of the results of Table 3. The

Table 3: Simplicity of Rule Sets Discovered by Ant-Miner vs. C4.5

Data set	No. of rules		No. of terms	
	Ant-Miner	C4.5	Ant-Miner	C4.5
Breast cancer (Ljubljana)	7.20 ± 0.60	6.2 ± 4.20	9.80 ± 1.47	12.8 ± 9.83
Breast cancer (Wisconsin)	6.20 ± 0.75	11.1 ± 1.45	12.2 ± 2.23	44.1 ± 7.48
Tic-tac-toe	8.50 ± 1.86	83.0 ± 14.1	10.0 ± 6.42	384.2 ± 73.4
Dermatology	7.00 ± 0.00	23.2 ± 1.99	81.0 ± 2.45	91.7 ± 10.64
Hepatitis	3.40 ± 0.49	4.40 ± 0.93	8.20 ± 2.04	8.50 ± 3.04
Heart disease (Cleveland)	9.50 ± 0.92	49.0 ± 9.4	16.2 ± 2.44	183.4 ± 38.94

rules discovered by Ant-Miner are organized into an ordered rule list. This means that, in order for a rule to be applied to a test case, the previous rules in the list must not cover that case. As a result, the rules discovered by Ant-Miner are not as modular and independent as the rules discovered by C4.5. This has the effect of reducing a little the simplicity of the rules discovered by Ant-Miner, by comparison with the rules discovered by C4.5. In any case, this effect seems to be quite compensated by the fact that, overall, the size of the rule list discovered by Ant-Miner is much smaller than the size of the rule set discovered by C4.5. Therefore, it seems safe to say that, overall, the rules discovered by Ant-Miner are simpler than the rules discovered by C4.5, which is an important point in the context of data mining.

Taking into account both the accuracy rate and rule set simplicity criteria, the results of our experiments can be summarized as follows.

In three data sets, namely Wisconsin breast cancer, Hepatitis and Heart disease, Ant-Miner discovered a rule set that is both simpler and more accurate than the rule set discovered by C4.5. In one data set, Ljubljana breast cancer, Ant-Miner was more accurate than C4.5, but the rule sets discovered by Ant-Miner and C4.5 have about the same level of simplicity. (C4.5 discovered fewer rules, but Ant-Miner discovered rules with a smaller number of terms.)

Finally, in two data sets, namely Tic-tac-toe and Dermatology, C4.5 achieved a better accuracy rate than Ant-Miner, but the rule set discovered by Ant-Miner was simpler than the one discovered by C4.5.

It is also important to notice that in all six data sets, the total number of terms of the rules discovered by Ant-Miner was smaller than C4.5's , which is strong evidence of the simplicity of the rules discovered by Ant-Miner.

These results were obtained for a Pentium II PC with clock rate of 333 MHz and 128 MB of main memory. Ant-Miner was developed in C++ language and it took about the same processing time as C4.5 (on the order of seconds for each data set) to obtain the results.

It is worthwhile to mention that the use of a high-performance programming language like C++, as well as an optimized code, is very important to improve the computational efficiency of Ant-Miner and data mining algorithms in general. The current C++ implementation of Ant-Miner is about three orders of magnitude (i.e., thousands of times) faster than a previous MatLab implementation.

CONCLUSIONS AND FUTURE WORK

This work has proposed an algorithm for rule discovery called Ant-Miner (Ant Colony-Based Data Miner). The goal of Ant-Miner is to extract classification rules from data. The algorithm is based on recent research on the behavior of real ant colonies as well as in some data mining concepts.

We have compared the performance of Ant-Miner with the performance of the well-known C4.5 algorithm in six public domain data sets. Overall the results show that, concerning predictive accuracy, Ant-Miner is competitive with C4.5. In addition, Ant-Miner has consistently found considerably simpler (smaller) rules than C4.5.

We consider these results very promising, bearing in mind that C4.5 is a well-known, sophisticated decision tree algorithm, which has been evolving from early decision tree algorithms for at least a couple of decades. By contrast, our Ant-Miner algorithm is in its first version, and the whole area of artificial Ant Colony Systems is still in its infancy, by comparison with the much more traditional area of decision-tree learning.

One research direction consists of performing several experiments to investigate the sensitivity of Ant-Miner to its user-defined parameters.

Other research direction consists of extending the system to cope with continuous attributes as well, rather than requiring that this kind of attribute be discretized in a preprocessing step.

In addition, it would be interesting to investigate the performance of other kinds of heuristic function and pheromone updating strategy.

REFERENCES

Aha, D. W. & Murphy P. M. (2000). *UCI Repository of Machine Learning Databases.* Retrieved August 05, 2000 from the World Wide Web: http://www.ics.uci.edu/~mlearn/MLRepository.html.

Bohanec, M. & Bratko, I. (1994). Trading accuracy for simplicity in decision trees. *Machine Learning, 15*, 223-250.

Bonabeau, E., Dorigo, M. & Theraulaz, G. (1999). *Swarm Intelligence: From Natural to Artificial Systems.* New York: Oxford University Press.

Brewlow, L.A. & Aha, D.W. (1997). Simplifying decision trees: a survey. *The Knowledge Engeneering Review, 12*(1), 1-40.

Catlett, J. (1991). Overpruning large decision trees. *Proc. 1991 Int. Joint Conf. on Artif. Intel. (IJCAI).* Sidney.

Cordón, O., Casillas, J. & Herrera, F. (2000). Learning fuzzy rules using ant colony optimization. *Proc. ANTS'2000 – From Ant Colonies to Artificial Ants: Second International Workshop on Ant Algorithms*, 13-21.

Cover, T. M. & Thomas, J. A. (1991). *Elements of Information Theory.* New York: John Wiley & Sons.

Dorigo, M., Colorni A. & Maniezzo V. (1996). The Ant System: Optimization by a colony of cooperating agents. *IEEE Transactions on Systems, Man, and Cybernetics-Part B, 26*(1), 1-13.

Dorigo, M., Di Caro, G. & Gambardella, L. M. (1999). Ant algorithms for discrete optimization. *Artificial Life, 5*(2), 137-172.

Fayyad, U. M., Piatetsky-Shapiro, G. & Smyth, P. (1996). From data mining to knowledge discovery: an overview. In: Fayyad, U.M., Piatetsky-Shapiro, G., Smyth, P. & Uthurusamy, R. (Eds.) *Advances in Knowledge Discovery & Data Mining*, 1-34. Cambridge: AAAI/MIT.

Freitas, A. A. & Lavington, S. H. (1998). *Mining Very Large Databases with Parallel Processing.* London: Kluwer.

Freitas, A.A. (2001). A survey of evolutionary algorithms for data mining and knowledge discovery. To appear in: Ghosh, A.; Tsutsui, S. (Eds.) *Advances in Evolutionary Computation.* Springer-Verlag.

Kohavi, R. & Sahami, M. (1996). Error-based and entropy-based discretization of continuous features. *Proc. 2nd Int. Conf. Knowledge Discovery and Data Mining*, 114-119.

Lopes, H. S., Coutinho, M. S. & Lima, W. C. (1997). An evolutionary approach to simulate cognitive feedback learning in Medical Domain. In: Sanches, E., Shibata, T. & Zadeh, L.A. (eds.) *Genetic Algorithms and Fuzzy Logic Systems: Soft Computing Perspectives*, Singapore: Word Scientific, 193-207.

Monmarche, N. (1999). On data clustering with artificial ants. In: Freitas, A.A. (Ed.) *Data Mining with Evolutionary Algorithms: Research Directions – Papers from the AAAI Workshop*. AAAI Press, 23-26.

Quinlan, J.R. (1987). Generating production rules from decision trees. *Proc. 1987 Int. Joint Conf. on Artif. Intel.(IJCAI)*, 304-307.

Quinlan, J.R. (1993). *C4.5: Programs for Machine Learning*. San Francisco: Morgan Kaufmann.

Stutzle, T. & Dorigo. M. (1999). ACO algorithms for the traveling salesman problem. In K. Miettinen, M. Makela, P. Neittaanmaki & J. Periaux. (Eds.), *Evolutionary Algorithms in Engineering and Computer Science*, New York: John Wiley & Sons.

Weiss, S.M. & Kulikowski, C.A. (1991). *Computer Systems That Learn*. San Francisco: Morgan Kaufmann.

Chapter XI

Artificial Immune Systems: Using the Immune System as Inspiration for Data Mining

Jonathan Timmis and Thomas Knight
University of Kent at Canterbury, UK

The immune system is highly distributed, highly adaptive, self-organising in nature, maintains a memory of past encounters and has the ability to continually learn about new encounters. From a computational view-point, the immune system has much to offer by way of inspiration. Recently there has been growing interest in the use of the natural immune system as inspiration for the creation of novel approaches to computational problems; this field of research is referred to as Immunological Computation (IC) or Artificial Immune Systems (AIS).

This chapter describes the physiology of the immune system and provides a general introduction to Artificial Immune Systems. Significant applications that are relevant to data mining, in particular in the areas of machine learning and data analysis, are discussed in detail. Attention is paid both to the salient characteristics of the application and the details of the algorithms. This chapter concludes with an evaluation of the current and future contributions of Artificial Immune Systems in data mining.

Over the years, biology has provided a rich source of inspiration for many different people in many different ways ranging from designing aircraft wings to bulletproof vests. Biology has also been used as a source of inspiration for computation problems, which can be classified as biologically motivated computing (Paton,1994). This is different from computationally motivated biology, where computing provides the source and inspiration for models in biology. The work described in this chapter is concerned with the former—biologically motivated computing applied to the field of data mining.

There has been much work done on the use of biological metaphors, for example neural networks, genetic algorithms and genetic programming. Recently, there has been increasing interest in using the natural immune system as a metaphor for computation in a variety of domains. This field of research, Immunological Computation (IC) or Artificial Immune Systems (AIS), has seen the application of immune algorithms to problems such as robotic control (Ishiguro et al., 1998), simulating behavior in robots (Lee et al.,1997), network intrusion detection (Kim and Bentley, 1998), fault diagnosis (Ishida, 1996) and machine learning (Hunt and Cooke,1995; Timmis and Neal,2000), to name a few. The immune system is a rich source of inspiration as it displays learning, adaptability and memory mechanisms that could be applied to many different computational tasks. It is proposed that the immune system, abstracted at a high level, can be thought of as a naturally occurring learning machine (Varela et al., 1988).

This chapter focuses on the use of these immune metaphor algorithms to the field of machine learning and data mining. The chapter begins with a look at the context of this work of relation to the field of data mining. Attention is then drawn to the salient features of the natural immune system that are used as inspiration to the field of AIS. The use of these features as metaphors is then detailed, by means of providing an overview of the current research within AIS, paying particular attention to a variety of machine learning algorithms inspired by the immune system. Observations are then made about the future direction for this work.

It is hoped that the reader will gain an appreciation for immunology and the way in which it can be utilized as an effective metaphor for computational techniques.

THE NATURAL IMMUNE SYSTEM

The immune system is a very complex "hunt and destroy" mechanism that works at the cellular level in our bodies. The immune system protects our bodies from infectious agents such as viruses, bacteria, fungi and other parasites. On the surface of these agents are antigens; it is these antigens that provoke an immune response. There are two types of immunity—innate and adaptive. Innate immunity (Janeway, 1993) is not directed in any way towards specific invaders into the body, but against any pathogens that enter the body. Certain blood proteins, called complement proteins, can bind to any other proteins, including those on bacteria. Immune system cells have the ability to inactivate this binding process, therefore removing the risk of the innate immune system attacking the bodies' cells. These proteins are able to kill off certain bacteria, but the innate immune system is by no means a complete solution to protecting the body.

Adaptive or acquired immunity, however, allows the immune system to launch an attack against any invader that the innate system cannot remove. The adaptive system is directed against specific invaders, and is modified by exposure to such invaders. The adaptive immune system is made up of lymphocytes, which are white blood cells, more specifically B and T cells. These cells aid in the process of recognizing and destroying specific substances. Any substance that is capable of generating such a response from the lymphocytes is called an antigen or immunogen. Antigens are not the invading microorganisms themselves; they are substances such as toxins or enzymes in the microorganisms that the immune system considers foreign. Immune responses are normally directed against the antigen that provoked them and are said to be antigen-specific. The immune system generalizes by virtue of the presence of the same antigens in more than one infectious agent. Many immunizations exploit this by presenting the immune system with an innocuous organism, which carries antigens, which are present in more dangerous organisms. Thus the immune system learns to react to a particular pattern of antigen.

The immune system is said to be adaptive, in that when an adaptive immune response is elicited, B cells undergo cloning in an attempt to produce sufficient antibodies to remove the infectious agent (Tizzard, 1988a, b; Burnet, 1959; Jerne, 1974b). When cloning, B cells undergo a stochastic process of somatic hypermutation (Kepler and Perelson, 1993) where an attempt is made by the immune system to generate a wider antibody repertoire so as to be able to remove the infectious agent from the body and prepare the body for infection from a similar but different infection, at some point in the future.

After the primary immune response, when the immune system first encounters a foreign substance and the substance has been removed from the system, a certain quantity of B cells remain in the immune system and acts as an immunological memory (Smith et al.,1998; Jerne, 1974a). This is to allow for the immune system to launch a faster attack against the infecting agent, called the secondary immune response.

Primary and Secondary Immune Responses

A primary response (Tizzard, 1988a) is provoked when the immune system encounters an antigen for the first time. A number of antibodies will be produced by the immune system in response to the infection, which will help to eliminate the antigen from the body. However, after a period of days, the levels of antibody begin to degrade, until the time when the antigen is encountered again. This secondary immune response is said to be specific to the antigen that first initiated the immune response and causes a very rapid growth in the quantity of B cells and antibodies. This second, faster response is attributed to *memory* cells remaining in the immune system, so that when the antigen, or similar antigen, is encountered, a new immunity does not need to be built up, it is already there. This means that the body is ready to combat any reinfection.

The amount of antibody is increased by the immune system generating a massive number of B cells through a process called clonal selection (Burnet, 1959), this is now discussed in relation to the B-cell in the immune system.

B Cells and Their Antibodies

The B cell is an integral part of the immune system. Through a process of recognition and stimulation, B cells will clone and mutate to produce a diverse set of antibodies in an attempt to remove the infection from the body. The antibodies are specific proteins that recognize and bind to another protein. The production and binding of antibodies is usually a way of signalling other cells to kill, ingest or remove the bound substance (de Castro, 1999). Each antibody has two paratopes and two epitopes that are the specialised part of the antibody that identify other molecules (Hunt and Cooke, 1996). Binding between antigens and antibodies is governed by how well the paratopes on the antibody matches the epitope of the antigen; the closer this match, the stronger the bind. Although it is the antibody strings that surround the B cell (Figure 1) that are responsible for recognising and attaching to antigen invaders, it is the B cell itself that has one of the most important roles in the immune system.

This is not the full story, as B cells are also affected by helper T cells during the immune response (Tizzard, 1988b). T cell paratopes are different from those on B cells in that they recognise fragments of antigens that have been combined with molecules found on the surfaces of the other cells. These molecules are called MHC molecules (Major Histocompatibility Complex). As T cells circulate through the body, they scan the surfaces of body cells for the presence of foreign antigens that have been picked up by the MHC molecules. This function is sometimes called immune surveillance. These helper T cells when bound to an antigen secrete interleukins that act on B cells helping to stimulate them.

Figure 1: The B-cells interact with an antigenic substance, become stimulated (activated) and clone, producing thousands of antibodies (adapted from Nossal, 1994).

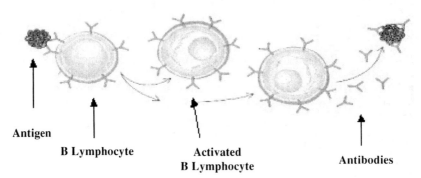

Antigen

B Lymphocyte

Activated
B Lymphocyte

Antibodies

Immune Memory

There are a variety of theories as to how immune memory is maintained (Tew and Mandel, 1979; Tew et al.,1980; Matzinger, 1994). The theory that is used greatly in AIS for inspiration is the theory first proposed by Jerne (1974a) and reviewed in Perelson (1989) called the Immune Network Theory. This theory states that B cells co-stimulate each other via idiotopes in such a way as to mimic antigens. An idiotope is made up of amino acids within the variable region of an antibody or T-cell. A network of B cells is thus formed and highly stimulated B cells survive and less stimulated B cells are removed from the system. It is further proposed that this network yields useful topological information about the relationship between antigens. For these reasons, this theory is examined in this chapter.

Immunological Memory via the Immune Network

Jerne (1974a) proposed that the immune system is capable of achieving immunological memory by the existence of a mutually reinforcing network of B cells. These cells not only stimulate each other, but also suppress the stimulation of connected B-Cells, though to a lesser degree. This suppression function is a mechanism by which to keep a control on the over stimulation of B cells in order to maintain a stable memory.

This network of B cells occurs due to the ability of paratopes, located on B cells, to match against idiotopes on other B cells. The binding between idiotopes and paratopes has the effect of stimulating the B cells. This is because the paratopes on B cells react to the idiotopes on similar B cells, as it would an antigen. However, to counter the reaction there is a certain amount of suppression between B cells to act as a regulatory mechanism. Figure 2 shows the basic principle of the immune network theory. Here B-cell 1 stimulates three other cells, B cells 2, 3 and 4, and also receives a certain amount of suppression from each one. This creates a network-type structure that provides a regulatory effect on neighboring B cells. The immune

Figure 2: Jernes' idiotypic network hypothesis

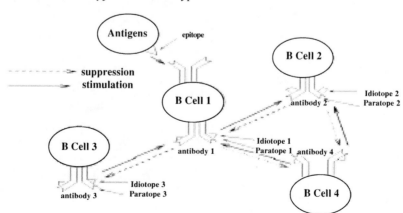

network acts as a self-organising and self-regulatory system that captures antigen information ready to launch an attack against any similar antigens.

Attempts have been made at creating a model for the immune system Farmer et al. (1986), Carneiro and Stewart (1995) to better understand its complex interactions. The work of Farmer et al. (1986) created a model to capture the essential characteristics of the immune network as described in Jerne (1974a) and identify memory mechanisms in it, whereas the work of Carneiro and Stewart (1995) observed how the immune system identifies self and non-self.

Both work by Farmer et al. (1986) and Perelson (1989) investigated Jernes' work of more depth and provide an insight into some of the mechanisms involved in the production and dynamics of the immune network. This section will summarise the salient features at a level appropriate for using the ideas as a metaphor for learning.

It is noted that this theory is somewhat contentious in the Immunological field. This, however, is not a problem for computer scientists when creating a metaphor-based algorithm. This is because it is the inspiration from the immune system that they seek, they do not seek to model it. Therefore, abstractions can be made from these models and fit into the respective areas of computer science.

Repertoire and Shape Space

Coutinho (1980) first postulated the idea of completeness of the repertoire. He stated that if the immune system's antibody repertoire is complete then antibodies with immunogenic idiotopes can be recognised by other antibodies and therefore an idiotypic network will be created.

However, in order to understand completeness, we must first understand the concept of shape space. Shape space (Figure 3) follows this theory; the immune system of a given person can be represented by a two-dimensional circle of volume V. This circle represents the finite number of gene combinations possible on an antibody's paratopes. Each antibody (A) can recognise a given number of genetic combinations and therefore can recognise a volume (V_e) of antigenic epitopes (x) in shape space. Therefore, it is conceivable that the repertoire of antibodies can be deemed complete if they cover the entire volume of the shape space.

In modelling shape space Perelson noted one thing, that there is

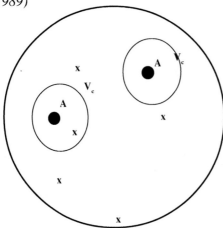

Figure 3: A diagrammatic representation of shape space (adapted from Perelson, 1989)

a trade off between good stability properties and good controllability properties. They also noted that the immune system is controlled by the same stability-controllability trade-off. As a general principle, they believed the immune system should be *stable but not too stable*. If this is the case, the immune system can remain insensitive to small random disturbances but yet be responsive to antigen challenge Jerne (1974a). Perelson argues that the repertoire will be complete if the following three hypotheses are satisfied:

1) Each antibody can recognise a set of related epitopes, each of which differs slightly in shape. The strengths of binding may differ for different epitopes and is accounted for by differences in affinity.

2) The antibodies in the repertoire have shapes that are randomly distributed throughout shape space.

3) The repertoire size is of order 10^6 or greater.

Learning within the Immune Network

It has been proposed that the immune network can be thought of as being cognitive Varela et al. (1988) and exhibits learning capabilities. The authors proposed four reasons as to why they consider immune systems to be cognitive: (i) they can recognise molecular shapes; (ii) they remember history of encounters; (iii) they define the boundaries of molecular self, and (iv) they can make inferences about molecular species they have yet to encounter. Taking these points, the chapter explores cognitive mechanisms of the immune system and proposes that the immune network can be thought of as a cognitive network, in a similar way to a neural network.

The work suggests that the immune network is capable of producing patterns over the entire network and that there is a self-regulatory mechanism working that helps to maintain this network structure. These emerging patterns within the immune network are characterised by increasing numbers of B cells that when in a response to an antigen undergo clonal selection. The authors use the term *metadynamics* of the immune system (see also Bersini and Valera, 1990). This can essentially be taken to mean the following. The immune system continually produces new antibodies and B cells that are a diverse representation of the invading antigen population. A large variety of new B cells will be produced, but not all will be a useful addition to the immune system and many will never enter into the dynamics of the immune system (interact with other B cells in the network) and will eventually die. The authors produced a simple model using these ideas and found that there are oscillations in many of the variables within their system, in particular the number of B cells that are produced. There would often be rapid production of B cells, followed by a sharp decline in number, which the authors argue is what you expect to see in the natural immune system. Coupled with this oscillatory pattern, the authors observed that a certain core and stable network structure did emerge over time. This structure emerges due to a topological self-organisation within the network, with the resulting network acting to record the history of encounters with antigens. Therefore, the authors concluded that the immune system is an excellent system for learning about new items and can support a memory of encounters by the use of complex pattern matching and a self-organising network structure and can thus be thought of as being cognitive.

Following on from work of Bersini and Valera (1990), work of Bersini and Valera (1994) provides an effective summary of work done on exploring the dynamics and metadynamics of the immune system. They claim that the metadynamics of the immune system allows the identity of the immune system to be preserved over time, but still allow itself to adapt to new situations. In this chapter, the authors propose seven general principles that can be extracted from the immune system that could be applied to creating a controlling system for the area of adaptive control, but they hope to other fields as well.

Clonal Selection Principle

When antibodies on a B-cell bind with an antigen, the B-cell becomes activated and begins to proliferate. New B-cell clones are produced that are an exact copy of the parent B-cell, but then undergo somatic hypermutation and produce antibodies that are specific to the invading antigen. The clonal selection principle Burnet (1978) is the term used to describe the basic properties of an adaptive immune response to an antigenic stimulus. It establishes the idea that only those cells capable of recognizing an antigenic stimulus will proliferate, thus being selected against those that do not. Clonal selection operates on both T-cells and B-cells.

The B-cells, in addition to proliferating or differentiating into plasma cells, can differentiate into long-lived B *memory cells*. Memory cells circulate through the blood, lymph and tissues, probably not manufacturing antibodies Perelson et al (1978). However, when exposed to a second antigenic stimulus they commence differentiating into large lymphocytes capable of producing high affinity antibody.

USING THE IMMUNE SYSTEM METAPHOR

The immune system is a valuable metaphor as it is self-organising, highly distributed and has no central point of control. Work summarised above reveals many interesting avenues for use of the immune system as a metaphor for developing an algorithm for use in data mining. These can be summarised as follows:

- *Using the idea of self-organisation.* Self-organisation is the ability of a natural or artificial system to adapt its internal structure to structures sensed in the input of the system. In the case of the natural immune system, the immune network adapts to new antigens it comes across and ultimately can be said to represent the antigens.
- *The metaphor of B cells and antigens.* B cells and their associated antibodies represent the antigens that they are exposed to. This leads to the possibility of using the B-cell and antigen to represent data. Antigens are exposed to B cells

to elicit a response, i.e. capture the patterns contained within.

- *The primary and secondary immune response.* It has been shown that more B cells are produced in response to continual exposure to antigens. This suggests that to learn on data using the immune system metaphor, the data may have to be presented a number of times in order for the patterns to be captured.

- *Using the idea of clonal selection.* As B cells become stimulated, they clone in order to create more antibodies to remove the antigen from the system. This causes clusters of B cells that are similar to appear. Clusters indicate similarity and could be useful in understanding common patterns in data, just as a large amount of specific B cells in the immune system indicate a certain antigen.

- *Adaptation and diversification.* Some B-cell clones undergo somatic hypermutation. This is an attempt by the immune system to develop a set of B cells and antibodies that cannot only remove the specific antigen, but also similar antigens. By using the idea of mutation, a more diverse representation of the data being learned is gained than a simple mapping of the data could achieve. This may be of benefit and reveal subtle patterns in data that may be missed. Additionally, through the use of more directed mutation and selection the immune system is capable of extracting more specific patterns.

- *The use of a network structure.* The immune network represents an effective way of achieving memory.

- *Metadynamics.* The oscillations of immune system variables, such as antibody concentration and B-cell population, as discussed in Varela (1988) indicate that a stable network representative of the data being learned could be possible.

SUMMARY

Immunology is a vast topic. Therefore, this chapter has introduced only those areas of immunology that are pertinent to its purpose. The immune system is a highly adaptive, distributed and self-organising system that is a rich source of inspiration to many. Through a process of matching between antibodies and antigens and the production of B cells through clonal selection (Burnet,1959) and somatic hypermutation (Kepler and Perelson, 1993), an immune response can be elicited against invading antigen and the antigen removed from the system. In order to remember which antigens the immune system has encountered, some form of immunological memory must be present. The pioneering work of Jerne (1974a), which first introduced the concept of a network of B cells supporting each other to form immunological memory, is central to much of the work of AIS at present. The work of Farmer et al. (1986) took a formal approach to that by Jerne (1974a) and created a simple equation that defined B-cell stimulation in the immune network.

This theoretical immunology has been simulated by other people (Perelson, 1989; Varela et al., 1988) where it was suggested that the immune network possesses some kind of learning and cognitive abilities. This leads many people to speculate that the immune system is an excellent learning system and that there are many mechanisms by which one could exploit the immune system for application to computer science. Work of the field of AIS attempts to capitalise on the immunology described in this chapter to create effective immune algorithms for data mining.

IMMUNOLOGICAL METAPHORS

There are a number of reasons why the immune system is of interest to computer scientists (Dasgupta, 1998), based on the basic principles given in the previous section. These can be summarised as follows:

- *Recognition*: The immune system has the ability to recognise and classify a vast number of different patterns and respond accordingly. Additionally, the immune system can differentiate between a foreign substance and its own immune system cells, therefore maintaining some sense of self.
- *Feature Extraction*: Through the use of Antigen Presenting Cells (APCs) the immune system has the ability to extract features of the antigen by filtering molecular noise from the antigen before being presented to the lymphocytes.
- *Diversity*: Through the process of somatic hypermutation, a diverse range of antibodies is created in response to an antigen, ensuring that not only the invading antigen is destroyed, but also the immune system is prepared for an attack by a slight variation of the same antigen.
- *Learning*: Through the interaction within the immune network, the immune system can be said to be a learning mechanism, adapting to antigens as they are presented by the creation of antibodies and ultimately removing them from the system. The mechanism of somatic hypermutation also allows the immune system to fine-tune its response to an invading pathogen.
- *Memory*: The immune system maintains a memory of its encounters with antigens.
- *Distributed detection*: There is inherent distribution within the immune system. There is no one point of overall control; each lymphocyte is specifically stimulated and responds to new antigens.
- *Self-regulation*: Immune systems dynamics are such that the immune system population is controlled by local interactions and not by a central point of control.

It is for the above reasons at least that the immune system has generated interest in applying some of these properties to data mining research. This section now examines some of these applications.

Learning with Artificial Immune Systems

Given the ability of the immune system to learn about new antigens and adapt to them, it was felt that the immune system would act as an excellent metaphor for machine learning. It was suggested earlier by theoretical immunologists that there were many mechanisms that could be used (Varela et al.,1988; Perelson, 1989) and some of these have been discussed previously.

BACKGROUND RESEARCH FOR IMMUNE-INSPIRED MACHINE LEARNING

The term machine learning covers a wide range of topics. Essentially, machine-learning techniques are computational methods that can be applied to data in order to learn or discover something new about that data, or alternatively, to predict an answer, based on some previous knowledge. Machine learning can be split into two categories, supervised and unsupervised techniques. Supervised techniques, such as neural networks, are used for example when one wishes to predict the classification of unseen items. Data is used to train a network with the ability to classify similar types of data into predefined classes. Unsupervised learning is the discovery of those classes in the first instance.

Some of the first work to be attempted at applying immune system metaphors to machine learning was performed by Cooke and Hunt (1995), Hunt and Cooke (1995) and Hunt and Cooke (1996). In these three papers, the authors describe their attempts to create a supervised machine learning mechanism to classify DNA sequences as either promoter or non-promoter classes, by creating a set of antibody strings that could be used for this purpose. Work had already been done on this classification problem using different approaches such as C4.5 (Quinlan, 1993), standard neural networks and a nearest neighbor algorithm (Kolodner, 1993). The authors claimed that their Artificial Immune System (AIS) achieved an error rate of only 3% on classification, which, when compared to the other established techniques, yielded superior performance. The system created used mechanisms such as B cells and B-cell stimulation, immune network theory, gene libraries, mutation and antibodies to create a set of antibody strings that could be used for classification.

Central to the work was the use of the Immune Network theory (Jerne,1974a). The system maintained a network of B cells, with two B cells being connected if they share an affinity for each other over a certain threshold. Each B-cell object contained a matching element, a library of genes for the creation of new antibodies, the DNA sequence, a number of intermediate DNA sequences and a record of the stimulation level. The system also used an antigen model, which is a string representation of DNA sequences to be learned. These were presented to the

Figure 4: Calculating the matching value. The match algorithm counts each bit, which matches (in a complementary fashion) between the antigen and the antibody and totals the number of bits, which match.

Antigen:	0 1 1 0 0 0 0 1 1 1 1 0 1 1 0
Antibody:	1 0 0 1 1 1 0 0 0 1 0 1 1 0 1
XOR:	1 1 1 1 1 1 0 1 1 0 1 1 0 1 1 => 12
Length:	6 2 2 2
Match Value:	$12 + 2^6 + 2^2 + 2^2 + 2^2$ => 88

matching elements (paratopes) of the B-cell objects. Initially, a random selection of the training data was extracted to create the B-cell network. The remainder is used as antigen training items. Antigens are then randomly selected from the training set and randomly presented to areas of the B-cell network where an attempt was made to bind the antigen with the closest two B cells and surrounding B cells up to a certain distance away in the network. If the bind was successful, then the B-cell was cloned and mutated. The matching mechanism employed can be seen in figure 4. If the match is above a certain threshold, then the antibody will bind to the antigen. The strength of this bind then directly determines how stimulated the B cell becomes.

A variety of mutation mechanisms were used in the system, including mimicking gene selection, folding, transcription and translation steps to random point mutation. Once a new B-cell had been created an attempt was made to integrate it into the network at the closest B cells. If the new B-cell could not be integrated, it was removed from the population. If no bind was successful, then a B-cell was generated using the antigen as a template and was then incorporated into the network. The algorithm for the system is shown:

Algorithm from the AIS created to recognise promoter sequence DNA (Hunt and Cooke, 1995)

> Load antigen population
> Randomly initialise the B-cell population
> Until termination condition is met do
>> Randomly select an antigen from the antigen population
>> Randomly select a point in the B-cell network to insert the antigen
>> Select a percentage of the B cells local to the insertion point
>> For each B-cell selected
>>> present the antigen to each B-cell and determine whether this
>>>> antigen can be bound
>>> by the antibody and if so, how stimulated the B-cell will become.
>>> If the B-cell is stimulated enough, clone the B cell
>> If no B-cell could bind the antigen
>>> generate a new B-cell, which can bind the antigen
>> Order these B cells by stimulation level
>> remove the weakest 5% of the population
>> Generate N new B cells (where N equals 25% of the population)
>> Select M B cells to join the immune network (where M equals 5% of
>>> the population)

A second important aspect to this work is the calculation of the B-cell stimulation. The stimulation level of a B-cell dictates whether the B-cell survives in the network. The authors used as a basis the equation proposed in Farmer (1986) and adapted it to the equation:

$$stimulation = c\left[\sum_{j=1}^{N}m(a,xe_j) - k_1\sum_{j=1}^{N}m(a,xp_j) + k_2\sum_{j=1}^{n}m(a,y)\right] - k_3$$

where N is the number of antibodies, n is the number of antigens, c is rate constant that depends on the number of comparisons per unit of time and the rate of antibody production stimulated by a comparison, a is the current B-cell object, xe_j represents the jth B cell's epitope, xp_j represents the jth B cell's paratope and y represents the current antigen. This equation takes into account matches between neighbors (both stimulation and suppression) and antigens. The antigen training data are being presented with a set for a number of times; once this is complete the antibodies are saved and can be used for classification. The authors claimed a certain amount of success for their technique, claiming a 90% success rate (on average) for classification of unseen items.

Based on the work of Hunt and Cooke (1995),the work of Hunt et al. (1996) took the application to case base reasoning and attempted to apply it directly to data mining. As the immune system creates generality in the fight against infection, the authors used this as inspiration to create the idea of a general case that would attempt to identify trends in data, as opposed to simply the data themselves. By introducing the idea of a generalised case, the authors created a system that could help in the customer-profiling domain; specifically, identifying people who are likely to buy PEPs. PEPs are Personal Equity Plans which were tax-free savings accounts available at the time. Each B-cell object contained customer profile data, such as marital status, ownership of cars and bank account details, etc. The authors claim 90% accuracy on identifying potential customers, but the benchmarking for these results is unclear, as are any real data to back up such claims. The authors employed a number of threshold values to tune algorithm performance. It was found that dramatic differences in the threshold values were needed for different applications, ranging from 50 to 1,500. The actual scale of this figure is unclear; this was a major drawback of the proposed algorithm since what is really desirable is an *independent* value that should not be predefined.

This algorithm was then applied to fraud detection (Hunt et al.,1996; Hunt et al., 1998; Neal et al.,1998). The work of Hunt et al (1996) simply proposed the idea that an AIS could be used to create a visual representation of loan and mortgage application data that could in some way aid the process of locating fraudulent behavior. An attempt at creating such a system was proposed by Hunt et al (1998). This system, called JISYS, called for the creation of a network of B-cell objects where each B-cell represented a loan application. A number of predefined initial parameters were required, some of which had been apparent in earlier research, such as setting the stimulation threshold (determining when a B-cell should clone), setting the match threshold (defining how good a match had to be before a bind between B-cell and antigen could occur) and setting the maximum number of links that a B-cell could have in the immune network. This work did not differ substantially from that described in Hunt et al. (1996), apart from the application and the inclusion of more sophisticated string matching techniques, such as trigram matching and the inclusion of weighting in order of the importance various fields in the B-cell object, taken from the weighted nearest neighbor idea (Kolodner, 1993). No real results were presented for this system.

Advances were made in the follow-up work of Neal et al. (1998) where results for fraud detection were presented. Known fraudulent patterns were placed in simulated loan application data to see if the JISYS system could produce a network of B-cell objects that could help a user identify these areas. The results from JISYS were positive, with the system identifying all known fraudulent patterns within the data and discovering other interesting relationships between other data items. This led to the notion that this algorithm was perhaps better suited to unsupervised learning, discovering patterns in data. However, it was acknowledged that the algorithm was very domain specific and deviated from immunological metaphors.

RECENT ADVANCES IN IMMUNE-INSPIRED DATA MINING

Generic Unsupervised Learning Algorithms

Timmis et al. (2000) developed an Artificial Immune System (AIS) inspired by the immune network theory, based on work undertaken by Hunt and Cooke (1996). This was undertaken in order to create an algorithm that was not domain dependant. Previous work had been shown to be quite domain dependant, but there was the potential of exploiting these metaphors across many different classes of problems. In order to achieve this the authors proposed a domain independent algorithm, based on immune system metaphors.

The proposed AIS consisted of a set of B cells, a set of antigen training data, links between those B cells and cloning and mutation operations that are performed on the B cell objects. The systems ability to extract meaningful clusters was tested on the well-known Fisher Iris data set (Fisher,1936). These clusters are visualised in a specially developed tool (Timmis, 2001) and can be used for exploratory analysis. It is proposed by the authors that these clusters could then be used to create a rule set, which in turn could be used for classification.

Each B cell in the AIS represented an individual data item that could be matched (by Euclidean distance) to an Antigen or another B cell in the network (following the theory that the immune network has some sort of feedback mechanism). The links between the B cells were calculated by a measure of affinity between the two matching cells, based on Euclidian distance. A link was created between the two B-cells if the affinity between the two was below a certain threshold, the NAT, (Network Affinity Threshold). The NAT is calculated as the average distance between all items in the data set being learned. A B cell also has a certain level of stimulation that is related to the number and to the strength of links a cell has. The AIS also had a cloning mechanism that produced randomly mutated

B cells from B cells that became stimulated above a certain threshold. The network was trained by repeatedly presenting the training set to the network.

The AIS produced some encouraging results when tested on the Fisher Iris data set. The proposed system successfully produced three distinct clusters, which when presented with a known data item could be classified. However, although the clusters were distinct, there was still a certain amount of connection between Iris Virginica and Iris Versicolor. The AIS also experienced an uncontrolled population explosion after only a few iterations, suggesting that the suppression mechanism (culling 5% of the B cell) could be improved.

This work was then taken further in Timmis and Neal (2000). In this paper the authors raise and address a number of problems concerning the work of Timmis et al. (2000). A number of initial observations were clear: the network underwent an exponential population explosion; the NAT eventually became so low that only very similar, if not identical clones can ever be connected; the number of B cells removed from the system lags behind the number created to such an extent that the population control mechanism was not effective in keeping the network population at a sensible level; the network grew so large that they become difficult to compute each iteration with respect to time; the resultant networks were so large, they were difficult to interpret, and were really too big to be a sensible representation of the data. With these concerns in mind, the authors proposed a new system called RLAIS (Resource Limited Artificial Immune System). This was later renamed AINE (Artificial Immune Network).

To summarize the work of Timmis and Neal (2001), AINE is initialised as a network of ARB (Artificial Recognition Balls) objects; T Cells, again, are ignored. Links between ARBs are created if they are below the Network Affinity Threshold (NAT), which is the average Euclidean distance between each item in the data set. The initial network is a cross section of the data set to be learned, the remainder makes up the antigen training set. Each member of this set is matched against each ARB in the network, again with the similarity being calculated on Euclidean distance. ARBs are stimulated by this matching process and by neighboring ARBs in the network. Again, a certain amount of suppression is included in the ARB-stimulation level calculation. The stimulation level of an ARB determines the survival of the B cell. The stimulation level also indicates if the ARB should be cloned and the number of clones that are produced for that ARB. Clones undergo a stochastic process of mutation in order to create a diverse network that can represent the antigen that caused the cloning as well as slight variations. There exists a number of parameters to the algorithm, those being: network affinity scalar, mutation rate and number of times the training data is presented to the network. Each one of these can be used to alter the algorithm performance (Timmis, 2000b).

Basic AINE algorithm (Timmis and Neal, 2000)

> Initialise AIN
> For each antigen
>> Present antigen to each ARB in the AIN
>> Calculate ARB stimulation level
>> Allocate B cells to ARBs, based on stimulation level
>> Remove weakest ARBs (ones that do not hold any B cells)
> Clone and mutate remaining ARBs
> Integrate new ARBs into AIN
> Check for termination condition
> Write out AIN to file

Each ARB contains a single piece of n-dimensional data and represents a number of identical B cells. This can be thought of as the center of its ball in shape space. B cells are therefore no longer explicitly represented in the network. AINE is limited to a maximum number of B cells, which may be shared among the ARBs. The main contents of an ARB are the data that it represents, a record of how many B cells it represents, a record the stimulation level of the ARB and some matching element that allows matching between ARB and antigens and other ARBs. An ARB undergoes stimulation level calculations as follows:

$$sl = \sum_{x=0}^{a} 1 - pd + \sum_{x=0}^{n}(1 - dis_x) - \sum_{x=0}^{n} dis_x$$

where pd is defined as the distance between the ARB and the antigen in the normalised data space, such that $0 \le pd \le 1$, and dis_x is the distance of the xth neighbor from the ARB. The population control mechanism, that replaced the 5% culling mechanism, forces ARBs to compete for survival based on a finite number of resources that AINE contains; the more stimulated an ARB, the more resources it can claim. Once an ARB no longer claims any B cells, it is removed from the AIN.

Previously, always 5% was removed. With AINE this is not the case, a predetermined number is not set for removal and the amount removed depends on the performance of the algorithm. This gives rise to a meta-dynamical system that eventually stabilises into a diverse core network structure that captures the main patterns contained within the data. This stability within AINE allows for the creation of a termination condition. Over a period of time, a core network emerges that captures the main patterns within the data set. The authors propose that AINE is a very effective learning algorithm, and on test data so far, very encouraging results have been obtained. The authors have tested the system on a simulated data set and the Iris data set. With the Iris data set, three distinct clusters can be obtained, unlike the original AIS proposed. Additionally, the networks produced by AINE are much smaller than the original system. In effect, AINE is acting as a compression facility, reducing the complexity of the networks, as to highlight the important information, or knowledge, that can be extracted from the data. More results pertaining to AINE can be found in Timmis (2000a).

The output from AINE can be considered as a disconnected graph, which is called an Artificial Immune Network (AIN). Data regarding the contents of each ARB is recorded, along with a list of all links in the network and the affinity between the connected ARBs. The networks evolved by AINE are ideally suited to visualisation. By visualising these networks, the user can build up a good impression of the topological make up of the data, enabling them to identify areas of similarity within the data and perform a more informed exploration of the results. Timmis (2001) proposes a tool called aiVIS, which allows for the effective visualisation of these networks and allows the user to interact with the networks to gain a fuller understanding of the data.

Similar to that work above has been undertaken by de Castro and von Zuben (2000). In this work the authors propose a system called aiNet, the driving force of which is data clustering and filtering redundant data. Chapter XII in this book explores this work in-depth.

A simple artificial immune system shell has been created that has been tested on various benchmark machine learning data sets Immune Networks (2001). At the time of writing, however, results and details of algorithms used were not available.

Supervised Learning with Immune Metaphors

Use was made of the immune network theory to produce a pattern recognition and classification system (Carter, 2000). This system was known as Immunos-81. The author's aim was to produce a supervised learning system that was implemented based on high levels of abstraction on the workings of the immune system. The algorithm can be seen below.

His model consisted of T cells, B cells, antibodies and an amino-acid library. Immunos-81 used the artificial T cells to control the production of B cells. The B cells would then in turn compete for the recognition of the "unknowns". The amino-acid library acts as a library of epitopes (or variables) currently in the system. When a new antigen is introduced into the system, its variables are entered into this library. The T cells then use the library to create their receptors that are used to identify the new antigen. During the recognition stage of the algorithm T cell paratopes are matched against the epitopes of the antigen, and then a B cell is created that has paratopes that match the epitopes of the antigen.

Immunos-81 was tested using two standard data sets, both of these from the medical field. The first set was the Cleveland data set, which consists of the results of a medical survey on 303 patients suspected of having coronary heart disease. This data set was then used as a training set for the second data set, a series of 200 unknown cases. Immunos-81 achieved an average classification rate of 83.2% on the Cleveland data set and approximately 73.5% on a second data set. When compared to other machine learning techniques, Immunos-81 performed very well. The best rival was a k-nearest neighbour classifier (Wettschereck et al.,1997), which averaged 82.4% on the Cleveland data set, other classification algorithms (Gennari et al.,1989) managed 78.9%, and using C4.5 only 77.9% accuracy was obtained. The authors therefore argue that Immunos-81 is an effective classifier system, the algorithm is simple and the results are transparent to the user. Immunos-81 also has the potential for the ability to learn in real-time and be embeddable. It has proved to be a good example of using the immune system as a metaphor for supervised machine learning systems.

Simulated Annealing Using Immune Metaphors

Simulated annealing is a search algorithm based loosely on the metaphor of the gradual cooling of a liquid until it freezes. Simulated annealing helps to prevent search algorithms from becoming stuck in local maximum points in the search space. This is achieved by a varying the amounts of randomness in gradually decreasing amounts within the search space. A novel approach at creating a simulated annealing algorithm based on the immune metaphor has been proposed by deCastro and von Zuben (2001) and applied to the problem of initialising feed forward neural networks (NNs). The initialisation of NN weight vectors is an important one, as the wrong initial choice could lead to a poor local minima being discovered by the network. To search the entire area for potential solutions is an unacceptably large computational overhead, so methods are created in order to reduce that search area. The authors argue that the correlation between the quality of initial network weights and the quality of the output from the network can be likened to the quality of the initial antibody repertoire and the quality of the immune response. The authors successfully extract the metaphors of creating antibody diversity and the idea of shape space to propose an algorithm called SAND (Simulated ANnealing for Diversity). The aim of the algorithm is to generate a set of initial weight vectors to be used in an NN that are diverse enough to reduce the likelihood of the NN's convergence to a local optimum. In SAND an antibody is considered to be a vector of weights of a given neuron in a single layer of the network. By the use of an *energy function* that maximises the distance (based on Euclidean distance) between antibodies a diverse population of antibodies, and thus weight vectors, emerges. The authors make comparisons to other similar algorithms such as BOERS (Boers and Kuiper,1992), WIDROW (Nguyen and Widrow,1990) and found that if the SAND algorithm was used to create the initial weight vectors, the NN required a reduced number of epochs on which to train. The authors claim to have shown that NN which have a more diverse and well-distributed set of initial weight vectors yield faster convergence rates, and SAND is a viable alternative to other established techniques.

SUMMARY

This chapter has introduced the idea of using the mammalian immune system as inspiration for creating machine-learning algorithms that can be used in the process of data mining. Salient features of the immune system were explained, such as B cells, immune response, immunological memory and the immune network theory. It was shown how research into modeling the immune system, in some way, acted as a catalyst for this area of research, highlighting areas of the immune system that could possibly be used for computational systems. Reasons why the immune system is a good metaphor were also explored, in order to create these Artificial Immune Systems (AIS).

A review was then presented of the most recent work of the field of AIS in relation to data mining. This included both unsupervised and supervised machine learning techniques, and other techniques used as part of the data mining process.

OBSERVATIONS FOR THE FUTURE

The field of AIS is rapidly expanding; in terms of computer science, the field is very new. There appears to be a growing rise in the popularity of investigating the mammalian immune system as a source of inspiration for solving computational problems. This is apparent not only in the increasing amount of work of the literature, but also the creation of special sessions on AIS at major international conferences and tutorials at such conferences.

This chapter has outlined some of the major algorithms in the field of machine learning and data mining. Other work on AIS has not been covered by this chapter, and it is acknowledged by the authors that there is a large body of work emerging. The authors feel that while these algorithms are a promising start to a very exciting field of research, it is clear that these algorithms need further and more detailed testing and examination. It is hoped that this chapter will go some way into acting as a catalyst for other researchers to use these ideas and put them to the test. This field is very promising, as the algorithms created offer the flexibility of being distributed, adaptable and in some cases self organising to allow for patterns in data to emerge and create a diverse representation of the data being learned. The strengths of the algorithms are clear, but as yet issues such as scalability and areas where they are have greater potential, have yet to be addressed.

ACKNOWLEDGMENTS

The authors would like to acknowledge the valuable input from Dr. Mark Neal from the University of Wales, Aberystwyth for his support in the early stages of their own work. The authors would also like to thank Sun Microsystems, USA for its continued financial support for Thomas Knight during his Ph.D. studies.

REFERENCES

Bersini, H. and Valera, F. (1994). The immune learning mechanisms: Reinforcement and recruitment and their applications. *Computing with Biological Metaphors*. Chapman-Hall. 166-192.

Bersini, H. and Varela, F. (1990). Hints for adaptive problem solving gleaned from immune networks. *Parallel Problem Solving from Nature and 1st Workshop PPSW 1.* Springer-Verlag. 343-354. Dortmund and Federal Republic of Germany.

Boers, E.G. and Kuiper, H. (1992). *Biological Metaphors and the Design of Modular Artificial Neural Networks.* Master Thesis, Leiden University Leiden, Netherlands.

Burnet, F. (1959). *The clonal selection theory of acquired immunity.* Cambridge University Press.

Burnet, F. M. (1978). Clonal Selection and After, In G. I. Bell, A. S. Perelson & G. H. Pimbley Jr. (Eds.), *Theoretical Immunology,* Marcel Dekker Inc., 63-85.

Carneiro, J and Stewart, J. (1995). Self and Nonself Revisited : Lessons from Modelling the Immune Network. *Third European Conference on Artificial Life.* 405-420. Springer-Verlag. Granada, Spain.

Carter, J.H. (2000). The Immune System as a Model for Pattern Recognition and Classification. *Journal of the American Medical Informatics Association,* 7(1).

Cooke, D. and Hunt, J. (1995). Recognising promoter sequences using an Artificial Immune System. 89-97 *Proceedings of Intelligent Systems in Molecular Biology.* AAAI Press.

Coutinho, A. (1980). The self non-self discrimination and the nature and acquisition of the antibody repertoire. *Annals of Immunology.* (Inst. Past.) 131D.

Dasgupta, D. (1998). An overview of artificial immune systems. *Artificial Immune Systems and Their Applications.* 3-19. Springer-Verlag

de Castro, L.N. (1999). Artificial Immune Systems: Part 1 – Basic Theory and Applications. Technical Report, RT-DCA 01/99.

deCastro, L and Von Zuben, F. (2000). An evolutionary immune network for data clustering. *SBRN'2000.* Rio de Janerio, November. IEEE Press.

deCastro, L and Von Zuben, F. (2001). An immunological approach to initialise feed forward neural network weights. To appear in proceedings of *International conference on Artificial Neural Networks and Genetic Algorithms.* Prague.

Farmer, J, Packard, N and Perelson, A. (1986). The immune system and adaptation and machine learning. *Physica D. 22,* 187-204.

Fisher, R. (1936). The use of multiple measurements in taxonomic problems. *Annual Eugenics. 7.* II. pp 179-188

Gennari, J.H. Langley, P and Fisher, D. (1989). Models of information concept formation. *Artificial Intelligence;* 40:11-61.

Hunt, J. and Cooke, D. (1995). An adaptive and distributed learning system based on the Immune system. 2494-2499 *Proceedings of IEEE International Conference on Systems Man and Cybernetics (SMC).* IEEE.

Hunt, J. and Cooke, D. (1996). Learning using an artificial immune system. *Journal of Network and Computer Applications: Special Issue on Intelligent Systems : Design and Application.* 19, 189-212

Hunt, J., King, C and Cooke, D (1996). Immunising against fraud. Proc. *Knowledge Discovery and Data Mining and IEE Colloquium.* IEEE. 38-45.

Hunt, J., Timmis, J, Cooke, D, Neal, M and King, C (1998). JISYS: Development of an Artificial Immune System for real world applications. *Artificial Immune Systems and their Applications.* 157-186. Springer-Verlag.

Immune Networks. (2000). http://www.immunenetworks.com.

Ishida, Y. (1996). Distributed and autonomous sensing based on immune network. *Proceedings of Artificial Life and Robotics.* Beppu. AAAI Press, 214-217.

Ishiguro, A., Ichikawa, S., Shibat, T. and Uchikawa, Y. (1998). Modernationsim in the immune system: Gait acquisition of a legged robot using the metadynamics function.

3827-3832 *Proceedings of IEEE International Conference on Systems and Man and Cybernetics (SMC).* San Diego, USA. IEEE.

Janeway, C. (1993). How the Immune Systems Recognises Invaders. *Life, Death and the Immune System, Scientific American Special Issue.* 27-36. Pub. Scientific America Inc.

Jerne, N. 1974a. Towards a network theory of the immune system. *Annals of Immunology (Inst. Pasteur). 125C,* 373-389.

Jerne, N. (1974b). Clonal Selection in a Lymphocyte Network. *Cellular Selection and Regulation in the Immune Response.* 39-48. Raven Press.

Kepler, T. and Perelson, A. (1993) Somatic Hypermutation in B cells : An Optimal Control Treatment. *Journal of Theoretical Biology. 164,* 37-64.

Kolodner, J. (1993). *Case Base Reasoning.* Morgan Kaufmann.

Kim, J and Bentley, P. (1998). The human immune system and network of trusion detection. *Proceedings of 7th European Congress on Intelligent Techniques - Soft Computing.* Aachan , Germany.

Lee, Dong-Wook and Sim, Kwee-Bo. 1997. Artificial immune network based co-operative control in collective autonomous mobile robots. 58-63 *Proceedings of IEEE International Workshop on Robot and Human Communication.* Sendai, Japan. IEEE.

Matzinger, P. (1994). Immunological memories are made of this? *Nature. 369,* 605-606

Neal, M., Hunt, J. and Timmis, J. (1998). Augmenting an Artificial Immune Network. *Proceedings of International Conference on Systems and Man and Cybernetics (SMC).* IEEE 3821-3826. San Diego, California, U.S.A.

Nossal, G.J.V (1994) Life, Death and the Immune System: Life, Death and the Immune System. *Scientific American, Special Issue.* W.H.Freeman and Company.

Nguyen, D. and Widrow, B. (1990). Improving the learning speed of two-layer neural networks by choosing initial values of the adaptive weights. *Proceedings of IJCNN'90. Vol. 3,*21-26.

Paton, R. (1994) *Computing with Biological Metaphors.* Chp. Introduction to computing with biological metaphors. Publisher Chapman and Hall, 1-9

Perelson, A. (1989). Immune Network Theory *Immunological Review,* 110, 5-36

Perelson, A. S., Mirmirani, M. & Oster, G. F. (1978). Optimal Strategies in Immunology II. B. Memory Cell Production, *J. Math. Biol., 5,* 213-256.

Quinlan, J. (1993). *C4.5: Programs for Machine Learning.* Morgan Kaufmann.

Smith, D., Forrest, S. and Perelson, A. (1998). Immunological Memory is Associative. Artificial Immune Systems and their Applications. Springer-Verlag.

Tew, J. and Mandel, T. (1979). Prolonged antigen half-life in the lymphoid follicles of antigen-specifically immunised mice. *Immunology. 37,* 69-76.

Tew, J., Phipps, J. and Mandel, T. (1980). The maintenance and regulation of the humoral immune response. Persisting antigen and the role of follicular antigen-binding dendritic cells. *Immunological Review.* 53, 175-211

Timmis, J., Neal, M. and Hunt, J. (2000). An Artificial Immune System for Data Analysis. *Biosystems. 55(1/3),* pp. 143-150

Timmis, J. and Neal, M. (2001). *Knowledge Based Systems,* 14(3-4), 121-130.

Timmis, J. (2000a). *Artificial Immune Systems : A novel data analysis technique inspired by the immune network theory.* Ph.D. Thesis. University of Wales, Aberystwyth. 2000.

Timmis, J. (2000b). *On parameter adjustment of the immune inspired machine learning algorithm AINE.* Jon Timmis. Technical Report 12-00, Computing Laboratory, University of Kent at Canterbury, Canterbury, Kent. CT2 7NF.

Timmis, J. (2001). aiVIS: Artificial Immune Network Visualisation. *Proceedings of*

EuroGraphics UK. Pp 61-69. UCL, London. ISBN 0-9540321-0-1.

Tizzard, I. (1988a). *Immunology : An Introduction* 2nd Edition. Pub. Saunders College Publishing . The Response of B Cells to Antigen, 199-223.

Tizzard, I. (1988b). *Immunology : An Introduction* 2nd edition The Response of T Cells to Antigen. Pages 224-260. Saunders College Publishing.

Varela, F., Coutinho, A., Dupire, B and Vaz, N. (1988). Cognitive Networks : Immune and Neural and Otherwise. *Theoretical Immunology : Part Two, SFI Studies in the Sciences of Complexity, 2*, 359-371.

Wettschereck, D., Aha, D.W, and Mohri, T. (1997). A review and empirical evaluation of feature weighting methods for a class of lazy learning algorithms. *Artificial Intelligence Review. 11*:273-314.

Chapter XII

aiNet: An Artificial Immune Network for Data Analysis

Leandro Nunes de Castro and Fernando J. Von Zuben
State University of Campinas, Brazil

This chapter shows that some of the basic aspects of the natural immune system discussed in the previous chapter can be used to propose a novel artificial immune network model with the main goals of clustering and filtering crude data sets described by high-dimensional samples. Our aim is not to reproduce with confidence any immune phenomenon, but demonstrate that immune concepts can be used as inspiration to develop novel computational tools for data analysis. As important results of our model, the network evolved will be capable of reducing redundancy and describing data structure, including their spatial distribution and cluster interrelations. Clustering is useful in several exploratory pattern analyses, grouping, decision-making and machine-learning tasks, including data mining, knowledge discovery, document retrieval, image segmentation and automatic pattern classification. The data clustering approach was implemented in association with hierarchical clustering and graph-theoretical techniques, and the network performance is illustrated using several benchmark problems. The computational complexity of the algorithm and a detailed sensitivity analysis of the user-defined parameters are presented. A trade-off among the proposed model for data analysis, connectionist models (artificial neural networks) and evolutionary algorithms is also discussed.

BASIC IDEAS AND RATIONALE

The previous chapter (Timmis, Knight, and Neal, 2001) presented a brief introduction to the natural immune system describing the most relevant immune principles from a computational perspective, and focusing on how these can be used as metaphors to develop machine learning and data analysis algorithms. In this chapter, we will assume that the reader is familiar with these immunological principles. Other sources of reference of immunology under a computer science perspective can be found in the works by de Castro and Von Zuben (1999a) and Hofmeyr (2000).

To develop our artificial immune network model, named aiNet, we will employ the immune network theory, and the clonal selection and affinity maturation principles. In summary, the immune network theory hypothesizes the activities of the immune cells, the emergence of memory and the discrimination between our own cells (known as self) and external invaders (known as nonself). It also suggests that the immune system has an internal image of all pathogens (infectious nonself) to which it was exposed during its lifetime. On the other hand, the clonal selection principle proposes a description of the way the immune system copes with the pathogens to mount an adaptive immune response. The affinity maturation principle is used to explain how the immune system becomes increasingly better at its task of recognizing and eliminating these pathogens (antigenic substances).

The aiNet model will consist of a set of cells, named antibodies, interconnected by links with associated connection strengths. The aiNet antibodies are supposed to represent the network internal images of the pathogens (input patterns) to which they are exposed. The connections between the antibodies will determine their inter-relations, providing a degree of similarity (in a given metric space) among them: the closer the antibodies, the more similar they are.

Based upon a set of unlabeled patterns $\mathbf{X} = \{x_1, x_2, ..., x_M\}$, where each pattern (object, or sample) x_i, $i = 1,...M$, is described by L variables (attributes or characteristics), a network will be constructed to answer questions like: (1) Is there a great amount of redundancy within the data set and, if there is, how can we reduce it? (2) Is there any group or subgroup intrinsic to the data? (3) How many groups are there within the data set? (4) What is the structure or spatial distribution of these data (groups)? (5) How can we generate decision rules to classify novel samples?

This chapter is organized as follows. In the second section, the artificial immune network model, named aiNet, is described. We then characterize and analyse the proposed network model and present the hierarchical clustering and graph-theoretical techniques used to define the network structure, and the aiNet simulation results for several benchmark tasks, including a comparison with the Kohonen self-organizing map (SOM) (Kohonen, 1995). A sensitivity analysis of the proposed algorithm in relation to the most critical user-defined parameters is given a the chapter concludes with a discussion of the network's main characteristics, potential applications and future trends.

AINET: AN ARTIFICIAL IMMUNE NETWORK FOR DATA ANALYSIS

In this section, we will present the aiNet learning algorithm focusing on its dynamics and metadynamics. A deeper analysis and useful hierarchical clustering and graph-theoretical techniques, proposed to determine the final network architecture, will be discussed in the next section.

In order to quantify immune recognition, it is appropriate to consider all immune events as occurring in a shape-space S, which is a multi-dimensional metric space where each axis stands for a physico-chemical measure associated with a molecular shape (Perelson & Oster, 1979). A point $s \in S$ will be assumed to represent a problem dependent set of L measurements, capable of characterizing a molecular configuration. Hence, a point in an L-dimensional space, called shape-space, specifies the set of features necessary to determine the antibody-antibody (Ab-Ab) and antigen-antibody (Ag-Ab) interactions. Mathematically, this shape (set of features that define either an antibody or an antigen) can be represented as an L-dimensional string, or vector. The possible interactions within the aiNet will be represented in the form of a connectivity graph. The proposed artificial immune network model can now be formally defined:

> *Definition 1:* aiNet is a *disconnected weighted graph* composed of a set of nodes, called *antibodies*, and sets of node pairs called *edges* with an assigned number called *weight*, or *connection strength*, associated with each edge.

The aiNet clusters will serve as *internal images (mirrors)* responsible for mapping existing clusters in the data set onto network clusters. As an illustration, suppose there is a data set composed of three regions with a high density of data, according to Figure 1(a). A hypothetical network architecture, generated by the learning algorithm to be presented, is shown in Figure 1(b). The numbers within the

Figure 1: aiNet illustration. (a) Available data set with three clusters of high data density. (b) Network of labeled cells with their connection strengths assigned to the links. The dashed lines indicate connections to be pruned in order to generate disconnected sub-graphs, each characterizing a different cluster in the network.

(a)   *(b)*

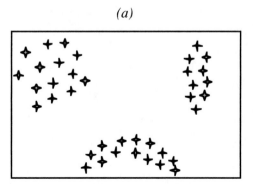
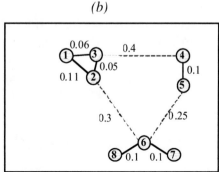

cells indicate their labels (the total number is generally higher than the number of clusters and much smaller than the number of samples); the numbers next to the connections represent their strengths, and dashed lines suggest connections to be pruned, in order to detect clusters and define the final network structure. Notice the presence of three distinct clusters of antibodies, each of which with a different number of antibodies, connections and strengths. These clusters map those of the original data set. Notice also that the number of antibodies in the network is much smaller than the number of data samples, characterizing an architecture suitable for data compression. Finally, the shape of the spatial distribution of antibodies gives proper insights about the original shape of the antigenic spatial distribution.

Similar to the models of Jerne (1974a,b) and Farmer, Packard and Perelson (1986), we make no distinction between the network cells and their surface molecules (antibodies). The Ag-Ab and Ab-Ab interactions are quantified through proximity (or similarity) measures. The goal is to use a distance metric to generate an antibody repertoire that constitutes the internal image of the antigens to be recognized, and evaluate the similarity degree among the aiNet antibodies, such that the cardinality of the repertoire can be controlled. Thus, the Ag-Ab affinity is inversely proportional to the distance between them: the smaller the distance, the higher the affinity, and vice-versa.

It is important to stress that, in the biological immune system, recognition occurs through a complementary match between a given antigen and the antibody. Nevertheless, in several artificial immune system applications (Hajela & Yoo, 1999; Hart & Ross, 1999; Oprea, 1999), the generation of an antibody repertoire with similar characteristics (instead of complementary) to the antigen set is a suitable choice, and will be adopted here.

As proposed in the original immune network theory, the existing cells will compete for antigenic recognition and those successful will lead to the network activation and cell proliferation (according to the clonal selection principle described in the next section), while those who fail will be eliminated. In addition, Ab-Ab recognition will result in network suppression. In our model, suppression is performed by eliminating the self-recognizing antibodies, given a suppression threshold σ_s. Every pair Ag_j-Ab_i, $j = 1,...,M$ and $i = 1,...,N$, will relate to each other within the shape-space S through the affinity $d_{i,j}$ of their interactions, which reflects the probability of starting a clonal response. Similarly, an affinity $s_{i,j}$ will be assigned to each pair Ab_j-Ab_i, $i,j = 1,...,N$, reflecting their interactions (similarity).

The following notation will be adopted:

- **Ab**: available antibody repertoire ($\mathbf{Ab} \in S^{N \times L}$, $\mathbf{Ab} = \mathbf{Ab}_{\{d\}} \cup \mathbf{Ab}_{\{m\}}$);
- $\mathbf{Ab}_{\{m\}}$: total memory antibody repertoire ($\mathbf{Ab}_{\{m\}} \in S^{m \times L}$, $m \leq N$);
- $\mathbf{Ab}_{\{d\}}$: d new antibodies to be inserted in $\mathbf{Ab}$ ($\mathbf{Ab}_{\{d\}} \in S^{d \times L}$);
- **Ag**: population of antigens ($\mathbf{Ag} \in S^{M \times L}$);
- f_j: vector containing the affinity of all the antibodies Ab_i ($i = 1,...N$) in relation to antigen Ag_j. The affinity is inversely proportional to the Ag-Ab distance;
- **S**: similarity matrix between each pair Ab_i-Ab_j, with elements $s_{i,j}$ ($i,j = 1,...,N$);

- **C**: population of N_c clones generated from **Ab** ($\mathbf{C} \in S^{N_c \times L}$);
- **C***: population **C** after the affinity maturation process;
- $\boldsymbol{d_j}$: vector containing the affinity between every element from the set **C*** with $\boldsymbol{Ag_j}$;
- ζ: percentage of the mature antibodies to be selected;
- $\mathbf{M}_j$: memory clone for antigen $\boldsymbol{Ag_j}$ (remaining from the process of clonal suppression);
- $\mathbf{M}_j^*$: resultant clonal memory for antigen $\boldsymbol{Ag_j}$;
- σ_d: natural death threshold; and
- σ_s: suppression threshold.

The aiNet learning algorithm aims at building a memory set that recognizes and represents the antigenic spatial distribution. The more specific the antibodies, the less parsimonious the network (low compression rate), whilst the more generalist the antibodies, the more parsimonious the network in relation to the number of antibodies (improved compression rate). The suppression threshold (σ_s) controls the specificity level of the antibodies, the clustering accuracy and network plasticity. In order to provide the user with important hints on how to set up the aiNet parameters, a sensitivity analysis of the algorithm in relation to the most critical user-defined parameters will be presented.

The aiNet learning algorithm can be described as follows:

1. At each iteration, do:
   1.1. For each antigenic pattern $\boldsymbol{Ag_j}, j = 1,...,M, (\boldsymbol{Ag_j} \in \mathbf{Ag})$, do:
      1.1.1. Determine the vector f_j composed of the affinities $f_{i,j}, i = 1,...,N,$ to all $\boldsymbol{Ab_i}. f_{i,j} = 1/D_{i,j}, i = 1,...,N$:

      $$D_{i,j} = \| \boldsymbol{Ab_i} - \boldsymbol{Ag_j} \|, \; i = 1,...,N ; \tag{1}$$

      1.1.2. A subset $\mathbf{Ab}_{\{n\}}$ composed of the n highest affinity antibodies is selected;
      1.1.3. The n selected antibodies are going to proliferate (clone) proportionally to their antigenic affinity $f_{i,j}$, generating a set **C** of clones: the higher the affinity, the larger the clone size, $i = 1,...,n$ for each of the n selected antibodies (see Equation (6));
      1.1.4. The set **C** is submitted to a directed affinity maturation process (guided mutation) generating a mutated set **C***, where each antibody k from **C*** will suffer a mutation with a rate α_k inversely proportional to the antigenic affinity $f_{i,j}$ of its parent antibody: the higher the affinity, the smaller the mutation rate:

      $$C_k^* = C_k + \alpha_k (\boldsymbol{Ag_j} - C_k); \; \alpha_k^i \propto 1/f_{i,j}; \; k = 1,...,; \; i = 1,..., N. \tag{2}$$

      1.1.5. Determine the affinity $d_{k,j} = 1/D_{k,j}$ among $\boldsymbol{Ag_j}$ and all the elements of **C***:

      $$D_{k,j} = \| C_k^* - \boldsymbol{Ag_j} \|, \; k = 1,...,N_c. \tag{3}$$

      1.1.6. From **C***, re-select $\zeta\%$ of the antibodies with highest $d_{k,j}$ and put them into a matrix $\mathbf{M}_j$ of clonal memory;

1.1.7. *Apoptosis*: eliminate all but one of the memory clones from $\mathbf{M}_j$ whose affinity $D_{k,j} > \sigma_d$:

1.1.8. Determine the affinity $s_{i,k}$ among the memory clones:

$$s_{i,k} = \| \mathbf{M}_{j,i} - \mathbf{M}_{j,k} \|, \forall i,k. \tag{4}$$

1.1.9. *Clonal suppression*: eliminate those memory clones whose $s_{i,k} < \sigma_s$:

1.1.10. Concatenate the total antibody memory matrix with the resultant clonal memory $\mathbf{M}_j^*$ for Ag_j: $\mathbf{Ab}_{\{m\}} \leftarrow [\mathbf{Ab}_{\{m\}}; \mathbf{M}_j^*]$;

1.2. Determine the affinity among all the memory antibodies from $\mathbf{Ab}_{\{m\}}$:

$$s_{i,k} = \| \mathbf{Ab}_{\{m\}}^j - \mathbf{Ab}_{\{m\}}^k \|, \forall i,k. \tag{5}$$

1.3. *Network suppression*: eliminate all the antibodies such that $s_{i,k} < \sigma_s$:

1.4. Build the total antibody matrix $\mathbf{Ab} \leftarrow [\mathbf{Ab}_{\{m\}}; \mathbf{Ab}_{\{d\}}]$

2. Test the stopping criterion.

Equations (1) and (3)-(5) use the Euclidean distance to determine the Ag-Ab and Ab-Ab affinities. The antigens were represented in a real-valued shape-space with the strings normalized over the interval [0, 1].

To determine the total clone size, N_c^i, generated for each antibody and each of the M antigens, the following equation was employed:

$$N_k^i = \sum_{i=1}^{n} round\left(N - D_{i,j}.N \right), \tag{6}$$

where N is the total amount of antibodies in $\mathbf{Ab}$, $round(\bullet)$ is the operator that rounds the value in parenthesis towards its closest integer and $D_{i,j}$ is the distance between the selected antibody i and the given antigen Ag_j, given by Equation (1).

In the above algorithm, Steps 1.1.1 to 1.1.7 describe the clonal selection and affinity maturation processes, as proposed by de Castro and Von Zuben (2000) in their computational implementation of the clonal selection principle. Steps 1.1.8 to 1.3 simulate the immune network activity.

As can be seen by the aiNet learning algorithm, a clonal immune response is elicited by each presented antigenic pattern. Notice also the existence of two suppressive steps in this algorithm (1.1.9 and 1.3) that we call *clonal suppression* and *network suppression*, respectively. As far as a different clone is generated to each antigenic pattern presented, a clonal suppression is necessary to eliminate intra-clonal self-recognizing antibodies. On the other hand, a network suppression is required to search for similarities between different sets of clones. After the learning phase, the network antibodies represent internal images of the antigens (or groups of antigens) presented to it.

The network outputs can be taken to be the matrix of memory antibodies' co-ordinates ($\mathbf{Ab}_{\{m\}}$) and their matrix of affinity ($\mathbf{S}$). While matrix $\mathbf{Ab}_{\{m\}}$ represents the network internal images of the antigens presented to the aiNet, matrix $\mathbf{S}$ is responsible for determining which network antibodies are connected to each other, describing the general network structure.

To evaluate the aiNet convergence, several alternative criteria can be proposed:

1. Stop the iterative process after a pre-defined number of iterations;
2. Stop the iterative process when the network reaches a pre-defined number of antibodies;
3. Evaluate the average error between all the antigens and the network memory antibodies ($\mathbf{Ab}_{\{m\}}$) by calculating the distance from each network antibody to each antigen (this strategy will be useful for less parsimonious solutions), and stop the iterative process if this average error is larger than a pre-specified threshold; and
4. Stop the iterative process if the average error between all the antigens and the aiNet memory antibodies rises after a pre-defined number of consecutive iterations.

AINET CHARACTERIZATION AND ANALYSIS

The aiNet model can be classified as a *connectionist*, *competitive* and *constructive network*, where the antibodies correspond to the network nodes and the antibody concentration and affinity are their states. The learning mechanism is responsible for the changes in antibody concentration and affinity. The connections among antibodies ($s_{i,k}$) correspond to the physical mechanisms that measure their affinity, quantifying the immune network recognition. The aiNet graph representation describes its architecture, with the definition of the final number and spatial distribution of clusters. The dynamics govern the plasticity of the aiNet, while the metadynamics are responsible for a broader exploration of the search-space and maintenance of diversity. The aiNet can also be classified as competitive, once its antibodies compete with each other for antigenic recognition and, consequently, survival. Antigenic competition is evident in Steps 1.1.2 and 1.1.6, while the competition for survival is performed in Step 1.1.7. Finally, the aiNet is plastic in nature, in the sense that its architecture, including number and relative role of cells, is adaptable according to the problem.

The aiNet general structure is different from neural network models (Haykin, 1999) if one considers the function of the nodes and their connections. In the aiNet case, the nodes work as internal images of ensembles of patterns (thus representing the acquired knowledge), and the connection strengths describe the similarities among these ensembles. On the other hand, in the neural network case, the nodes are processing elements while the connection strengths may represent the knowledge.

As discussed by de Castro and Von Zuben (2000), the immune clonal selection pattern of antigenic response can be seen as a microcosm of Darwinian evolution. The processes of simulated evolution (Holland, 1998) try to mimic some aspects of the original theory of evolution. Regarding the aiNet learning algorithm, it is possible to notice several features in common with simulated evolution (evolutionary algorithms). First, the aiNet is population based: an initial set of candidate solutions (antibodies), properly coded, is available at the beginning of the learning process. Second, a function to evaluate these candidate solutions has to be defined: an affinity measure as given by Equations (1) and (3)-(5). Third, the genetic encoding of the generated offspring (clones) is altered through a hypermutation mechanism. Finally, several parameters have to be defined, like the number of highest affinity antibodies to be selected, and the natural death and suppression thresholds.

Related Immune Network Models

The proposed artificial immune network model also follows the general immune network structure presented in Perelson (1989), in which the rate of population variation is proportional to the sum of the network novel antibodies (Step 1.4), minus the death of unstimulated antibodies (Step 1.1.7), plus the reproduction of stimulated antibodies (Step 1.1.3). As a complement, we suppress self-recognizing antibodies (Steps 1.1.9 and 1.3). Nevertheless, the essence of the aiNet model is different from the existing ones in two respects. First, and most important, it is a discrete (iterative) instead of a continuous model. Second, our network model may not be directly reproducing any biological immune phenomenon. The goal is to use the immune network paradigm, together with the clonal selection behavior of antigenic responses, as inspiration to develop an adaptive system capable of solving complex information processing tasks, like data compression, pattern recognition, classification and clustering. The proposed artificial immune network is problem dependent, in the sense that it is built according to the antigen set.

Hunt and Cooke (1996) proposed an artificial immune system (AIS) model, based upon the immune network theory, to perform machine learning. The key features they tried to explore were a mechanism to construct the antibodies, a content-addressable memory, the immune recognition (matching) mechanism and its self-organizing properties. Like in the aiNet case, they did not intend to provide a deep association between their proposed model and the vertebrate immune system. Instead, computationally appealing features were explored for the development of problem-solving tools. Their model was based on the following elements with their respective roles and characteristics:

1. *bone marrow:* generates antibodies, decides where in the network to insert the antigen, decides which B cell dies and triggers the addition of cells to the network;
2. *B cells:* carry the genetic information to build antibodies (and the antibodies themselves) along with their stimulation level;
3. *antibodies:* possess the paratope pattern;
4. *antigen:* possesses a single epitope; and
5. *stimulation level:* evaluates the strength of the Ag-Ab match and the affinity between different B cells.

Table 1: Trade-off between aiNet and the network model of Hunt and Cooke (1996).

Attribute	Model	
	aiNet	**Hunt & Cooke**
Nodes	Antibodies	B cells
Coding	Real-valued vectors	Binary strings
Network initialization	Random with small influence in the final network	Critical for the processing time
Antigenic presentation	To all the network	To a randomly chosen part of the network
Affinities	Euclidean distance	Proportional to the number of matching bits
Cell death	Suppressing antibodies with low antigenic and high antibody affinities	Suppressing B cell with low stimulation levels
Hypermutation	Directed aiming at learning	Undirected aiming at promoting diversity

Table 1 compares aiNet with the AIS model of Hunt and Cooke (1996).

Analysis of the Algorithm

Analysis of an algorithm refers to the process of deriving estimates for the time and memory space needed during execution. Complexity of an algorithm refers to the worst-case amount of time and memory space required during execution (Johnsonbaugh, 1997). Determining the performance parameters of a computer program is a difficult task and depends on a number of factors, such as the computer architecture being used, the way the data are represented, how and with which programming language the code is implemented. The time needed to execute an algorithm is also a function of the input. In our case, instead of dealing directly with the input, we may use parameters that characterize its size, like the number of variables (L) of each input vector and the amount of samples (patterns) (M) available. In addition, the total number of network cells N, the number of cell clones N_c^i and the network final number of memory cells (m) will be necessary to evaluate the complexity. The most computational-intensive step of the aiNet learning algorithm is the determination of the affinity between all the network antibodies (Step 1.2). The computation time required to compare all the elements of a matrix of size m is $O(m^2)$. Due to the asymptotic nature of the computational complexity, the total cost of the algorithm is taken to be $O(m^2)$. It is important to notice that m may vary along the learning iterations, such that at each generation the algorithm may have a different computational cost.

KNOWLEDGE EXTRACTION AND STRUCTURE OF A TRAINED AINET

The aiNet memory antibodies $\mathbf{Ab}_{\{m\}}$ represent internal images of the antigens to which it is exposed. This feature demands a representation in the same shape-space for the network of antibodies and for the antigens. Hence, visualizing the network for antigens (and antibodies) with $L > 3$ becomes a difficult task. In order to alleviate this difficulty, we suggest the use of several hierarchical clustering techniques to interpret the generated network. These techniques will help us to define the aiNet structure.

The aiNet structure could simply be determined by fully connecting all the network cells according to matrix $\mathbf{S}$, but it would not contribute to the process of network interpretation and knowledge extraction. One way of simply reducing the complexity of a fully connected network of cells is to suppress all those connections whose strength extrapolates a pre-defined threshold. This idea, though simple, does not account for any information within the network antibodies (indirectly in the data set) and might lead to erroneous interpretations of the resultant network. It is the main purpose here, to supply the user with formal and robust network interpretation strategies. Explicitly speaking, the goals are to determine (1) the number of *clusters*, or classes (whenever a cluster corresponds to a class), (2) the spatial distribution of each cluster, and (3) the network antibodies belonging to each of the identified clusters. To do so, the network output is used, which is composed of the number m of memory antibodies, the matrix $\mathbf{Ab}_{\{m\}}$ of memory antibodies, and the upper triangular matrix $\mathbf{S}$ of distances among these memory antibodies, along with some principles from cluster analysis. The problem is stated as follows.

Given a network with m memory antibodies (matrix $\mathbf{Ab}_{\{m\}}$), each being a vector of dimension L ($\mathbf{Ab}_{\{m\}} \in \Re^{m \times L}$) and their interconnections (matrix $\mathbf{S}$), devise a clustering scheme to detect inherent separations between subsets (clusters) of $\mathbf{Ab}_{\{m\}}$, given a distance metric.

The algorithms to be presented here are well known from the statistical literature, but will suffer a series of adaptations and will demand new interpretations in order to be applied to the immune network paradigm. Thus, the aiNet becomes responsible for extracting knowledge from the data set, while hierarchical cluster analysis techniques will be used to detect clusters in the resultant network, i.e., to interpret the aiNet. The network can be seen as a pre-processing for the cluster analysis technique, being a powerful tool to filter out redundant data from a given data set.

Hierarchical Clustering and Graph-Theoretical Techniques

To illustrate the methods that will be used and the ones to be proposed, consider one of the simplest problems of data clustering presented in Figure 2(a).

There are 50 samples subdivided into five clusters (non-overlapping classes) of 10 samples each. Figure 2(b) depicts the automatically generated network cells, considering the following aiNet training parameters: $n = 4$, $\zeta = 0.2$, $\sigma_d = 1.0$, $\sigma_s = 0.14$ and $d = 10$. The stopping criterion is a fixed number of generations: $N_{gen} = 10$. The resulting network contains only 10 cells, reducing the problem to 20% of its original size, what corresponds to a compression rate $CR = 80\%$.

Hierarchical techniques may be subdivided into agglomerative methods, which proceed by a series of successive fusions of the m entities (antibodies) into groups, and divisive methods, which partition the set of m entities (antibodies) successively into finer partitions. The results of both agglomerative and divisive techniques may be represented in the form of a dendrogram, which is a two-dimensional diagram illustrating the fusions or partitions which have been made at each successive level (Everitt, 1993).

In this work, we will focus on the agglomerative methods, more specifically the nearest-neighbor (or single-link) method, and the centroid cluster analysis. As the aiNet may be seen as an interconnected graph of antibodies, it will be interpreted based on some graph-theoretical strategies for detecting and describing clusters, in particular the minimal spanning tree, MST.

The aiNet outputs are m, the matrix $\mathbf{S}$ of dimension $\Re^{m \times m}$ and matrix $\mathbf{Ab}_{\{m\}}$ of dimension $S^{m \times L}$. Hence, the application of hierarchical methods for the construction of a dendrogram, like the nearest and furthest neighbor and centroid, is straightforward.

Given matrix $\mathbf{S}$, we wish to construct a tree, or a nested set of clustering of the objects, in order to provide a striking visual display of similarity groupings of the network cells.

Definition 2: A *dendrogram* is defined as a rooted weighted tree where all terminal nodes are at the same distance (path length) from the root (Lapointe & Legendre, 1991).

We will not get into details on how to construct a dendrogram from a similarity matrix. The interested reader shall refer to Hartigan (1967) and Hubert, Arabie and

Figure 2. Illustrative example. (a) Learning data. (b) Resulting network antibodies.

(a)   *(b)*

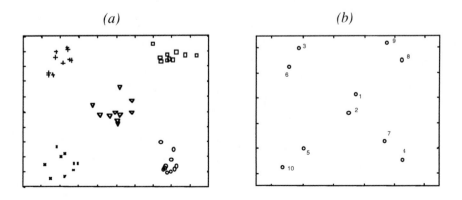

Meulman (1998). For the purposes of this chapter, three characteristics can adequately describe a dendrogram: its topology, labels and cluster heights (Lapointe & Legendre, 1995). Figure 3 illustrates the dendrogram representation for the centroid cluster strategy and the aiNet antibodies depicted in Figure 2(b). Notice the topology, cell labels, and cluster heights, representing the Ab-Ab affinities.

Virtually all clustering procedures provide little, if any, information concerning the number of clusters present in data. Nonhierarchical procedures usually require the user to specify this parameter before any clustering is accomplished (that is the reason why we chose to use hierarchical methods instead of nonhierarchical ones), and hierarchical methods routinely produce a series of solutions ranging from m clusters to a solution with only one cluster present. As can be seen from Figure 3, the dendrogram can be broken at different levels to yield different clusterings of the network antibodies. In this case, the large variations in heights allow us to distinguish five clusters among the network antibodies, in accordance with the network depicted in Figure 2(b). This procedure is called *stepsize* and involves examining the differences in *fusion values* between hierarchy levels. A broad review of several different methods for determining the number of clusters in a set of objects can be found in Milligan and Cooper (1985).

Keeping track of the nearest-neighbor hierarchical clustering technique, we can find the *minimal spanning tree* (MST) of a graph to be a powerful mechanism to search for a locally adaptive interconnecting strategy for the network cells (Zahn, 1971). The MST will serve as another aid to detect and describe the structure of the aiNet clusters.

Figure 3: Dendrogram of the aiNet antibodies for the centroid method depicting large differences in the fusion values (for instance, ① in relation to ②).

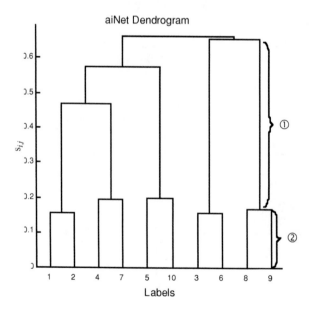

Definition 3: A tree is a *spanning tree* of a graph if it is a sub-graph containing all the vertices of the graph. A *minimal spanning tree* of a graph is a spanning tree with minimum weight. The weight of a tree is defined as the sum of the weights of its constituent edges (Leclerc, 1995).

Figure 4(a) depicts the minimal spanning tree (MST) for the constructed network. The visualization of this tree is only feasible for $L \leq 3$, but the applicability of the method is not restricted to lower dimensional spaces. By using the algorithm known as Prim's algorithm (Prim, 1957) to build the MST, we can draw a bar graph (see Figure 4(b)) representing the distances between neighboring cells.

Definition 4: A *minimax path* is the path between a pair of nodes that minimizes, over all paths, the cost, which is the maximum weight of the path (Carroll, 1995).

This definition is important in the aiNet context, once the preference for minimax paths in the MST forces it to connect two nodes i and j belonging to a tight cluster without straying outside the cluster. If the MST of a graph G is unique, then the set of minimax links of G defines this MST, else it defines the union of all MSTs of G.

Up to this point, notice that the MST is used to define the number of network clusters, which will be equal to the number of higher peaks in the bar graph of Figure 4(b) plus one, indicating large variations in the minimax distances between cells. When the aiNet learning algorithm generates more than one antibody for each cluster (which is the case of every population-based approach), the number of clusters can also be measured as the number of valleys of the respective histogram. On the other hand, the dendrograms allow us not only to define the number of clusters but also to identify the elements (nodes or antibodies) belonging to each cluster. In order to automatically define both the number and nodes composing each cluster of an MST, we can use some of the techniques proposed by Zahn (1971).

Figure 4: The minimal spanning tree and its histogram. (a) Edges to be removed (dashed lines) based upon the factor *criteria,* r = 2. *(b) Number of clusters (Peaks + 1, or Valleys) for this MST.*

(a)   *(b)*

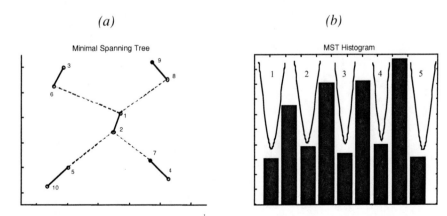

It is quite helpful that the MST does not break up the real clusters in $\mathbf{Ab}_{\{m\}}$, but at the same time neither does it force breaks where real gaps exist in the geometry of the network. A spanning tree is forced by its nature to span all the nodes in a network, but at least the MST jumps across the smaller gaps first.

There is the problem of deleting edges from an MST so that the resulting connected subtrees correspond to the observable clusters. In the example of Figure 4(a), we need an algorithm that can detect the appropriateness of deleting the edges (1,6), (1,8), (2,5) and (2,7). The following criterion is used.

An MST edge (i,k) whose weight $s_{i,k}$ is significantly larger than the average of nearby edge weights on both sides of the edge (i,k) should be deleted. This edge is called inconsistent.

There are two natural ways to measure the significance referred to. One is to see how many sample standard deviations separate $s_{i,k}$ from the average edge weights on each side. The other is to calculate the *factor* or *ratio* (r) between $s_{i,k}$ and the respective averages.

To illustrate this criterion, let us assume that all edges whose $s_{i,k}$ is greater than the average of nearby edges plus two standard deviations will be deleted, i.e., a factor $r = 2$ is chosen. Edges (1,6), (1,8), (2,5) and (2,7) will be selected for deletion (dashed lines in Figure 4(a)).

After determining the edges to be deleted, we can determine the number (p) of existing clusters (c_i, $i = 1,...,p$) in the aiNet and their respective components (antibodies). In this case, $c_1 = [6,3]$, $c_2 = [8,9]$, $c_3 = [1,2]$, $c_4 = [5,10]$ and $c_5 = [4,7]$.

The discussed criterion would fail to determine the correct number of network clusters in cases where the network reaches its minimal size for the given data set and the clusters are approximately uniformly distributed over the search space. As an example, for the proposed problem (Figure 2(a)), suppose a minimal network

Figure 5: The resultant network is composed of five separate sub-graphs (sub-networks), each corresponding to a different cluster. The stars represent the centroids of each cluster.

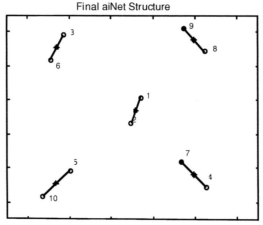

Final aiNet Structure

with five antibodies was found. This would result in the detection of a single cluster by the MST factor criterion. On the other hand, all the remaining network antibodies could be seen as internal images of the data clusters, implying that its number is equal to the number of antibodies, each of which represents a single cluster.

As one last aspect of clustering to be discussed, consider the problem of cluster representation. Assume that each cluster can be uniquely represented by its *center of mass* $(v_k, k = 1,...,p)$, or *centroid*, and the distance between clusters defined as the distance between the cluster centroids. Figure 5 depicts the resultant network antibodies defined by the aiNet learning algorithm and the network determined by the MST clustering algorithm described above for $r = 2$. The stars represent the centroids of each cluster. The use of the centroid to represent a cluster works well when the clusters are compact or isotropic. However, when the clusters are elongated or non-isotropic, this scheme fails to represent them properly, as will be discussed in the case of two examples to be presented further. Representing clusters by their centroids allows us to assign membership levels to each aiNet antibody in relation to the determined clusters, yielding a *fuzzy clustering* scheme.

aiNet Fuzzy Clustering

The presented clustering approaches generate partitions. In a partition, each cell belongs to one and only one cluster. Thus, the clusters in this hard clustering scheme are disjoint. Fuzzy clustering extends this notion to associate each cell (antibody) with every cluster using a membership function (Bezdek & Pal, 1992). The most well known fuzzy clustering techniques are the *fuzzy k-means* and the *fuzzy c-means* algorithms, that iteratively update the cluster centers according to an actual proximity matrix (**U**), until a small variation in **U** is achieved. A brief exposition of fuzzy partition spaces is given by Bezdek and Pal (1992):

Let M be an integer, $1 < c < M$, and let $\mathbf{X} = \{x_1, x_2,... x_M\}$ denote a set of M unlabeled feature vectors in $\Re^L$. Given $\mathbf{X}$, we say that p fuzzy subsets $\{u_i: \mathbf{X} \rightarrow [0,1]\}$ are a fuzzy p-partition of $\mathbf{X}$ in case the (pM) values $\{u_{i,k} = u_i(x_k), 1 \leq k \leq M, 1 \leq i \leq p\}$ satisfy three conditions:

$$0 \leq u_{i,k} \leq 1 \qquad \text{for all } i, k; \qquad (7a)$$
$$\Sigma\, u_{i,k} = 1 \qquad \text{for all } k; \qquad (7b)$$
$$0 < \Sigma\, u_{i,k} < 1 \qquad \text{for all } i. \qquad (7c)$$

Each set of (pM) values satisfying conditions (7a-c) can be arrayed as a $(p \times M)$ matrix $\mathbf{U} = [u_{i,k}]$. The set of all such matrices is the nondegenerate fuzzy c-partitions of $\mathbf{X}$.

After the number and members of each (hard) cluster are defined, and the network clusters are represented by their centers of mass, it is possible to apply a fuzzy clustering concept to the aiNet, where each antibody will have a measurable membership value to each of the determined clusters (centroids). In the aiNet context, the fuzzy clustering relaxes the membership of the network antibodies to the cluster centers, $\mathbf{U} = [u_{i,k}]$, which in this case can assume any value over the interval $[0,1]$. Conditions (7b) and (7c) are also relaxed, so that the sum of memberships is not required to be one.

Matrix $\mathbf{U}$ for the aiNet can be determined by calculating the distance between all the network memory antibodies $\mathbf{Ab}^i_{\{m\}}$, $i = 1,...,m$, and the centroids of the clusters v_k, $k = 1,...,p$, $\mathbf{U}^*$, normalizing its rows over the interval $[0,1]$ and then passing it through a squashing function, such that the smaller the distance between the aiNet antibodies and their respective centroids, the closer its membership value to unity. This can be achieved by applying a sigmoidal function to $\mathbf{U} = 1./\mathbf{U}^*$, where the ./ operator means that each value of the $\mathbf{U}$ matrix will be determined by dividing one by the respective element of $\mathbf{U}^*$.

The proximity matrix $\mathbf{U}$ assigning the membership of each network antibody to the determined centroids is presented in Table 2. It is possible to see that cells c_1 and c_2 belong to cluster v_1 with membership 1.0, to cluster v_2 with membership 0.58 and 0.63 ($u_{2,1}$ and $u_{2,2}$), respectively, and so on.

EMPIRICAL RESULTS

In order to evaluate the performance of the aiNet, three benchmark problems were considered: SPIR, CHAINLINK, 5-NLSC, according to Figure 6. Note that, though the samples are labeled in the picture, they are unlabeled for the aiNet. Each task has its own particularity and will serve to evaluate several network features, among which we can stress cluster partition and representation, and its potential to reduce data redundancy. Table 3 presents the aiNet training parameters for all problems. The stopping criterion was a maximum number of generations N_{gen}.

Two-Spirals Problem: SPIR

In the three cases, the aiNet performance was compared to that of the

Table 2: Membership values for each cell c_i, $i = 1,...,10$, in relation to each cluster centroid v_j, $j = 1,...,5$.

Centroid	Cell									
	c_1	c_2	c_3	c_4	c_5	c_6	c_7	c_8	c_9	c_{10}
v_1	1.00	1.00	0.67	0.71	0.76	0.69	0.84	0.75	0.71	0.66
v_2	0.58	0.63	0.50	1.00	0.68	0.50	1.00	0.60	0.56	0.64
v_3	0.67	0.50	0.63	0.56	0.50	0.58	0.57	1.00	1.00	0.50
v_4	0.50	0.55	0.54	0.62	1.00	0.57	0.64	0.50	0.50	1.00
v_5	0.60	0.50	1.00	0.50	0.59	1.00	0.50	0.60	0.56	0.64

Kohonen self-organizing map (SOM), which is also an unsupervised technique broadly used in clustering tasks (Kohonen, 1995). The SOM was implemented with a 0.9 geometrical decreasing learning rate (at each five iterations) with an initial value $\alpha_0 = 0.9$, and final value $\alpha_f = 10^{-3}$ as the stopping criterion. The weights were initialized using a uniform distribution over the interval [-

Table 3: Training parameters for the aiNet learning algorithm.

Problem	Parameter					
	σ_s	σ_d	n	d	$\zeta(\%)$	N_{gen}
SPIR	0.07	1.0	4	10	10	40
CHAINLINK	0.15	1.0	4	10	10	40
5-NLSC	0.20	1.0	4	10	20	10

Figure 6: Test problems for the aiNet, where M is the number of samples. (a) SPIR, M = 190. (b) CHAINLINK, M = 1000. (c) 5-NLSC, M = 200.

(a)   *(b)*

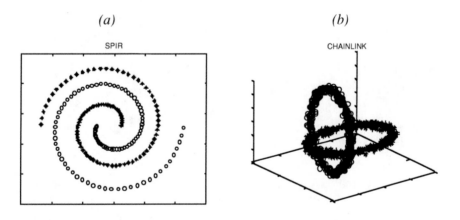

(c)

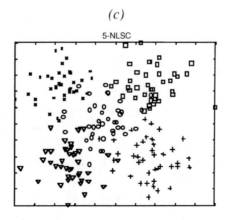

Figure 7: aiNet applied to the 2-spirals problem. (a) Minimal spanning tree, in which the dashed line represents the connection to be pruned. (b) MST histogram indicating two clusters. (c) aiNet dendrogram. (d) Final network structure, determining the spatial distribution of the 2 clusters.

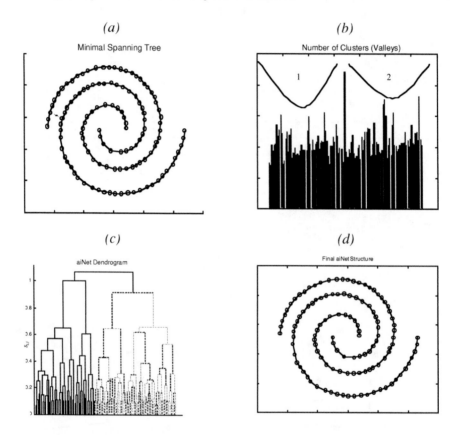

0.1,+0.1]. The output grid is uni-dimensional with a variable output number of neurons according to the problem under evaluation. At the end of the SOM learning phase, all those output neurons that do not classify any input datum will be pruned from the network.

The first problem was the so-called 2-spirals problem, illustrated in Figure 6(a). This training set is composed of 190 samples in $\Re^2$. This task aims at testing the aiNet capability to detect non-linearly separable clusters.

Figures 7(a) and (b) depict the MST and its corresponding histogram. From the histogram we can detect the existence of two different clusters in the network, which are automatically obtained using a factor $r = 2$. In this case, the resultant memory matrix was composed of $m = 121$ antibodies, corresponding to a $CR = 36.32\%$ reduction in the size of the sample set. Note that the compression was superior in regions where the amount of redundancy is larger, i.e., the centers of the spirals (see Figure 6(a)). The network dendrogram also allows us to detect two large clusters of data, as differentiated by the solid and dashed parts of Figure 7(c).

Figure 8: Results obtained by the application of the SOM to the SPIR problem. (a) Final network configuration and weight neighborhood, m *= 105. (b) U-matrix.*

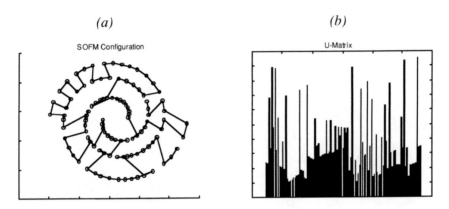

(a) *(b)*

SOFM Configuration   U-Matrix

Figures 8(a) and (b) present the results for the SOM with an initial number m = 121 neurons, i.e., the same number of units obtained with the aiNet. Sixteen neurons that have not classified any input datum were pruned after learning (m = 105). The network final configuration and the resultant U-matrix (Ultsch, 1995) indicate the way the neurons were distributed. According to their neighborhood, the SOM would not be able to appropriately solve this problem, since the final neighborhood configuration of the weight vectors leads to an incorrect clustering.

The ChainLink Problem: CHAINLINK

A number of 1,000 data points in the $\Re^3$-space were arranged such that they form the shape of two intertwined 3-D rings, of whom one is extended along the *x-y* direction and the other one along the *x-z* direction. The two rings can be thought of as two links of a chain with each one consisting of 500 data points. The data is provided by a random number generator whose values are inside two toroids with radius R = 1.0 and r = 0.1 (see Figure 6(b)).

Figures 9(a) and (b) depict the MST and its corresponding histogram when the aiNet is applied to the CHAINLINK problem. From the histogram we can detect the existence of two different clusters in the network, which are automatically obtained using a factor $r = 2$.

Note that, in this case, the evaluation of the fusion values (*stepsize*) of the network dendrogram (Figure 9(c)) represents a difficult task, and may lead to an incorrect clustering. The compression rate of this problem was at the order of CR = 94.5% (m = 55).

Figures 10(a) and (b) depict the final SOM configuration taking into account the neurons' neighborhood and the U-matrix, respectively, for m = 46 output neurons (four output neurons were pruned after learning, since they represent no input datum). In this case, note that the U-matrix is composed of five valleys, indicating five different clusters, which is not in accordance with the correct number

Figure 9. aiNet application to the CHAINLINK problem. (a) Minimal spanning tree with the dashed connection to be pruned. (b) MST histogram indicating the presence of two well separated clusters. (c) aiNet dendrogram. (d) Final network architecture.

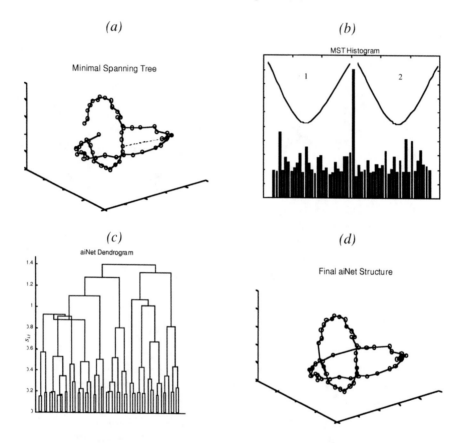

of clusters. Notice also, from Figure 10(a), that the five clusters can be obtained by drawing five hyperplanes cutting each of the rings in its respective parts.

Five Non-Linearly Separable Classes: 5-NLSC

As a last example, consider the problem illustrated in Figure 6(c). This example is particularly interesting, because the distinction among all the classes is not clear, even for a human observer. Note that, as in the previous examples, though the samples are labeled in the picture, they are unlabeled for the aiNet. This example has already been used by de Castro and Von Zuben (1999b) to evaluate the performance of a pruning method for the Kohonen SOM, named PSOM.

Figures 11(a) and (b) depict the MST and its corresponding histogram, respectively. The aiNet presented a compression rate $CR = 96\%$, with a final memory size $m = 8$.

As discussed previously, when the final number of network antibodies is close to its minimal size ($m = 5$ in this case), the MST method might not be able to produce

Figure 10: Uni-dimensional SOM applied to the CHAINLINK problem. (a) Final network configuration and neighborhood. (b) U-matrix.

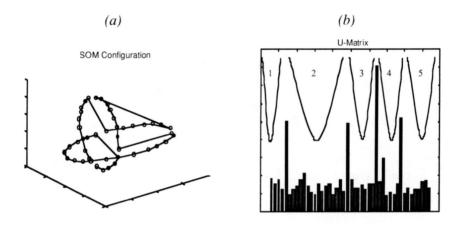

(a)

SOM Configuration

(b)

U-Matrix

Figure 11: aiNet applied to the 5-NLSC problem. (a) MST and its corresponding histogram (b). (c) Network dendrogram. (d) Final network structure with the centroids depicted, and the Voronoi diagram in relation to the centers of the clusters.

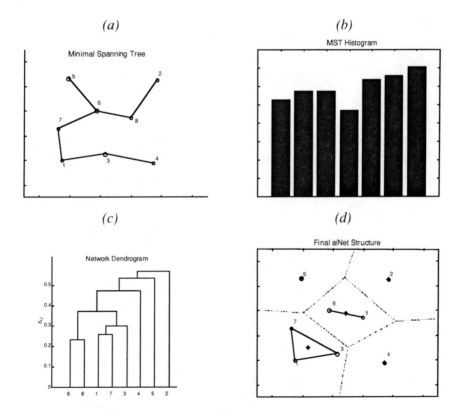

(a)

Minimal Spanning Tree

(b)

MST Histogram

(c)

Network Dendrogram

(d)

Final aiNet Structure

an accurate cluster separation and the network dendrogram might serve as an alternative. This is clear in this example, where by looking at Figures 11(a) and (b) we cannot conclude anything about the final number of network clusters. In this case, the aiNet dendrogram (Figure 11(c)) served the purpose of correctly determining the number and members of each cluster. Figure 11(d) presents the final network configuration, the centroids of the clusters and the Voronoi diagram plotted in relation to the centroids of the clusters.

For the purpose of fuzzy clustering, Table 4 shows the membership values for each network cell (c_i, $i = 1,...,8$) in relation to the five clusters (v_i, $i = 1,...,5$), and Figure 12 depicts the Voronoi diagram of Figure 11(d) together with the data set of Figure 6(c).

We used a SOM to solve the 5-NLSC problem with the same parameters as used in all the other examples. The number of output units was chosen to be $m = 20$, and

Table 4: Membership values for each cell c_i, $i = 1,...,8$, in relation to each cluster centroid v_j, $j = 1,...,5$.

Centroid	Cell							
	c_1	c_2	c_3	c_4	c_5	c_6	c_7	c_8
v_1	1.00	0.50	1.00	0.50	0.50	0.76	1.00	0.63
v_2	0.80	0.50	0.66	0.50	0.50	1.00	0.77	1.00
v_3	0.65	0.50	0.55	0.50	1.00	0.79	0.84	0.50
v_4	0.71	0.50	0.80	1.00	0.50	0.50	0.59	0.72
v_5	0.50	1.00	0.50	0.50	0.50	0.63	0.50	0.80

Figure 12: Decision surface (Voronoi diagram), taken from Figure 11(d), for the data set of Figure 6(c).

Trainning Patterns and Decision Surface

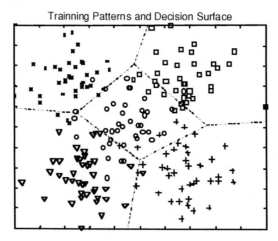

Figure 13: Results of the SOM to the 5-NLSC problem m = *20. (a) Network configuration and neighborhood. (b) U-matrix.*

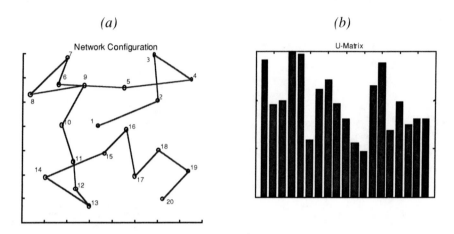

(a)   *(b)*

the results are presented in Figure 13. Note that, from the U-matrix, we cannot infer anything about the number of clusters in the resultant SOM.

SENSITIVITY ANALYSIS

To apply the aiNet to a broad class of data analysis problems, a number of parameters has to be defined by the user, as can be seen in Table 3. In this section, we intend to discuss and analyse how sensitive the aiNet is to some of these user-defined parameters. In particular, we will study the influence of the parameters σ_s, σ_d, n and ζ in the convergence speed, final network size and recognition accuracy.

Figure 14 shows the trade-off between the suppression threshold σ_s and the final number N of output cells in the aiNet for the SPIR and CHAINLINK problems. As discussed previously, σ_s controls the final network size and is responsible for the network plasticity. Larger values for σ_s indicate more generalist antibodies, while smaller values result in highly specific antibodies. This parameter is critical, because the choice of a high value for σ_s might yield a misleading clustering. For the problems tested, the limiting values for σ_s that lead to correct results are $\sigma_s = 0.08$, $\sigma_s = 0.2$ and $\sigma_s = 0.2$, respectively. Higher values resulted in wrong clustering for some trials.

The pruning threshold (σ_d) is responsible for eliminating antibodies with low antigenic affinity. Without loss of generality, if we consider the illustrative problem presented in Section 5 (5-LSC), we can evaluate the relevance of this parameter for the aiNet learning. Table 5 shows the amount of antibodies pruned from the network at the first generation. The results presented were taken from 10 different runs. In all runs, this parameter pruned network antibodies only at the first generation, and in the following generations no antibody was pruned by σ_d. This can be explained by the fact that the initial population of antibodies is randomly generated, but after

Figure 14: Trade-off between the final number of output units (N) and the suppression threshold (σ_s). The results are the maximum, minimum, mean and standard deviation taken over 10 runs.

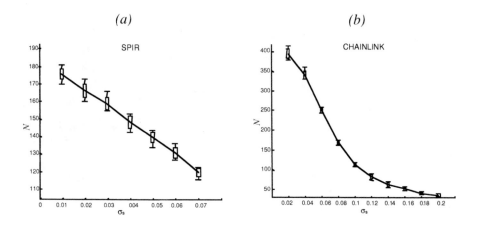

Table 5 *Number of antibodies pruned (Np) from the aiNet, at the first generation, for problem 5-LSC along ten runs.*

	Run										Average
	1	*2*	*3*	*4*	*5*	*6*	*7*	*8*	*9*	*10*	
Np	74	87	73	60	81	54	55	58	62	77	68.1±11.7

the first generation, some of these antibodies were already selected, reproduced and maturated to recognize the antigens (input patterns). Hence, we can conclude that the selection pressure and learning imposed by the algorithm are strong enough to properly guide the initial network towards a reasonable representation of the antigens in a single generation.

It is known that immune recognition is performed by a complementary Ag-Ab match. On the other hand, if we suppose that the aiNet main goal is to reproduce (build internal images of) the antigens to be recognized, it is possible to define as the stopping criterion an average distance between the aiNet antibodies and the antigens and try to minimize this distance. In Steps 1.1.2 and 1.1.6 we minimize the Ag-Ab distance in order to maximize their affinity.

To properly study the aiNet sensitivity in relation to parameters n and ζ, a value was chosen for the suppression threshold that would lead to a final network with approximately 50 antibodies. Based on this idea, one can test the aiNet potential to appropriately learn the antigens by simply defining as the stopping criterion (SC) a small value for the Ag-Ab average distance (10^{-2}, for example).

While evaluating the aiNet sensitivity to n, the following parameters were chosen: $\sigma_s = 0.01$, $\sigma_d = 1.0$, $n = 1..10$, $\zeta = 10\%$ and $SC = 10^{-2}$. Figure 15(a) depicts the trade-off between n and N (final network size), and Figure 15(b) illustrates the trade-off between n and the final number of generations for convergence. Note that the larger n, the larger the network size N, indicating that n has a direct influence on the network plasticity (see Figure 15(a)). On the other hand, from Figure 15(b) we can conclude that the larger n, the smaller the number of generations required for convergence (learning). The results presented are the maximum, minimum and mean taken over 10 runs.

Figure 15: aiNet sensitivity to the number n *of highest affinity cells to be selected for the next generation; Maximum, minimum and mean taken over ten runs. (a) Trade-off* n $\times$ N. *(b) Trade-off* n $\times N_{gen}$.

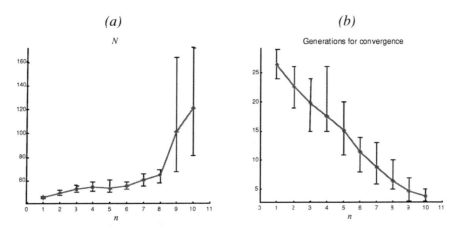

Figure 16: Trade-off among ζ, N *and the number of generations for convergence (average over ten runs).*

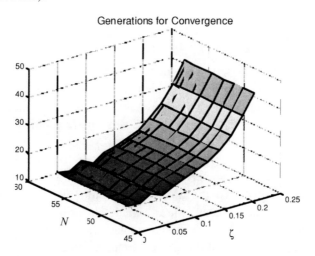

Finally, to study the aiNet sensitivity to ζ, we chose the parameters $\sigma_s = 0.01$, $\sigma_d = 1.0$, $n = 4$, and $SC = 10^{-2}$; ζ was varied from 2% to 24% with steps of size 2%. Figure 16 shows the trade-off between ζ, N and the final number of generations for convergence (mean value taken over 10 runs). From this picture we can notice that ζ does not have a great influence on the final network size, but larger values of ζ imply slower convergence.

About the Network Clusters and Parameters

The definition of a suppression threshold (σ_s) parameter is crucial to the determination of the final network size and consequently the number and shapes of the final cluster generated by the minimal spanning tree. This parameter has been determined in an ad hoc fashion, and as a further extension of this model we suggest the co-evolution of σ_s together with the network antibodies.

The amount of highest affinity antibodies to be selected for reproduction (n) also demonstrated to be decisive for the final network size. Nevertheless, the authors kept most of the parameters fixed for all problems, as can be seen from Table 3. In the most computationally intensive problems (SPIR and CHAINLINK), ζ was set to 10% in order to increase the learning speed. The only parameter that seemed to be really critical for the network clustering was the suppression threshold. It is also important to mention that in all the problems tested, the network demonstrated to be rather insensitive to the initial antibody repertoire, i.e., initial conditions.

As can be seen from Figures 7(d) and 9(d), the resulting aiNet clusters present a very peculiar spatial distribution. If we tried to represent these clusters by their respective centers of mass to perform the aiNet fuzzy clustering, the membership value of most of the antibodies would be incorrect, once the centroids are not representative of the real distribution of the classes.

In the SOM network case, the apriori definition of the network size may impose a network architecture not capable of correctly mapping the input data into the output nodes. Several models have been proposed to overcome this drawback (Fritzke, 1994; Cho, 1997; de Castro & Von Zuben, 1999b).

CONCLUDING REMARKS

In this chapter, an artificial immune network model, named aiNet, was proposed to solve data clustering problems. The resulting learning algorithm was formally described, and related to other connectionist and evolutionary models. In addition, the aiNet was applied to several benchmark problems and the obtained results compared to those of the Kohonen self-organizing neural network. As there is a great amount of user-defined parameters associated with the aiNet training, a sensitivity analysis was also performed.

The general purposes of the aiNet are: the automation of knowledge discovery, the mining of redundant data and the automatic clustering partition, even under the presence of noisy data. This way, we can make use of antibodies and input patterns to be recognized (antigens) of the same dimension. One of the main reasons to take this decision, is that the aiNet can maintain the original topology of the classes, which is usually lost when a dimensionality reduction is promoted.

On the one hand, the two main goals of the SOM are to reduce data dimensionality and to preserve the metric and topological relationships of the input patterns (Kohonen, 1995). On the other hand, the aiNet reduces data redundancy, not dimensionality, and allows the reconstruction of the metric and topological relationships after the definition of the spatial distribution. Due to the possibility of reproducing the topological relationships, similar information (based upon a distance metric) are mapped into closer antibodies, eventually the same one, characterizing the quantization and clustering of the input space.

By the time the immune network theory was proposed, the selective view of immune recognition (clonal selection principle) was already well established and accepted. This immune network paradigm was in conflict with the selective theory, and network models did not take into account a clonal selection pattern of antigenic response. The network model being presented in this chapter is different from the existing ones in the sense that it is discrete, instead of continuous, and it brings together the two originally conflicting theories: clonal selection and immune network. Moreover, the aiNet model takes into account the same processes covered by most of the continuous models found in the literature, but does not aim at directly mimicking any immune phenomenon.

In the aiNet model, clonal selection controls the amount and shapes of the network antibodies (its dynamics and metadynamics), while hierarchical and graph-theoretical clustering techniques are used to define the final network structure. The learning algorithm is generic, but the resultant networks are problem dependent, i.e., the set of patterns (antigens) to be recognized will guide the search for the network structure and shape of clusters. As its main drawbacks, we can mention the high number of user-defined parameters and the high computational cost per iteration, $O(m^2)$, in relation to the number, m, of memory antibodies.

As possible extensions and future trends we can stress the application of the aiNet to real-world benchmark problems of dimension $L > 3$, its application to combinatorial optimization problems, the treatment of feasibility in the shape-space and its possible hybridization with local search techniques. In addition, the aiNet can be augmented to take into account adaptive parameters, aiming at reducing the amount of user-defined parameters.

In the context of artificial immune systems, aiNet is interesting for it is a successful attempt to bring together the two previously conflicting paradigms of clonal selection and network theory. Together with Timmis' network (Timmis, 2000), it is one of the most influential discrete immune network models available currently.

ACKNOWLEDGMENTS

Leandro Nunes de Castro would like to thank FAPESP (Proc. n. 98/11333-9) for the financial support. Fernando Von Zuben would like to thank FAPESP (Proc. n. 98/09939-6) and CNPq (Proc. n. 300910/96-7) for their financial support.

REFERENCES

Bezdek, J. C., & Pal, S. K. (1992). *Fuzzy Models for Pattern Recognition: Methods that Search for Structures in Data*, New York, IEEE.

Carrol, J. D. (1995). 'Minimax Length Links' of a Dissimilarity Matrix and Minimum Spanning Trees, *Psychometrika, 60* (3), 371-374.

Cho, S.B. (1997). Self-Organizing Map withDynamical Node Splitting: Application to Handwritten Digit Recognition, *Neural Computation, 9*, 1345-1355.

de Castro, L. N., & Von Zuben, F. J. (2000). The Clonal Selection Algorithm with Engineering Applications, In *Workshop Proceedings of the GECCO 2000*, 36-37. Retrieved January 20, 2001 from the World Wide Web: http://www.dca.fee.unicamp.br/~lnunes/immune.html.

de Castro, L. N. & Von Zuben, F. J. (1999a). Artificial Immune Systems: Part I – Basic Theory and Applications, *Technical Report – RT DCA 01/99*, p. 95. Retrieved January 20, 2001 from the World Wide Web: http://www.dca.fee.unicamp.br/~lnunes/immune.html.

de Castro, L. N., & Von Zuben, F. J. (1999b). An Improving Pruning Technique with Restart for the Kohonen Self-Organizing Feature Map, In *Proceedings of International Joint Conference on Neural Networks, 3* (pp. 1916-1919). Washington D.C., USA.

Everitt, B. (1993). *Cluster Analysis*, Heinemann Educational Books.

Farmer, J. D., Packard, N. H., & Perelson, A. S. (1986). The Immune System, Adaptation, and Machine Learning, *Physica 22D*, 187-204.

Fritzke, B. (1994). Growing Cell Structures—A Self-Organizing Network for Unsupervised and Supervised Learning, *Neural Networks*, 7(9), 1441-1460.

Hajela, P., & Yoo, J. S. (1999). Immune Network Modelling in Design Optimization, In D. Corne, M. Dorigo, & F. Glover (Eds.). *New Ideas in Optimization* (pp. 203-215). McGraw Hill, London.

Hart, E., & Ross, P. (1999). The Evolution and Analysis of a Potential Antibody Library for Use in Job-Shop Scheduling, In D. Corne, M. Dorigo, & F. Glover (Eds.). *New Ideas in Optimization* (pp. 185-202). McGraw Hill, London.

Hartigan, J. A. (1967). Representations of Similarity Matrices by Trees, *Journal of the American Statistical Association, 62*, 1440-1158.

Haykin S. (1999). *Neural Networks – A Comprehensive Foundation* (2nd ed.). Prentice Hall.

Hofmeyr S. A. (2000). An Interpretative Introduction to the Immune System, In I. Cohen, & L. A. Segel (Eds.). *Design Principles for the Immune System and Other Distributed Autonomous Systems*. Oxford University Press.

Holland, J. H. (1998). *Adaptation in Natural and Artificial Systems* (5th ed.). MIT Press.

Hubert, L., Arabie, P., & Meulman, J. (1998). Graph-Theoretic Representations for Proximity Matrices Through Strongly-Anti-Robinson or Circular Strongly-Anti-Robinson Matrices, *Psychometrika, 63* (4), 341-358.

Hunt, J. E., & Cooke, D. E. (1996). Learning Using an Artificial Immune System, *Journal of Network and Computer Applications, 19*, 189-212.

Jerne, N. K. (1974a). Towards a Network Theory of the Immune System, *Ann. Immunol. (Inst. Pasteur) 125C*, 373-389.

Jerne, N. K. (1974b). Clonal Selection in a Lymphocyte Network. In G. M. Edelman (Ed.). *Cellular Selection and Regulation in the Immune Response* (p. 39). Raven Press, New

York.

Johnsonbaugh, R. (1997). *Discrete Mathematics* (4th ed.). Prentice Hall.

Kohonen T. (1995). *Self-Organizing Maps*. Berlin: Springer-Verlag.

Lapointe, F-J., & Legendre, P. (1995). Comparison Tests for Dendrograms: A Comparative Evaluation, *Journal of Classification, 12*, 265-282.

Lapointe, F-J., & Legendre, P. (1991). The Generation of Random Ultrametric Matrices Representing Dendrograms, *Journal of Classification, 8*, 177-200.

Leclerc, B. (1995). Minimum Spanning Trees for Tree Metrics: Abridgements and Adjustments, *Journal of Classification, 12*, 207-241.

Milligan, G. W., & Cooper, M. C. (1985). An Examination of Procedures for Determining the Number of Clusters in a Data Set, *Psychometrika, 50* (2). 159-179.

Oprea, M. (1999). Antibody Repertoires and Pathogen Recognition: The Role of Germline Diversity and Somatic Hypermutation (Ph.D. Dissertation, University of New Mexico, Albuquerque, New Mexico, USA).

Perelson, A. S. (1989). Immune Network Theory, *Immunological Review, 110*, 5-36.

Perelsen, A. S., & Oster, G. F. (1979). Theoretical Studies of Clonal Selection: Minimal Antibody Repertoire Size and Reliability of Self-Nonself Discrimination, *Journal of Theoretical Biololgy, 81*, 645-670.

Prim, R. C. (1957). Shortest Connection Networks and Some Generalizations, *Bell System Technology Journal*, 1389-1401.

Timmis, J. I., Knight, T., & Neal, M. (2001). Artificial Immune Systems: Using the Immune System as Inspiration for Data Mining, (this volume).

Timmis, J. I. (2000). Artificial Immune Systems: A Novel Data Analysis Technique Inspired by the Immune Network Theory (Ph.D. Dissertation, University of Wales, Aberystwyth, UK).

Ultsch, A. (1995). Self-Organizing Neural Networks Perform Different from Statistical k-means, *Gesellschaft für Klassification*.

Zahn, C. T. (1971). Graph-Theoretical Methods for Detecting and Describing Gestalt Clusters, *IEEE Transactions on Computers, C-20* (1), 68-86.

PART FIVE:

PARALLEL DATA MINING

Chapter XIII

Parallel Data Mining

David Taniar
Monash University, Australia

J. Wenny Rahayu
La Trobe University, Australia

Data mining refers to a process on nontrivial extraction of implicit, previously unknown and potential useful information (such as knowledge rules, constraints, regularities) from data in databases. With the availability of inexpensive storage and the progress in data capture technology, many organizations have created ultra-large databases of business and scientific data, and this trend is expected to grow. Since the databases to be mined are likely to be very large (measured in terabytes and even petabytes), there is a critical need to investigate methods for parallel data mining techniques. Without parallelism, it is generally difficult for a single processor system to provide reasonable response time. In this chapter, we present a comprehensive survey of parallelism techniques for data mining. Parallel data mining offers new complexity as it incorporates techniques from parallel databases and parallel programming. Challenges that remain open for future research will also be presented.

INTRODUCTION

Data mining refers to a process on nontrivial extraction of implicit, previously unknown and potential useful information (such as knowledge rules, constraints, regularities) from data in databases. Techniques for data mining include mining association rules, data classification, generalization, clustering, and searching for patterns (Chen, Han, & Yu, 1996). The focus of data mining is to reveal information that is hidden and unexpected, as there is little value in finding patterns and relationships that are already intuitive. By discovering hidden patterns and relationships in the data, data mining enables users to extract greater value from their data than simple query and analysis approaches. To discover the hidden patterns in data, we need to build a model consisting of independent variables (e.g., income, marital status) that can be used to determine a dependent variable (e.g., credit risk). Building a data mining model consists of identifying the relevant independent variables and minimizing the generalization error. To identify the model that has the least error and is the best predictor may require building hundreds of models in order to select the best one.

We have now reached a point in terms of computational power, storage capacity and cost that enables us to gather, analyze and mine unprecedented amounts of data. Due to their size or complexity, a high performance data mining product is critically required. High performance in data mining literally means to take advantage of parallel database management systems and additional CPUs in order to gain performance benefits. By adding additional processing elements, more data can be processed, more models can be built and accuracy of the models can be improved.

In this chapter, we are going to present a study of how parallelism can be achieved in data mining. To explain this, we need to study parallelism in more details. We also need to highlight data mining techniques. The merging between these two technologies, namely parallelism and data mining, are then presented, which includes various existing parallel data mining algorithms. Finally, we highlight the challenges including research topics that still have to be investigated.

PARALLELISM

In *Parallel Data Mining*, one of the most important keywords is *"Parallel."* In the following sections, we describe what the architectures of parallel technology are, what forms of parallelism are available in data mining, what the objectives of parallelism are, and what the obstacles of employing parallelism in data mining are.

Parallel Technology

The motivation for the use of parallel technology in data mining is not only influenced by the need for performance improvement, but also the fact that parallel computers are no longer a monopoly of supercomputers but are now in fact available in many forms, such as systems consisting of a small number but powerful processors (e.g., SMP machines), clusters of workstations (e.g., loosely coupled shared-nothing architectures), massively parallel processors (MPP), and clusters of SMP machines (i.e., hybrid architectures) (Almasi & Gottlieb, 1994). It is common that parallel architectures especially used for data-intensive applications, including data mining, are classified into several categories, namely *shared-memory*, *shared-disk*, *shared-nothing*, and *shared-something* architectures (Bergsten, Couprie &

Valduriez, 1993; Valduriez, 1993).

Shared-memory architecture is an architecture where all processors share a common main memory and secondary memory. In *shared-disk* architecture, all processors, each of which has its own local main memory, share the disks. In the context of computing platform, *shared-memory* and *shared-disk* architectures are normally found in *Symmetric Multi Processor* (*SMP*) machines. A typical SMP machine consists of several CPUs ranging from two to 16 CPUs. A larger number of CPUs is not too common due to the scaling up limitation. Each CPU maintains its own cache, and the main-memory is shared among all the CPUs. Multiple disks may be attached to an SMP machine, and all CPUs have the same access to them. The operating system normally allocates tasks according to the schedule. Once a processor is idle, a task in the queue will be immediately allocated to it. In this way, balancing is relatively easy to achieve. Figure 1(a) gives an illustration of an SMP architecture.

A *shared-nothing* architecture provides each processor with a local main memory and disks. Because each processor is independent of others, it is often claimed that scaling up the number of processors without adversely affecting performance is achievable. Shared-nothing architecture stretches from workstations farm to *Massively Parallel Processors* (*MPP*) machines. The range is basically divided by the speed of the network, which connects the processing units (i.e. CPUs containing primary and secondary memory). For workstations, the network is a slower Ethernet, whereas for *MPP* the interconnection is done via fast network or system bus. Whether it is a slow or fast network, the processing units communicate among each other via network, as they do not share common data storage (i.e., primary or secondary memory). Due to the fact that the data storage is not shared but localized, shared-nothing architecture is often called *distributed-memory* architecture. Figure 1(b) shows a typical shared-nothing architecture.

Finally, a *shared-something* (or *hybrid*) architecture is a mixture between shared-memory and shared-nothing architectures. There are a number of variations to this architecture, but basically each *node* is shared-memory architecture connected to an interconnection network via shared-nothing. As each shared-memory (i.e., SMP machine) maintains a group of processing elements, collection of these groups is often called *"Cluster,"* or in this case *clusters of SMP* architecture (Pfister, 1998). Figure 1(c) shows architecture of clusters of *SMP*. Obvious features of a shared-something architecture include flexibility in the configuration (i.e., number of nodes, size of nodes) and lower network communication traffic as the number of nodes is reduced.

The popularity of cluster architectures is also influenced by the fact that processor technology is moving rapidly (Patterson & Hannessy, 1994; Pfister, 1998). This also means that a powerful computer today will be out of date within a few years. Consequently, computer pricing is falling due to not only the competitiveness but also the above facts. Therefore, it becomes sensible to be able to plug in new processing elements to the current system and to take out the old ones. To some degree this can be done to *SMP machines*, considering their scaling limitations and only identical processors can be added into. *MPP* machines although theoretically do not impose scaling limitations, their configurations are difficult to alter, and hence cannot keep up with up-to-date technology, let alone the high pricing of *MPP* machines. On the other hand, *SMP* machines are getting popular because of competitiveness in pricing and power; it becomes easier and more feasible to add *SMP* machines on an interconnection network. Therefore, cluster of *SMP* becomes demanding.

Figure 1: Parallel Architectures

a) SMP:

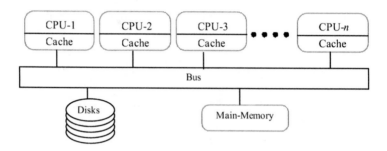

b) Shared-Nothing:

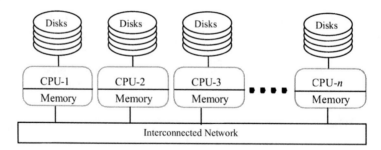

c) Clusters of SMP:

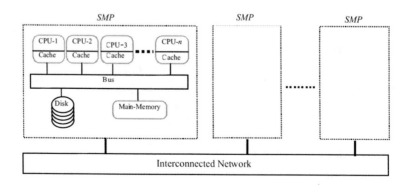

Forms of Parallelism

There are different forms of parallelism in data mining depending on the context of the problem. The first one is *inter-model* and *intra-model* parallelism, parallelism from a viewpoint of the model built by data mining tools (Small & Eledstein, 1997). The other is *data parallelism* and *control parallelism*, parallelism from a viewpoint of data or program/process (Freitas, 1998).

Figure 2. Inter-model and Intra-model Parallelism

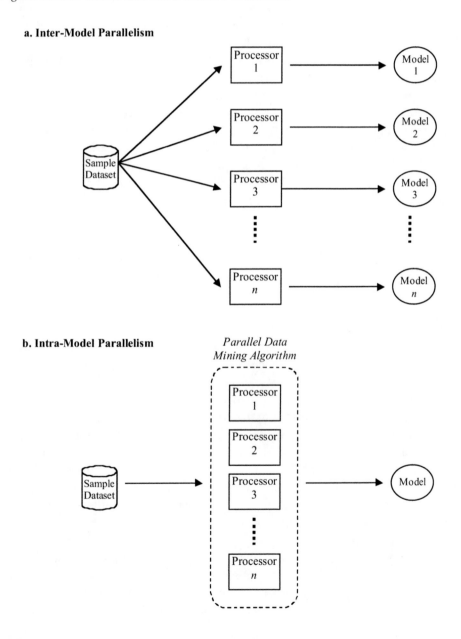

a. Inter-Model Parallelism

b. Intra-Model Parallelism

Inter-Model and Intra-Model Parallelism

A data mining process starts by taking a sample from a database and building a model. Building a complex model with many variables, even when sample size is small, may be computationally intensive and will therefore benefit from parallelism. In all data mining applications, extra variables can introduce noise and reduce the model's accuracy. At the same time, important variables that can increase the accuracy or simplify the application of the model to new data should not be left out. Consequently, it is often needed to do additional analysis and build different models to ensure that the right variables are used. Furthermore, searching for the best model may require building and testing many different models, sometimes numbering in the hundreds, before the best solution can be found. In some cases, each model built requires a significant elapsed time. Hence, building multiple models may sometimes be restricted due to limited time. Clearly, if it takes a long time to build each model, or the number of models that must be built is large, the only way to effectively mine a database is simply with parallelism techniques.

There are two forms of parallelism in this context, namely *inter-model parallelism* and *intra-model parallelism* (Small & Eledstein, 1997). *Inter-model parallelism* is a method where multiple models are concurrently built and each model is assigned to a different processor. The idea is that the more processors, the more models can be constructed without reducing throughput. Therefore, this kind of scale-up is useful in building multiple independent models. *Intra-model parallelism* is a method where each model is built by using multiple processors. This is particularly applicable when building each model takes a long time. The model is broken into tasks; these tasks are executed on separate processors, and then recombine them for the answer. Figure 2 gives a graphical illustration of inter-model and intra-model parallelism.

Data Parallelism and Control Parallelism

Data parallelism refers to the execution of the same operation or instruction on multiple large data subsets at the same time. This is in contrast to *control parallelism* (or *operation parallelism* or *task parallelism*), which refers to the concurrent execution of multiple operations or instructions.

From a data mining viewpoint, data parallelism has several main advantages over control parallelism. First, data parallelism lends itself to a kind of automatic parallelization. The control flow of a data parallel program is essentially the same as the control flow of a serial program – only the access to the data is parallelized in the former. Hence, a lot of previously written serial code can be reused in a data parallel fashion. This simplifies programming and leads to a development time significantly smaller than the one associated with control parallel programming.

Second, data parallelism has a higher degree of machine architecture independence, in comparison with control parallelism. Since the control flow of a data parallel algorithm is still serial, there is no need to tailor the control flow of the algorithm to the underlying parallel architecture. This is in contrast with control parallelism, where this kind of tailoring is one of the major challenges of parallel programming. Note that the problem of machine architecture dependence is not completely eliminated in data parallelism. This problem is simply pushed down to a lower layer of software, hidden from the applications programmer, which leads to an increase in programmer productivity.

Third, intuitively data parallelism has better scalability for large databases than control parallelism. In most database applications, including data mining, the amount of data can increase arbitrarily fast, while the number of lines of code typically increases at a much slower rate. To put it in simple terms, the more data is available, the more opportunity to exploit data parallelism. In principle we can add to the system a number of processing elements proportionally to the amount of data increase, to keep the response time nearly constant (i.e., linear scale-up).

Despite the above advantages of data parallelism, it should be emphasized that the exploitation of control parallelism is also useful in data mining. For instance, in the rule induction paradigm, a pure data parallel approach would search the rule space in a sequential fashion, evaluating/modifying candidate rules one at a time. Hence, data parallelism does not address the problem of very large rule spaces. This problem is better dealt with by using control parallelism.

To summarize, data parallelism addresses the problem of very large databases, whereas control parallelism addresses the problem of very large search spaces (e.g., very many candidate rules). Note that data and control parallelism are not mutually exclusive. If a large enough number of processors is available, both types of parallelism can be exploited at the same time, which can greatly speed up the execution of data mining algorithms.

Parallelism Objectives

The primary objective of parallelism is to gain performance improvement. There are two main measures of performance improvement. The first is *throughput* – the number of tasks that can be completed in a given time interval. The second is *response time* – the amount of time it takes to complete a single task from the time it is submitted. These two measures are normally quantified by the following metrics: *speed up* and *scale up*.

Speed up refers to performance improvement gained because of extra hardware added. Speed up can be measured by dividing the elapsed time of a job on uniprocessor with the elapsed time of the job on multiprocessors. The ultimate goal is *linear speed up*, which refers to performance improvement growing linearly with additional resources and is an indicator to show the efficiency of data processing on multiprocessors. Performance in this environment is bound to, particularly, *workload partitioning* and *load imbalance*. In parallel systems, equal workload (load balance) among all processing elements is one of the critical factors to achieve linear speed up. When the load of one processing element is heavier than those of others, the total elapsed time for a particular task will be determined by this processing element. This situation is certainly undesirable.

The other metric is *scale up*, which refers to handling larger tasks by increasing the degree of parallelism. For a given application, we would like to examine whether it is visible to add more resources when the workload is increased in order to maintain its performance. Scale up can be determined by dividing the elapsed time on a small system and the elapsed time on a large system. *Linear scale up* refers to the ability to maintain the same level of performance when both the workload and the resources are proportionally added. There are two kinds of scale up that are relevant to parallel data mining, depending on how the size of the task is measured. The first is called *data scale up*, where the size of the data to be mined increases. The second is called *task scale up*, where the rate at which tasks are submitted to the data mining tool increases. The size of the database may also increase proportionally to the task submission rate.

Figure 3 shows graphs to demonstrate linear/sub-linear speed up and linear/ sub-linear scale up.

Parallel Obstacles

A number of factors work against efficient parallel operation and can diminish both speed up and scale up.

Start-up cost. There is a start-up cost associated with initiating a single process. In parallel operation consisting of multiple processes, the start-up time may overshadow the actual processing time, affecting speed up adversely.

Interference. Since processes executing in a parallel system often access shared resources, a slowdown may result from the interference of each new process as it competes with existing processes for commonly held resources. Both speed up and scale up are affected by this phenomenon.

Communication. Very often one process may have to communicate with other processes. In a synchronized environment, the process wanting to communicate with others may be forced to wait for other processes to be ready for communication.

Figure 3: Speed up and Scale up

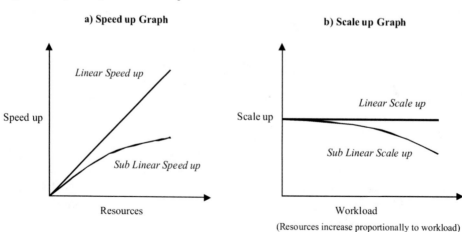

a) Speed up Graph

Linear Speed up

Speed up

Sub Linear Speed up

Resources

b) Scale up Graph

Linear Scale up

Scale up

Sub Linear Scale up

Workload

(Resources increase proportionally to workload)

This waiting time may affect the whole process, as some tasks are idle waiting for other tasks.

Skew. Skew refers to the variance being greater than the mean. In short, skew refers to unevenness of workload partitioning. Since performance of parallel systems is dependent upon how the workload is divided, uniform workload among processors is most desirable. In the presence of skew, overall execution time depends on the most heavily loaded processors, and those processors finishing early would have to wait.

Consolidation. Parallel processing normally starts with breaking up the main task into multiple sub tasks in which each sub task is carried out by a different processing element. After these sub tasks are completed, it is necessary to consolidate the results produced by each sub task to be presented to the user. Since the consolidation process is usually carried out by a single processing element, normally by the host processor, no parallelism is applied, and consequently, affects the speed up of the overall process.

DATA MINING TECHNIQUES

There are many data mining techniques being proposed in the literature. The most common ones, which will be included in this section, are *association rules* (Agrawal & Srikant, 1994), *sequential patterns* (Agrawal & Srikant 1995; Srikant & Agrawal, 1996; Zaki 1998), *classification* (Agrawal, Ghosh, Imielinski, Iyer, & Swami, 1992; Alsabti, Ranka, & Singh, 1998; Mehta, Agrawal & Rissanen, 1996; Shafer, Agrawal, & Mehta, 1996), and *clustering* (Aggarwal, Procopiuc, Wolf, Yu, & Park, 1999; Agrawal, Gehrke, Gunopulos, & Raghavan, 1998; Cheng, Fu & Zhang, 1999; Guha, Rastogi & Shim, 1998; Ng & Han, 1994; Zhang, Ramakrishnan & Livny, 1996).

An *association rule* is a rule that implies certain association relationships among a set of objects (such as "occur together" or "one implies the other") in a database. Given a set of transactions, where each transaction is a set of items, an association rule is an expression of the form X Y, where X and Y are sets of items. The intuitive meaning of such a rule is that transactions of the database which contain X then contain Y. An example of an association rule is "25% of transactions that contain instant noodles also contain Coca Cola; 3% of all transactions contain both of these items". Here 25% is called the confidence of the rule and 3% the support of the rule. The problem is to find all association rules that satisfy user-specified minimum support and minimum confidence constraints.

Sequential patterns are to find a sequence of items shared across time among a large number of transactions in a given database. An example of such pattern is that customers of a bookshop typically buy *The Brethren*, then *The Jury*, and then *Falling Leaves*. Note that these purchases need not be consecutive. Customers who bought some other books in between also support this sequential pattern. Elements of a sequential pattern need not be simple items. They can be composite items, such as "wine glasses and dinner sets", followed by "mugs", then followed by "mugs and spoons and forks and woks".

The database to be mined in the above examples consists of customer transactions, whereby each transaction contains the following fields: customer-id, transaction-time and items purchased. No customer has more than one transaction with the same transaction-time. All transactions of a customer can together be viewed as a sequence, where each transaction corresponds to a set of items, and the list of transactions, ordered by increasing transaction-time, corresponds to a sequence. Mining sequential patterns is to find the maximal sequences among all sequences that have a certain user-specified minimum support.

Comparing with association rules, sequential patterns focus on *inter-transaction* patterns, whereas association rules concentrate on *intra-transaction* patterns. Patterns in the former are ordered, and that's why it is called a sequential or has a sequence, whereas those in the latter are not in any particular order.

In *classification*, we are given a set of example records, called a training set, where each record consists of several fields or attributes. Attributes are either continuous, coming from an ordered domain or categorical coming from an unordered domain. One of the attributes called the classifying attribute indicates the class to which each example belongs. The objective of classification is to build a mode of the classifying attribute based upon the other attributes. Once a model is built, it can be used to determine the class of future unclassified records. Several classification models have been proposed over the years, such as neural networks, statistical models like linear/quadratic discriminants, decision trees, and genetic models. Among these models, decision trees are particularly suited for data mining. Decision trees can be constructed relatively fast compared to other methods. Another advantage is that decision tree models are simple and easy to understand. Decision tree classifiers obtain similar and sometimes better accuracy when compared with other classification methods.

Clustering finds dense regions in a sparse multidimensional data set. The attribute values and ranges of these regions characterize the clusters. Clustering techniques can be broadly classified into two categories: *partitional* and *hierarchical*. Given a set of objects and a clustering criterion, partitional clustering contains a partition of the objects into clusters such that the objects in a cluster are more similar to each other than to objects in different clusters. A hierarchical clustering is a sequence of partitions in which each partition is nested into the next partition in the sequence. An agglomerative, hierarchical clustering starts by placing each object in its own cluster, and then merges these atomic clusters into larger and larger clusters until all objects are in a single cluster. Divisive, hierarchical clustering reverses the process by starting with all objects in a cluster and subdividing into smaller pieces.

PARALLEL DATA MINING TECHNIQUES

Recent algorithmic work has been very successful in showing the benefits of parallelism in many of the common data mining tasks including *association rules* (Agrawal & Shafer, 1996; Cheung & Xiao, 1998, 1999; Cheung, Ng, Fu, & Fu, 1996; Cheung, Hu, & Xia, 1998, 2001; Han, Karypis, & Kumar, 1997; Parthasarathy, Zaki, & Li, 1998; Shintani & Kitsuregawa, 1998; Zaki, et al, 1996; Zaki, Parthasarathy, Ogihara, & Li, 1997), *sequential patterns* (Shintani & Kitsuregawa, 1998; Zaki, 1999), *classification* (Mehta, et al, 1996; Shafer, et al, 1996; Zaki, Ho, & Agrawal, 1998, 1999), and *clustering* (Foti, Lipari, Pizzuti, & Talia, 2000; Dhillon & Modha, 1999). These are summarized in the following sections.

Parallel Association Rules

There are several main streams in parallel mining of association rules (Zaki, 1999a). The most prominent ones are based on *Apriori* (Agrawal & Srikant, 1994). Apriori is an iterative algorithm that counts itemsets of a specific length in a given database pass. The process starts by scanning all transactions in the database and computing the frequent items. Next, a set of potentially frequent candidate 2-itemsets is formed from the frequent items. Another database scan is made to obtain their supports. The frequent 2-itemsets are retained for the next pass, and the process is repeated until all frequent itemsets have been enumerated.

The second group of parallel association rules algorithms is based on *Dynamic Itemset Counting (DIC)* (Brin, Motwani, Ullman, & Tsur, 1997), which is a generalized Apriori. It counts multiple-length candidates in the same pass, as opposed to counting k-length candidates in iteration k. The database is divided into equal-sized partitions such that each partition fits in memory. In partition 1, supports of single items are gathered. Locally found frequent items are used to generate 2-itemsets candidates. Then partition 2 is read and supports for all current candidates are obtained. This process is repeated for the remaining partitions. After the last partition has been processed, the processing wraps around to partition 1 again. The global support of a candidate is known once the processing wraps around the database and reaches the partition where it was first generated. If no new candidates are generated from the current partition, and all previous candidates have been counted, the program terminates.

The last group of parallel association rules algorithms to be discussed in the section is based on the family of *Eclat* and *Clique* (Zaki, Parthasarathy & Li, 1997). There are four algorithms in the family: *Eclat*, *MaxEclat*, *Clique* and *MaxClique*. Unlike the other methods, which adopt horizontal partitioning, these methods utilize a vertical partitioning. The main advantage of using a vertical partitioning is that by simply intersecting the *id* of any two of its $(k-1)$ length subsets, the support of any k-itemsets can be determined. The algorithm makes use of the first two $(k-1)$ length subsets that share a common prefix to compute the support of new k length itemsets. Using a simple check on the cardinality of the results can tell whether or not the new itemset is frequent. Among these four algorithms, both Eclat and MaxEclat use prefix-based classes, whereas Clique and MaxClique use clique-based classes. Eclat and Clique use bottom-up search, whereas their Max versions use hybrid search.

Apriori-Based Parallel Association Rules Algorithms

There are a number of versions of parallel association rules algorithms based on Apriori, including *Count/Data/Candidate Distribution* (Agrawal & Shafer, 1996), *Intelligent/Hybrid Data Distribution* (Han, et al., 1997), *Fast Parallel Mining (FPM)* (Cheung & Xiao, 1998, 1999; Cheung et al., 1996), *Non-Partitioned/ Hash-Partitioned/Hierarchical-Partitioned* (Shintani & Kitsuregawa, 1998a), and *Common Candidate Partitioned Database / Partitioned Candidate Common Database (CCPD/PCCD)* (Parthasarathy, et al., 1998; Zaki, Ogihara, Parthasarthy, & Li, 1996). All of these parallel algorithms, but CCPD/PCCD, were implemented in a shared-nothing/distributed-memory architecture. CCPD/PCCD were implemented in a shared-memory architecture.

Count Distribution, Data Distribution and Candidate Distribution

In the *Count Distribution* (Agrawal & Shafer, 1996), each processor computes how many times all the candidates appear in the locally stored transactions. This is done by building the entire hash tree that corresponds to all the candidates and then by performing a single pass over the locally stored transactions to collect the counts. The global counts of the candidates are computed by summing these individual counts using a global reduction operation. Since each processor needs to build a hash tree for all the candidates, these hash trees are identical at each processor. Thus, excluding global reduction, each processor executes the serial Apriori algorithm on the locally stored transactions. This algorithm needs to communicate with the other processors only once at the end of the computation step. Additionally, this algorithm works well only when the hash trees can fit into the main memory of each processor.

The *Data Distribution* (Agrawal & Shafer, 1996) partitions the candidate itemsets among the processors. Each processor is responsible for computing the counts of its locally stored subset of the candidate itemsets for all the transactions in the database. Each processor needs to scan the portions of the transactions assigned to the other processors as well as its locally stored portion of the transactions. It thus suffers from high communication overhead and performs poorly when compared with Count Distribution.

The *Candidate Distribution* (Agrawal & Shafer, 1996) partitions the candidates during the iteration, so that each processor can generate disjoint candidates independently of other processors. At the same time the database is selectively replicated so that a processor can generate global counts independently. Each processor asynchronously broadcasts the local frequent set to other processors during each iteration. In terms of its performance, it is worse than Count Distribution. Candidate Distribution pays the cost of redistributing the database.

To summarise, the *Count Distribution* algorithm had delivered the best performance among the three algorithms.

Intelligent Data Distribution and Hybrid Data Distribution

The *Intelligent Data Distribution* algorithm (Han, et al., 1997) is based on the Data Distribution algorithm (Agrawal & Shafer, 1996). Han, et al. (1997) observed that the Data Distribution algorithm uses an expensive multicast to send the local database portion to every other processor. Although the candidates are equally divided among the processors, it fails to divide the work done on each transaction. The Intelligent Data Distribution is improved by using a linear time ring-based multicast for communication, by switching to Count Distribution once the candidates fit in memory, and by performing a single item prefix-based partitioning (instead of round-robin). Before processing a transaction, they make sure that it contains the relevant prefixes. If not, the transactions are discarded. The entire database is still communicated, but the transactions may not be processed if they do not contain relevant items.

The *Hybrid Distribution* is a combination of Count Distribution and Intelligent Data Distribution. In the Hybrid Distributions, processors are grouped into equal sized groups. Within each group of processors, the Count Distribution algorithm is used. Within the group, the Intelligent Data Distribution is employed. The database is horizontally partitioned among the groups, and the candidates are partitioned among the processors within each group. The number of groups is decided dynamically for each pass. The experimentations show that it has the same performance as Count Distribution, but can handle much larger databases.

Fast Parallel Mining

Fast Parallel Mining (FPM) (Cheung & Xiao, 1998; 1999) is also based on the Count Distribution algorithm. FPM incorporates two candidate pruning techniques: distributed pruning and global pruning, to reduce the number of candidates at each iteration. The first iteration of FPM is the same as Count Distribution. Each processor scans its local partition to find the local support counts of all size-1 itemsets and uses one round of count exchange to compute the global support counts. For subsequent iterations, each processor performs distributed pruning and global pruning, scans local partition to find the local support counts for all remaining candidates, exchanges with all other processors to get the global support counts, computes minimum supports and returns the frequent itemsets.

Non-Partitioned, Hash-Partitioned, Hierarchical-Partitioned

Shintani and Kitsuregawa (1997) proposed three parallel algorithms: *Non-Partitioned Generalized association rule Mining* (NPGM), *Hash-Partitioned Gen-*

eralized association rule Mining (HPGM) and *Hierarchical HPGM* (H-HPGM). The NPGM is essentially the same as Count Distribution. It copies itemsets among the processors. The HPGM is similar to Candidate Distribution. It partitions the candidate itemsets among the nodes using a hash function like in the hash join, which eliminates broadcasting. The H-HPGM also partitions the candidate itemsets among the nodes, but unlike HPGM, it takes the classification hierarchy into account so that all the candidate itemsets whose root items are identical be allocated to the identical processor, which eliminates communication of the ancestor items. Thus the communication overhead can reduce significantly compared with the original HPGM.

Common Candidate Partitioned Database and Partitioned Candidate Common Database

Zaki et al. (1996) proposed two algorithms for shared-memory environment: *Common Candidate Partitioned Database* (CCPD) and *Partitioned Candidate Common Database* (PCCD). CCPD algorithm uses a common candidate hash tree across all processors, while the database is logically split among them. The hash tree is built in parallel. Each processor then traverses its local database and counts the support for each itemset. Finally, the master process selects the large itemsets.

PCCD has a partitioned candidate hash tree, but a common database. In this approach, we construct a local candidate hash tree per processor. Each processor then traverses the entire database and counts support for itemsets only in its local tree. Finally, the master process performs the reduction and selects the large itemsets for the next iteration.

DIC-Based Parallel Association Rules Algorithms

Cheung, Hu, and Xia (1998, 2001) proposed the *Asynchronous Parallel Mining (APM)*, which is based on DIC. APM logically divides the database into many small, equal-sized, virtual partitions, which is independent to the number of processors, but usually larger than the processors available. The partitions are further grouped into clusters, such that inter-cluster distance is maximized and intra-cluster distance is minimized.

After this, APM is ready to apply DIC in parallel. The database is divided into homogeneous partitions, and each processor independently applies DIC to its local partition. When all processors have processed all candidates (e.g., locally generated or generated somewhere else), and when no new candidates are generated, the program terminates. In each processor, the local partitions are further divided into sub-partitions. Inter-processor partitions and intra-processor sub-partitions must be as homogeneous as possible. This can be achieved by assigning the virtual partitions, from each of the clusters of the first pass, in a round-robin manner among the processors–resulting in each processor receiving an equal mix of virtual partitions from separate clusters. The same technique is applied to sub-partitions in each processor to create homogeneous sub-partitions.

Eclat/Clique-based Parallel Association Rules Algorithms

Zaki, Parthasarathy, and Li (1997) proposed four parallel algorithms, namely *ParEclat*, *ParMaxEclat*, *ParClique* and *ParMaxClique*, which are based on their respective serial algorithms. These parallel algorithms were implemented on a shared-nothing architecture. These algorithms apply a vertical partitioning, and each partition is distributed among the processing nodes – that is each node gets an entire *idlist* for a single item and the total length of local *idlist*s is roughly equal on all nodes. Each processing node further splits the local *idlist*s into several vertical partitions. This kind of partitioning is certainly suitable for a shared-something architecture, so that each processor within a shared-memory node has its own local vertical partition.

There are three main phases in the algorithms: the *initialisation* phase, the *asynchronous* phase, and the *reduction* phase. The *initialisation* phase performs computation and data partitioning.

The host processor generates the parent classes using prefix or clique-based partitioning. These parent classes are then scheduled among all available processors using a greedy algorithm. Each class is assigned a weight based on its cardinality. They are sorted based on their weights and assigned, in turn, to the processor with the least total weight. After the parent class scheduling, *idlist*s are selectively replicated on each shared-memory node, so that all items *idlist*s, part of some assigned class on a processor, are available on the shared-memory node's local disk. The communication is purely carried out by the host processor only.

The *asynchronous* phase independently generates frequent itemsets. No communication or synchronization is required, as each processor has the classes assigned to it and the *idlist*s for all items. All available memory of the system is used, no in-memory hash or prefix trees are needed, and only simple intersection operations are required for itemsets enumeration.

Finally, the *reduction* phase aggregates the final results.

Parallel Sequential Patterns

There are two main streams in parallel sequential patterns. One is based on *GSP* (*Generalized Sequential Patterns*) (Agrawal & Srikant 1995; Srikant & Agrawal, 1996), and the other is based on *SPADE* (Zaki, 1998). The parallelized versions of the former were implemented in a shared-nothing architecture (Shintani & Kitsuregawa, 1998b) and the latter run on shared-memory machines (Zaki, 1999b).

GSP-Based Parallel Sequential Patterns Algorithms

Generalized Sequential Patterns (GSP) algorithm (Srikant & Agrawal, 1996) consists of several iterations (or passes).

Iteration-1
>
> Scan the database to count the support-count for each item
>
> All items, which satisfy the minimum support threshold, are picked out (This is called frequent 1-sequences items)

Iteration-k ($k \geq 2$)
>
> Use large (k-1) sequences from the previous pass to generate candidate k-sequences
>
> Count the support-count by scanning the database
>
> Check the candidate k-sequences whether they satisfy the minimum support condition
>
> Determine the frequent k-sequences that satisfy the minimum support

The parallel version of sequential patterns based on GSP proposed by Shintani and Kitsuregawa (1998b) come in three versions: *Non Partitioned Sequential Pattern Mining (NPSPM)*, *Simply Partitioned Sequential Pattern Mining (SPSPM)*, and *Hash Partitioned Sequential Pattern Mining (HPSPM)*.

In the *Non-Partitioned* method (NPSPM), the candidate sequences are simply copied among all the nodes. In the case where all of the candidate sequences do not fit within the local memory of single node, the candidate sequences are partitioned into fragments, each of which fits in the memory size of single node. At this time, the Non-Partitioned method makes multiple passes over the customer-sequence database in one pass. Each node determines the frequent sequences by exchanging the support count values among all the nodes. Though each node can work independently in count support processing, each node has to examine all the candidate sequences.

In the *Simply-Partitioned* method (SPSPM), the candidate sequences are partitioned equally over the memory space of all the nodes using a round-robin fashion. As it partitions the candidate sequences among the nodes, each node has to broadcast the customer-sequences stored in its local disk to all the other nodes for count support processing.

In the *Hash-Partitioned* method (HPSPM), it partitions the candidate sequences among the nodes using the hash function. This consequently eliminates the need for customer-sequence broadcasting and can reduce the comparison workload significantly.

SPADE-Based Parallel Sequential Patterns Algorithms (*pSPADE*)

SPADE (Sequential Pattern Discovery using Equivalence classes) (Zaki, 1998) adopts a vertical partitioning, as opposed to the more common horizontal partitioning. In vertical partitioning, we maintain a disk-based *idlist* for each item, consisting of all customer-id and transactions-id pairs. Given the sequence *idlists*, we can determine the support of any k-sequence by simply intersecting the *idlists* of any two of its (k-1) length subsequences. In particular, we use the two (k-1) length subsequences that share a common suffix to compute the support of a new k length sequence. A simple check on the cardinality of the resulting *idlist* tells us whether the new sequence is frequent or not.

To use only a limited amount of main-memory SPADE breaks up the sequence search space into small, independent, manageable chunks, which can be processed in memory. This is accomplished via suffix-based partition. k length sequences are in the same equivalence class or partition if they share a common k-1 length suffix. SPADE recursively decomposes the sequences at each new level into even smaller independent classes.

Unlike GSP which makes multiple database scans and uses complex hash tree structures that tend to have sub-optimal locality, SPADE decomposes the original problem into smaller sub-problems using equivalence classes on frequent sequences. SPADE usually makes only three database scans – one for frequent 1-sequences, another for frequent 2-sequences, and one more for generating all frequent k-sequences ($k \geq 3$). SPADE uses only simple intersection operations, and is thus ideally suited for direct integration with a DBMS.

Parallel SPADE (pSPADE) (Zaki, 1999b) comes into two major versions – one using a *data parallelism* approach, and the other using a *task parallelism* approach. In the data parallelism approach, processors work on distinct portions of the database, but synchronously process the global computation tree. In task parallelism, the processors share the database, but work on different classes in parallel, asynchronously processing the computation tree.

In parallel SPADE, *data parallelism* comes in two flavours: *idlist parallelism*, and *join parallelism*. There are two ways of implementing the *idlist parallelism*. In the first method, each intersection is performed in parallel among the processors. Each processor performs the intersection over its customer-id range, and increments support in a shared variable. The second method uses a level-wise approach. At each new level of the computation tree, each processor processes all the classes at that level, performing intersection for each candidate, but only over its local database portion. The local supports are stored in a local array to prevent false sharing among processors. After a barrier synchronization signals that all processors have finished processing the current level, a sum-reduction is performed in parallel to determine the global support of each candidate. The frequent sequences are then retained for the next level, and the same process is repeated for other levels until no more frequent sequences are found. In *join parallelism*, each processor performs intersection for different sequences within the same class. Once the current class has been processed, the processors must synchronize before moving on to the next class.

In *task parallelism*, since all processors work on separate classes, load balancing is a major issue. There are basically several load balancing methods: *static load balancing*, *inter-class dynamic load balancing* and *recursive dynamic load balancing*. *Static load balancing* is achieved by assigning a weight to each equivalence class based on the number of elements in the class. The main problem of this method is that, given the irregular nature of the computation tree, there is no way to accurately determining the amount of work per class statically. To get better load balancing, *inter-class dynamic load balancing* is utilized. Instead of a static or fixed class assignment, as in the previous method, each processor dynamically picks a new class to work on from the list of classes not yet processed. While the inter-class dynamic load balancing is better than the static one, it does so only at the inter-class level, which may be too coarse grained to achieve a good workload balance. The *recursive dynamic load balancing* addresses this by exploiting both inter and intra-class parallelism.

Parallel Classification

Among other techniques for data classification, decision trees are the most popular ones. A decision tree is a class discriminator that recursively partitions the training set until each partition consists entirely or dominantly of examples from one class. Each non-leaf node of the tree contains a split point, which is a test on one or more attributes and determines how the data is partitioned.

A decision tree classifier is built in two phases: a *growth* phase and a *prune* phase. In the *growth* phase, the tree is built by recursively partitioning the data until each partition is either pure (all members belong to the same class) or sufficiently small (a parameter set by the user). This form of the split used to partition the data depends on the type of the attribute used in the split, whether it is continuous or categorical. Once the tree has been fully grown, it is *pruned* to generalize the tree by removing dependence on statistical noise or variation that may be particular only to the training set.

The tree growth phase is computationally much more expensive than pruning, since data is scanned multiple times during the growth phase. Pruning requires access only to the fully grown decision tree. Therefore, most parallel versions of classification algorithms based on decision tree focus on the parallelization of the growth phase. Basically, the growth phase algorithm is as follows:

Partition (Data *S*)
  If (all points in *S* are of the same class) then
      Return;
  For each attribute *A* do
      Evaluate splits on attribute *A*
  Use best split found to partition *S* into *S1* and *S2*;
  Partition (*S1*)   // recursive call
  Partition (*S2*)   // recursive call

There are several versions of parallel algorithms based on decision trees: *Parallel SPRINT* (Shafer et al., 1996), *Parallel SLIQ* (Mehta et al., 1996), and *Moving-Window-k* (*MWK*) and *SUBTREE* (Zaki et al., 1998, 1999).

Parallel SPRINT

The parallel version of SPRINT focuses on the parallelization of tree-growth. The primary problems remain finding good split-points and partitioning the data using the discovered split points. Parallel SPRINT was designed for an implementation in a shared-nothing architecture (Shafer et al., 1996). The algorithm starts with partitioning. The partitioning is achieved by first distributing the training-set examples equally among all the processors. Each processor then generates its own attribute list partitions in parallel by projecting out each attribute from training set examples it was assigned. List for categorical attributes are evenly partitioned and require no further processing. Continuous attribute lists must be sorted and repartitioned into contiguous sorted sections. In this case, parallel sorting must be applied. The result of this sorting is that each processor gets fairly equal-sized sorted sections of each attribute list.

Finding split points in parallel SPRINT is very similar to the serial algorithm. In the serial version, processors scan the attribute lists either evaluating split points for continuous attributes or collecting distribution counts for categorical attributes. This does not change in the parallel version, as no extra work or communication is required while each processor is scanning its attribute list partitions. Hence, we get the full advantage of having multi processors worked simultaneously and independently.

Having determined the winning split points, splitting the attribute lists for each leaf is nearly identical to the serial algorithm, with each processor responsible for splitting its own attribute list partitions. The only additional step is that before building the probe structure, we will need to collect record-ids from all the processors. Thus, after partitioning the list of a leaf's splitting attribute, the record-ids collected during the scan are exchanged with all other processors. After the exchange, each processor continues independently, constructing a probe-structure with all the record-ids and using it to split the leaf's remaining attribute lists.

Parallel SLIQ

SLIQ (Mehta et al., 1996) classification algorithm addresses several issues in building a fast scalable classifier. SLIQ gracefully handles disk-resident data that is too large to fit in memory. It does not use small memory-sized datasets obtained via sampling or partitioning, but builds a single decision tree using the entire training set. However, SLIQ does require that some data per record stay memory-resident all the time. Since the size of this in-memory data structure grows in direct proportion to the number of input records, this limits the amount of data that can be classified by SLIQ.

Parallelization of SLIQ is complicated by its use of a centralized, memory-resident data structure; that is class list, because the class list requires random access and frequent updating, and hence parallel algorithms based on SLIQ require that the class list be kept memory-resident. There are two approaches for parallelizing SLIQ: one is where the class list is replicated in the memory of every processor, and the other where it is distributed such that each processor's memory holds only a portion of the entire list.

SLIQ/R (Replicated Class List)

In SLIQ/R, the class list for the entire training set is replicated in the local memory of every processor. Split points are evaluated by exchanging count metrices and by properly initialising the class histograms. Performing the splits requires updating the class list for each training example. Since every processor must maintain a consistent copy of the entire class list, every class-list update must be communicated to and applied to every processor. Thus, the time for this part of tree growth will increase with the size of the training set, even if the amount of data at each node remains fixed. On the other hand, each processor has a full copy of the class list; SLIQ/R can efficiently process a training set only if the class list for the entire database can fit in the memory of every processor. This is true regardless of the number of processors used.

SLIQ/D (Distributed Class List)

SLIQ/D relieves the problem memory limitation by partitioning the class list over the multiprocessor. Each processor therefore contains only 1/Nth of the class list. The partitioning of the class list has no correlation with the partitioning of the continuous attribute lists; the class label corresponding to an attribute value could reside on a different processor. This implies that communication is required to look up a non-local class label. Since the class list is created from the original partitioned training set, it will be perfectly correlated with categorical attribute lists. Thus, communication is only required for continuous attributes. SLIQ/D has high communication costs while evaluating continuous split points. As each attribute list is scanned, we need to look up the corresponding class label and tree-pointer for each attribute value. This implies that each processor will be required for communication for $N-1/N$ of its data. Also, each processor will have to service lookup requests from other processors in the middle of scanning its attribute lists.

Moving-Window-k (MWK) and SUBTREE

Zaki et al. (1998, 1999) proposed parallel classification algorithms for SMP machines. There are two versions: one is based on *data parallelism* approach (which they called *Moving-Window-k (MWK)*) and the other is based on *task parallelism* approach (which they called *SUBTREE*).

Data Parallel Approach for Parallel Classification

Data parallel approach used for parallel classification is based on *attribute data parallelism*, where the attributes are divided equally among the different processors so that each processor is responsible for $1/P$ attributes. Zaki et al. (1998, 1999) proposed the Moving-Window-k (MWK), which is based on attribute data parallelism.

The other data parallelism approach, called *record data parallelism*, where each processor is responsible for processing roughly 1/*P* fraction of each attribute list is not well suited to SMP system since it is likely to cause excessive synchronization, and replication of data structures (Kubota, Nakase, Sakai & Oyanagi, 2000).

The MWK algorithm is described as follows: starting with the root node, executes the following code for each new tree level:

Forall attributes in parallel
    For each block of *k* leaves
        For each leaf i
            If (last block's *i*-th leaf not done) then wait
            Evaluate attributes
            If (last processor finishing on leaf *i*) then
                Get winning attribute
                Form hash probe
                Signal that *i*-th leaf is done
Barrier
Forall attributes in parallel
    For each leaf
        Split attributes

Before evaluating leaf *i*, a check is made whether the *i*-th leaf of the previous block has been processed. If not, the processor goes to sleep on the conditional variable. Otherwise, it proceeds with the current leaf. The last processor to finish the evaluation of leaf *i* from the previous block constructs the hash probe, and then signals the conditional variable, so that any sleeping processors wake up.

Task Parallel Approach for Parallel Classification

The data parallel approaches target the parallelism available among the different attributes. On the other hand, the *task parallel* approach is based on the parallelism that exists in different subtrees. The algorithm is called SUBTREE, which is as follows:

    SubTree (Processor Group *P*, Left Frontier *L*)
        Apply simple algorithm on L with P processors
        NewL = {*l*1, *l*2, ..., *l*m} // new leaf frontier
        If (NewL is empty) then
            Put self in Free queue
        Elseif (group master) then
            Get Free processors; NewP = {*p*1, *p*2, ..., *p*n}
            If (only one leaf remaining) then
                SubTree(NewP, *l*1)
            Elseif (only one processor in group) then
                SubTree (*p*1, NewL)

        Else

                Split NewL into $L1$ and $L2$

                Split NewP into $P1$ and $P2$

                SubTree $(P1, L1)$

                SubTree $(P2, L2)$

        Wakeup processors in NewP

    Else

        Go to sleep

At any given point in the algorithm, there may be multiple processor groups working on distinct subtrees. Each group independently executes the following steps once the basic algorithm has been applied to the current subtree. First, the new subtree leaf frontier is constructed. If there are no children remaining, then each processor inserts itself in the free queue, ensuring mutually exclusive access via locking. If there is more work to be done, then all processors except the master go to sleep on a conditional variable. The group master checks if there are any new arrivals in the free queue and grabs all free processors in the queue.

If there is only one leaf remaining, then all processors are assigned to that leaf. If there is only one processor in the previous group and there is no processor in the free queue, then it forms a group on its own and works on the current leaf frontier. Lastly if there are multiple leaves and multiple processors, the group master splits the processor set into two parts, and also splits the leaves into two parts. The two newly formed processor sets become the new groups and work on the corresponding leaf sets. Finally, the master wakes up all relevant processors – from the original groups and those acquired from the free queue.

Parallel Clustering

There are a number of versions of parallel clustering, including parallel clustering based on k-means (*parallel k-means*) (Dhillon & Modha, 1999), and parallel clustering based on AutoClass algorithms called *P-AutoClass* (Foti et al., 2000).

Parallel k-means

Parallel k-means algorithm (Dhillon & Modha, 1999) was implemented on a shared-nothing architecture, using the MPI library. The algorithm can be explained as follows:

Parallel k-means

// a. Initialization process

    Identify the number of processes

    For each process

        Select k initial cluster centroid

Broadcast the cluster centroid from the host to all other processes
End For
// b. *Distance calculation*: each process concentrates on the portion of data
assigned to it
For each data point
Compute its Euclidean distance to each cluster centroid
Find the closest cluster centroid
End For
// c. Centroid Recalculation
Recompute cluster centroid as the average of data points assigned to it
// d. Convergence Condition
Repeat steps b and c until convergence.

In *Distance Calculation*, since each process concentrates on the portion of data assigned to it, it is inherently data parallel, that is, in principle; they can be executed asynchronously and in parallel for each data point. In this context, a simple, but effective, parallelization strategy is to divide the data points so that each process receives an equal share of data points. In other words, as a benefit of parallelization, we expect the computational burden to be shared equally by all processors. However, there is also a price attached to this benefit, namely the associated communication cost, which is imposed in the *Centroid Recalculation*. Before the new iteration of k-means can begin, which takes place in step Distance Calculation, all processors must communicate to recompute the centroids. This global communication (and also synchronization) is done in the *Centroid Recalculation* step in the program. In the *Convergence Condition*, it ensures that each of the processes has a local copy of the total mean-squared-error, hence each process can independently decide on the convergence condition; that is when to exit the program.

In conclusion, each iteration of the parallel k-means algorithm consists of an asynchronous computation phase, followed by a synchronous communication phase.

P-AutoClass

P-AutoClass is a parallel version of AutoClass, a clustering algorithm based on Bayesian method (Foti et al., 2000). The algorithm was designed for a shared-nothing architecture. In order to explain P-AutoClass, let's examine the serial AutoClass algorithm, which is as follows:

AutoClass
Files reading and data structure initialisation
Loop
Select the number of classes
Perform new classification try
Eliminate duplicates

Select the best classification
Store partial results
Until the stopping conditions are met
Store results on the output files.

In the above algorithm, the *Perform new classification try* step is the most computationally intensive (i.e., around 99.5% of the total time), where it computes the weights of each item for each class and computes the parameters of the classification. The *Perform new classification try* step actually performs three functions: *update weights*, *update parameters*, and *update approximation*. The first two functions are time consuming whereas the last function is negligible. Therefore, only the first two functions are parallelized.

The parallel version of the *updated weights* function first calculates on each processing element the weights for each item belonging to the local partition of the data set and sum the weights of each class relative to its own data. Then all the partial weight values are exchanged among all the processors and summed in each of them to have the same value in every processor. To implement the total exchange of the weight values, a global reduction operation is used, which sums all local copies in the all processes (reduction operation) and places the results on all the processors (broadcast operation).

The *update parameters* function computes for each class a set of class posterior parameter values, which specify how the class is distributed along the various attributes. The function is composed of three nested loops: the external loop scans all the classes, then for each class all the attributes are analysed, and in the inter loop all items are read and their values are used to compute the class parameters. In the parallel version, partial computation of parameters is executed in parallel on all processors, and then all the local values are collected on each processor before utilizing them for computing the global values of the classification parameters. To implement the total exchange of the parameter values, global reduction operation is also used, which sums all the local copies in all processes and places the results on every processor.

CHALLENGES

Most of existing work, as described in the previous section, focuses on the development of parallel algorithms for data mining techniques. Parallel data mining imposes many challenges, which are still to be explored. These are some of them.

Parallel Versions of Existing Serial Algorithms

The typical trend in parallel algorithms for data mining is to start with a serial algorithm and pose various parallel formulation, implement them and conduct a performance evaluation. While this is very important, it is a very costly process. After all, the parallel design space is vast and the problem becomes even worse when a new and improved serial algorithm is found, and we are forced to come up with new parallel formulations. Therefore, there is a critical need to investigate new ways for parallel paradigm in data mining. One solution might be a formulation of cost models to quantitatively analyse the proposed parallel algorithms. Skillicorn (1999) provides some initial work in performance modelling of parallel data mining algorithms.

Parallel Databases

Most of data mining systems employ special mining engines and do not use the query processing capability of SQL in RDBMS. On the other hand, it is realized that integration of data mining system with RDBMS provides many benefits, including easier system maintenance, flexibility and portability. Also the ability to perform data mining using standard SQL queries will benefit data warehouses with a better integration with RDBMS. Moreover, most data warehouses today make use of parallel database management systems. Therefore, the use of parallel database systems for data mining seems feasible. Very little work has been reported where parallel databases and SQL have been used in data mining, such as Freitas (1997), Freitas and Lavington (1996), Linoff (1998), Pramudiono, Shintani, Tamura, and Kitsuregawa (1999) and Thomas and Chakravarthy (1999).

It is usually a good idea to create a data mart for purposes of mining data from data warehouses, since data mining process may involve data from multiple databases or subsets of data from a data warehouse, and with data mart, the problem of preparing data for data mining may be avoided. The size of the data mart or allowing for growth in the size of the data mart will require the data store to be parallelized.

Parallel Data Mining Using Complex Data Structure

Traditionally, access to data in data mining applications is file based, and data is typically viewed as tabular. In contrast, scientific, engineering and business data is usually structured. Object-oriented databases and object warehouses have been developed to work with more structured data. The goal of this research is to use the appropriate data management infrastructure so that natural structure inherent in data can be exploited efficiently, without having to reassemble and recompute the structures, which were thrown away when data is flattened into files in tabular format. Therefore, an important challenge is to develop integrated data analysis, data mining and data management systems for structured and semi-structured data with complex data types.

Inter-Model Parallelism

Traditionally parallel data mining is applied to intra-model parallelism, in which parallelism is employed in building a data mining model. There is also the need to investigate how construction of multiple models can make use of parallelism. The issues of multiple models include whether the models are totally independent to each other, or there are some hierarchies among the models, etc. At the other end, the issues relating to parallelism of such process include resource allocation, models scheduling, load balancing, etc.

Parallelism for Model Testing and Validation

A model built by any techniques needs to be tested and validated, which means calculating an error rate based on data independent of that used to build the model. There are various testing methods, such as *simple validation, cross validation, n-fold cross validation* and *bootstrapping*. Model testing and validation is a complex process, even when only a single model is built. Validation on even simple models may need to be performed multiple of times. Moreover, complex testing schemes make heavy use of the computer and are one of the reasons parallelism is required.

Parallelism in Searching for Best Model

To get a good model, it is commonly required to build multiple models. Once these models are built and validated, we need to search for the best model to be deployed. Searching the best model may require parallelism.

Parallelism in the Deployment of Data Mining Models

The main task of data mining algorithms is to build good data mining models. Once a good model is developed, it can be deployed for new transactions to use the model. Even after the data mining model is built, there may be a need for parallel computing to apply the model.

In some situations, the data mining model is applied to one event or transaction at a time, such as scoring a loan application for risk. The amount of time to process each new transaction, and the rate at which new transactions arrive, will determine whether a parallel algorithm is needed. Thus, while the loan applications can probably be easily evaluated on modest sized computers, monitoring credit card transactions or mobile telephone calls for fraud would require a parallel system to deal with the high transaction rate.

Often a data mining model is applied to a batch of data such as an existing customer database, a newly purchased mailing list or a monthly record of transactions from a retail store. In this case, the large quantity of data to be processed would also require that a parallel solution be deployed.

REFERENCES

Aggarwal, C., Procopiuc, C., Wolf, J.L., Yu, P.S., & Park, J.S. (1999). A Framework for Finding Projected Clusters in High Dimensional Spaces. *Proceedings of the ACM SIGMOD International Conference on Management of Data.*

Agrawal, R., Ghosh, S., Imielinski, T., Iyer, B., & Swami, A. (1992). An interval classifier for database mining applications. *Proceedings of the Very Large Data Bases Conference.*

Agrawal, R., & Srikant, R. (1994). Fast Algorithms for Mining Association Rules.

Proceedings of the 20th International Conference on Very Large Data Bases.

Agrawal, R., & Srikant, R. (1995). Mining Sequential Patterns. *Proceedings of the 11th International Conference on Data Engineering*, 3-14.

Agrawal, R., & Shafer, J.C. (1996). Parallel Mining of Association Rules. *IEEE Transactions on Knowledge and Data Engineering, 8*(6), 962-969.

Agrawal, R, Gehrke, J., Gunopulos, D., & Raghavan, P. (1998). Automatic subspace clustering of high dimensional data for data mining applications. *Proceedings of the ACM SIGMOD International Conference on Management of Data.*

Almasi G., & Gottlieb, A. (1994). *Highly Parallel Computing* (2nd ed.), The Benjamin/ Cummings Publishing Company Inc.

Alsabti, K., Ranka, S., & Singh, V. (1998). CLOUDS: A decision tree classifier for large datasets. *Proceedings of the 4th International Conference on Knowledge Discovery and Data Mining.*

Bergsten, B., Couprie, M., & Valduriez, P. (1993). Overview of Parallel Architecture for Databases. *The Computer Journal, 36*(8), 734-740.

Brin, S., Motwani, R., Ullman, J.D., & Tsur, S. (1997). Dynamic itemset counting and implication rules for market basket data. *Proceedings of the ACM SIGMOD Conference*, 255-264.

Chen, M.-S., Han, J., & Yu, P.S. (1996). Data Mining: An Overview from a Database Perspective. *IEEE Transactions on Knowledge and Data Engineering, 8*(6), 866-883.

Cheng, C., Fu, A., & Zhang, Y. (1999). Entropy-based subspace clustering for mining numerical data. *Proceedings of the ACM SIGKDD International Conference on Knowledge Discovery and Data Mining.*

Cheung, D.W., Ng, V.T., Fu, A.W., & Fu, Y. (1996). Efficient Mining of Association Rules in Distributed Databases. *IEEE Transaction on TKDE, 8*(6), 911-922.

Cheung, D.W., Hu, K., & Xia, S. (1998). Asynchronous Parallel Algorithm for Mining Association Rules on a Shared-Memory Multi-Processors. *Proceedings of the 10th Annual ACM Symposium on Parallel Algorithms and Architectures SPAA'98.*

Cheung, D.W., & Xiao, Y. (1998). Effect of Data Skewness in Parallel Mining of Association Rules. *Proceedings of the PAKDD Conference*, 48-60.

Cheung, D.W., & Xiao, Y. (1999). Effect of Data Distribution in Parallel Mining of Associations. *Data Mining and Knowledge Discovery International Journal, 3*, 291-314.

Cheung, D.W., Hu, K., & Xia, S. (2001). An Adaptive Algorithm for Mining Association Rules on Shared-Memory Parallel Machines. *Distributed and Parallel Databases International Journal.*

DeWitt, D.J. & Gray, J. (1992). Parallel Database Systems: The Future of High Performance Database Systems. *Communications of the ACM, 35*(6), 85-98.

Dhillon, I.S., & Modha, D.S. (1999). A Data-Clustering Algorithm on Distributed Memory Multiprocessors. *Proceedings of the Workshop on Large-Scale Parallel KDD Systems.*

Foti, D., Lipari, D., Pizzuti, C., & Talia, D. (2000). Scalable Clustering for Data Mining on Multicomputers. *Proceedings of the High Performance Data Mining Workshop.*

Freitas, A.A., & Lavington, S.H. (1996). Parallel data mining for very large relational databases. *Proceedings of the International Conference on High Performance Computing and Networking HPCN Europe'96*, LNCS 1067, Springer-Verlag, 158-163.

Freitas, A.A. (1997). Towards Large-Scale Knowledge Discovery in Databases (KDD) by Exploiting Parallelism in Generic KDD Primitives. *Proceedings of the 3rd International Workshop on Next Generation Information Technologies and Systems*, 33-43.

Freitas, A.A. (1998). A Survey of Parallel Data Mining. *Proceedings of the 2nd International Conference on the Practical Applications of Knowledge Discovery and Data Mining*, 287-300.

Guha, S., Rastogi, R., & Shim, K. (1998). CURE: An efficient clustering algorithm for large databases. *Proceedings of the ACM SIGMOD International Conference on Management of Data*.

Han, E.-H., Karypis, G., & Kumar, V. (1997). Scalable Parallel Data Mining for Association Rules. *Proceedings of the ACM SIGMOD Conference*, 277-288.

Kubota, K., Nakase, A., Sakai, H., & Oyanagi, S. (2000). Parallelization of Decision Tree Algorithm and its Performance Evaluation. *Proceedings of the HPCAsia Conference*, IEEE Computer Society Press, 574-579.

Linoff, G. (1998). NT Clusters: Data Mining Motherlode. *Database Programming and Design*, Online Extra Edition, June.

Mehta, M., Agrawal, R., & Rissanen, J. (1996). SLIQ: A fast scalable classifier for data mining. *Proceedings of the 5th International Conference on Extending Database Technology*.

Ng, R., & Han, J. (1994). Efficient and Effective Clustering Methods for Spatial Data Mining. *Proceedings of the 20th International Conference on Very Large Databases*.

Olson, C.F. (1995). Parallel Algorithms for Hierarchical Clustering. *Parallel Computing International Journal, 21*, 1313-1325.

Parthasarathy, S., Zaki, M.J. & Li, W. (1998). Memory Placement Techniques for Parallel Association Mining. *Proceedings of the 4th International Conference on Knowledge Discovery and Data Mining KDD*, 304-308.

Patterson, D.A., & Hennessy, J.L. (1994). *Computer Organization & Design: The Hardware/Software Interface*, Morgan Kaufmann.

Pfister, G.F. (1998). *In Search of Clusters: The Ongoing Battle in Lowly Parallel Computing*, (2nd ed.), Prentice Hall.

Pramudiono, I., Shintani, T., Tamura, T., & Kitsuregawa, M. (1999). Mining Generalized Association Rules Using Parallel RDB Engine on PC Cluster. *Proceedings of DaWak'99 Conference*, 281-292.

Shafer, J., Agrawal, R., & Mehta, M. (1996). SPRINT: A Scalable Parallel Classifier for Data Mining. *Proceedings of the 22nd VLDB Conference*.

Shintani, T., & Kitsuregawa, M. (1998a). Parallel Mining Algorithms for Generalized Association Rules with Classification Hierarchy. *Proceedings of the ACM SIGMOD Conference*, 25-36.

Shintani, T. & Kitsuregawa, M. (1998b). Mining algorithms for sequential patterns in parallel: Hash based approach. *Proceedings of the Pacific-Asia Conference on Knowledge Discovery and Data Mining*.

Skillicorn, D.B. (1999). Strategies for Parallel Data Mining. *IEEE Concurrency, Special Issue on Parallel Mechanism for Data Mining, 7(4)*.

Small, R.D. & Edelstein, H.A. (1997). *Scalable Data Mining*, White Paper, Two Crows Company.

Srikant, R. & Agrawal, R. (1996). Mining sequential patterns: Generalizations and performance improvements. *Proceedings of the 5th International Conference on Extending Database Technology*.

Thomas, S., & Chakravarthy, S. (1999). Performance Evaluation and Optimization of Join Queries for Association Rule Mining. *Proceedings of DaWak'99 Conference*, 241-250.

Valduriez, P. (1993). Parallel Database Systems: The Case for Shared-Something. *Proceed-*

ings of the International Conference on Data Engineering, 460-465.

Zaki, M.J., Ogihara, M., Parthasarathy, S., & Li, W. (1996). Parallel Data Mining for Association Rules on Shared-Memory Multi-Processors. *Student Technical Paper, Supercomputing'96 Conference.*

Zaki, M.J., Parthasarathy, S., & Li, W. (1997). New algorithms for fast discovery of association rules. *Proceedings of the 3rd International Conference on Knowledge Discovery and Data Mining.*

Zaki, M.J., Parthasarathy, S., Ogihara, M., & Li, W. (1997). Parallel Algorithms for Discovery of Association Rules. *Data Mining and Knoweldge Discovery, 1.*

Zaki, M.J. (1998). Efficient enumeration of frequent sequences. *Proceedings of the 7th International Conference on Information and Knowledge Management.*

Zaki, M.J., Ho, C-T., & Agrawal, R. (1998). Parallel Classification on SMP Systems. *Proceedings of the 1st Workshop on High Performance Data Mining.*

Zaki, M.J., Ho, C-T., & Agrawal, R. (1999). Parallel Classification for Data Mining on Shared-Memory Multiprocessors. *Proceedings of the IEEE International Conference on Data Engineering*, 198-205.

Zaki, M.J. (1999a). Parallel and Distributed Association Mining: A Survey. *IEEE Concurrency, Special Issue on Parallel Mechanism for Data Mining, 7(4)*, 14-25.

Zaki, M.J. (1999b). Parallel Sequence Mining on Shared-Memory Machines. *Proceedings of the 2nd Workshop on High Performance Data Mining HPDM.*

Zhang, T., Ramakrishnan, R., & Livny, M. (1996). BIRCH: An efficient data clustering method for very large databases. *Proceedings of the ACM SIGMOD International Conference on Management of Data.*

About the Authors

Hussein A. Abbass gained his Ph.D. in Computer Science from the Queensland University of Technology, Brisbane, Australia. He also holds several degrees including Business, Operational Research, a and Constraint Logic Programming, from Cairo University, Egypt, and Artificial Intelligence, from the University of Edinburgh, UK. From 1994 to 2000, he worked at the Department of Computer Science, Institute of Statistical Studies and Research, Cairo University, Egypt. In 2000, he joined the School of Computer Science, University of New South Wales, ADFA Campus, Australia. His research interests include Swarm Intelligence, Evolutionary Algorithms and biological agents where he develops approaches for the Satisfiability problem, Evolving Artificial Neural Networks, Data Mining and war gamming.

Erick Cantú-Paz received a B.S. degree in computer engineering from the Instituto Tecnológico Autónomo de México in 1994 and a Ph.D. in computer science from the University of Illinois at Urbana-Champaign in 1999. Currently, he works in the Lawrence Livermore National Laboratory on scalable data mining of scientific data. He is the author of a book on parallel genetic algorithms and over 25 peer-reviewed publications. He is an associate editor for the *Journal of Heuristics* and member of the editorial board of *Computational Optimization and Applications*. His research interests include theoretical foundations and practical applications of evolutionary algorithms, machine learning, and data mining. He is a member of ACM, IEEE, and the International Society of Genetic and Evolutionary Computation, where he serves as chair of the Council of Authors.

Neil Dunstan received a master's degree from the University of Newcastle in 1991 and a PhD from the University of New England in 1997. Current research interests include signal processing and application specific parallel processing devices.

A.P. Engelbrecht is an associate professor in Computer Science at the University of Pretoria, South Africa. He obtained the M.Sc and PhD degrees in Computer Science from the University of Stellenbosch, South Africa in 1994 and 1999 respectively. He is production editor for the *South African Computer Journal*, serves on the editorial board of the International Journal on Computers, Systems and Signals, and has been guest editor of a special issue on data mining for the same journal. Prof. Engelbrecht serves as chair for the INNS SIG AFRICA, chair of the South African Section of IAAMSAD, and is a member of INNS and IEEE. His research interests include artificial neural networks, evolutionary computing, swarm intelligence and data mining.

Vladimir Estivill-Castro graduated with his Ph.D. in 1991 from the University of Waterloo, after having obtained his B.Sc. and MSc from Universidad Nacional Autónoma de México in 1985 and 1987, respectively. After spending several years as a project leader in industry, he returned to academia at Griffith University in Australia in 1996. He has made many scholarly contributions in the areas of algorithmics and machine learning, as well as knowledge discovery and data mining. He has been a member of ACM and the IEEE Computer Society since 1990. He is the author of a book on computational geometry, and a co-author of several book chapters. In 2000, he was the conference chair of the annual international COCOON conference on computing and combinatorics, held in Sydney. He has also served recently on the program committees of several other international conferences, including DaWaK (data warehousing), ISADS (advanced distributed systems), and MICAI (artificial intelligence).

Alex A. Freitas received his B.Sc. and M.Sc. degrees in Computer Science from FATEC-SP (Faculdade de Tecnologia de Sao Paulo) and UFSCar (Universidade Federal de Sao Carlos), both in Brazil, in 1989 and 1993, respectively. He received his Ph.D. degree in Computer Science, doing research on data mining, from the University of Essex, England, in 1997. His publications include a scientific book on data mining and over 40 research papers. He is currently an associate professor at PUC-PR (Pontificia Universidade Catolica do Parana), in Curitiba, Brazil. His main research interests are data mining and evolutionary algorithms. He is a member of AAAI, ACM-SIGKDD, IEEE, ISGEC, and BCS-SGES.

Michael E. Houle obtained his Ph.D. degree from McGill University in 1989, on the topic of separability in computational geometry. After spending several years as a research associate in Japan, at Kyushu University and then at the University of Tokyo, he moved to the University of Newcastle in Australia in 1992. He has broad interests in design and analysis of algorithms, with international journal and conference publications in computational geometry, parallel computing, distributed computing, data mining, facility location, and visualization. Currently, he is a Visiting Scientist at IBM Japan's Tokyo Research Laboratory, on leave from the University of Sydney.

Beatriz de la Iglesia received the BSc Honours degree in Applied Computing from the University of East Anglia, Norwich, in 1994. Since then, she has worked part-time on a PhD degree in Computing Science, which was submitted in 2001. In this same period, she worked on a variety of research projects, including data mining for a large financial sector company as part of a two-year Teaching Company Scheme, and more recently, on a BBSRC funded project in the area of bioinformatics. She is also involved with teaching undergraduate and post-graduate courses at the University. Her current research interests include data mining, optimization, bioinformatics,and dealing with uncertainty.

Iñaki Inza received his M.Sc. degree in Computer Science from the University of the Basque Country in 1997. He is a lecturer of Statistics and Artificial Intelligence at the Computer Sciences and Artificial Intelligence Department of the University of the Basque Country. His research interests reside in evolutionary algorithms, Bayesian networks and supervised classifiers.

Chandrika Kamath is a computer scientist at the Center for Applied Scientific Computing at the Lawrence Livermore National Laboratory. She received the Ph.D. degree in computer science from the University of Illinois at Urbana-Champaign in 1986. Prior to joining LLNL in 1997, Dr. Kamath was a Consulting Software Engineer at Digital Equipment Corporation developing high-performance mathematical software. Her research interests are in large-scale data mining and pattern recognition, including image processing, feature extraction, dimension reduction, and classification and clustering algorithms. She is also interested in the practical application of these techniques. Since January 1998, she has been the project lead and an individual contributor for Sapphire, a project in large scale data mining at LLNL.

Thomas Knight is currently studying at the University of Kent at Canterbury towards a Ph.D. in Artificial Intelligence; concentrating on an Artificial Immune System for Document Classification, under the supervision of Dr. Jonathan Timmis. He previously gained a BSc Honours Degree in Geography at the University of Wales, Aberystwyth, before obtaining an MSc in Computer Science at the same institution.

Pedro Larrañaga received his M.Sc. degree in Mathematics from the University of Valladolid, Spain and his Ph.D. degree in Computer Science from the University of the Basque Country. He is currently Professor at the Department of Computer Science and Artificial Intelligence of the University of the Basque Country. His current research interests are in the fields of Bayesian networks, combinatorial optimization and data analysis with applications to medicine, molecular biology, cryptoanalysis and finance.

Heitor S. Lopes received a degree in electrical engineering and M.Sc. from CEFET-PR (Centro Federal de Educacao Tecnologica do Parana), Curitiba, in 1984 and 1990, respectively. He received his Ph.D. in electrical engineering in 1996 from the Universidade Federal de Santa Catarina. Since 1987, he has been a lecturer at the Department of Electronics of CEFET-PR, where he is currently an associate professor. In 1997, he founded the Bioinformatics Laboratory at the CEFET-PR. He is a member of IEEE SMC and EMB societies and his current research interests are evolutionary computation, data mining, and biomedical engineering.

Jorge Muruzábal holds a Licenciatura in Mathematics from the Universidad Complutense de Madrid (Spain), and a Ph. D. in Statistics from the University of Minnesota. His 1992 doctoral dissertation explored a machine learning approach to regularity detection based on an evolutionary algorithm. Besides evolutionary algorithms, his research interests include data mining, neural computation, multivariate analysis and outlier detection. He has previously served on Program Committees of several major conferences. He is currently a member of EVONET, ACM's SIG on Data Mining and Knowledge Discovery, and the European Chapter on Metaheuristics.

Charles S. Newton is the Head of Computer Science, University of New South Wales (UNSW) at the Australian Defence Force Academy (ADFA) campus, Canberra. Prof. Newton is also the Deputy Rector (Education). He obtained his Ph.D. in Nuclear Physics from the Australian National University, Canberra in 1975. He joined the School of Computer Science in 1987 as a Senior Lecturer in Operations Research. In May 1993, he was appointed Head of School and became Professor of Computer Science in November 1993. Prior to joining at ADFA,he spent nine years in the Analytical Studies Branch of the Department of Defence. From 1989-91, Prof. Newton was the National President of the Australian Society for Operations Research. His research interests encompass group decision support systems, simulation, wargaming, evolutionary computation, data mining and operations research applications. He has published extensively in national and international journals, books and conference proceedings.

Leandro Nunes de Castro is an Electrical Engineer from the Federal University of Goiás (Brazil), He has an M.Sc. in Automation and a Ph.D. in Computer Engineering from the State University of Campinas (Brazil). His current main work interests are Artificial Immune Systems, Artificial Neural Networks and Evolutionary Computation. He is a valued IEEE member since 1998, an INNS member since 1998, and also a member of SBA (Brazilian Society on Automation) since 1999.

Rafael S. Parpinelli received his B.Sc. and M.Sc. degrees in Computer Science from UEM (Universidade Estadual de Maringa) and CEFET-PR (Centro Federal de Educacao Tecnologica do Parana – Curitiba), both in Brazil, in 1999 and 2001, respectively. He is currently a Ph.D. student in Computer Science at CEFET-PR. His main research interests are data mining and all kinds of biology-inspired algorithms (mainly evolutionary algorithms and ant colony algorithms).

Michael de Raadt undertook undergraduate study initially at Maquarie University and then at the University of Western Sydney. He graduated with distinction. His Honours work in Genetic Algorithms earned him First Class Honours and the UWS Nepean University Medal. He was the recipient of the ACS Award for Highest Achievement. He has worked with the CSIRO's RoboCup development team. He is currently undertaking PhD study with interests in Online Learning aand Teaching Programming

J. Wenny Rahayu received a PhD in Computer Science from La Trobe University, Australia, in 2000. Her thesis, supervised by Professor Tharam Dillon, was in the area of Object-Relational Database Design and Transformation, and she received the 2001 Computer Science Association Australia Best PhD Thesis Award. Dr Rahayu is currently a Senior Lecturer at La Trobe University. She has published two books and numerous research articles.

Victor J. Rayward-Smith read Mathematics at Oxford and obtained his doctorate in Formal Language Theory from the University of London. He was appointed lecturer in Computing at the University of East Anglia, Norwich, in 1973 and, except for sabbatical periods in Colorado, in California and at Simon Fraser has remained at Norwich ever since. He was appointed professor in 1991 and is now Dean of the School of Information Systems. He is well known for his research into optimization (especially in scheduling and for work on the Steiner tree problem) and, more recently, for exploiting optimization techniques in KDD. He has written over 150 research articles, ten books and is editor-in-chief of the *International Journal of Mathematical Algorithms.*

Sonja Rouwhorst recently finished her Masters in Artificial Intelligence at the Department of Mathematics and Computer Science of the Vrije Universiteit Amsterdam in The Netherlands. Part of the research presented in Chapter 9 was performed at the department of Computer Science of the University of Pretoria in South Africa, under the supervision of Prof AP Engelbrecht. At the moment she is working as an ICT-consultant for Ordina Public Utopics (The Netherlands).

Ruhul A. Sarker received his Ph.D. in 1991 from DalTech, Dalhousie University, Halifax, Canada, and is currently a Senior Lecturer in Operations Research at the School of Computer Science, University of New South Wales, ADFA Campus, Canberra, Australia. Before joining at UNSW in February 1998, Dr. Sarker worked with Monash University, Victoria, and the Bangladesh University of Engineering and Technology, Dhaka. His main research interests are Evolutionary Optimization, Data Mining and Applied Operations Research. He is currently involved with four edited books either as editor or co-editor, and has published more than 60 refereed papers in international journals and conference proceedings. He is also the editor of ASOR Bulletin, the national publication of the Australian Society for Operations Research.

Peter W.H. Smith was born in Sheffield, UK and completed his M.Sc. in

Computer Science at Essex University before working in industry for some time. He completed a Ph.D. in Speech Act Theory at Leeds University and accepted a lectureship at City University, London where he is currently employed. His research interests include genetic programming and he has published several papers on code growth in genetic programming. His other research interests include alternative neural network architectures, stylometric analysis of Elizabethan literary texts and secondary protein structure. He also works with a company on modelling operational risk in financial institutions.

L. Schoeman is currently a lecturer in Computer Science at the University of Pretoria, South Africa. Before this position she was a lecturer in Computer Studies at the Pretoria Technikon. She received the degrees of B.Sc from the University of Stellenbosch, B.Sc Hons from the University of South Africa, and M.Sc from the Rands Afrikaanse University. Her current research interests include artificial intelligence, evolutionary computing and medical informatics.

Basilio Sierra received his M.Sc. degree in Computer Science from the University of the Basque Country in 1990. He received a Master degree in Computer Sciences and Technologies in 1992. He has been a lecturer of Statistics and Artificial Intelligence at the Department of Computer Science and Artificial Intelligence of the University of the Basque Country since 1996. His current research interests are in the fields of Bayesian networks, Nearest Neighbor algorithm and combination of supervised classifiers.

David Taniar received his PhD in Computer Science from Victoria University, Australia, in 1997 under the supervision of Professor Clement Leung. He is currently a Senior Lecturer at the School of Business Systems, Monash University, Australia. His research interests are in the areas of applications of parallel/distributed/high performance computing in data mining/data warehousing/databases/business systems. He has published four computing books, and numerous research articles. He is also a Fellow of the Royal Society of Arts, Manufactures and Commerce.

Jonathan Timmis has a first class honours degree in Computer Science from the University of Wales, Aberystwyth (UWA). He was employed as a research associate for two years, investigating the use of immune metaphors for machine learning and visualisation at UWA. He went on to complete his PhD in Artificial Immune Systems from UWA and since June 2000 has been employed as a lecturer in the Computing Laboratory, University of Kent at Canterbury. His main research interests are in the area of biologically inspired computation, in particular using the immune system as a metaphor for solving computational problems. Current research projects include investigating immune metaphors for machine learning, the application of AIS in data mining and AIS applied to hardware and software engineering.

Fernando J. Von Zuben received his B.Sc. degree in Electrical Engineering in 1991. In 1993, he received his M.Sc. degree, and in 1996, his Ph.D. degree, both in Automation from the Faculty of Electrical and Computer Engineering, State University of Campinas, SP, Brazil. Since 1997, he has been an Assistant Professor with the Department of Computer Engineering and Industrial Automation, of the State University of Campinas, SP, Brazil. The main topics of his research are artificial neural networks, artificial immune systems, evolutionary computation, nonlinear control systems, and multivariate data analysis. Dr. Von Zuben is a member of IEEE and INNS.

Index